THE CAMBRIDGE EDITION OF THE WORKS OF
F. SCOTT FITZGERALD

Two Wrongs

by F. Scott Fitzgerald.

"Look at those shoes," said Bill, "twenty eight dollars."

Mr. Brancusi looked.

"Purty".

"Made to order."

" I always knew you were a great swell. You didn't get me up here to show me those shoes, did you?"

"I am not a great swell. Who said I was a great swell?" demanded Bill, "Just because I've got more education than most people in show business."

"But then you're a handsome young fellow," said Brancusi drily.

"Sure I am — compared to you anyhow, you dirty little kyke. The girls all think I must be an actor till they find out. Got

First page of the surviving typescript of "Two Wrongs." The anti-semitic slur in the last two lines did not appear in the *Saturday Evening Post*.
Princeton University Libraries.

TAPS AT REVEILLE

* * *

F. SCOTT FITZGERALD

Edited by
JAMES L. W. WEST III

CAMBRIDGE
UNIVERSITY PRESS

University Printing House, Cambridge CB2 8BS, United Kingdom

Cambridge University Press is part of the University of Cambridge.

It furthers the University's mission by disseminating knowledge in the pursuit of education, learning, and research at the highest international levels of excellence.

www.cambridge.org
Information on this title: www.cambridge.org/9781107470378

First published 2014
Paperback edition 2014

Printed in the United States of America by Sheridan Books, Inc.

A catalogue record for this publication is available from the British Library

ISBN 978-0-521-76603-6 Hardback
ISBN 978-1-107-47037-8 Paperback

CONTENTS

Acknowledgments *page* vii
Illustrations viii

Introduction ix
1. Background ix
2. Publication and reception xv
3. Post-publication corrections xvi
4. Editorial principles xx
5. Regularizations xxii
6. Restorations xxiii

TAPS AT REVEILLE

Crazy Sunday 5

Two Wrongs 24

The Night of Chancellorsville 45

The Last of the Belles 50

Majesty 67

Family in the Wind 87

A Short Trip Home 107

One Interne 129

The Fiend 150

Babylon Revisited 157

ADDITIONAL STORIES, December 1928–July 1931

Outside the Cabinet-Maker's 181

The Rough Crossing 186

At Your Age 207

The Swimmers 223

The Bridal Party 244

One Trip Abroad 263

The Hotel Child 288

Indecision 310

A New Leaf 328

Record of Variants 345

Explanatory Notes 363

Illustrations 391

Appendix 1 Thank You for the Light 397

Appendix 2 Author's Foreword 402

Appendix 3 Composition, publication, and earnings 403

ACKNOWLEDGMENTS

I am grateful to Eleanor Lanahan and Chris Byrne, the Trustees of the F. Scott Fitzgerald Estate, for their support and assistance. I thank Phyllis Westberg of Harold Ober Associates, Inc., for continuing help with permissions and copyrights.

Most of the pre-publication documents used in establishing the texts for this volume are among the F. Scott Fitzgerald Papers in the Manuscript Division, Department of Rare Books and Special Collections, Princeton University Library. My thanks as always to Don Skemer, Curator of Manuscripts at Princeton, and to his staff. An early typescript of "The Swimmers" and a copy of *Taps at Reveille* annotated by Fitzgerald are both in the Bruccoli Collection, Thomas Cooper Library, University of South Carolina. I am grateful to Patrick Scott and Elizabeth Sudduth for permission to consult these materials. The setting-copy typescript of "The Fiend" is part of the Fitzgerald collection at the Albert and Shirley Small Special Collections Library, University of Virginia. I thank the staff there for access and cooperation. I am grateful to Donald Mennerich of the Manuscripts and Archives Division, New York Public Library, for answering a query about "Crazy Sunday."

For continuing support at Penn State I thank Susan Welch, Dean of the College of the Liberal Arts, and Mark Morrisson, Head of the Department of English. Linda Patterson Miller, Professor of English at the Abington campus of Penn State, helped with the identification of one of Gerald Murphy's paintings. Willa Z. Silverman, my colleague in the Department of French and Francophone Studies, gave much assistance with the French language; Martina Kolb in the Department of German and Slavic Languages and Literatures helped with idiomatic German. Research and proofreading labors for this volume were provided by Jeanne Alexander (who drafted several of the historical annotations), Gregg Baptista, Michael DuBose, Ethan Mannon, and Bethany Ober.

J. L. W. W. III

ILLUSTRATIONS

(*Beginning on p. 391*)

Frontispiece. First page, surviving typescript of “Two Wrongs.”

1. Page 5, working typescript of “One Trip Abroad.”
2. Page 7, working typescript of “The Hotel Child.”
3. Page 17, working typescript of “The Bridal Party.”
4. Page 12, working typescript of “Babylon Revisited.”

INTRODUCTION

1. BACKGROUND

F. Scott Fitzgerald's short-story collection *Taps at Reveille* has a complicated textual history. On 15 May 1934, a little more than a month after the formal publication of his novel *Tender Is the Night*, Fitzgerald wrote to Maxwell Perkins, his editor at Charles Scribner's Sons, offering four plans for a new book to be published in the fall. The practice at Scribners was to follow a novel or other major book with a collection of shorter pieces—usually, for fiction writers, a collection of short stories. One sees this pattern in Fitzgerald's career and in the careers of other authors of his period, both at Scribners and at other publishing houses. The aim was to keep the author's name in the public eye for the next publishing season and, not incidentally, to generate a second round of income for work that had already been sold on the magazine market.

In his 15 May letter Fitzgerald presented Perkins with four ideas. The first was to publish an omnibus volume "including both new stories and the pick of the other three collections"—that is, previously uncollected stories plus the best stories from Fitzgerald's three published volumes of short fiction—*Flappers and Philosophers* (1920), *Tales of the Jazz Age* (1922), and *All the Sad Young Men* (1926).[1] The second suggestion was for a volume that would bring together the eight Basil Duke Lee stories and the five Josephine Perry stories, two series that Fitzgerald had published in the *Saturday Evening Post* between 1928 and 1931. Third was a book of previously uncollected short fiction, chosen from the approximately forty stories that Fitzgerald had on hand. And fourth was a

[1] The letters between Fitzgerald and Perkins in the account that follows are quoted from John Kuehl and Jackson R. Bryer, eds., *Dear Scott/Dear Max: The Fitzgerald–Perkins Correspondence* (New York: Scribners, 1971): 195–218.

nonfiction collection comprised of personal essays and travel writings from throughout Fitzgerald's career.[2]

After consulting with his colleagues at Scribners, Perkins wrote back on 17 May urging Fitzgerald to make a collection of the Basil and Josephine stories, which Perkins had read in the *Post* and had very much liked—especially the Basil stories. Perkins thought that Fitzgerald could probably produce copy for the printers fairly quickly, in "not more than six weeks say," and that the collection, featuring two attractive young characters, would appeal to readers and have a brisk sale. Fitzgerald reread the Basil and Josephine stories and reported to Perkins on the 21st that they were "not as good as I thought." Making the stories into a collection would require "a tremendous amount of work and a good deal of new invention," especially since Fitzgerald wanted to write a final story for the volume, a story in which Basil and Josephine would meet and fall in love. Fitzgerald also feared that the Scribners sales department would market the collection "to some extent as a novel," undercutting his credibility with book critics and the reading public.

Fitzgerald therefore settled on a plan to merge his second and third ideas into a single collection. He decided to republish the best of the Basil and Josephine stories and to add eight or ten other stories to fill out the volume. His working title was "More Tales of the Jazz Age," though on 8 June he suggested several other titles to Perkins, including "Basil, Josephine and Others," "When Grandma Was a Boy," "Last Year's Steps," "The Salad Days," "Many Blues," "Just Play One More," and "A Dance Card." Eventually Fitzgerald chose "Taps at Reveille" as his title, though he continued to fret about the matter. A few weeks before publication he suggested "Last Night's Moon," "In the Last Quarter of the Moon," "Golden Spoons," or "Moonlight in My Eyes." By then, Perkins informed him, it was too late. The collection would be published as *Taps at Reveille*.

Perkins wanted Fitzgerald to gather his energies and send in revised copy as soon as possible. Perkins promised to put the volume into production immediately. He would have the stories typeset

[2] This fourth proposal by Fitzgerald is made incarnate in *My Lost City: Personal Essays, 1920–1940* (Cambridge University Press, 2005).

as they came in and would release the collection in October. "My personal idea of it would be that we should publish the book of stories as soon as we could," he wrote to Fitzgerald on 20 August. "I think it urgently important that you should bring out these stories close to 'Tender Is the Night' for I think that the reviewers will be impressed by them. . . . Besides, the stories themselves show more sides of you than 'Tender Is the Night.'" Fitzgerald must have seen the wisdom of Perkins' suggestion, but he doubted his ability to deliver copy on schedule. Fitzgerald was still in debt to Scribners for past advances and owed a great deal of money to his literary agent, Harold Ober. He was living modestly, in an apartment in Baltimore, where he could be near his wife, Zelda, who was undergoing treatment for mental illness at the Phipps Psychiatric Clinic of Johns Hopkins Hospital. The treatments were expensive, and Zelda's condition was uncertain. Fitzgerald had to concentrate his primary energies on new writing for the magazine market in order to meet his financial obligations. He was producing a series of stories about a medieval count named Philippe and selling these to *Redbook* as he finished them. He was also attempting to write other stories for the *Post*. His health, never strong, had been weakened by his recent ordeals, and his drinking had increased. He asked Scribners for advances on royalties in order to meet his expenses while he prepared *Taps at Reveille* for press—but the publisher, unwilling to advance further money to Fitzgerald until he had squared his existing debts, turned him down (*Dear Scott/DearMax*, 207–08).

Fitzgerald decided to delay the publication of *Taps at Reveille*. "I am not in the proper condition either physically or financially to put over the kind of rush job that this would be," he wrote to Perkins in an undated letter sent toward the end of August. "I have got to get myself out of this morass of debt," he added. "I am terribly unhappy in debt and do not get much comfort out of my personal life if I feel any such shadow over me." Further, Fitzgerald had discovered in rereading his stories that he had "bled" them (his term) of some of their best phrases and passages for reuse in *Tender Is the Night*. He deleted or rewrote these parts when he recognized them, but he could not identify all the passages. The problem, he explained to Perkins on 26 June, was that "there were so many revisions of 'Tender' that I don't know what I left in it and what I didn't leave in it finally." Perkins counseled Fitzgerald not to worry overly much about the problem. "There is no reason a writer should not repeat a little," he wrote to Fitzgerald on 20 August. "Hem has done it." Fitzgerald was unpersuaded. "The fact that Ernest has let himself repeat here and there a phrase would be no possible justification for my doing the same," he replied on 24 August. "Each of us has his virtues and one of mine happens to be a great sense of exactitude about my work. He might be able to afford a lapse in that line where I wouldn't be and after all I have got to be the final judge of what is appropriate in these cases." Fitzgerald spent much time during the months that followed comparing the texts of his stories to the text of *Tender Is the Night*. He cut and revised many doublings but did not identify them all, leading to problems after *Taps at Reveille* appeared in print.[3]

Fitzgerald's initial choices for the collection were the Basil stories "The Scandal Detectives," "The Freshest Boy," "He Thinks He's Wonderful," and "The Perfect Life"; the Josephine stories "First Blood" and "A Woman with a Past"; and the additional stories "Crazy Sunday," "Two Wrongs," "Jacob's Ladder," "Majesty," "Family in the Wind," "A Short Trip Home," "One Interne," "The Last of the Belles," "A New Leaf," and "Babylon Revisited"—sixteen stories in all. He began submitting revised copy in late June. Perkins had these first stories set in type, but Fitzgerald was slow to address the galley proofs. When he did, he revised heavily—creating difficulties for the Scribners compositors and proofreaders. One of the best stories he had selected, "Jacob's Ladder," was sent to him in fresh galleys, but he found as he entered corrections that he had incorporated numerous passages from the story into *Tender Is the Night*, passages that he had not noticed at first. He began to

[3] George Anderson, "F. Scott Fitzgerald's Use of Story Strippings in *Tender Is the Night*," in Matthew J. Bruccoli with Judith S. Baughman, *Reader's Companion to F. Scott Fitzgerald's* Tender Is the Night (Columbia: University of South Carolina Press, 1996): 1–48.

mark heavy revisions on these galleys, which survive in his papers at Princeton, but quickly gave up the task, deciding instead to drop the story. This pattern held over the remaining months before publication. Fitzgerald withdrew stories from the lineup, sometimes after they had been set in type, and added other stories that Perkins thought inferior to the withdrawn stories. He was slow with the proofs, entering heavy revisions when he did turn his attention to them.

Fitzgerald apologized frequently to Perkins in letters, explaining always that his primary energies were going toward new magazine writing for immediate payment. Much of this writing, however, was not selling, and Fitzgerald's debts continued to grow. Perkins was indulgent at first but eventually lost patience. Editorial and make-ready expenses for *Taps at Reveille* were mounting, with no publication date in sight. Stories were being held in standing type for long periods at the Scribners printing plant, and the junking of already-typeset stories was adding further to production costs. This might have been acceptable if Fitzgerald had been working on a book with strong sales potential—a full-length novel, perhaps—but a collection of short fiction, even by Fitzgerald, was not likely to sell in significant numbers, especially in one of the darkest years of the Great Depression, when book sales were down for all publishers. Indeed, the production of *Taps at Reveille* was beginning to resemble the production of *Tender Is the Night*—a complicated business that had stretched over six months in 1933 and 1934, with cost overruns and extra corrections charges and with numerous errors in the text when the novel finally appeared.

For immediate expenses Fitzgerald was writing for *Esquire*, a new magazine edited by Arnold Gingrich, a talented young literary man who had sought him out and had flattered him with praise and attention. As a kind of reward to Gingrich, Fitzgerald added two of these *Esquire* stories, "The Fiend" and "The Night of Chancellorsville," to *Taps at Reveille*, cutting "Her Last Case," a *Post* story. Perkins now bore down on Fitzgerald and insisted that he make up his mind about which stories he wanted to include. Eventually Fitzgerald complied, settling on the Basil stories "The Scandal Detectives,"

"The Freshest Boy," "He Thinks He's Wonderful," "The Captured Shadow," and "The Perfect Life"; the Josephine stories "First Blood," "A Nice Quiet Place," and "A Woman with a Past"; and the additional stories "Crazy Sunday," "Two Wrongs," "The Night of Chancellorsville," "The Last of the Belles," "Majesty," "Family in the Wind," "A Short Trip Home," "One Interne," "The Fiend," and "Babylon Revisited."

This table of contents has not been followed for the Cambridge *Taps at Reveille*. All of the Basil stories (including "That Kind of Party," a story that remained unpublished during Fitzgerald's lifetime) and all of the Josephine stories have been published in the Cambridge volume *The Basil, Josephine, and Gwen Stories* (2009). The appearance of these stories together, in an earlier volume of this series, has made it impossible to follow Fitzgerald's arrangement for the 1935 *Taps at Reveille*. The ten additional stories from the original Scribners collection are published here in the order in which Fitzgerald arranged them; to these stories have been added nine others from the 1928–1931 period, presented chronologically by date of serial publication. These stories are "Outside the Cabinet-Maker's," "The Rough Crossing," "At Your Age," "The Swimmers," "The Bridal Party," "One Trip Abroad," "The Hotel Child," "Indecision," and "A New Leaf."[4]

This strategy shows the high quality of many of the stories that Fitzgerald did *not* include in the original *Taps at Reveille*, either because he had used passages from them in *Tender Is the Night* or because they were too close in theme and characterization to that novel. Among these rejected stories are several that are as good as any he produced during this period. If he had lived longer, Fitzgerald might have reprinted these stories in later collections, but because he died early—in 1940, at the age of 44—the stories were unknown and unread until later editors exhumed them and included them in miscellaneous collections that were, in some cases, published decades after Fitzgerald's death. Appreciation of his skill and craftsmanship as a writer of short fiction was held back by the

[4] For dates of composition and publication for these stories, see Appendix 3.

accidents and exigencies that came into play during the preparation of *Taps at Reveille*. With this Cambridge volume, the record is filled out, allowing readers to see and appreciate Fitzgerald's considerable achievement in short fiction during the late 1920s and early 1930s.

2. PUBLICATION AND RECEPTION

Taps at Reveille was formally published on 20 March 1935 at $2.50 per copy. Scribners manufactured 5,100 copies of the first impression. The publisher did not sell the last copies of this print run until 1960, twenty years after Fitzgerald's death. Fitzgerald's royalties did not square his debts with Scribners; he owed money to the firm until 1938, when he was finally able to pay off his indebtedness, and his much greater debt to Harold Ober, from his Metro-Goldwyn-Mayer earnings during his last stint in Hollywood. Fitzgerald expended much effort on *Taps at Reveille*, but in the short run this labor did nothing to help his finances.

Taps at Reveille was not widely reviewed. Most of the notices appeared in regional newspapers, though there were some reviews in major metropolitan outlets. John Chamberlain, writing for the *New York Times*, called Fitzgerald "our only poet of the upper middle class" but complained that he "cannot explain the tragedy of his characters" (27 March). Elizabeth Hart, in the *New York Herald Tribune Book Review*, singled out "Babylon Revisited" as a story written "in full relation to the contemporary scene" (31 March). Edith H. Walton, reviewing for the *New York Times Book Review*, offered mixed praise: "The characteristic seal of his brilliance stamps the entire book," she wrote, "but it is a brilliance which sputters off too frequently into mere razzle-dazzle" (31 March). William Troy, writing in the *Nation*, found the "moral interest" in the stories to be "acute" but saw little else to praise (17 April). Some negative notices appeared: the reviewer for the *New York Sun* found Fitzgerald's characters "as remote today as the neanderthal man" (5 April); and T. S. Matthews, in a review for the *New Republic*, felt that Fitzgerald had sold his characters "down the river for a good price" (10 April). Gilbert Seldes, an old friend of Fitzgerald's, praised the collection in the *New York Evening Journal*, calling "Babylon Revisited" the "saddest and truest" of the many stories Fitzgerald had written (11 April).[5]

3. POST-PUBLICATION CORRECTIONS

The haphazard production and proofing of *Taps at Reveille* left marks on the published text. The stories were disfigured by numerous misspellings and typographical errors, including "base" for "bass," "Tschaikowsky" for "Tchaikovsky," "Stravinksi" for "Stravinski," "Greenwhich" for "Greenwich," "Assis" for "Assisi," "permaturely" for "prematurely," "Bernaise" for "Béarnaise," and "*de toute*" for "*à tout*." Two slugs of linotype at 346.7–8 of the first edition were switched, creating a jumble of text. "One Interne" was marred by two near-nonsensical passages. At 350.5–7 one finds: "he need not base himself on the adding machine-calculating machine-probability machine-St. Francis of Assis machine any longer." And at 351.29–30 the text reads: "'Oh, catch it—oh, catch it and take it—oh, catch it,' she sighed." Fitzgerald noticed these passages soon after publication and sent corrections to Perkins. For page 350 he asked that the text be made to read: "need not base himself upon that human mixture of adding machines and St. Francis of Assis [sic] any longer." And for page 351 he requested that the sentence read: "'Oh, things like that happen whenever there are a lot of men together.'" So far as can be determined from the surviving evidence, the readings that displeased Fitzgerald were his own fault. Perkins, knowing that *Taps at Reveille* was unlikely to sell in high enough numbers to make necessary a second printing, had the corrections introduced into the remaining bound stock by having the printers prepare a second state of the first printing—a fussy and expensive business. The erroneous text was chiseled off the printing plates for

[5] Annotated references to the reviews of *Taps at Reveille* can be found in Jackson R. Bryer, *The Critical Reputation of F. Scott Fitzgerald* (Hamden, Conn.: Archon Books, 1967): 90–98. The major reviews have been reprinted in Jackson R. Bryer, ed., *F. Scott Fitzgerald: The Critical Reception* (New York: Burt Franklin, 1978): 337–53.

pages 350 and 351 (a facing verso and recto). The corrected text, typeset and electrotyped, was mortised in. New leaves for pages 349–50 and 351–52 were printed (that is to say, these leaves had to be printed on both sides) using the same paper stock that had been employed for the first state. These new leaves, which a bibliographer would call "cancellantia," or simply "cancels," were now run through a paper cutter and reduced to the trim size of the book. (In bibliographical terms these were leaves 5 and 6 of the twenty-third gathering of the volume.) Next came handwork at the bindery: the leaves bearing the offending readings were removed from the remaining copies of *Taps at Reveille* with a cutting tool, leaving stubs in the gutters where these leaves had been. Glue was applied to the corrected leaves along the inner edges, and these leaves were inserted into the books by hand so that the inner edges would be glued to the stubs. (In printer's language the leaves were "tipped in.") For a descriptive bibliographer this creates a second state of the first impression; the copies with the uncorrected leaves bound integrally constitute the first state.

Making corrections in this fashion was common in eighteenth- and nineteenth-century book publishing, but by 1935 it was unusual for a publisher to go to such trouble and expense, especially for a book with limited sales potential. If *Taps at Reveille* had been likely to go into subsequent impressions, Perkins would simply have had the printing plates altered and waited until it was time to order a reprint, which would have been executed from these corrected plates. This had been done for some of Fitzgerald's previous books, including *This Side of Paradise*, *Tales of the Jazz Age*, and *The Great Gatsby*, creating plate variants, instead of different states, for a bibliographer. The meticulous labor required to correct the plates and the handwork needed to excise the offending leaves and tip in the corrected leaves can be interpreted as a gesture by Perkins indicating his high regard for Fitzgerald's writing, or at least as an effort by the editor to soothe Fitzgerald's feelings over the nonsensical text. Fitzgerald's corrected readings for "One Interne" have been accepted for the Cambridge text and are recorded in the emendations list for the story.

Fitzgerald discovered another error, a significant one, in "Babylon Revisited."[6] On page 384 of the Scribners text one finds the following two paragraphs:

> Outside, the fire-red, gas-blue, ghost-green signs shone smokily through the tranquil rain. It was late afternoon and the streets were in movement; the *bistros* gleamed. At the corner of the Boulevard des Capucines he took a taxi. The Place de la Concorde moved by in pink majesty; they crossed the logical Seine, and Charlie felt the sudden provincial quality of the left bank.
>
> Charlie directed his taxi to the Avenue de l'Opera, which was out of his way. But he wanted to see the blue hour spread over the magnificent façade, and imagine that the cab horns, playing endlessly the first few bars of *Le Plus qu Lent*, were the trumpets of the Second Empire. They were closing the iron grill in front of Brentano's Book-store, and people were already at dinner behind the trim little bourgeois hedge of Duval's. He had never eaten at a really cheap restaurant in Paris. Five-course dinner, four francs fifty, eighteen cents, wine included. For some odd reason he wished that he had.

These paragraphs present a problem. The taxi-cab in which Charlie Wales is riding appears to cross the River Seine twice going in the same direction, from the Right Bank to the Left Bank. This illogicality originated in the fact that Fitzgerald had used phrases in the first paragraph in *Tender Is the Night*, on page 97 of the 1934 first edition. (The text in question appears on page 85 of the Cambridge edition of the novel.) He wanted to cut the first paragraph. He wrote

[6] For commentary on the text of "Babylon Revisited," see Bernth Lindfors, "Paris Revisited," *Fitzgerald Newsletter*, 16 (1962): 3–4; Richard R. Griffith, "A Note on Fitzgerald's 'Babylon Revisited,'" *American Literature*, 35 (1963): 236–39; William White, "Two Versions of F. Scott Fitzgerald's 'Babylon Revisited,'" *Papers of the Bibliographical Society of America*, 60 (1966): 439–52; Kenneth McCollum, "'Babylon Revisited' Revisited," *Fitzgerald/Hemingway Annual*, 2 (1971): 314–16; Garry N. Murphy and William C. Slattery, "The Flawed Text of 'Babylon Revisited,'" *Studies in Short Fiction*, 18 (1981): 315–18; Christa E. Daugherty and James L. W. West III, "Josephine Baker, Petronius, and the Text of 'Babylon Revisited,'" *F. Scott Fitzgerald Review*, 1 (2002): 3–15; and Allison E. Krebs, "The 'Human Ingenuity and Effort Expended in' Fitzgerald's 'Revisiting' of his 'Babylon,'" University honors thesis, Kent State University, 2003. My thanks to Ms. Krebs for sending me a copy of her thesis.

a new paragraph, the second paragraph above, to replace the first paragraph. In a letter dated 15 April, Fitzgerald told Perkins that he had deleted the first paragraph on the proofs: "I'd carefully elided it and written the paragraph beneath it to replace it, but the proof readers slipped and put them both in."[7] Perkins would probably have ordered a correction to the plates if Fitzgerald had insisted, but Fitzgerald did not supply substitute text for the first paragraph. No correction was ever made. Fitzgerald remained aware of the error, however, and in at least one instance deleted the first paragraph in a copy of *Taps at Reveille*, writing "Used in Tender" in the margin of the page. This copy was inscribed by Fitzgerald to Anthony Buttitta, an aspiring writer whom he befriended in Asheville, North Carolina, in 1935.[8] The letter to Perkins, together with the copy emended in Fitzgerald's hand, are compelling evidence that Fitzgerald wanted the paragraph to be removed.

This, however, has not happened. "Babylon Revisited" has become one of Fitzgerald's best-known and most frequently anthologized stories. All texts of "Babylon Revisited" known to this editor publish both paragraphs, one after the other, as they appeared in the 1935 first edition. It might be argued that the erroneous text has become fixed by the numerous reprintings and that the text for this Cambridge edition should not alter what readers are accustomed to seeing. This argument, however, is more than counterbalanced by Fitzgerald's letter to Perkins and by his markings in the Buttitta copy. For the text of "Babylon Revisited" presented here, the first paragraph has been deleted. The second paragraph stands alone, as Fitzgerald intended. The first paragraph is preserved in the emendations list for the story.

Another problem with the text of "Babylon Revisited" has been identified by Barbara Sylvester in "Whose 'Babylon Revisited' Are We Teaching? Cowley's Fortunate Corruption—and Others Not

[7] Fitzgerald to Perkins, 15 April 1935, in Matthew J. Bruccoli with Judith S. Baughman, eds., *F. Scott Fitzgerald: A Life in Letters* (New York: Simon & Schuster, 1994): 279.

[8] This copy is in the Bruccoli Collection of F. Scott Fitzgerald at the Thomas Cooper Library, University of South Carolina.

So Fortunate."[9] The reading under examination occurs near the beginning of the story, in a passage of meditation by Charlie Wales. In all surviving typescripts and in the *Post* text, the passage reads: "He believed in character; he wanted to jump back a whole generation and trust in character again as the eternally valuable element. Everything wore out now." In revising for *Taps at Reveille*, Fitzgerald deleted the word "now" to make the sentence read "Everything wore out." As Sylvester explains, the revision was likely dictated by Fitzgerald's deletion of the two sentences that follow the words "wore out now." Fitzgerald almost surely removed these sentences because part of the first sentence had been used in *Tender Is the Night*. Depending upon one's interpretation of the passage, this deletion might cause the referent of "Everything" in the *Taps at Reveille* text to be unclear. The editor and critic Malcolm Cowley seems to have thought so. In preparing the text of "Babylon Revisited" for his edition of *The Stories of F. Scott Fitzgerald*, published by Scribners in 1951, Cowley added the word "else" to make the sentence read "Everything else wore out." This is the "fortunate corruption" of Sylvester's title; after Cowley's emendation, "character" is not among the traits that wear out.[10] Cowley's emendation has not been adopted for the Cambridge text; Fitzgerald's revision of the *Post* text has been preserved. The reading is not confusing as it stands. Fitzgerald might indeed have meant to say that character, like other human traits, can become depleted, causing psychic enervation and emotional bankruptcy.

4. EDITORIAL PRINCIPLES

For editorial purposes the stories in this volume have been divided into two groups. In the first group are the stories (other than the Basil and Josephine stories) that Fitzgerald chose for the Scribners

[9] In *F. Scott Fitzgerald: New Perspectives*, ed. Jackson R. Bryer, Alan Margolies, and Ruth Prigozy (Athens: University of Georgia Press, 2000): 180–91.

[10] Sylvester makes it clear in the rest of her examination that other silent emendations by Cowley, and changes presumably made at the *Post* (especially in punctuation), are not so fortunate and alter the texture and meaning of several important passages.

edition of *Taps at Reveille*. He revised these texts for a second outing, working with tearsheets of the serial appearances and with proofs from Scribners. The base texts for these stories—that is, the texts against which emendations have been recorded—are the Scribners versions. The Scribners texts have been collated against the serial versions and against any surviving typescripts. The collations have uncovered readings, both substantive and accidental, that have been restored, either because of alterations, cuts, and bowdlerizations by magazine editors or because of typist or compositorial error.

In the second group of stories are those that Fitzgerald did not collect in *Taps at Reveille*. These stories survive in serial form and, in most instances, in final revised typescripts sent by Fitzgerald to Ober before magazine publication. Here the base texts are the serial texts. These versions have been collated against the Ober typescripts in search of mistranscriptions by typists, alterations by magazine editors, and typographical errors by compositors. Restorations and corrections have been recorded in the apparatus.

No copy-texts have been declared for these stories. The editorial procedure followed is that described by G. Thomas Tanselle in "Editing without a Copy-Text," *Studies in Bibliography*, 47 (1994): 1–22. This seminal article has guided the editorial policy of the Cambridge edition since the first volume under the current editor's direction, *This Side of Paradise*, published in 1995. Under this approach, equal authority is vested in the manuscript, typescript, serial, and collected texts—this in order to avoid dominance by any single witness. The evidence that survives for each story is described at the head of the emendations list for that story in the apparatus. The authority of each extant version is commented upon, and the strategy for emendation is set forth. Each story presents a separate editorial problem.

No evidence of editorial interference at Scribners has emerged, other than the styling of Fitzgerald's punctuation, capitalization, and orthography—the "accidentals," in editorial parlance. For Fitzgerald's earlier books with Scribners, and especially for *This Side of Paradise* (1920) and *The Beautiful and Damned* (1922), Scribners had imposed a quasi-British style of pointing and orthography that was alien to his prose. By 1935 the Scribners house style had been adjusted to favor American spellings, but the Scribners copy-editors still exercised a heavy hand with punctuation. Fitzgerald's revised typescripts are of some help here, but he could not himself type and relied on hired stenographers, both in Europe and in the United States. Some of the typists he employed in France and elsewhere automatically imposed British spelling, punctuation, and word division on his texts—single quotation marks in dialogue, for example, or *–ise* and *–our* spellings, or abbreviations not followed by full stops. Fitzgerald's substantive revisions on these typescripts carry his authority, as do his handwritten changes in punctuation and spelling; but the texture of *typed* accidentals in these versions has been regarded with skepticism, especially when the usages are contrary to Fitzgerald's usual practices in holograph.

Fitzgerald kept personal copies of some of his books and marked corrections and revisions into them. These alterations have been incorporated into earlier volumes of the Cambridge series. For *Taps at Reveille*, however, no personal copy is known to survive. The changes introduced into the second state of the Scribners *Taps at Reveille* have been adopted. Because Scribners executed only one impression of the book during Fitzgerald's lifetime, there are no impressions subsequent to the first to be subjected to a machine collation, and therefore no plate variants to consider. For some of his books Fitzgerald ordered corrections for a British edition, but no British edition of *Taps at Reveille* was ever published. Extra tearsheets of some of the stories are preserved in Fitzgerald's papers, but these tearsheets do not bear post-publication revisions. The tearsheets on which he entered revisions for Scribners do not survive and were likely discarded once fresh typescripts had been made, or galley proofs pulled.

5. REGULARIZATIONS

Fitzgerald used American spellings for most words, though he did favor some British forms—"grey" and "theatre," for example. These forms have been allowed to stand. He was inconsistent about word division, as most authors are, but study of his holographs has established his preferences for most words—for example, "taxi-cab," "band leader," and "deckhouse." Compound words in this volume have been regularized to Fitzgerald's customary forms. Question marks and exclamation points are italicized when they follow italicized words. Structural breaks indicated by roman or Arabic numerals are followed; nonstructural divisions signified in magazines by blank space and a display cap, inserted to break up the text visually, have been ignored unless they correspond to similar breaks in an extant typescript.

Years are given in Arabic numerals; seasons of the year are rendered in lower-case. Numbered avenues in New York City (Fifth Avenue) are spelled out; numbered cross-streets (59th Street) are in Arabic numerals. All dashes are one em in length. The convention of three ellipsis points within sentences and four at the ends of sentences has been followed unless Fitzgerald, in typescript, used three points at the end of a sentence to indicate interrupted speech or unfinished thought.

Fitzgerald punctuated dialogue inconsistently—sometimes correctly and sometimes in this fashion: "I'm in the sunroom," she said, "please join me." In such cases the second comma has been editorially emended to a period and, when necessary, the first word in the second clause has been capitalized. Fitzgerald often omitted the comma between two adjectives of equal weight, and he usually left out the comma between the last two elements in a series. Sometimes he did not employ a comma before the conjunction in a compound sentence. These practices are preserved in the Cambridge texts unless they cause confusion in meaning. Emendations have been recorded in the apparatus.

This approach to emendation has introduced a measure of consistency to the pointing of the Cambridge texts. No effort has been made, however, to create and impose a new house style on Fitzgerald's texts. The effect, for the Cambridge texts, is to present a slightly irregular texture of accidentals that is nevertheless faithful to Fitzgerald's usages during this period of his career.

6. RESTORATIONS

In his commercial fiction, Fitzgerald avoided or downplayed certain themes and subjects that, he knew from experience, were *verboten*—not only at the *Post* but at other mass-circulation magazines. These included alcoholism, suicide, open adultery, incest, racial prejudice, mental illness, homosexuality, and violent crime. One does not find frank treatments of these subjects in very many of Fitzgerald's commercial stories. He does take them up, all of them, in his novels. There is plentiful evidence to indicate that, during the late 1920s and early 1930s, Fitzgerald was writing mature stories on adult themes for the *Post* but that these stories were being edited at that magazine to remove forbidden elements. Any sexual innuendo, however faint, was eliminated. Nearly all profanity was cut. Almost all blasphemy, even mild oaths such as "Christ!" or "By God," was taken out. Passages having to do with racial or ethnic prejudice were cut or muted—likewise for drunkenness and alcoholism, unless the drinker was a candidate for reformation.

No purpose is served by criticizing the *Post* for adjusting Fitzgerald's texts. These were the rules of the marketplace: Fitzgerald, as a professional author, accepted them. The *Post* aimed for a broad middle-class readership and avoided potential offense to readers or advertisers. As Fitzgerald composed and revised, he included language or situations in his stories that he surely knew might be softened or deleted with the blue pencil. During this period, the *Post* was paying him between $3,500 and $4,000 for each story, its top price. To arrive at an estimate of the buying power of these sums today, one should multiply by a factor of at least ten or eleven, perhaps higher. Fitzgerald needed the money because he supported his family on literary earnings. He had no trust fund or inheritance or other source of income; his wife did not come from a wealthy family. Especially after 1930, Fitzgerald depended on the *Post* to keep going. He was able to provide what the *Post* wanted to publish, though sometimes only after scrubbings and bleachings had been carried out.

During these years, the late 1920s and early 1930s, Fitzgerald's habit was to set down a holograph first draft of a story and then to put it through successive typescripts, usually three of them, each of which he would revise, augment, cut, and polish. As mentioned, he worked with hired stenographers. His typical practice was to make wholesale revisions on the first typescript (often triple-spaced), then revise the second typescript somewhat less heavily, and finally put the third typescript into publishable shape.

The final typescripts always bore handwritten revisions, often fairly extensive ones. These typescripts, which were typically smudged and untidy, were unsuitable for submission on the fiction market. Fitzgerald sent these final typescripts to Harold Ober in New York; Ober had clean typescripts made and submitted them to the *Post* or to other magazines. The typescripts that Fitzgerald had sent to Ober, the last typescripts to bear his handwritten revisions, would be placed in Ober's files. Ober kept these typescripts; eventually they made their way to the Fitzgerald Papers at Princeton. These documents have been exceptionally valuable in editing the stories in this Cambridge volume. Fitzgerald kept files of tearsheets for his stories—the pages of printed text, torn out of magazine issues—but these tearsheets preserved the texts *after* they had been altered. The revised typescripts from Ober's files represent the stories as last revised by Fitzgerald, as last *touched* by him, before the publication process began.[11]

Collation of these typescripts against the published *Post* texts uncovers a great deal. Most references to sex, race, and alcohol were excised. Profanity was cut or muted. Fitzgerald was not allowed to use the names of real hotels, restaurants, or other businesses—for fear that such establishments might object if some fictional unpleasantness took place on their premises. Such editing was not fatal to the stories. It diminished the force of some exclamations and robbed the stories of verisimilitude, but the plots and characters remained the same.

Some of the editing, however, went deeper. This happened with several of the stories in this Cambridge volume. A good example is "Two Wrongs," a story written by Fitzgerald in October and November of 1929 and sold by Ober to the *Post* shortly thereafter. "Two Wrongs" appeared in the *Post* on 18 January 1930. It was

[11] For elaboration of this point, see James L. W. West III, "Editorial Theory and the Act of Submission," *Papers of the Bibliographical Society of America*, 83 (1989): 169–85; reprinted in West, *Making the Archives Talk* (University Park, Pa.: Penn State Press, 2011): 17–28.

one of the stories that Fitzgerald revised and included in *Taps at Reveille*. The protagonist of "Two Wrongs" is Bill McChesney, a theatrical producer who has had a recent string of hits on Broadway. Bill is typical of many of Fitzgerald's leading men: he comes from modest beginnings, is of Irish extraction, attends an elite Eastern university (Harvard, in this instance), encounters snobbishness there, and succeeds in the world of art or entertainment after he has left college. Success has made Bill cocky, abrasive, and obnoxious. He meets an aspiring dancer, a beautiful redheaded Southern girl named Emmy Pinkard, and tries to seduce her. He fails, but out of backhanded respect he gives her a small part in one of his productions, perhaps as a way of keeping her around. Bill and Emmy see a good deal of each other in the months that follow; eventually they fall in love and marry.

They move to London, where Bill is overseeing successful British productions of his Broadway hits. (His new shows in New York, however, have been failures.) He makes money in London, but on old productions. His behavior deteriorates: he has affairs with other women, begins to associate with louche aristocrats, smokes incessantly, and drinks heavily. Emmy becomes pregnant; on a night when Bill is out carousing with his friends, she goes into early labor. She makes her way to the hospital alone and gives birth to a stillborn child. Somehow Bill and Emmy make it past this disaster, and he resolves to be a better husband.

Bill and Emmy return to New York, but he has only mixed success with his productions there. Emmy, having regained her health, begins to pursue ballet seriously. She attracts notice from a star dancer named Paul Makova and has an offer to perform with him at the Metropolitan Opera House. Meanwhile Bill's health deteriorates from excessive drinking and smoking, and he falls ill with tuberculosis. Emmy, a saintly woman, offers to give up her ambitions for the ballet so that she can accompany Bill to a sanitarium in Denver, Colorado. Bill, sensing that it is Emmy's turn to enjoy success, decides to go alone. At the end of the story he leaves her to pursue a career, and possibly a romance, with Makova in New York.

"Two Wrongs" is similar to several stories Fitzgerald wrote around this time, narratives that drew on his and Zelda's personal lives. After a late start, Zelda was pursuing ballet fervently, determined to make of herself something other than a celebrated flapper girl, a role that Fitzgerald had created for her but which she had outgrown. Fitzgerald was ambivalent about Zelda's efforts in the ballet. Her lessons were expensive, and he was supporting her by writing stories for the *Post* instead of working on his next novel, the one that became *Tender Is the Night*. Fitzgerald was not convinced that Zelda had the talent to achieve anything more than a modest success in the world of dance. He understood her frustrations and wanted her to remake herself, but unfortunately his own career had stalled. He had been unable to advance on his novel for several years, his own health was on the downslide, and his smoking and drinking were increasing, causing a flare-up of what he thought might be tuberculosis.

Bill McChesney, in "Two Wrongs," is based partly on Fitzgerald. One discerns a touch of authorial self-punishment here: Bill needs to be taught a lesson—and is, in the end. Readers of popular fiction must be made to dislike a character who is going to take a fall. Thus it is interesting to note that Bill, in the typescript that Fitzgerald sent to Ober, is anti-semitic.[12] This is apparent in scenes between Bill and one of his friends, a Jewish producer named Brancusi. This anti-semitism is one of Bill's most unattractive traits. Brancusi has played an important role in Bill's successes, co-producing several of his first Broadway hits. Brancusi likes Bill and understands that his abrasive behavior comes as much from his personal insecurities as from his innate character. Brancusi absorbs the anti-semitic comments the first time they occur. Only six paragraphs into the narrative, Brancusi says to Bill, with mild irony, "You're a handsome young fellow." Bill responds, in typescript: "Sure I am—compared to you anyhow, you dirty little kyke." Brancusi seems to recognize that this is rough kidding, perhaps marginally acceptable at the time, and does not take open offense.

[12] One recalls that Anthony Patch in *The Beautiful and Damned* is anti-semitic, and that Tom Buchanan in *The Great Gatsby* places great faith in the quasi-science of eugenics. One of Joel Coles' major faux pas in "Crazy Sunday" (a story in this volume) is to perform a mildly anti-semitic comedy routine at a gathering of Hollywood royalty.

Three years pass. Bill is in London, managing his old shows there and planning a return to New York. Brancusi has come over to visit him; the two men are sitting together in the Savoy Grill. Brancusi, who has worries about Bill, tells him that he is drinking too much. We learn from Brancusi that the flops in New York resulted from a quarrel between Bill and an erstwhile friend of his named Aronstael, another producer.[13] Brancusi criticizes Bill, telling him to slow down and to treat his friends with more consideration. Bill says, "Shut your trap, you lousy little kyke." This time Brancusi reacts differently. He sees that Bill has become artistically and personally bankrupt. Fitzgerald tells us that Brancusi "made a decision, then and there, that McChesney was on the down grade; it was quite typical of him that at that point he erased him from his mind forever." Brancusi has judged correctly: Bill will soon experience illness and defeat. The point is more strongly made when readers see that Bill is callous to the feelings of others, even to the point of using anti-semitic language. The *Post*, however, cut out both "dirty little kyke" and "lousy little kyke." Bill still rejects Brancusi's advice, but after the cuts Bill only seems rude and abrupt rather than anti-semitic.

Other editing of "Two Wrongs" occurred at the *Post*. Bill and Emmy have returned to New York, and, as the story approaches its conclusion, Emmy comes home to Bill one evening after her dancing practice. He must tell her that he has been diagnosed with tuberculosis. She is about to take a bath; before he can reveal his condition, she invites him to sit and talk with her while she bathes. This is a charged sexual situation and is presented that way by Fitzgerald. Emmy steps into the running bath, and Bill watches as she sponges herself. She tells him about her offer to dance at the Metropolitan, and about Paul Makova's personal interest in her. Bill wonders whether Makova's attentions might grow into something more, just as his gift of a small part to Emmy, shortly after he had met her, had done. Emmy finishes her bath, steps out of the tub,

[13] Suggestively Jewish names, such as Aronstael, are significant in the story. Fitzgerald probably took Brancusi's name from the sculptor Constantin Brancusi, who was of Romanian Jewish descent. Paul Makova, who later in the story will invite Emmy to dance with him professionally at the Metropolitan Opera House, bears the name of an Hasidic dynasty.

and begins to dry her dancer's body. She throws a wet arm around Bill, but he does not embrace or touch her. His desires are dead; he can think only of his sickness and alcoholism. He reveals his illness to her, and the story moves quickly to its conclusion.

The *Post* altered the bath scene. After the editing, Bill and Emmy have their conversation with her fully clothed, before she bathes. In the Ober typescript, she urges him to "cut out smoking and drinking," but in the *Post* text even this reference to alcohol has been removed. Thus, in the magazine text, Bill's sexual diminishment is not apparent, Emmy's sexual allure is gone, and his debilitation seems to come only from smoking.

One does not want to make more of these cuts and bleachings than is reasonable. Even with the cuts, "Two Wrongs" is an effective story. The tension between Bill and Brancusi is discernible, and the complex feelings between Bill and Emmy are present. But Fitzgerald was a master of subtlety: one must pay attention to details and dialogue in his fiction and stay alert for suggestions and inferences. Certainly that is true of "Two Wrongs" in its unbowdlerized state. The story is more forceful if the two instances in which Bill calls Brancusi a "kyke" are left as Fitzgerald wrote them. The narrative is stronger if we see that Bill has ruined himself with alcohol, and it is more complex if he watches his wife's naked body and imagines what will happen if she remains in New York with Paul Makova.

Fitzgerald's typescript, bearing his last round of revisions, is the authoritative document for "Two Wrongs." The *Post* text has been bowdlerized. The setting copy for the story, prepared in Ober's offices, and on which any alterations would have been marked by the *Post* editors, does not survive. Nearly all of the *Post* files from this period were destroyed when the magazine ceased publication in 1969. Fitzgerald was living in Paris when the *Post* was preparing this story for the press. He might conceivably have seen the proofs and made these alterations himself, but there is no indication in the surviving correspondence that proofs were passing back and forth across the Atlantic between Fitzgerald and the *Post*—either for "Two Wrongs" or for other stories that he wrote during his expatriate years in Europe.

Similar patterns of bowdlerization have been uncovered for several of the other stories in this volume. ("The Hotel Child" is a particularly good example.) In each case a typescript bearing Fitzgerald's final handwritten revisions was sent to Ober. After a clean typescript had been made for the *Post*, the typescript revised by Fitzgerald was preserved in Ober's files, and this copy is today at Princeton. For these stories, the published texts in the *Post* differ from the typescripts only in the ways that have been described above. That is to say, no other variants that can be attributed to Fitzgerald have emerged—no new stylistic touches or added details of characterization and description that might have been added in proof. Variants involving profanity, sexual suggestiveness, real names for buildings and businesses, inebriation, and racial or ethnic prejudice have been revealed in collation. The material has been reinstated for the Cambridge texts; emendations have been recorded in the apparatus.

If Fitzgerald had wanted to restore the anti-semitic comments and the bathing scene to the text of "Two Wrongs," why did he not do so when he prepared the story for *Taps at Reveille*? The texts were being freshly typeset by Scribners for the collection; Fitzgerald could have altered "Two Wrongs" in any way he chose. The likely explanation is that in 1934 and 1935, when he was preparing copy for *Taps at Reveille*, he no longer possessed the earlier versions of "Two Wrongs" or of the other stories for reference. The unbowdlerized texts were in Ober's files in New York, where they stayed until after Fitzgerald's death. For most of the stories that he included in *Taps at Reveille*, he had on hand only the magazine tearsheets, which would have given him only the bowdlerized texts to work with.

The *Post* text of "Two Wrongs" is a good example of a socially constructed document. It is a collaborative work of fiction produced by Fitzgerald, his typists, Harold Ober, Ober's typist, the editors at the *Post*, and their typesetters and proofreaders. The text of the story in *Taps at Reveille* incorporates further revisions by Fitzgerald and adds a new group of collaborators: Maxwell Perkins, the Scribners copy-editors, and the compositors and printers at the Scribners printing plant in New York. Such a socially constructed text can be read and critiqued as a product of its times, an utterance of its culture. And, one might add, "Two Wrongs" can now be understood more thoroughly because the details of its composition, marketing, and bowdlerization have been brought to light by these collations.

This Cambridge edition of *Taps at Reveille* puts into play restored texts, also socially constructed, for "Two Wrongs" and for several other stories in this volume. Scholars and critics can now read these stories as Fitzgerald originally wrote and revised them and not in the compromised texts published in the *Post*.

TAPS AT REVEILLE

TO

HAROLD OBER

CRAZY SUNDAY

It was Sunday—not a day, but rather a gap between two other days. Behind, for all of them, lay sets and sequences, the long waits under the crane that swung the microphone, the hundred miles a day by automobiles to and fro across a county, the struggles of rival ingenuities in the conference rooms, the ceaseless compromise, the clash and strain of many personalities fighting for their lives. And now Sunday, with individual life starting up again, with a glow kindling in eyes that had been glazed with monotony the afternoon before. Slowly as the hours waned they came awake like "Puppenfeen" in a toy shop: an intense colloquy in a corner, lovers disappearing to neck in a hall. And the feeling of "Hurry, it's not too late, but for God's sake hurry before the blessed forty hours of leisure are over."

Joel Coles was writing continuity. He was twenty-eight and not yet broken by Hollywood. He had had what were considered nice assignments since his arrival six months before and he submitted his scenes and sequences with enthusiasm. He referred to himself modestly as a hack but really did not think of it that way. His mother had been a successful actress; Joel had spent his childhood between London and New York trying to separate the real from the unreal, or at least to keep one guess ahead. He was a handsome man with the pleasant cow-brown eyes that in 1913 had gazed out at Broadway audiences from his mother's face.

When the invitation came it made him sure that he was getting somewhere. Ordinarily he did not go out on Sundays but stayed sober and took work home with him. Recently they had given him a Eugene O'Neill play destined for a very important lady indeed. Everything he had done so far had pleased Miles Calman, and Miles Calman was the only director on the lot who did not work under a supervisor and was responsible to the money men alone. Everything was clicking into place in Joel's career. ("This is Mr. Calman's secretary. Will you come to tea from four to six Sunday—he lives in Beverly Hills, number—.")

Joel was flattered. It would be a party out of the top-drawer. It was a tribute to himself as a young man of promise. The Marion Davies crowd, the high-hats, the big currency numbers, perhaps even Dietrich and Garbo and the Marquise, people who were not seen everywhere, would probably be at Calman's.

"I won't take anything to drink," he assured himself. Calman was audibly tired of rummies, and thought it was a pity the industry could not get along without them.

Joel agreed that writers drank too much—he did himself, but he wouldn't this afternoon. He wished Miles would be within hearing when the cocktails were passed to hear his succinct, unobtrusive, "No, thank you."

Miles Calman's house was built for great emotional moments—there was an air of listening, as if the far silences of its vistas hid an audience, but this afternoon it was thronged, as though people had been bidden rather than asked. Joel noted with pride that only two other writers from the studio were in the crowd, an ennobled limey and, somewhat to his surprise, Nat Keogh, who had evoked Calman's impatient comment on drunks.

Stella Calman (Stella Walker, of course) did not move on to her other guests after she spoke to Joel. She lingered—she looked at him with the sort of beautiful look that demands some sort of acknowledgment and Joel drew quickly on the dramatic adequacy inherited from his mother:

"Well, you look about sixteen! Where's your kiddy car?"

She was visibly pleased; she lingered. He felt that he should say something more, something confident and easy—he had first met her when she was struggling for bits in New York. At that moment a tray slid up and Stella put a cocktail glass into his hand.

"Everybody's afraid, aren't they?" he said, looking at it absently. "Everybody watches for everybody else's blunders, or tries to make sure they're with people that'll do them credit. Of course that's not true in your house," he covered himself hastily. "I just meant generally in Hollywood."

Stella agreed. She presented several people to Joel as if he were very important. Reassuring himself that Miles was at the other side of the room, Joel drank the cocktail.

"So you have a baby?" he said. "That's the time to look out. After a pretty woman has had her first child, she's very vulnerable, because she wants to be reassured about her own charm. She's got to have some new man's unqualified devotion to prove to herself she hasn't lost anything."

"I never get anybody's unqualified devotion," Stella said rather resentfully.

"They're afraid of your husband."

"You think that's it?" She wrinkled her brow over the idea; then the conversation was interrupted at the exact moment Joel would have chosen.

Her attentions had given him confidence. Not for him to join safe groups, to slink to refuge under the wings of such acquaintances as he saw about the room. He walked to the window and looked out toward the Pacific, colorless under its sluggish sunset. It was good here—the American Riviera and all that, if there were ever time to enjoy it. The handsome, well-dressed people in the room, the lovely girls, and the—well, the lovely girls. You couldn't have everything.

He saw Stella's fresh boyish face, with the tired eyelid that always drooped a little over one eye, moving about among her guests and he wanted to sit with her and talk a long time as if she were a girl instead of a name; he followed her to see if she paid anyone as much attention as she had paid him. He took another cocktail—not because he needed confidence but because she had given him so much of it. Then he sat down beside the director's mother.

"Your son's gotten to be a legend, Mrs. Calman—Oracle and a Man of Destiny and all that. Personally, I'm against him but I'm in a minority. What do you think of him? Are you impressed? Are you surprised how far he's gone?"

"No, I'm not surprised," she said calmly. "We always expected a lot from Miles."

"Well now, that's unusual," remarked Joel. "I always think all mothers are like Napoleon's mother. My mother didn't want me to have anything to do with the entertainment business. She wanted me to go to West Point and be safe."

"We always had every confidence in Miles. . . . "

He stood by the built-in bar of the dining room with the good-humored, heavy-drinking, highly paid Nat Keogh.

"—I made a hundred grand during the year and lost forty grand gambling, so now I've hired a manager."

"You mean an agent," suggested Joel.

"No, I've got that too. I mean a manager. I make over everything to my wife and then he and my wife get together and hand me out the money. I pay him five thousand a year to hand me out my money."

"You mean your agent."

"No, I mean my manager, and I'm not the only one—a lot of other irresponsible people have him."

"Well, if you're irresponsible why are you responsible enough to hire a manager?"

"I'm just irresponsible about gambling. Look here—"

A singer performed; Joel and Nat went forward with the others to listen.

II

The singing reached Joel vaguely; he felt happy and friendly toward all the people gathered there, people of bravery and industry, superior to a bourgeoisie that outdid them in ignorance and loose living, risen to a position of the highest prominence in a nation that for a decade had wanted only to be entertained. He liked them—he loved them. Great waves of good feeling flowed through him.

As the singer finished his number and there was a drift toward the hostess to say good-bye, Joel had an idea. He would give them "Building It Up," his own composition. It was his only parlor trick, it had amused several parties and it might please Stella Walker. Possessed by the hunch, his blood throbbing with the scarlet corpuscles of exhibitionism, he sought her.

"Of course," she cried. "Please! Do you need anything?"

"Someone has to be the secretary that I'm supposed to be dictating to."

"I'll be her."

As the word spread the guests in the hall, already putting on their coats to leave, drifted back and Joel faced the eyes of many strangers. He had a dim foreboding, realizing that the man who had just performed was a famous radio entertainer. Then someone said "Sh!" and he was alone with Stella, the center of a sinister Indian-like half-circle. Stella smiled up at him expectantly—he began.

His burlesque was based upon the cultural limitations of Mr. Dave Silverstein, an independent producer; Silverstein was presumed to be dictating a letter outlining a treatment of a story he had bought.

"—a story of divorce, the younger generators and the Foreign Legion," he heard his voice saying, with the intonations of Mr. Silverstein. "But we got to build it up, see?"

A sharp pang of doubt struck through him. The faces surrounding him in the gently molded light were intent and curious, but there was no ghost of a smile anywhere; directly in front the Great Lover of the screen glared at him with an eye as keen as the eye of a potato. Only Stella Walker looked up at him with a radiant, never faltering smile.

"If we make him a Menjou type, then we get a sort of Michael Arlen only with a Honolulu atmosphere."

Still not a ripple in front, but in the rear a rustling, a perceptible shift toward the left, toward the front door.

"—then she says she feels this sex appil for him and he burns out and says 'Oh go on destroy yourself'—"

At some point he heard Nat Keogh snicker and here and there were a few encouraging faces, but as he finished he had the sickening realization that he had made a fool of himself in view of an important section of the picture world, upon whose favor depended his career.

For a moment he existed in the midst of a confused silence, broken by a general trek for the door. He felt the undercurrent of derision that rolled through the gossip; then—all this was in the space of ten seconds—the Great Lover, his eye hard and empty as the eye of a needle, shouted "Boo! Boo!" voicing in an overtone what he felt was the mood of the crowd. It was the resentment of the professional toward the amateur, of the community toward the stranger, the thumbs-down of the clan.

Only Stella Walker was still standing near and thanking him as if he had been an unparalleled success, as if it hadn't occurred to her that anyone hadn't liked it. As Nat Keogh helped him into his overcoat, a great wave of self-disgust swept over him and he clung desperately to his rule of never betraying an inferior emotion until he no longer felt it.

"I was a flop," he said lightly, to Stella. "Never mind, it's a good number when appreciated. Thanks for your cooperation."

The smile did not leave her face—he bowed rather drunkenly and Nat drew him toward the door....

The arrival of his breakfast awakened him into a broken and ruined world. Yesterday he was himself, a point of fire against an industry, today he felt that he was pitted under an enormous disadvantage, against those faces, against individual contempt and collective sneer. Worse than that, to Miles Calman he was become one of those rummies, stripped of dignity, whom Calman regretted he was compelled to use. To Stella Walker, on whom he had forced a martyrdom to preserve the courtesy of her house—her opinion he did not dare to guess. His gastric juices ceased to flow and he set his poached eggs back on the telephone table. He wrote:

DEAR MILES:

You can imagine my profound self-disgust. I confess to a taint of exhibitionism, but at six o'clock in the afternoon, in broad daylight! Good God! My apologies to your wife.

Yours ever,

JOEL COLES.

Joel emerged from his office on the lot only to slink like a malefactor to the tobacco store. So suspicious was his manner that one of the studio police asked to see his admission card. He had decided to eat lunch outside when Nat Keogh, confident and cheerful, overtook him.

"What do you mean you're in permanent retirement? What if that Three Piece Suit did boo you?

"Why, listen," he continued, drawing Joel into the studio restaurant. "The night of one of his premiers at Grauman's, Joe Squires kicked his tail while he was bowing to the crowd. The ham said Joe'd hear from him later but when Joe called him up at eight o'clock next day and said, 'I thought I was going to hear from you,' he hung up the phone."

The preposterous story cheered Joel, and he found a gloomy consolation in staring at the group at the next table, the sad, lovely Siamese twins, the mean dwarfs, the proud giant from the circus picture. But looking beyond at the yellow-stained faces of pretty women, their eyes all melancholy and startling with mascara, their ball gowns garish in full day, he saw a group who had been at Calmans' and winced.

"Never again," he exclaimed aloud, "absolutely my last social appearance in Hollywood!"

The following morning a telegram was waiting for him at his office:

YOU WERE ONE OF THE MOST AGREEABLE PEOPLE AT OUR PARTY. EXPECT YOU AT MY SISTER JUNE'S BUFFET SUPPER NEXT SUNDAY.

STELLA WALKER CALMAN.

The blood rushed fast through his veins for a feverish minute. Incredulously he read the telegram over.

"Well, that's the sweetest thing I ever heard of in my life!"

III

Crazy Sunday again. Joel slept until eleven, then he read a newspaper to catch up with the past week. He lunched in his room on trout, avocado salad and a pint of California wine. Dressing for the tea, he selected a pin-check suit, a blue shirt, a burnt orange tie. There were dark circles of fatigue under his eyes. In his second-hand car he drove to the Riviera apartments. As he was introducing himself to Stella's sister, Miles and Stella arrived in riding clothes—they had been quarrelling fiercely most of the afternoon on all the dirt roads back of Beverly Hills.

Miles Calman, tall, nervous, with a desperate humor and the unhappiest eyes Joel ever saw, was an artist from the top of his curiously shaped head to his niggerish feet. Upon these last he stood firmly—he had never made a cheap picture though he had sometimes paid heavily for the luxury of making experimental flops. In spite of his excellent company, one could not be with him long without realizing that he was not a well man.

From the moment of their entrance Joel's day bound itself up inextricably with theirs. As he joined the group around them Stella turned away from it with an impatient little tongue click—and Miles Calman said to the man who happened to be next to him:

"Go easy on Eva Goebel. There's hell to pay about her at home." Miles turned to Joel, "I'm sorry I missed you at the office yesterday. I spent the afternoon at the analyst's."

"You being psychoanalyzed?"

"I have been for months. First I went for claustrophobia, now I'm trying to get my whole life cleared up. They say it'll take over a year."

"There's nothing the matter with your life," Joel assured him.

"Oh, no? Well, Stella seems to think so. Ask anybody—they can all tell you about it," he said bitterly.

A girl perched herself on the arm of Miles' chair; Joel crossed to Stella, who stood disconsolately by the fire.

"Thank you for your telegram," he said. "It was darn sweet. I can't imagine anybody as good-looking as you are being so good-humored."

She was a little lovelier than he had ever seen her and perhaps the unstinted admiration in his eyes prompted her to unload on him—it did not take long, for she was obviously at the emotional bursting point.

"—and Miles has been carrying on this thing for two years, and I never knew. Why, she was one of my best friends, always in the house. Finally when people began to come to me, Miles had to admit it."

She sat down vehemently on the arm of Joel's chair. Her riding breeches were the color of the chair and Joel saw that the mass of her hair was made up of some strands of red gold and some of pale gold, so that it could not be dyed, and that she had on no make-up. She was that good-looking—

Still quivering with the shock of her discovery, Stella found unbearable the spectacle of a new girl hovering over Miles; she led Joel into a bedroom, and seated at either end of a big bed they went on talking. People on their way to the washroom glanced in and made wisecracks, but Stella, emptying out her story, paid no attention. After awhile Miles stuck his head in the door and said, "There's no use trying to explain something to Joel in half an hour that I don't understand myself and the psychoanalyst says will take a whole year to understand."

She talked on as if Miles were not there. She loved Miles, she said—under considerable difficulties she had always been faithful to him.

"The psychoanalyst told Miles that he had a mother complex. In his first marriage he transferred his mother complex to his wife, you see—and then his sex turned to me. But when we married the thing repeated itself—he transferred his mother complex to me and all his libido turned toward this other woman."

Joel knew that this probably wasn't gibberish—yet it sounded like gibberish. He knew Eva Goebel; she was a motherly person, older and probably wiser than Stella, who was a golden child.

Miles now suggested impatiently that Joel come back with them since Stella had so much to say, so they drove out to the mansion in Beverly Hills. Under the high ceilings the situation seemed more dignified and tragic. It was an eerie bright night with the dark very clear outside all the windows and Stella all rose-gold raging and crying around the room. Joel did not quite believe in picture actresses' grief. They have other preoccupations—they are beautiful rose-gold figures blown full of life by writers and directors, and after hours they sit around and talk in whispers and giggled innuendoes, and the ends of many adventures flow through them.

Sometimes he pretended to listen and instead thought how well she was got up—sleek breeches with a matched set of legs in them, an Italian-colored sweater with a little high neck, and a short brown chamois coat. He couldn't decide whether she was an imitation of an English lady or an English lady was an imitation of her. She hovered somewhere between the realest of realities and the most blatant of impersonations.

"Miles is so jealous of me that he questions everything I do," she cried scornfully. "When I was in New York I wrote him that I'd been to the theatre with Eddie Baker. Miles was so jealous he phoned me ten times in one day."

"I was wild," Miles snuffled sharply, a habit he had in times of stress. "The analyst couldn't get any results for a week."

Stella shook her head despairingly. "Did you expect me just to sit in the hotel for three weeks?"

"I don't expect anything. I admit that I'm jealous. I try not to be. I worked on that with Dr. Bridgebane, but it didn't do any good. I was jealous of Joel this afternoon when you sat on the arm of his chair."

"You were?" She started up. "You were! Wasn't there somebody on the arm of your chair? And did you speak to me for two hours?"

"You were telling your troubles to Joel in the bedroom."

"When I think that that woman"—she seemed to believe that to omit Eva Goebel's name would be to lessen her reality—"used to come here—"

"All right—all right," said Miles wearily. "I've admitted everything and I feel as bad about it as you do." Turning to Joel he began talking about pictures, while Stella moved restlessly along the far walls, her hands in her breeches pockets.

"They've treated Miles terribly," she said, coming suddenly back into the conversation as if they'd never discussed her personal affairs. "Dear, tell him about old Beltzer trying to change your picture."

As she stood hovering protectively over Miles, her eyes flashing with indignation in his behalf, Joel realized that he was in love with her. Stifled with excitement he got up to say good-night.

With Monday the week resumed its workaday rhythm, in sharp contrast to the theoretical discussions, the gossip and scandal of Sunday; there was the endless detail of script revision—"Instead of a lousy dissolve, we can leave her voice on the sound track and cut to a medium shot of the taxi from Bell's angle or we can simply pull the camera back to include the station, hold it a minute and then pan to the row of taxis"—by Monday afternoon Joel had again forgotten that people whose business was to provide entertainment were ever privileged to be entertained. In the evening he phoned Miles' house. He asked for Miles but Stella came to the phone.

"Do things seem better?"

"Not particularly. What are you doing next Saturday evening?"

"Nothing."

"The Perrys are giving a dinner and theatre party and Miles won't be here—he's flying to South Bend to see the Notre Dame-California game. I thought you might go with me in his place."

After a long moment Joel said, "Why—surely. If there's a conference I can't make dinner but I can get to the theatre."

"Then I'll say we can come."

Joel walked to his office. In view of the strained relations of the Calmans, would Miles be pleased, or did she intend that Miles shouldn't know of it? That would be out of the question—if Miles didn't mention it Joel would. But it was an hour or more before he could get down to work again.

Wednesday there was a four-hour wrangle in a conference room crowded with planets and nebulæ of cigarette smoke. Three men and a woman paced the carpet in turn, suggesting or condemning, speaking sharply or persuasively, confidently or despairingly. At the end Joel lingered to talk to Miles.

The man was tired—not with the exaltation of fatigue but life-tired, with his lids sagging and his beard prominent over the blue shadows near his mouth.

"I hear you're flying to the Notre Dame game."

Miles looked beyond him and shook his head.

"I've given up the idea."

"Why?"

"On account of you." Still he did not look at Joel.

"What the hell, Miles?"

"That's why I've given it up." He broke into a perfunctory laugh at himself. "I can't tell what Stella might do just out of spite—she's invited you to take her to the Perrys', hasn't she? I wouldn't enjoy the game."

The fine instinct that moved swiftly and confidently on the set, muddled so weakly and helplessly through his personal life.

"Look, Miles," Joel said frowning. "I've never made any passes whatsoever at Stella. If you're really seriously cancelling your trip on account of me, I won't go to the Perrys' with her. I won't see her. You can trust me absolutely."

Miles looked at him, carefully now.

"Maybe." He shrugged his shoulders. "Anyhow there'd just be somebody else. I wouldn't have any fun."

"You don't seem to have much confidence in Stella. She told me she'd always been true to you."

"Maybe she has." In the last few minutes several more muscles had sagged around Miles' mouth. "But how can I ask anything of her after what's happened? How can I expect her—" He broke off and his face grew harder as he said, "I'll tell you one thing, right or wrong and no matter what I've done, if I ever had anything on her I'd divorce her. I can't have my pride hurt—that would be the last straw."

His tone annoyed Joel, but he said:

"Hasn't she calmed down about the Eva Goebel thing?"

"No." Miles snuffled pessimistically. "I can't get over it either."

"I thought it was finished."

"I'm trying not to see Eva again, but you know it isn't easy just to drop something like that—it isn't some girl I kissed last night in a taxi! The psychoanalyst says—"

"I know," Joel interrupted. "Stella told me." This was depressing. "Well, as far as I'm concerned if you go to the game I won't see Stella. And I'm sure Stella has nothing on her conscience about anybody."

"Maybe not," Miles repeated listlessly. "Anyhow I'll stay and take her to the party. Say," he said suddenly, "I wish you'd come too. I've got to have somebody sympathetic to talk to. That's the trouble—I've influenced Stella in everything. Especially I've influenced her so that she likes all the men I like—it's very difficult."

"It must be," Joel agreed.

IV

Joel could not get to the dinner. Self-conscious in his silk hat against the unemployment, he waited for the others in front of the Hollywood Theatre and watched the evening parade: obscure replicas of bright, particular picture stars, spavined men in polo coats, a stomping dervish with the beard and staff of an apostle, a pair of chic Filipinos in collegiate clothes, reminder that this corner of the Republic opened to the seven seas, a long fantastic carnival of young shouts which proved to be a fraternity initiation. The line split to pass two smart limousines that stopped at the curb.

There she was, in a dress like ice-water, made in a thousand pale-blue pieces, with icicles trickling at the throat. He started forward.

"So you like my dress?"

"Where's Miles?"

"He flew to the game after all. He left yesterday morning—at least I think—" She broke off. "I just got a telegram from South Bend saying that he's starting back. I forgot—you know all these people?"

The party of eight moved into the theatre.

Miles had gone after all and Joel wondered if he should have come. But during the performance, with Stella a profile under the pure grain of light hair, he thought no more about Miles. Once he turned and looked at her and she looked back at him, smiling and meeting his eyes for as long as he wanted. Between the acts they smoked in the lobby and she whispered:

"They're all going to the opening of Jack Johnson's night club—I don't want to go, do you?"

"Do we have to?"

"I suppose not." She hesitated. "I'd like to talk to you. I suppose we could go to our house—if I were only sure—"

Again she hesitated and Joel asked:

"Sure of what?"

"Sure that—oh, I'm haywire I know, but how can I be sure Miles went to the game?"

"You mean you think he's with Eva Goebel?"

"No, not so much that—but supposing he was here watching everything I do. You know Miles does odd things sometimes. Once he wanted a man with a long beard to drink tea with him and he sent down to the casting agency for one, and drank tea with him all afternoon."

"That's different. He sent you a wire from South Bend—that proves he's at the game."

After the play they said good-night to the others at the curb and were answered by looks of amusement. They slid off along the golden garish thoroughfare through the crowd that had gathered around Stella.

"You see he could arrange the telegrams," Stella said, "very easily."

That was true. And with the idea that perhaps her uneasiness was justified, Joel grew angry: if Miles had trained a camera on them he felt no obligations toward Miles. Aloud he said:

"That's nonsense."

There were Christmas trees already in the shop windows and the full moon over the boulevard was only a prop, as scenic as the giant boudoir lamps of the corners. On into the dark foliage of Beverly Hills that flamed as eucalyptus by day, Joel saw only the flash of a white face under his own, the arc of her shoulder. She pulled away suddenly and looked up at him.

"Your eyes are like your mother's," she said. "I used to have a scrapbook full of pictures of her."

"Your eyes are like your own and not a bit like any other eyes," he answered.

Something made Joel look out into the grounds as they went into the house, as if Miles were lurking in the shrubbery. A telegram waited on the hall table. She read aloud:

CHICAGO.

HOME TOMORROW NIGHT. THINKING OF YOU. LOVE.

MILES.

"You see," she said, throwing the slip back on the table, "he could easily have faked that." She asked the butler for drinks and sandwiches and ran upstairs, while Joel walked into the empty reception rooms. Strolling about he wandered to the piano where he had stood in disgrace two Sundays before.

"Then we could put over," he said aloud, "a story of divorce, the younger generators and the Foreign Legion."

His thoughts jumped to another telegram.

"You were one of the most agreeable people at our party—"

An idea occurred to him. If Stella's telegram had been purely a gesture of courtesy then it was likely that Miles had inspired it, for it was Miles who had invited him. Probably Miles had said:

"Send him a wire—he's miserable—he thinks he's queered himself."

It fitted in with "I've influenced Stella in everything. Especially I've influenced her so that she likes all the men I like." A woman would do a thing like that because she felt sympathetic—only a man would do it because he felt responsible.

When Stella came back into the room he took both her hands.

"I have a strange feeling that I'm a sort of pawn in a spite game you're playing against Miles," he said.

"Help yourself to a drink."

"And the odd thing is that I'm in love with you anyhow."

The telephone rang and she freed herself to answer it.

"Another wire from Miles," she announced. "He dropped it, or it says he dropped it, from the airplane at Kansas City."

"I suppose he asked to be remembered to me."

"No, he just said he loved me. I believe he does. He's so very weak."

"Come sit beside me," Joel urged her.

It was early. And it was still a few minutes short of midnight a half-hour later, when Joel walked to the cold hearth, and said tersely:

"Meaning that you haven't any curiosity about me?"

"Not at all. You attract me a lot and you know it. The point is that I suppose I really do love Miles."

"Obviously."

"And tonight I feel uneasy about everything."

He wasn't angry—he was even faintly relieved that a possible entanglement was avoided. Still as he looked at her, the warmth and softness of her body thawing her cold blue costume, he knew she was one of the things he would always regret.

"I've got to go," he said. "I'll phone a taxi."

"Nonsense—there's a chauffeur on duty."

He winced at her readiness to have him go, and seeing this she kissed him lightly and said, "You're sweet, Joel." Then suddenly three things happened: he took down his drink at a gulp, the phone rang loud through the house and a clock in the hall struck in trumpet notes.

Nine—ten—eleven—twelve—

V

It was Sunday again. Joel realized that he had come to the theatre this evening with the work of the week still hanging about him like cerements. He had made love to Stella as he might attack some matter to be cleaned up hurriedly before the day's end. But this was Sunday—the lovely, lazy perspective of the next twenty-four hours unrolled before him—every minute was something to be approached with lulling indirection, every moment held the germ of innumerable possibilities. Nothing was impossible—everything was just beginning. He poured himself another drink.

With a sharp moan, Stella slipped forward inertly by the telephone. Joel picked her up and laid her on the sofa. He squirted soda-water on a handkerchief and slapped it over her face. The telephone mouthpiece was still grinding and he put it to his ear.

"—the plane fell just this side of Kansas City. The body of Miles Calman has been identified and—"

He hung up the receiver.

"Lie still," he said, stalling, as Stella opened her eyes.

"Oh, what's happened?" she whispered. "Call them back. Oh, what's happened?"

"I'll call them right away. What's your doctor's name?"

"Did they say Miles was dead?"

"Lie quiet—is there a servant still up?"

"Hold me—I'm frightened."

He put his arm around her.

"I want the name of your doctor," he said sternly. "It may be a mistake but I want someone here."

"It's Doctor— Oh, God, is Miles dead?"

Joel ran upstairs and searched through strange medicine cabinets for spirits of ammonia. When he came down Stella cried:

"He isn't dead—I know he isn't. This is part of his scheme. He's torturing me. I know he's alive. I can feel he's alive."

"I want to get hold of some close friend of yours, Stella. You can't stay here alone tonight."

"Oh, no," she cried. "I can't see anybody. You stay. I haven't got any friend." She got up, tears streaming down her face. "Oh, Miles is my only friend. He's not dead—he can't be dead. I'm going there right away and see. Get a train. You'll have to come with me."

"You can't. There's nothing to do tonight. I want you to tell me the name of some woman I can call: Lois? Joan? Carmel? Isn't there somebody?"

Stella stared at him blindly.

"Eva Goebel was my best friend," she said.

Joel thought of Miles, his sad and desperate face in the office two days before. In the awful silence of his death all was clear about him. He was the only American-born director with both an interesting temperament and an artistic conscience. Meshed in an industry, he had paid with his ruined nerves for having no resilience, no healthy cynicism, no refuge—only a pitiful and precarious escape.

There was a sound at the outer door—it opened suddenly, and there were footsteps in the hall.

"Miles!" Stella screamed. "Is it you, Miles? Oh, it's Miles."

A telegraph boy appeared in the doorway.

"I couldn't find the bell. I heard you talking inside."

The telegram was a duplicate of the one that had been phoned. While Stella read it over and over, as though it were a black lie, Joel telephoned. It was still early and he had difficulty getting anyone; when finally he succeeded in finding some friends he made Stella take a stiff drink.

"You'll stay here, Joel," she whispered, as though she were half-asleep. "You won't go away. Miles liked you—he said you—" She shivered violently, "Oh, my God, you don't know how alone I feel."

Her eyes closed, "Put your arms around me. Miles had a suit like that." She started bolt upright. "Think of what he must have felt. He was afraid of almost everything, anyhow."

She shook her head dazedly. Suddenly she seized Joel's face and held it close to hers.

"You won't go. You like me—you love me, don't you? Don't call up anybody. Tomorrow's time enough. You stay here with me tonight."

He stared at her, at first incredulously, and then with shocked understanding. In her dark groping Stella was trying to keep Miles alive by sustaining a situation in which he had figured—as if Miles' mind could not die so long as the possibilities that had worried him still existed. It was a distraught and tortured effort to stave off the realization that he was dead.

Resolutely Joel went to the phone and called a doctor.

"Don't, oh, don't call anybody!" Stella cried. "Come back here and put your arms around me."

"Is Doctor Bales in?"

"Joel," Stella cried. "I thought I could count on you. Miles liked you. He was jealous of you—Joel, come here."

Ah then—if he betrayed Miles she would be keeping him alive—for if he were really dead how could he be betrayed?

"—has just had a very severe shock. Can you come at once, and get hold of a nurse?"

"Joel!"

Now the door-bell and the telephone began to ring intermittently, and automobiles were stopping in front of the door.

"But you're not going," Stella begged him. "You're going to stay, aren't you?"

"No," he answered. "But I'll be back, if you need me."

Standing on the steps of the house which now hummed and palpitated with the life that flutters around death like protective leaves, he began to sob a little in his throat.

"Everything he touched he did something magical to," he thought. "He even brought that little gamin alive and made her a sort of masterpiece."

And then:

"What a hell of a hole he leaves in this damn wilderness—already!"

And then with a certain bitterness, "Oh, yes, I'll be back—I'll be back!"

TWO WRONGS

"Look at those shoes," said Bill—"twenty-eight dollars."

Mr. Brancusi looked.

"Purty."

"Made to order."

"I knew you were a great swell. You didn't get me up here to show me those shoes, did you?"

"I am not a great swell. Who said I was a great swell?" demanded Bill. "Just because I've got more education than most people in show business."

"And then, you know, you're a handsome young fellow," said Brancusi dryly.

"Sure I am—compared to you anyhow, you dirty little kyke. The girls think I must be an actor, till they find out .... Got a cigarette? What's more, I look like a man—which is more than most of these pretty boys round Times Square do."

"Good-looking. Gentleman. Good shoes. Shot with luck."

"You're wrong there," objected Bill. "Brains. Three years—nine shows—four big hits—only one flop. Where do you see any luck in that?"

A little bored, Brancusi just gazed. What he would have seen—had he not made his eyes opaque and taken to thinking about something else—was a fresh-faced young Irishman exuding aggressiveness and self-confidence until the air of his office was thick with it. Presently, Brancusi knew, Bill would hear the sound of his own voice and be ashamed and retire into his other humor—the quietly superior, sensitive one, the patron of the arts, modelled on the intellectuals of the Theatre Guild. Bill McChesney had not quite decided between the two; such blends are seldom complete before thirty.

"Take Ames, take Hopkins, take Harris—take any of them," Bill insisted. "What have they got on me? What's the matter? Do you want a drink?"—seeing Brancusi's glance wander toward the cabinet on the opposite wall.

"I never drink in the morning. I just wondered who was it keeps on knocking. You ought to make it stop it. I get a nervous fidgets, kind of half crazy, with that kind of thing."

Bill went quickly to the door and threw it open.

"Nobody," he said . . . "Hello! What do you want?"

"Oh, I'm so sorry," a voice answered; "I'm terribly sorry. I got so excited and I didn't realize I had this pencil in my hand."

"What is it you want?"

"I want to see you, and the clerk said you were busy. I have a letter for you from Alan Rogers, the playwright—and I wanted to give it to you personally."

"I'm busy," said Bill. "See Mr. Cadorna."

"I did, but he wasn't very encouraging, and Mr. Rogers said—"

Brancusi, edging over restlessly, took a quick look at her. She was very young, with beautiful red hair, and more character in her face than her chatter would indicate; it did not occur to Mr. Brancusi that this was due to her origin in Delaney, South Carolina.

"What shall I do?" she inquired, quietly laying her future in Bill's hands. "I had a letter to Mr. Rogers, and he just gave me this one to you."

"Well, what do you want me to do—marry you?" exploded Bill.

"I'd like to get a part in one of your plays."

"Then sit down and wait. I'm busy . . . . Where's Miss Cohalan?" He rang a bell, looked once more, crossly, at the girl and closed the door of his office. But during the interruption his other mood had come over him, and he resumed his conversation with Brancusi in the key of one who was hand in glove with Reinhardt for the artistic future of the theatre.

By 12:30 he had forgotten everything except that he was going to be the greatest producer in the world and that he had an engagement to tell Sol Lincoln about it at lunch. Emerging from his office, he looked expectantly at Miss Cohalan.

"Mr. Lincoln won't be able to meet you," she said. "He jus 'is minute called."

"Just this minute," repeated Bill, shocked. "All right. Just cross him off that list for Thursday night."

Miss Cohalan drew a line on a sheet of paper before her.

"Mr. McChesney, now you haven't forgotten me, have you?"

He turned to the red-headed girl.

"No," he said vaguely, and then to Miss Cohalan: "That's all right; ask him for Thursday anyhow. To hell with him."

He did not want to lunch alone. He did not like to do anything alone now, because contacts were too much fun when one had prominence and power.

"If you would just let me talk to you two minutes—" she began.

"Afraid I can't now." Suddenly he realized that she was the most beautiful person he had ever seen in his life.

He stared at her.

"Mr. Rogers told me—"

"Come and have a spot of lunch with me," he said, and then, with an air of great hurry, he gave Miss Cohalan some quick and contradictory instructions and held open the door.

They stood on 42nd Street and he breathed his preempted air—there is only enough air there for a few people at a time. It was November and the first exhilarating rush of the season was over, but he could look east and see the electric sign of one of his plays, and west and see another. Around the corner was the one he had put on with Brancusi—the last time he would produce anything except alone.

They went to the Bedford, where there was a to-do of waiters and captains as he came in.

"Two cocktails," he ordered. "I mean shake up three. You don't want one? Well, then, two."

"This is ver tractive restaurant," she said, impressed and on company behavior.

"This is hams' paradise." He nodded to several people. "Hello, Jimmy—Bill.... Hello there, Jack.... That's Jack Dempsey.... I don't eat here much. I usually eat up at the Harvard Club."

"Oh, did you go to Harvard? I used to know—"

"Yes." He hesitated; there were two versions about Harvard, and he decided suddenly on the true one. "Yes, and they had me down for a hick there, but not anymore. About a week ago I was out on Long Island at the Gouverneer Haights—very fashionable people—and a couple of Gold Coast boys that never knew I was alive up in Cambridge began pulling this 'Hello, Bill, old boy' on me."

He hesitated and suddenly decided to leave the story there.

"What do you want—a job?" he demanded. He remembered suddenly that she had holes in her stockings. Holes in stockings always moved him, softened him.

"Yes, or else I've got to go home," she said. "I want to be a dancer—you know, Russian ballet. But the lessons cost so much, so I've got to get a job. I thought it'd give me stage presence anyhow."

"Hoofer, eh?"

"Oh, no, serious."

"Well, Pavlova's a hoofer, isn't she?"

"Oh, no." She was shocked at this profanity, but after a moment she continued: "I took with Miss Campbell—Georgia Berriman Campbell—back home—maybe you know her. She took from Ned Wayburn, and she's really wonderful. She—"

"Yeah?" he said abstractedly. "Well, it's a tough business—casting agencies bursting with people that can all do anything, till I give them a try. How old are you?"

"Eighteen."

"I'm twenty-six. Came here four years ago without a cent."

"My!"

"I could quit now and be comfortable the rest of my life."

"My!"

"Going to take a year off next year—get married.... Ever hear of Irene Rikker?"

"I should say! She's about my favorite of all."

"We're engaged."

"My!"

When they went out into Times Square after awhile he said carelessly, "What are you doing now?"

"Why, I'm trying to get a job."

"I mean right this minute."

"Why, nothing."

"Do you want to come up to my apartment on 46th Street and have some coffee, or a drink?"

Their eyes met, and Emmy Pinkard made up her mind she could take care of herself.

It was a great bright studio apartment with a ten-foot divan, and after she had coffee and he a highball, his arm dropped round her shoulder.

"Why should I kiss you?" she demanded. "I hardly know you, and besides, you're engaged to somebody else."

"Oh, that! She doesn't care."

"No, really!"

"You're a good girl."

"Well, I'm certainly not an idiot."

"All right, go on being a good girl."

She stood up, but lingered a minute, very fresh and cool, and not upset at all.

"I suppose this means you won't give me a job?" she asked pleasantly.

He was already thinking about something else—about an interview and a rehearsal—but now he looked at her again and saw that she still had holes in her stockings. He telephoned:

"Joe, this is the Fresh Boy. . . . You didn't think I knew you called me that, did you? . . . It's all right. . . . Say, have you got those three girls for the party scene? Well, listen; save one for a Southern kid I'm sending around today."

He looked at her jauntily, conscious of being such a good fellow.

"Well, I don't know how to thank you. And Mr. Rogers," she added audaciously. "Good-bye, Mr. McChesney."

He disdained to answer.

II

During rehearsal he used to come around a great deal and stand watching with a wise expression, as if he knew everything in people's minds; but actually he was in a haze about his own good fortune and didn't see much and didn't for the moment care. He spent most of his weekends on Long Island with the fashionable people who had "taken him up." When Brancusi referred to him as the "big social butterfly," he would answer, "Well, what about it? Didn't I go to Harvard? You think they found me in a Grand Street apple cart, like you?" He was well liked among his new friends for his good looks and good nature, as well as his success.

His engagement to Irene Rikker was the most unsatisfactory thing in his life; they were tired of each other but unwilling to put an end to it. Just as, often, the two richest young people in a town are drawn together by the fact, so Bill McChesney and Irene Rikker, borne side by side on waves of triumph, could not spare each other's nice appreciation of what was due such success. Nevertheless, they indulged in fiercer and more frequent quarrels, and the end was approaching. It was embodied in one Frank Llewellen, a big, fine-looking actor playing opposite Irene. Seeing the situation at once, Bill became bitterly humorous about it; from the second week of rehearsals there was tension in the air.

Meanwhile Emmy Pinkard, with enough money for crackers and milk, and a friend who took her out to dinner, was being happy. Her friend, Easton Hughes from Delaney, was studying at Columbia to be a dentist. He sometimes brought along other lonesome young men studying to be dentists, and at the price, if it can be called that, of a few casual kisses in taxi-cabs, Emmy dined when hungry. One afternoon she introduced Easton to Bill McChesney at the stage door, and afterward Bill made his facetious jealousy the basis of their relationship.

"I see that dental number has been slipping it over on me again. Well, don't let him give you any laughing gas is my advice."

Though their encounters were few, they always looked at each other. When Bill looked at her he stared for an instant as if he had not seen her before, and then remembered suddenly that she was to be teased. When she looked at him she saw many things—a bright day outside, with great crowds of people hurrying through the streets; a very good new limousine that waited at the curb for two people with very good new clothes, who got in and went somewhere that was just like New York, only away, and more fun there.

Many times she wished she had kissed him, but just as many times she was glad she hadn't, since, as the weeks passed, he grew less romantic, tied up, like the rest of them, to the play's laborious evolution.

They were opening in Atlantic City. A sudden moodiness, apparent to everyone, came over Bill. He was short with the director and sarcastic with the actors. This, it was rumored, was because Irene Rikker had come down with Frank Llewellen on a different train. Sitting beside the author on the night of the dress rehearsal, he was an almost sinister figure in the twilight of the auditorium; but he said nothing until the end of the second act, when, with Llewellen and Irene Rikker on the stage alone, he suddenly called:

"We'll go over that again—and cut out the mush!"

Llewellen came down to the footlights.

"What do you mean—cut out the mush?" he inquired. "Those are the lines, aren't they?"

"You know what I mean—stick to business."

"I don't know what you mean."

Bill stood up. "I mean all that damn whispering."

"There wasn't any whispering. I simply asked—"

"That'll do—take it over."

Llewellen turned away furiously and was about to proceed, when Bill added audibly: "Even a ham has got to do his stuff."

Llewellen whipped about. "I don't have to stand that kind of talk, Mr. McChesney."

"Why not? You're a ham, aren't you? When did you get ashamed of being a ham? I'm putting on this play and I want you to stick to your stuff." Bill got up and walked down the aisle. "And when you don't do it, I'm going to call you just like anybody else."

"Well, you watch out for your tone of voice—"

"What'll you do about it?"

Llewellen jumped down into the orchestra pit.

"I'm not taking anything from you!" he shouted.

Irene Rikker called to them from the stage, "For heaven's sake, are you two crazy?" And then Llewellen swung at him, one short, mighty blow. Bill pitched back across a row of seats, fell through one, splintering it, and lay wedged there. There was a moment's wild confusion, then people holding Llewellen, then the author, with a white face, pulling Bill up, and the stage manager crying: "Shall I kill him, chief? Shall I break his fat face?" and Llewellen panting and Irene Rikker frightened.

"Get back there!" Bill cried, holding a handkerchief to his face and teetering in the author's supporting arms. "Everybody get back! Take that scene again, and no talk! Get back, Llewellen!"

Before they realized it they were all back on the stage, Irene pulling Llewellen's arm and talking to him fast. Someone put on the auditorium lights full and then dimmed them again hurriedly. When Emmy came out presently for her scene, she saw in a quick glance that Bill was sitting with a whole mask of handkerchiefs over his bleeding face. She hated Llewellen and was afraid that presently they would break up and go back to New York. But Bill had saved the show from his own folly, since for Llewellen to take the further initiative of quitting would hurt his professional standing. The act ended and the next one began without an interval. When it was over, Bill was gone.

Next night, during the performance, he sat on a chair in the wings in view of everyone coming on or off. His face was swollen and bruised, but he neglected to seem conscious of the fact and there were no comments. Once he went around in front, and when he returned, word leaked out that two of the New York agencies were making big buys. He had a hit—they all had a hit.

At the sight of him to whom Emmy felt they all owed so much, a great wave of gratitude swept over her. She went up and thanked him.

"I'm a good picker, red-head," he agreed grimly.

"Thank you for picking me."

And suddenly Emmy was moved to a rash remark.

"You've hurt your face so badly!" she exclaimed. "Oh, I think it was so brave of you not to let everything go to pieces last night."

He looked at her hard for a moment and then an ironic smile tried unsuccessfully to settle on his swollen face.

"Do you admire me, baby?"

"Yes."

"Even when I fell in the seats, did you admire me?"

"You got control of everything so quick."

"That's loyalty for you. You found something to admire in that fool mess."

And her happiness bubbled up into, "Anyhow, you behaved just wonderfully." She looked so fresh and young that Bill, who had had a wretched day, wanted to rest his swollen cheek against her cheek.

He took both the bruise and the desire with him to New York next morning; the bruise faded, but the desire remained. And when they opened in the city, no sooner did he see other men begin to crowd around her beauty than she became this play for him, this success, the thing that he came to see when he came to the theatre. After a good run it closed just as he was drinking too much and needed someone on the grey days of reaction. They were married suddenly in Connecticut, early in June.

III

Two men sat in the Savoy Grill in London, waiting for the Fourth of July. It was already late in May.

"Is he a nice guy?" asked Hubbel.

"Very nice," answered Brancusi; "very nice, very handsome, very popular." After a moment, he added: "I want to get him to come home."

"That's what I don't get about him," said Hubbel. "Show business over here is nothing compared to home. What does he want to stay here for?"

"He goes around with a lot of dukes and ladies."

"Oh?"

"Last week when I met him he was with three ladies—Lady this, Lady that, Lady the other thing."

"I thought he was married."

"Married three years," said Brancusi, "got a fine child, going to have another."

He broke off as McChesney came in, his very American face staring about boldly over the collar of a box-shouldered topcoat.

"Hello, Mac; meet my friend Mr. Hubbel."

"J'doo," said Bill. He sat down, continuing to stare around the bar to see who was present. After a few minutes Hubbel left, and Bill asked:

"Who's that bird?"

"He's only been here a month. He ain't got a title yet. You been here six months, remember."

Bill grinned.

"You think I'm high-hat, don't you? Well, I'm not kidding myself anyhow. I like it; it gets me. I'd like to be the Marquis of McChesney."

"Maybe you can drink yourself into it," suggested Brancusi.

"Shut your trap, you lousy little kyke. Who said I was drinking? Is that what they say now? Look here; if you can tell me any American manager in the history of the theatre who's had the success that I've had in London in less than eight months, I'll go back to America with you tomorrow. If you'll just tell me—"

"It was with your old shows. You had two flops in New York."

Bill stood up, his face hardening.

"Who do you think you are?" he demanded. "Did you come over here to talk to me like that?"

"Don't get sore now, Bill. I just want you to come back. I'd say anything for that. Put over three seasons like you had in '22 and '23, and you're fixed for life."

"New York makes me sick," said Bill moodily. "One minute you're a king; then you have two flops, they go around saying you're on the toboggan."

Brancusi shook his head.

"That wasn't why they said it. It was because you had that quarrel with Aronstael, your best friend."

"Friend hell!"

"Your best friend in business anyhow. Then—"

"I don't want to talk about it." He looked at his watch. "Look here; Emmy's feeling bad so I'm afraid I can't have dinner with you tonight. Come around to the office before you sail."

Five minutes later, standing by the cigar counter, Brancusi saw Bill enter the Savoy again and descend the steps that led to the tea room.

"Grown to be a great diplomat," thought Brancusi; "he used to just say when he had a date. Going with these dukes and ladies is polishing him up even more."

Perhaps he was a little hurt, though it was not typical of him to be hurt. At any rate he made a decision, then and there, that McChesney was on the down grade; it was quite typical of him that at that point he erased him from his mind forever.

There was no outward indication that Bill was on the down grade; a hit at the New Strand, a hit at the Prince of Wales, and the weekly grosses pouring in almost as well as they had two or three years before in New York. Certainly a man of action was justified in changing his base. And the man who, an hour later, turned into his Hyde Park house for dinner had all the vitality of the late twenties. Emmy, very tired and clumsy, lay on a couch in the upstairs sitting room. He held her for a moment in his arms.

"Almost over now," he said. "You're beautiful."

"Don't be ridiculous."

"It's true. You're always beautiful. I don't know why. Perhaps because you've got character, and that's always in your face, even when you're like this."

She was pleased; she ran her hand through his hair.

"Character is the greatest thing in the world," he declared, "and you've got more than anybody I know."

"Did you see Brancusi?"

"I did, the little louse! I decided not to bring him home to dinner."

"What was the matter?"

"Oh, just snooty—talking about my row with Aronstael, as if it was my fault."

She hesitated, closed her mouth tight, and then said quietly, "You got into that fight with Aronstael because you were drinking."

He rose impatiently.

"Are you going to start—"

"No, Bill, but you're drinking too much now. You know you are."

Aware that she was right, he evaded the matter and they went in to dinner. On the glow of a bottle of claret he decided he would go on the wagon tomorrow till after the baby was born.

"I always stop when I want, don't I? I always do what I say. You never saw me quit yet."

"Never yet."

They had coffee together, and afterward he got up.

"Come back early," said Emmy.

"Oh, sure. . . . What's the matter, baby?"

"I'm just crying. Don't mind me. Oh, go on; don't just stand there like a big idiot."

"But I'm worried, naturally. I don't like to see you cry."

"Oh, I don't know where you go in the evenings; I don't know who you're with. And that Lady Sybil Combrinck who kept phoning. It's all right, I suppose, but I wake up in the night and I feel so alone, Bill. Because we've always been together, haven't we, until recently?"

"But we're together still. . . . What's happened to you, Emmy?"

"I know—I'm just crazy. We'd never let each other down, would we? We never have—"

"Of course not."

"Come back early, or when you can."

He looked in for a minute at the Prince of Wales Theatre; then he went into the hotel next door and called a number.

"I'd like to speak to her Ladyship. Mr. McChesney calling."

Like all small enclosures the booth smelled of molasses; it was some time before Lady Sybil answered:

"This is rather a surprise. It's been several weeks since I've been lucky enough to hear from you."

Her voice was flip as a whip and cold as automatic refrigeration, in the mode grown familiar since British ladies took to piecing themselves together out of literature. It had fascinated Bill for awhile, but just for awhile. He had kept his head.

"I haven't had a minute," he explained easily. "You're not sore, are you?"

"I should scarcely say 'sore.'"

"I was afraid you might be; you didn't send me an invitation to your party tonight. My idea was that after we talked it all over we agreed—"

"You talked a great deal," she said; "possibly a little too much."

Suddenly, to Bill's astonishment, she hung up.

"Going British on me," he thought. "A little skit entitled The Daughter of a Thousand Earls."

The snub roused him, the indifference revived his waning interest. Usually women forgave his changes of heart because of his obvious devotion to Emmy, and he was remembered by various ladies with a not unpleasant sigh. But he had detected no such sigh upon the phone.

"I'd like to clear up this mess," he thought. Had he been wearing evening clothes, he might have dropped in at the dance and talked it over with her; still he didn't want to go home. Upon consideration it seemed important that the misunderstanding should be fixed up at once, and presently he began to entertain the idea of going as he was; Americans were excused unconventionalities of dress. In any case, it was not nearly time, and, in the company of several highballs, he considered the matter for an hour.

At midnight he walked up the steps of her Mayfair house. The coat-room attendants scrutinized his tweeds disapprovingly and a footman peered in vain for his name on the list of guests. Fortunately his friend Sir Humphrey Dunn arrived at the same time and convinced the footman it must be a mistake.

Inside, Bill immediately looked about for his hostess.

She was a very tall young woman, half American and all the more intensely English. In a sense, she had discovered Bill McChesney, vouched for his savage charms; his retirement was one of her most humiliating experiences since she had begun being bad.

She stood with her husband at the head of the receiving line—Bill had never seen them together before. He decided to choose a less formal moment for presenting himself.

As the receiving went on interminably, he became increasingly uncomfortable. He saw a few people he knew, but not many, and he was conscious that his clothes were attracting a certain attention; he was aware also that Lady Sybil saw him and could have relieved his embarrassment with a wave of her hand, but she made no sign. He was sorry he had come, but to withdraw now would be absurd, and going to a buffet table, he took a glass of champagne.

When he turned around she was alone at last, and he was about to approach her when the butler spoke to him:

"Pardon me, sir. Have you a card?"

"I'm a friend of Lady Sybil's," said Bill impatiently. He turned away, but the butler followed.

"I'm sorry, sir, but I'll have to ask you to step aside with me and straighten this up."

"There's no need. I'm just about to speak to Lady Sybil now."

"My orders are different, sir," said the butler firmly.

Then, before Bill realized what was happening, his arms were pressed quietly to his sides and he was propelled into a little anteroom back of the buffet.

There he faced a man in a pince-nez in whom he recognized the Combrinck's private secretary.

The secretary nodded to the butler, saying, "This is the man," whereupon Bill was released.

"Mr. McChesney," said the secretary, "you have seen fit to force your way here without a card, and His Lordship requests that you leave his house at once. Will you kindly give me the check for your coat?"

Then Bill understood, and the single word that he found applicable to Lady Sybil sprang to his lips; whereupon the secretary gave a sign to two footmen, and in a furious struggle Bill was carried through a pantry where busy bus boys stared at the scene, down a long hall, and pushed out a door into the night. The door closed; a moment later it was opened again to let his coat billow forth and his cane clatter down the steps.

As he stood there, overwhelmed, stricken aghast, a taxi-cab stopped beside him and the driver called:

"Feeling ill, gov'nor?"

"What?"

"I know where you can get a good pick-me-up, gov'nor. Never too late." The door of the taxi opened on a nightmare. There was a cabaret that broke the closing hours; there was being with strangers he had picked up somewhere; then there were arguments, and trying to cash a check, and suddenly proclaiming over and over that he was William McChesney, the producer, and convincing no one of the fact, not even himself. It seemed important to see Lady Sybil right away and call her to account; but presently nothing was important at all. He was in a taxi-cab whose driver had just shaken him awake in front of his own home.

The telephone was ringing as he went in, but he walked stonily past the maid and only heard her voice when his foot was on the stair.

"Mr. McChesney, it's the hospital calling again. Mrs. McChesney's there and they've been phoning every hour."

Still in a daze, he held the receiver up to his ear.

"We're calling from the Midland Hospital, for your wife. She was delivered of a stillborn child at nine this morning."

"Wait a minute." His voice was dry and cracking. "I don't understand."

After awhile he understood that Emmy's child was dead and she wanted him. His knees sagged groggily as he walked down the street, looking for a taxi.

The room was dark; Emmy looked up and saw him from a rumpled bed.

"Oh, my God, it's you!" she cried. "I thought you were dead! Where did you go?"

He threw himself down on his knees beside the bed, but she turned away.

"Oh, you smell awful," she said. "It makes me sick."

But she kept her hand in his hair, and he knelt there motionless for a long time.

"I'm done with you," she muttered, "but it was awful when I thought you were dead. Everybody's dead. I wish I was dead."

A curtain parted with the wind, and as he rose to arrange it, she saw him in the full morning light, pale and terrible, with rumpled clothes and bruises on his face. This time she hated him instead of those who had hurt him. She could feel him slipping out of her heart, feel the space he left, and all at once he was gone, and she could even forgive him and be sorry for him. All this in a minute.

She had fallen down at the door of the hospital, trying to get out of the taxi-cab alone.

IV

When Emmy was well, physically and mentally, her incessant idea was to learn to dance; the old dream inculcated by Miss Georgia Berriman Campbell of South Carolina persisted as a bright avenue leading back to first youth and days of hope in New York. To her, dancing meant that elaborate blend of tortuous attitudes and formal pirouettes that evolved out of Italy several hundred years ago and reached its apogee in Russia at the beginning of this century. She wanted to use herself on something she could believe in, and it seemed to her that the dance was woman's interpretation of music; instead of strong fingers, one had limbs with which to render Tchaikovsky and Stravinski; and feet could be as eloquent in *Chopiniana* as voices in *The Ring*. At the bottom, it was something sandwiched in between the acrobats and the trained seals; at the top it was Pavlova and art.

Once they were settled in an apartment back in New York, she plunged into her work like a girl of sixteen—four hours a day at bar exercises, attitudes, *sauts*, arabesques and pirouettes. It became the realest part of her life, and her only worry was whether or not she was too old. At twenty-six she had ten years to make up, but she was a natural dancer with a fine body—and that lovely face.

Bill encouraged it; when she was ready he was going to build the first real American ballet around her. There were even times when he envied her her absorption; for affairs in his own line were more difficult since they had come home. For one thing, he had made many enemies in those early days of self-confidence; there were exaggerated stories of his drinking and of his being hard on actors and difficult to work with.

It was against him that he had always been unable to save money and must beg a backing for each play. Then, too, in a curious way, he was intelligent, as he was brave enough to prove in several uncommercial ventures, but he had no Theatre Guild behind him, and what money he lost was charged against him.

There were successes, too, but he worked harder for them, or it seemed so, for he had begun to pay a price for his irregular life. He always intended to take a rest or give up his incessant cigarettes, but there was so much competition now—new men coming up, with new reputations for infallibility—and besides, he wasn't used to regularity. He liked to do his work in those great spurts, inspired by black coffee, that seem so inevitable in show business, but which took so much out of a man after thirty. He had come to lean, in a way, on Emmy's fine health and vitality. They were always together, and if he felt a vague dissatisfaction that he had grown to need her more than she needed him, there was always the hope that things would break better for him next month, next season.

Coming home from ballet school one November evening, Emmy swung her little grey bag, pulled her hat far down over her still damp hair, and gave herself up to pleasant speculation. For a month she had been aware of people who had come to the studio especially to watch her—she was ready to dance. Once she had worked just as hard and for as long a time on something else—her relations with Bill—only to reach a climax of misery and despair, but here there was nothing to fail her except herself. Yet even now she felt a little rash in thinking: "Now it's come. I'm going to be happy."

She hurried, for something had come up today that she must talk over with Bill.

Finding him in the living room, she called him to come back while she took her bath— As she heard him enter she began to talk without looking around:

"Listen what happened!" Her voice was loud, to compete with the water running in the tub. "Paul Makova wants me to dance with him at the Metropolitan this season; only it's not sure, so it's a secret—even I'm not supposed to know."

"That's great."

"The only thing is whether it wouldn't be better for me to make a début abroad? Anyhow Donilof says I'm ready to appear. What do you think?"

"I don't know."

"You don't sound very enthusiastic."

"I've got something on my mind. I'll tell you about it later. Go on."

"That's all, dear. If you still feel like going to Germany for a month, like you said, Donilof would arrange a début for me in

Berlin, but I'd rather open here and dance with Paul Makova. Just imagine—" She broke off, feeling suddenly through the thick skin of her elation how abstracted he was. "Tell me what you've got on your mind."

"I went to Doctor Kearns this afternoon."

"What did he say?" She stepped into the hot tub; her mind was still singing with her own happiness. Bill's intermittent attacks of hypochondria had long ceased to worry her.

"I told him about that blood this morning, and he said what he said last year—it was probably a little broken vein in my throat. But since I'd been coughing and was worried, perhaps it was safer to take an X-ray and clear the matter up. Well, we cleared it up all right. My left lung is practically gone."

"Bill!"

"Luckily there are no spots on the other."

She waited, horribly afraid.

"It's come at a bad time for me," he went on steadily, "but it's got to be faced. He thinks I ought to go to the Adirondacks or to Denver for the winter, and his idea is Denver. That way it'll probably clear up in five or six months."

"Of course we'll have to—" she stopped suddenly.

"I wouldn't expect you to go—especially if you have this opportunity."

"Of course I'll go," she said quickly. "Your health comes first. We've always gone everywhere together."

"Oh, no."

"Why, of course." She made her voice strong and decisive. "We've always been together. I couldn't stay here without you. When do you have to go?"

"As soon as possible. I went in to see Brancusi to find out if he wanted to take over the Richmond piece, but he didn't seem enthusiastic." His face hardened. "Of course there won't be anything else for the present, but I'll have enough, with what's owing—"

"Oh, if I was only making some money!" Emmy cried. "You work so hard, and here I've been spending two hundred dollars a week for just my dancing lessons alone—more than I'll be able to earn for years."

"Of course in six months I'll be as well as ever—he says."

"Sure, dearest; we'll get you well. We'll start as soon as we can."

She was out of the tub drying herself; she put a damp arm around him and kissed his cheek.

"I'm just an old parasite," she said. "I should have known my darling wasn't well."

He reached automatically for a cigarette, and then stopped.

"I forgot—I've got to cut out smoking and drinking." He rose to the occasion suddenly: "No, baby, I've decided to go alone. You'd go crazy with boredom out there, and I'd just be thinking I was keeping you away from your dancing."

"Don't think about that. The thing is to get you well."

They discussed the matter hour after hour for the next week, each of them saying everything except the truth—that he wanted her to go with him and that she wanted passionately to stay in New York. She talked it over guardedly with Donilof, her ballet master, and found that he thought any postponement would be a terrible mistake. Seeing other girls in the ballet school making plans for the winter, and imagining the barren vistas of Colorado, she wanted to die rather than go, and Bill saw all the involuntary indications of her misery. For awhile they talked of compromising on the Adirondacks, whither she would commute by aeroplane for the week-ends, but he was running a little fever now and he was definitely ordered West.

Bill settled it all one gloomy Sunday night, with that rough, generous justice that had first made her admire him, that made him rather tragic in his adversity, as he had always been bearable in his overweening success:

"It's just up to me, baby. I got into this mess because I didn't have any self-control—you seem to have all of that in this family—and now it's only me that can get me out. You've worked hard at your stuff for three years and you deserve your chance—and if you came out there now you'd have it on me the rest of my life." He grinned. "And I couldn't stand that. Besides, it wouldn't be good for the kid."

Eventually she gave in, ashamed of herself, miserable—and glad. For the world of her work, where she existed without Bill, was bigger to her now than the world in which they existed together. There was more room to be glad in one than to be sorry in the other.

Two days later, with his ticket bought for that afternoon at five, they passed the last hours together, talking of everything hopeful. She protested still, and sincerely; had he weakened for a moment she would have gone. But the shock had done something to him, and he showed more character under it than he had for years. Perhaps it would be good for him to work it out alone.

"In the spring!" they said.

Then in the station with little Billy, and Bill saying: "I hate these grave-side partings. You leave me here. I've got to make a phone call from the train before it goes."

They had never spent more than a night apart in six years, save when Emmy was in the hospital; save for the time in England they had a good record of faithfulness and of tenderness toward each other, even though she had been alarmed and often unhappy at this insecure bravado from the first. After he went through the gate alone, Emmy was glad he had a phone call to make and tried to picture him making it.

She was a good woman; she had loved him with all her heart. When she went out into 33rd Street, it was just as dead as dead for awhile, and the apartment he paid for would be empty of him, and she was here, about to do something that would make her happy.

She stopped after a few blocks, thinking: "Why, this is terrible—what I'm doing! I'm letting him down like the worst person I ever heard of. I'm leaving him flat and going off to dinner with Donilof and Paul Makova, whom I like for being beautiful and for having the same color eyes and hair. Bill's on the train alone."

She swung little Billy around suddenly as if to go back to the station. She could see him sitting in the train, with his face so pale and tired, and no Emmy.

"I can't let him down," she cried to herself as wave after wave of sentiment washed over her. But only sentiment—hadn't he let her down—hadn't he done what he wanted in London?

"Oh, poor Bill!"

She stood irresolute, realizing for one last honest moment how quickly she would forget this and find excuses for what she was doing. She had to think hard of London, and her conscience cleared. But with Bill all alone in the train it seemed terrible to think that way. Even now she could turn and go back to the station and tell him that she was coming, but still she waited, with life very strong in her, fighting for her. The sidewalk was narrow where she stood; presently a great wave of people, pouring out of the theatre, came flooding along it, and she and little Billy were swept along with the crowd.

In the train. Bill telephoned up to the last minute, postponed going back to his stateroom, because he knew it was almost certain that he would not find her there. After the train started he went back and, of course, there was nothing but his bags in the rack and some magazines on the seat.

He knew then that he had lost her. He saw the set-up without any illusions—this Paul Makova, and months of proximity, and loneliness—afterward nothing would ever be the same. When he had thought about it all a long time, reading *Variety* and *Zit's* in between, it began to seem, each time he came back to it, as if Emmy somehow were dead.

"She was a fine girl—one of the best. She had character." He realized perfectly that he had brought all this on himself and that there was some law of compensation involved. He saw, too, that by going away he had again become as good as she was; it was all evened up at last.

He felt beyond everything, even beyond his grief, an almost comfortable sensation of being in the hands of something bigger than himself; and grown a little tired and unconfident—two qualities he could never for a moment tolerate—it did not seem so terrible if he were going West for a definite finish. He was sure that Emmy would come at the end, no matter what she was doing or how good an engagement she had.

THE NIGHT OF CHANCELLORSVILLE

I tell you I didn't have any notion what I was getting into or I wouldn't of gone down there. They can have their army—it seems to me they were all a bunch of yella-bellies. But my friend Nell said to me: "Nora, Philly is as dead as Baltimore and we've got to eat this summer." She just got a letter from a girl that said they were living fine down there in "Ole Virginia." The soldiers were getting big pay-offs and figuring maybe they'd stay there all summer, at least till the Johnny Rebs gave up. They got their pay regular too, and a good clean-looking girl could ask—well, I forget now, because, after what happened to us, I guess you can't expect me to remember anything.

I've always been used to decent treatment—somehow when I meet a man, no matter how fresh he is in the beginning, he comes to respect me in the end, and I've never had things done to me like some girls—getting left in a strange town or had my purse stolen.

Well, I started to tell you how I went down to the army in "Ole Virginia." Never again! Wait'll you hear.

I was used to travelling nice—once when I was a little girl my daddy took me on the cars to Baltimore—we lived in York, Pa. And we couldn't have been more comfortable; we had pillows and the men came through with baskets of oranges and apples. You know, singing out: "Want to buy some oranges or apples—or beer?"

You know what they sell—but I never took any beer because—

Oh I know, I'll go on—You only want to talk about the war, like all you men. But if this is your idea what a war is—

Well, they stuck us all in one car and a fresh fella took our tickets, and winked and said:

"Oh you're going down to Hooker's army."

The lights were terrible in the car, smoky and full of bugs, so everything looked sort of yella. And say, that car was so old it was falling to pieces.

There must of been forty gay girls in it, a lot of them from Baltimore and Philly. Only there were three or four that weren't gay—I mean they were more, oh, you know, rich people, and sat up front. Every once in awhile an officer would pop in from the next car and ask them if they wanted anything. I was in the seat behind with Nell and we heard him whisper: "You're in terrible company, but we'll be there in a few hours. And we'll go right to headquarters, and I guarantee you some solid comfort."

I never will forget that night. None of us had any food except some girls behind us had some sausages and bread, and they gave us what they had left. There was a spigot you turned but no water came out. After about two hours—stopping every two minutes it seemed to me—a couple of lieutenants, drunk as monkeys, came in from the next car and offered Nell and me some whiskey out of a bottle. Nell took some and I pretended to, and they set on the side of our seats. One of them started to make up to Nell, but just then the officer that had spoken to the women, pretty high up I guess, a major or a general, came back again and asked:

"You all right? Anything I can do?"

One of the ladies kind of whispered to him, and he turned to the one that was talking to Nell and made him go back in the other car. After that there was only one officer with us; he wasn't really so drunk, just feeling sick.

"This certainly is a happy looking gang," he said. "It's good you can hardly see them in this light. They look as if their best friend just died."

"What if they do," Nell answered back quick. "How would you look yourself if you come all the way from Philly and then got in a buggy like this?"

"I come all the way from The Seven Days, sister," he answered. "Maybe I'd be more pretty for you if I hadn't lost an eye at Gaines' Mill."

Then we noticed he *had* lost an eye. He kept it sort of closed so we hadn't remarked it before. Pretty soon he left and said he'd try and get us some water or coffee, that was what we wanted most.

The car kept rocking and it made us both feel funny. Some of the girls was sick and some was asleep on each other's shoulders.

"Hey, where *is* this army?" Nell said. "Down in Mexico?"

I was kind of half asleep myself by that time and didn't answer.

The next thing I knew I was woke up by a storm, the car was stopped again, and I said, "It's raining."

"Raining!" said Nell. "That's cannons—they're having a battle."

"Oh!" I got awake. "Well, after *this* ride I don't care who wins."

It seemed to get louder all the time, but out the windows you couldn't see anything on account of the mist.

In about half an hour another officer came in the car—he looked pretty messy as if he'd just crawled out of bed: his coat was still unbuttoned and he kept hitching up his trousers as if he didn't have any suspenders on.

"All you ladies outside," he said. "We need this car for wounded."

"Hey!"

"We paid for our tickets, didn't we?"

"We need all the cars for the wounded and the other cars are filled up."

"Hey! We didn't come down to fight in any battle!"

"It doesn't matter what you came down for—you're in a hell of a battle."

I was scared, I can tell *you*. I thought maybe the Rebs would capture us and send us down to one of those prisons you hear about, where they starve you to death unless you sing Dixie all the time and kiss niggers.

"Hurry up!"

But another officer had come in who looked more nice.

"Stay where you are, ladies," he said. And then he said to the officer, "What do you want to do? leave them standing on the siding! If Sedgwick's Corps is broken, like they say, the Rebs may come up in this direction!"

Some of the girls began crying out loud.

"These are northern women after all," he said.

"These are—"

"Shut up and go back to your command! I'm detailed to this transportation job—I'm taking these girls back to Washington with us."

I thought they were going to hit each other, but they both walked off together. And we girls sat wondering what we were going to do.

What happened next I don't remember exact. The cannons were sometimes very loud and then sometimes more far away, but there was firing of shots right near us—and a girl down the car had her window smashed like a hole in the center, sort of, all smashed you know, not like when you break a glass, more like ice in cold weather, just a hole and streaks around—you know. I heard a whole bunch of horses gallop by our windows, but I still couldn't see anything.

That went on half an hour—galloping and more shots. We couldn't tell how far away but they sounded like up by the engine.

Then it got quiet—and two men came into our car—we all knew right away they were Rebels, not officers, just plain private ones, with muskets. One had on a old brown blouse sort of thing and one had on a blue thing—all spotted—I know I could never of let *that* man make love to me. It had spots—it was too short—anyway, it was out of style. Oh it was disgusting. I was surprised because I thought they always wore grey. They were disgusting looking and very dirty; one had a big pot of jam smeared all over his face and the other one had a big box of crackers.

"Hi ladies."

"What you gals doin' down here?"

"Kain't you see, Steve, this is old Joe Hooker's staff."

"Reckin' we ought to take 'em back to the General?"

They talked outlandish like that—I could hardly understand, they talked so funny.

One of the girls got historical she was so scared, and that made them kind of shy. They were just kids under those beards, and one of them tipped his hat or cap or whatever the old thing was.

"We're not fixin' to hurt you."

At that moment there was a whole bunch more shooting down by the engine and the Rebs turned and ran.

We were glad, I can tell you.

Then, about fifteen minutes later, in came one of our officers. This was another new one.

"You better duck down!" he shouted to us. "They may fire on this train. We're starting you off as soon as we unload two more ambulances."

Half of us was on the floor already. The rich women sitting ahead of Nell and me had gone up into the car ahead where the wounded were—to see if they could do anything. Nell thought she'd look in too, but she came back holding her nose. She said it smelled awful in there.

It was lucky she didn't go in, because two of the girls did from our car. People that is sick can never seem to get much consideration for other people who happen to be well. The nurses sent them right back—as if they was dirt under their feet.

After I don't know how long the train began to move. A soldier come in and poured oil out of all our lights except one, and took it into the wounded car. So now we could hardly see at all.

If the trip down was slow the trip back was slower— The wounded began making so much noise, grunting and all, that we could hear it and couldn't get a decent sleep.

We stopped everywhere.

When we got in Washington at last there was a lot of people in the station and they were all anxious about what had happened to the army, but I said You can search me. All I wanted was my little old room and my little old bed. I never been treated like that in my life.

One of the girls said she was going to write to President Lincoln about it.

And in the papers next day they never said anything about how our train got attacked, or about us girls at all! Can you beat it?

THE LAST OF THE BELLES

After Atlanta's elaborate and theatrical rendition of Southern charm, we all underestimated Tarleton. It was a little hotter than anywhere we'd been—a dozen rookies collapsed the first day in that Georgia sun—and when you saw herds of cows drifting through the business streets, hi-yaed by colored drovers, a trance stole down over you out of the hot light; you wanted to move a hand or foot to be sure you were alive.

So I stayed out at camp and let Lieutenant Warren tell me about the girls. This was fifteen years ago, and I've forgotten how I felt, except that the days went along, one after another, better than they do now, and I was empty-hearted, because up North she whose legend I had loved for three years was getting married. I saw the clippings and newspaper photographs. It was "a romantic wartime wedding," all very rich and sad. I felt vividly the dark radiance of the sky under which it took place, and as a young snob, was more envious than sorry.

A day came when I went into Tarleton for a haircut and ran into a nice fellow named Bill Knowles, who was in my time at Harvard. He'd been in the National Guard division that preceded us in camp; at the last moment he had transferred to aviation and been left behind.

"I'm glad I met you, Andy," he said with undue seriousness. "I'll hand you on all my information before I start for Texas. You see, there're really only three girls here—"

I was interested; there was something mystical about there being three girls.

"—and here's one of them now."

We were in front of a drug store and he marched me in and introduced me to a lady I promptly detested.

"The other two are Ailie Calhoun and Sally Carrol Happer."

I guessed from the way he pronounced her name, that he was interested in Ailie Calhoun. It was on his mind what she would be doing while he was gone; he wanted her to have a quiet, uninteresting time.

At my age I don't even hesitate to confess that entirely unchivalrous images of Ailie Calhoun—that lovely name—rushed into my mind. At twenty-three there is no such thing as a preempted beauty; though, had Bill asked me, I would doubtless have sworn in all sincerity to care for her like a sister. He didn't; he was just fretting out loud at having to go. Three days later he telephoned me that he was leaving next morning and he'd take me to her house that night.

We met at the hotel and walked uptown through the flowery, hot twilight. The four white pillars of the Calhoun house faced the street, and behind them the verandah was dark as a cave with hanging, weaving, climbing vines.

When we came up the walk a girl in a white dress tumbled out of the front door, crying, "I'm so sorry I'm late!" and seeing us, added: "Why, I thought I heard you come ten minutes—"

She broke off as a chair creaked and another man, an aviator from Camp Harry Lee, emerged from the obscurity of the verandah.

"Why, Canby!" she cried. "How you?"

He and Bill Knowles waited with the tenseness of open litigants.

"Canby, I want to whisper to you, honey," she said, after just a second. "You'll excuse us, Bill."

They went aside. Presently Lieutenant Canby, immensely displeased, said in a grim voice, "Then we'll make it Thursday, but that means sure." Scarcely nodding to us, he went down the walk, the spurs with which he presumably urged on his aeroplane gleaming in the lamplight.

"Come in y'all,—I don't just know your name—"

There she was—the Southern type in all its purity. I would have recognized Ailie Calhoun if I'd never heard Ruth Draper or read "Marse Chan." She had the adroitness sugarcoated with sweet, voluble simplicity, the suggested background of devoted fathers, brothers and admirers stretching back into the South's heroic age, the unfailing coolness acquired in the endless struggle with the heat.

There were notes in her voice that ordered slaves around, that withered up Yankee captains, and then soft, wheedling notes that mingled in unfamiliar loveliness with the night.

I could scarcely see her in the darkness, but when I rose to go—it was plain that I was not to linger—she stood in the orange light from the doorway. She was small and very blonde; there was too much fever-colored rouge on her face, accentuated by a nose dabbed clownish white, but she shone through that like a star.

"After Bill goes I'll be sitting here all alone night after night. Maybe you'll take me to the country-club dances." The pathetic prophecy brought a laugh from Bill. "Wait a minute," Ailie murmured. "Your guns are all crooked."

She straightened my collar pin, looking up at me for a second with something more than curiosity. It was a seeking look, as if she asked, "Could it be you?" Like Lieutenant Canby, I marched off unwillingly into the suddenly insufficient night.

Two weeks later I sat with her on the same verandah, or rather she half lay in my arms and yet scarcely touched me—how she managed that I don't remember. I was trying unsuccessfully to kiss her, and had been trying for the best part of an hour. We had a sort of joke about my not being sincere. My theory was that if she'd let me kiss her I'd fall in love with her. Her argument was that I was obviously insincere.

In a lull between two of these struggles she told me about her brother who had died in his senior year at Yale. She showed me his picture—it was a handsome, earnest face with a Leyendecker forelock—and told me that when she met someone who measured up to him she'd marry. I found this family idealism discouraging; even my brash confidence couldn't compete with the dead.

The evening and other evenings passed like that, and ended with my going back to camp with the remembered smell of magnolia flowers and a mood of vague dissatisfaction. I never kissed her. We went to the vaudeville and to the country club on Saturday nights, where she seldom took ten consecutive steps with one man, and she took me to barbecues and rowdy watermelon parties, and never thought it was worth while to change what I felt for her into love. I see now that it wouldn't have been hard, but she was a wise nineteen and she must have seen that we were emotionally incompatible. So I became her confidant instead.

We talked about Bill Knowles. She was considering Bill; for, though she wouldn't admit it, a winter at school in New York and a prom at Yale had turned her eyes North. She said she didn't think she'd marry a Southern man. And by degrees I saw that she was consciously and voluntarily different from these other girls who sang nigger songs and shot craps in the country-club bar. That's why Bill and I and others were drawn to her. We recognized her.

June and July, while the rumors reached us faintly, ineffectually, of battle and terror overseas, Ailie's eyes roved here and there about the country-club floor, seeking for something among the tall young officers. She attached several, choosing them with unfailing perspicacity—save in the case of Lieutenant Canby, whom she claimed to despise, but, nevertheless, gave dates to "because he was so sincere"—and we apportioned her evenings among us all summer.

One day she broke all her dates—Bill Knowles had leave and was coming. We talked of the event with scientific impersonality—would he move her to a decision? Lieutenant Canby, on the contrary, wasn't impersonal at all; made a nuisance of himself. He told her that if she married Knowles he was going to climb up six thousand feet in his aeroplane, shut off the motor and let go. He frightened her—I had to yield him my last date before Bill came.

On Saturday night she and Bill Knowles came to the country club. They were very handsome together and once more I felt envious and sad. As they danced out on the floor the three-piece orchestra was playing "After You've Gone," in a poignant incomplete way that I can hear yet, as if each bar were trickling off a precious minute of that time. I knew then that I had grown to love Tarleton, and I glanced about half in panic to see if some face wouldn't come in for me out of that warm, singing, outer darkness that yielded up couple after couple in organdie and olive drab. It was a time of youth and war, and there was never so much love around.

When I danced with Ailie she suddenly suggested that we go outside to a car. She wanted to know why didn't people cut in on her tonight? Did they think she was already married?

"Are you going to be?"

"I don't know, Andy. Sometimes, when he treats me as if I were sacred, it thrills me." Her voice was hushed and far away. "And then—"

She laughed. Her body, so frail and tender, was touching mine, her face was turned up to me, and there, suddenly, with Bill Knowles ten yards off, I could have kissed her at last. Our lips just touched experimentally; then an aviation officer turned a corner of the verandah near us, peered into our darkness and hesitated.

"Ailie."

"Yes."

"You heard about this afternoon?"

"What?" She leaned forward, tenseness already in her voice.

"Horace Canby crashed. He was instantly killed."

She got up slowly and stepped out of the car.

"You mean he was killed?" she said.

"Yes. They don't know what the trouble was. His motor—"

"Oh-h-h!" Her rasping whisper came through the hands suddenly covering her face. We watched her helplessly as she put her head on the side of the car, gagging dry tears. After a minute I went for Bill, who was standing in the stag line, searching anxiously about for her, and told him she wanted to go home.

I sat on the steps outside. I had disliked Canby, but his terrible, pointless death was more real to me then than the day's toll of thousands in France. In a few minutes Ailie and Bill came out. Ailie was whimpering a little, but when she saw me her eyes flexed and she came over swiftly.

"Andy"—she spoke in a quick, low voice—"of course you must never tell anybody what I told you about Canby yesterday. What he said, I mean."

"Of course not."

She looked at me a second longer as if to be quite sure. Finally she was sure. Then she sighed in such a quaint little way that I could hardly believe my ears, and her brow went up in what can only be described as mock despair.

"*An*-dy!"

I looked uncomfortably at the ground, aware that she was calling my attention to her involuntarily disastrous effect on men.

"Good-night, Andy!" called Bill as they got into a taxi.
"Good-night," I said, and almost added: "You poor fool."

II

Of course I should have made one of those fine moral decisions that people make in books, and despised her. On the contrary, I don't doubt that she could still have had me by raising her hand.

A few days later she made it all right by saying wistfully, "I know you think it was terrible of me to think of myself at a time like that, but it was such a shocking coincidence."

At twenty-three I was entirely unconvinced about anything, except that some people were strong and attractive and could do what they wanted, and others were caught and disgraced. I hoped I was of the former. I was sure Ailie was.

I had to revise other ideas about her. In the course of a long discussion with some girl about kissing—in those days people still talked about kissing more than they kissed—I mentioned the fact that Ailie had only kissed two or three men, and only when she thought she was in love. To my considerable disconcertion the girl figuratively just lay on the floor and howled.

"But it's true," I assured her, suddenly knowing it wasn't. "She told me herself."

"Ailie Calhoun! Oh, my heavens! Why, last year at the Tech spring house party—"

This was in September. We were going over-seas any week now, and to bring us up to full strength a last batch of officers from the fourth training camp arrived. The fourth camp wasn't like the first three—the candidates were from the ranks; even from the drafted divisions. They had queer names without vowels in them, and save for a few young militiamen, you couldn't take it for granted that they came out of any background at all. The addition to our company was Lieutenant Earl Schoen from New Bedford, Massachusetts; as fine a physical specimen as I have ever seen. He was six-foot-three, with black hair, high color and glossy dark-brown eyes. He wasn't very smart and he was definitely illiterate, yet he was a good officer, high-tempered and commanding, and with that becoming touch of vanity that sits well on the military. I had an idea that New Bedford was a country town, and set down his bumptious qualities to that.

We were doubled up in living quarters and he came into my hut. Inside of a week there was a cabinet photograph of some Tarleton girl nailed brutally to the shack wall.

"She's no jane or anything like that. She's a society girl; goes with all the best people here."

The following Sunday afternoon I met the lady at a semi-private swimming pool in the country. When Ailie and I arrived, there was Schoen's muscular body rippling out of a bathing suit at the far end of the pool.

"Hey, lieutenant!"

When I waved back at him he grinned and winked, jerking his head toward the girl at his side. Then, digging her in the ribs, he jerked his head at me. It was a form of introduction.

"Who's that with Kitty Preston?" Ailie asked, and when I told her she said he looked like a street-car conductor, and pretended to look for her transfer.

A moment later he crawled powerfully and gracefully down the pool and pulled himself up at our side. I introduced him to Ailie.

"How do you like my girl, lieutenant?" he demanded. "I told you she was all right, didn't I?" He jerked his head toward Ailie, this time to indicate that his girl and Ailie moved in the same circles. "How about let's us all having dinner together down at the hotel some night?"

I left them in a moment, amused as I saw Ailie visibly making up her mind that here, anyhow, was not the ideal. But Lieutenant Earl Schoen was not to be dismissed so lightly. He ran his eyes cheerfully and inoffensively over her cute, slight figure, and decided that she would do even better than the other. Then minutes later I saw them in the water together, Ailie swimming away with a grim little stroke she had, and Schoen wallowing riotously around her and ahead of her, sometimes pausing and staring at her, fascinated, as a boy might look at a nautical doll.

While the afternoon passed he remained at her side. Finally Ailie came over to me and whispered, with a laugh: "He's following me around. He thinks I haven't paid my carfare."

She turned quickly. Miss Kitty Preston, her face curiously flustered, stood facing us.

"Ailie Calhoun, I didn't think it of you to go out and delib'ately try to take a man away from another girl."

An expression of distress at the impending scene flitted over Ailie's face.

"I thought you considered yourself above anything like that," continued Kitty.

Her voice was low, but it held that tensity that can be felt farther than it can be heard, and I saw Ailie's clear lovely eyes glance about in panic. Luckily, Earl himself was ambling cheerfully and innocently toward us.

"If you care for him you certainly oughtn't to belittle yourself in front of him," said Ailie in a flash, her head high.

It was her acquaintance with the traditional way of behaving against Kitty Preston's naïve and fierce possessiveness, or if you prefer it, Ailie's "breeding" against the other's "commonness." She turned away.

"Wait a minute, kid!" cried Earl Schoen. "How about your address? Maybe I'd like to give you a ring on the phone."

She looked at him in a way that should have indicated to Kitty her entire lack of interest.

"I'm very busy at the Red Cross this month," she said, her voice as cool as her slicked-back blonde hair. "Good-bye."

On the way home she laughed. Her air of having been unwittingly involved in a contemptible business vanished.

"She'll never hold that young man," she said. "He wants somebody new."

"Apparently he wants Ailie Calhoun."

The idea amused her.

"He could give me his ticket punch to wear, like a fraternity pin. What fun! If mother ever saw anybody like that come in the house, she'd just lay down and die."

And to give Ailie credit, it was fully a fortnight before he did come in her house, although he rushed her until she pretended to be annoyed at the next country-club dance.

"He's the biggest tough, Andy," she whispered to me. "But he's so sincere."

She used the word "tough" without the conviction it would have carried had he been a Southern boy. She only knew it with her mind; her ear couldn't distinguish between one Yankee voice and another. And somehow Mrs. Calhoun didn't expire at his appearance on the threshold. The supposedly ineradicable prejudices of Ailie's parents were a convenient phenomenon that disappeared at her wish. It was her friends who were astonished. Ailie, always a little above Tarleton, whose beaux had been very carefully the "nicest" men of the camp—Ailie and Lieutenant Schoen! I grew tired of assuring people that she was merely distracting herself—and indeed every week or so there was someone new—an ensign from Pensacola, an old friend from New Orleans—but always, in between times, there was Earl Schoen.

Orders arrived for an advance party of officers and sergeants to proceed to the port of embarkation and take ship to France. My name was on the list. I had been on the range for a week and when I got back to camp, Earl Schoen buttonholed me immediately.

"We're giving a little farewell party in the mess. Just you and I and Captain Craker and three girls."

Earl and I were to call for the girls. We picked up Sally Carrol Happer and Nancy Lamar, and went on to Ailie's house, to be met at the door by the butler with the announcement that she wasn't home.

"Isn't home?" Earl repeated blankly. "Where is she?"

"Didn't leave no information about that; just said she wasn't home."

"But this is a darn funny thing!" he exclaimed. He walked around the familiar dusky verandah while the butler waited at the door. Something occurred to him. "Say," he informed me—"say, I think she's sore."

I waited. He said sternly to the butler, "You tell her I've got to speak to her a minute."

"How'm I goin' tell her that when she ain't home?"

Again Earl walked musingly around the porch. Then he nodded several times and said:

"She's sore at something that happened downtown."

In a few words he sketched out the matter to me.

"Look here; you wait in the car," I said. "Maybe I can fix this." And when he reluctantly retreated: "Oliver, you tell Miss Ailie I want to see her alone."

After some argument he bore this message and in a moment returned with a reply:

"Miss Ailie say she don't want to see that other gentleman about nothing never. She say come in if you like."

She was in the library. I had expected to see a picture of cool, outraged dignity, but her face was distraught, tumultuous, despairing. Her eyes were red-rimmed, as though she had been crying slowly and painfully, for hours.

"Oh, hello, Andy," she said brokenly. "I haven't seen you for so long. Has he gone?"

"Now, Ailie—"

"Now, Ailie!" she cried. "Now, Ailie! He spoke to me, you see. He lifted his hat. He stood there ten feet from me with that horrible—that horrible woman—holding her arm and talking to her, and then when he saw me he raised his hat. Andy, I didn't know what to do. I had to go in the drug store and ask for a glass of water, and I was so afraid he'd follow in after me that I asked Mr. Rich to let me go out the back way. I never want to see him or hear of him again."

I talked. I said what one says in such cases. I said it for half an hour. I could not move her. Several times she answered by murmuring something about his not being "sincere," and for the fourth time I wondered what the word meant to her. Certainly not constancy; it was, I half suspected, some special way she wanted to be regarded.

I got up to go. And then, unbelievably, the automobile horn sounded three times impatiently outside. It was stupefying. It said as plainly as if Earl were in the room, "All right, go to the devil then! I'm not going to wait here all night."

Ailie looked at me aghast. And suddenly a peculiar look came into her face, spread, flickered, broke into a teary, hysterical smile.

"Isn't he awful?" she cried in helpless despair. "Isn't he terrible?"

"Hurry up," I said quickly. "Get your cape. This is our last night."

And I can still feel that last night vividly, the candlelight that flickered over the rough boards of the mess shack, over the frayed paper decorations left from the supply company's party, the sad mandolin down a company street that kept picking "My Indiana Home" out of the universal nostalgia of the departing summer. The three girls lost in this mysterious men's city felt something, too—a bewitched impermanence as though they were on a magic carpet that had lighted on the Southern countryside, and any moment the wind would lift it and waft it away. We toasted ourselves and the South. Then we left our napkins and empty glasses and a little of the past on the table, and hand in hand went out into the moonlight itself. Taps had been played; there was no sound but the far-away whinny of a horse, and a loud persistent snore at which we laughed, and the leathery snap of a sentry coming to port over by the guardhouse. Craker was on duty; we others got into a waiting car, motored into Tarleton and left Craker's girl.

Then Ailie and Earl, Sally and I, two and two in the wide back seat, each couple turned from the other, absorbed and whispering, drove away into the wide, flat darkness.

We drove through pine woods heavy with lichen and Spanish moss, and between the fallow cotton fields along a road white as the rim of the world. We parked under the broken shadow of a mill where there was the sound of running water and restive squawky birds and over everything a brightness that tried to filter in anywhere—into the lost nigger cabins, the automobile, the fastnesses of the heart. The South sang to us—I wonder if they remember. I remember—the cool pale faces, the somnolent amorous eyes and the voices:

"Are you comfortable?"

"Yes, are you?"

"Are you sure you are?"

"Yes."

Suddenly we knew it was late and there was nothing more. We turned home.

Our detachment started for Camp Mills next day, but I didn't go to France after all. We passed a cold month on Long Island, marched aboard a transport with steel helmets slung at our sides and then marched off again. There wasn't any more war. I had missed the war. When I came back to Tarleton I tried to get out of the Army, but I had a regular commission and it took most of the winter. But Earl Schoen was one of the first to be demobilized. He wanted to find a good job "while the picking was good." Ailie was noncommittal, but there was an understanding between them that he'd be back.

By January the camps, which for two years had dominated the little city, were already fading. There was only the persistent incinerator smell to remind one of all that activity and bustle. What life remained centered bitterly about divisional headquarters building, with the disgruntled regular officers who had also missed the war.

And now the young men of Tarleton began drifting back from the ends of the earth—some with Canadian uniforms, some with crutches or empty sleeves. A returned battalion of the National Guard paraded through the streets with open ranks for their dead, and then stepped down out of romance forever and sold you things over the counters of local stores. Only a few uniforms mingled with the dinner coats at the country-club dance.

Just before Christmas, Bill Knowles arrived unexpectedly one day and left the next—either he gave Ailie an ultimatum or she had made up her mind at last. I saw her sometimes when she wasn't busy with returned heroes from Savannah and Augusta, but I felt like an outmoded survival—and I was. She was waiting for Earl Schoen with such a vast uncertainty that she didn't like to talk about it. Three days before I got my final discharge he came.

I first happened upon them walking down Market Street together, and I don't think I've ever been so sorry for a couple in my life—though I suppose the same situation was repeating itself in every city where there had been camps. Exteriorly Earl had about everything wrong with him that could be imagined. His hat was green, with a radical feather; his suit was slashed and braided in a grotesque fashion that national advertising and the movies have put an end to. Evidently he had been to his old barber, for his hair bloused neatly on his pink, shaved neck. It wasn't as though he had been shiny and poor, but the background of mill-town dance halls and outing clubs flamed out at you—or rather flamed out at Ailie. For she had never quite imagined the reality; in these clothes even the natural grace of that magnificent body had departed. At first he boasted of his fine job; it would get them along all right until he could "see some easy money." But from the moment he came back into her world on its own terms he must have known it was hopeless. I don't know what Ailie said or how much her grief weighed against her stupefaction. She acted quickly—three days after his arrival, Earl and I went North together on the train.

"Well, that's the end of that," he said moodily. "She's a wonderful girl, but too much of a highbrow for me. I guess she's got to marry some rich guy that'll give her a great social position. I can't see that stuck-up sort of thing." And then, later: "She said to come back and see her in a year, but I'll never go back. This aristocrat stuff is all right if you got the money for it, but—"

"But it wasn't real," he meant to finish. The provincial society in which he had moved with so much satisfaction for six months already appeared to him as affected, "dude-ish" and artificial.

"Say, did you see what I saw getting on the train?" he asked me after awhile. "Two wonderful janes, all alone. What do you say we mosey into the next car and ask them to lunch? I'll take the one in blue." Halfway down the car he turned around suddenly. "Say, Andy," he demanded, frowning; "one thing—how do you suppose she knew I used to command a street car? I never told her that."

"Search me."

III

This narrative arrives now at one of the big gaps that stared me in the face when I began. For six years, while I finished at Harvard Law and built commercial aeroplanes and backed a pavement block that went gritty under trucks, Ailie Calhoun was scarcely more than a name on a Christmas card, something that blew a little in my mind on warm nights when I remembered the magnolia flowers. Occasionally an acquaintance of Army days would ask me, "What became of that blonde girl who was so popular?" but I didn't know. I ran into Nancy Lamar at the Montmartre in New York one evening and learned that Ailie had become engaged to a man in Cincinnati, had gone North to visit his family and then broken it off. She was lovely as ever and there was always a heavy beau or two. But neither Bill Knowles nor Earl Schoen had ever come back.

And somewhere about that time I heard that Bill Knowles had married a girl he met on a boat. There you are—not much of a patch to mend six years with.

Oddly enough, a girl seen at twilight in a small Indiana station started me thinking about going South. The girl, in stiff pink organdie, threw her arms about a man who got off our train and hurried him to a waiting car, and I felt a sort of pang. It seemed to me that she was bearing him off into the lost midsummer world of my early twenties, where time had stood still and charming girls, dimly seen like the past itself, still loitered along the dusky streets. I suppose that poetry is a Northern man's dream of the South. But it was months later that I sent off a wire to Ailie, and immediately followed it to Tarleton.

It was July. The Jefferson Hotel seemed strangely shabby and stuffy—a boosters' club burst into intermittent song in the dining room that my memory had long dedicated to officers and girls. I recognized the taxi-driver who took me up to Ailie's house, but his "Sure, I do, lieutenant," was unconvincing. I was only one of twenty thousand.

It was a curious three days. I suppose some of Ailie's first young lustre must have gone the way of such mortal shining, but I can't bear witness to it. She was still so physically appealing that you wanted to touch the personality that trembled on her lips. No—the change was more profound than that.

At once I saw she had a different line. The modulations of pride, the vocal hints that she knew the secrets of a brighter, finer antebellum day, were gone from her voice; there was no time for them now as it rambled on in the half-laughing, half-desperate banter of the newer South. And everything was swept into this banter in order to make it go on and leave no time for thinking—the present, the future, herself, me. We went to a rowdy party at the house of some young married people, and she was the nervous, glowing center of it. After all, she wasn't eighteen, and she was as attractive in her role of reckless clown as she had ever been in her life.

"Have you heard anything from Earl Schoen?" I asked her the second night, on our way to the country-club dance.

"No." She was serious for a moment. "I often think of him. He was the—" She hesitated.

"Go on."

"I was going to say the man I loved most, but that wouldn't be true. I never exactly loved him, or I'd have married him any old how, wouldn't I?" She looked at me questioningly. "At least I wouldn't have treated him like that."

"It was impossible."

"Of course," she agreed uncertainly. Her mood changed; she became flippant: "How the Yankees did deceive us poor little Southern girls. Ah, me!"

When we reached the country club she melted like a chameleon into the—to me—unfamiliar crowd. There was a new generation upon the floor, with less dignity than the ones I had known, but none of them were more a part of its lazy, feverish essence than Ailie. Possibly she had perceived that in her initial longing to escape from Tarleton's provincialism she had been walking alone, following a generation which was doomed to have no successors. Just where she lost the battle, waged behind the white pillars of her verandah, I don't know. But she had guessed wrong, missed out somewhere. Her wild animation, which even now called enough men around her to rival the entourage of the youngest and freshest, was an admission of defeat.

I left her house, as I had so often left it that vanished June, in a mood of vague dissatisfaction. It was hours later, tossing about my bed in the hotel, that I realized what was the matter, what had always been the matter—I was deeply and incurably in love with her. In spite of every incompatibility, she was still, she would always be to me, the most attractive girl I had ever known. I told her so next afternoon. It was one of those hot days I knew so well, and Ailie sat beside me on a couch in the darkened library.

"Oh, no, I couldn't marry you," she said, almost frightened; "I don't love you that way at all. . . . I never did. And you don't love me. I didn't mean to tell you now, but next month I'm going to marry another man. We're not even announcing it, because I've done that twice before." Suddenly it occurred to her that I might be hurt: "Andy, you just had a silly idea, didn't you? You know I couldn't ever marry a Northern man."

"Who is he?" I demanded.

"A man from Savannah."

"Are you in love with him?"

"Of course I am." We both smiled. "Of *course* I am! What are you trying to make me say?"

There were no doubts, as there had been with other men. She couldn't afford to let herself have doubts. I knew this because she had long ago stopped making any pretensions with me. This very naturalness, I realized, was because she didn't consider me as a suitor. Beneath her mask of an instinctive thoroughbred she had always been on to herself, and she couldn't believe that anyone not taken in to the point of uncritical worship could really love her. That was what she called being "sincere"; she felt most security with men like Canby and Earl Schoen, who were incapable of passing judgments on the ostensibly aristocratic heart.

"All right," I said, as if she had asked my permission to marry. "Now, would you do something for me?"

"Anything."

"Ride out to camp."

"But there's nothing left there, honey."

"I don't care."

We walked downtown. The taxi-driver in front of the hotel repeated her objection: "Nothing there now, cap."

"Never mind. Go there anyhow."

Twenty minutes later he stopped on a wide unfamiliar plain powdered with new cotton fields and marked with isolated clumps of pine.

"Like to drive over yonder where you see the smoke?" asked the driver. "That's the new state prison."

"No. Just drive along this road. I want to find where I used to live."

An old race course, inconspicuous in the camp's day of glory, had reared its dilapidated grandstand in the desolation. I tried in vain to orient myself.

"Go along this road past that clump of trees, and then turn right—no, turn left."

He obeyed, with professional disgust.

"You won't find a single thing, darling," said Ailie. "The contractors took it all down."

We rode slowly along the margin of the fields. It might have been here—

"All right. I want to get out," I said suddenly.

I left Ailie sitting in the car, looking very beautiful with the warm breeze stirring her long, curly bob.

It might have been here. That would make the company streets down there and the mess shack, where we dined that night, just over the way.

The taxi-driver regarded me indulgently while I stumbled here and there in the knee-deep underbrush, looking for my youth in a clapboard or a strip of roofing or a rusty tomato can. I tried to sight on a vaguely familiar clump of trees, but it was growing darker now and I couldn't be quite sure they were the right trees.

"They're going to fix up the old race course," Ailie called from the car. "Tarleton's getting quite doggy in its old age."

No. Upon consideration they didn't look like the right trees. All I could be sure of was this place that had once been so full of life and effort was gone, as if it had never existed, and that in another month Ailie would be gone, and the South would be empty for me forever.

MAJESTY

The extraordinary thing is not that people in a lifetime turn out worse or better than we had prophesied; particularly in America that is to be expected. The extraordinary thing is how people keep their levels, fulfill their promises, seem actually buoyed up by an inevitable destiny.

One of my conceits is that no one has ever disappointed me since I turned eighteen and could tell a real quality from a gift for sleight of hand, and even many of the merely showy people in my past seem to go on being blatantly and successfully showy to the end.

Emily Castleton was born in Harrisburg in a medium-sized house, moved to New York at sixteen to a big house, went to the Briarly School, moved to an enormous house, moved to a mansion at Tuxedo Park, moved abroad, where she did various fashionable things and was in all the papers. Back in her debutante year one of those French artists who are so dogmatic about American beauties included her with eleven other public and semipublic celebrities as one of America's perfect types. At the time numerous men agreed with him.

She was just faintly tall, with fine, rather large features, eyes with such an expanse of blue in them that you were really aware of it whenever you looked at her, and a good deal of thick blonde hair—arresting and bright. Her mother and father did not know very much about the new world they had commandeered so Emily had to learn everything for herself, and she became involved in various situations and some of the first bloom wore off. However, there was bloom to spare. There were engagements and semi-engagements, short passionate attractions, and then a big affair at twenty-two that embittered her and sent her wandering the continents looking for happiness. She became "artistic" as most wealthy unmarried girls do at that age, because artistic people seem to have some secret, some inner refuge, some escape. But most of her friends were married now, and her life was a great disappointment to her father; so, at twenty-four, with marriage in her head if not in her heart, Emily came home.

This was a low point in her career and Emily was aware of it. She had not done well. She was one of the most popular, most beautiful girls of her generation with charm, money and a sort of fame, but her generation was moving into new fields. At the first note of condescension from a former schoolmate, now a young "matron," she went to Newport and was won by William Brevoort Blair. Immediately she was again the incomparable Emily Castleton. The ghost of the French artist walked once more in the newspapers; the most-talked-of leisure-class event of October was her wedding day.

Splendor to mark society nuptials.... Harold Castleton sets out a series of five-thousand-dollar pavilions arranged like the interconnecting tents of a circus, in which the reception, the wedding supper and the ball will be held.... Nearly a thousand guests, many of them leaders in business, will mingle with those who dominate the social world.... The wedding gifts are estimated to be worth a quarter of a million dollars....

An hour before the ceremony, which was to be solemnized at St. Bartholomew's, Emily sat before a dressing-table and gazed at her face in the glass. She was a little tired of her face at that moment and the depressing thought suddenly assailed her that it would require more and more looking after in the next fifty years.

"I ought to be happy," she said aloud, "but every thought that comes into my head is sad."

Her cousin, Olive Mercy, sitting on the side of the bed, nodded. "All brides are sad."

"It's such a waste," Emily said.

Olive frowned impatiently.

"Waste of what? Women are incomplete unless they're married and have children."

For a moment Emily didn't answer. Then she said slowly, "Yes, but whose children?"

For the first time in her life, Olive, who worshipped Emily, almost hated her. Not a girl in the wedding party but would have been glad of Brevoort Blair—Olive among the others.

"You're lucky," she said. "You're so lucky you don't even know it. You ought to be paddled for talking like that."

"I shall learn to love him," announced Emily facetiously. "Love will come with marriage. Now, isn't that a hell of a prospect?"

"Why so deliberately unromantic?"

"On the contrary, I'm the most romantic person I've ever met in my life. Do you know what I think when he puts his arms around me? I think that if I look up I'll see Garland Kane's eyes."

"But why, then—"

"Getting into his plane the other day I could only remember Captain Marchbanks and the little two-seater we flew over the Channel in, just breaking our hearts for each other and never saying a word about it because of his wife. I don't regret those men; I just regret the part of me that went into caring. There's only the sweepings to hand to Brevoort in a pink wastebasket. There should have been something more; I thought even when I was most carried away that I was saving something for the one. But apparently I wasn't." She broke off and then added: "And yet I wonder."

The situation was no less provoking to Olive for being comprehensible, and save for her position as a poor relation, she would have spoken her mind. Emily was well spoiled—eight years of men had assured her they were not good enough for her and she had accepted the fact as probably true.

"You're nervous." Olive tried to keep the annoyance out of her voice. "Why not lie down for an hour?"

"Yes," answered Emily absently.

Olive went out and downstairs. In the lower hall she ran into Brevoort Blair, attired in a nuptial cutaway even to the white carnation, and in a state of considerable agitation.

"Oh, excuse me," he blurted out. "I wanted to see Emily. It's about the rings—which ring, you know. I've got four rings and she never decided and I can't just hold them out in the church and have her take her pick."

"I happen to know she wants the plain platinum band. If you want to see her anyhow—"

"Oh, thanks very much. I don't want to disturb her."

They were standing close together, and even at this moment when he was gone, definitely preëmpted, Olive couldn't help thinking how alike she and Brevoort were. Hair, coloring, features—they might have been brother and sister—and they shared the same shy serious temperaments, the same simple straightforwardness. All this flashed through her mind in an instant, with the added thought that the blonde, tempestuous Emily, with her vitality and amplitude of scale, was, after all, better for him in every way; and then, beyond this, a perfect wave of tenderness, of pure physical pity and yearning swept over her and it seemed that she must step forward only half a foot to find his arms wide to receive her.

She stepped backward instead, relinquishing him as though she still touched him with the tips of her fingers and then drew the tips away. Perhaps some vibration of her emotion fought its way into his consciousness, for he said suddenly:

"We're going to be good friends, aren't we? Please don't think I'm taking Emily away. I know I can't own her—nobody could—and I don't want to."

Silently, as he talked, she said good-bye to him, the only man she had ever wanted in her life.

She loved the absorbed hesitancy with which he found his coat and hat and felt hopefully for the knob on the wrong side of the door.

When he had gone she went into the drawing-room, gorgeous and portentous; with its painted bacchanals and massive chandeliers and the eighteenth-century portraits that might have been Emily's ancestors, but weren't, and by that very fact belonged the more to her. There she rested, as always, in Emily's shadow.

Through the door that led out to the small, priceless patch of grass on 60th Street now inclosed by the pavilions, came her uncle, Mr. Harold Castleton. He had been sampling his own champagne.

"Olive so sweet and fair." He cried emotionally, "Olive, baby, she's done it. She was all right inside, like I knew all the time. The good ones come through, don't they—the real thoroughbreds? I began to think that the Lord and me, between us, had given her too much, that she'd never be satisfied, but now she's come down to earth just like a"—he searched unsuccessfully for a simile—"like a thoroughbred, and she'll find it not such a bad place after all." He came closer. "You've been crying, little Olive."

"Not much."

"It doesn't matter," he said magnanimously. "If I wasn't so happy I'd cry too."

Later, as she embarked with two other bridesmaids for the church, the solemn throbbing of a big wedding seemed to begin with the vibration of the car. At the door the organ took it up, and later it would palpitate in the cellos and bass viols of the dance, to fade off finally with the sound of the car that bore bride and groom away.

The crowd was thick around the church, and ten feet out of it the air was heavy with perfume and faint clean humanity and the fabric smell of new clean clothes. Beyond the massed hats in the van of the church the two families sat in front rows on either side. The Blairs—they were assured a family resemblance by their expression of faint condescension, shared by their in-laws as well as by true Blairs—were represented by the Gardiner Blairs, senior and junior; Lady Mary Bowes Howard, née Blair; Mrs. Potter Blair; Mrs. Princess Potowki Parr Blair, née Inchbit; Miss Gloria Blair, Master Gardiner Blair III, and the kindred branches, rich and poor, of Smythe, Bickle, Diffendorfer and Hamn. Across the aisle the Castletons made a less impressive showing—Mr. Harold Castleton, Mr. and Mrs. Theodore Castleton and children, Harold Castleton Junior, and, from Harrisburg, Mr. Carl Mercy, and two little old aunts named O'Keefe hidden off in a corner. Somewhat to their surprise the two aunts had been bundled off in a limousine and dressed from head to foot by a fashionable *couturière* that morning.

In the vestry, where the bridesmaids fluttered about like birds in their big floppy hats, there was a last lip rouging and adjustment of pins before Emily should arrive. They represented several stages of Emily's life—a schoolmate at Briarly, a last unmarried friend of debutante year, a travelling companion of Europe, and the girl she had visited in Newport when she met Brevoort Blair.

"They've got Wakeman," this last one said, standing by the door listening to the music. "He played for my sister, but I shall never have Wakeman."

"Why not?"

"Why, he's playing the same thing over and over—'At Dawning.' He's played it half a dozen times."

At this moment another door opened and the solicitous head of a young man appeared around it. "Almost ready?" he demanded of the nearest bridesmaid. "Brevoort's having a quiet little fit. He just stands there wilting collar after collar—"

"Be calm," answered the young lady. "The bride is always a few minutes late."

"A few minutes!" protested the best man. "I don't call it a few minutes. They're beginning to rustle and wriggle like a circus crowd out there, and the organist has been playing the same tune for half an hour. I'm going to get him to fill in with a little jazz."

"What time is it?" Olive demanded.

"Quarter of five—ten minutes of five."

"Maybe there's been a traffic tie-up." Olive paused as Mr. Harold Castleton, followed by an anxious curate, shouldered his way in, demanding a phone.

And now there began a curious dribbling back from the front of the church, one by one, then two by two, until the vestry was crowded with relatives and confusion.

"What's happened?"

"What on earth's the matter?"

A chauffeur came in and reported excitedly. Harold Castleton swore and, his face blazing, fought his way roughly toward the door. There was an attempt to clear the vestry, and then, as if to balance the dribbling, a ripple of conversation commenced at the rear of the church and began to drift up toward the altar, growing louder and faster and more excited, mounting always, bringing people to their feet, rising to a sort of subdued roar. The announcement from the altar that the marriage had been postponed was scarcely heard, for by that time everyone knew that they were participating in a front-page scandal, that Brevoort Blair had been left waiting at the altar and Emily Castleton had run away.

II

There were a dozen reporters outside the Castleton house on 60th Street when Olive arrived, but in her absorption she failed even to hear their questions; she wanted desperately to go and comfort a certain man whom she must not approach, and as a sort of substitute she sought her Uncle Harold. She entered through the interconnecting five-thousand-dollar pavilions, where caterers and servants still stood about in a respectful funereal half-light, waiting for something to happen, amid trays of caviar and turkey's breast and pyramided wedding cake. Upstairs, Olive found her uncle sitting on a stool before Emily's dressing-table. The articles of make-up spread before him, the repertoire of feminine preparation in evidence about, made his singularly inappropriate presence a symbol of the mad catastrophe.

"Oh, it's you." His voice was listless; he had aged in two hours. Olive put her arm about his bowed shoulder.

"I'm so terribly sorry, Uncle Harold."

Suddenly a stream of profanity broke from him, died away, and a single large tear welled slowly from one eye.

"I want to get my massage man," he said. "Tell McGregor to get him." He drew a long broken sigh, like a child's breath after crying, and Olive saw that his sleeves were covered with a dust of powder from the dressing-table, as if he had been leaning forward on it, weeping, in the reaction from his proud champagne.

"There was a telegram," he muttered. "It's somewhere." And he added slowly, "From now on *you*'re my daughter."

"Oh, no, you mustn't say that!"

Unrolling the telegram, she read:

I CAN'T MAKE THE GRADE I WOULD FEEL LIKE A FOOL EITHER WAY BUT THIS WILL BE OVER SOONER SO DAMN SORRY FOR YOU

EMILY

When Olive had summoned the masseur and posted a servant outside her uncle's door, she went to the library, where a confused secretary was trying to say nothing over an inquisitive and persistent telephone.

"I'm so upset, Miss Mercy," he cried in a despairing treble. "I do declare I'm so upset I have a frightful headache. I've thought for half an hour I heard dance music from down below."

Then it occurred to Olive that she, too, was becoming hysterical; in the breaks of the street traffic a melody was drifting up, distinct and clear:

"—Is she fair
Is she sweet
I don't care—cause
I can't compete –
Who's the—"

She ran quickly downstairs and through the drawing-room, the tune growing louder in her ears. At the entrance of the first pavilion she stopped in stupefaction.

To the music of a small but undoubtedly professional orchestra a dozen young couples were moving about the canvas floor. At the bar in the corner stood additional young men, and half a dozen of the caterer's assistants were busily shaking cocktails and opening champagne.

"Harold!" she called imperatively to one of the dancers. "Harold!"

A tall young man of eighteen handed his partner to another and came toward her.

"Hello, Olive. How did father take it?"

"Harold, what in the name of—"

"Emily's crazy," he said consolingly. "I always told you Emily was crazy. Crazy as a loon. Always was."

"What's the idea of this?"

"This?" He looked around innocently. "Oh, these are just some fellows that came down from Cambridge with me."

"But—*dan*cing!"

"Well, nobody's dead, are they? I thought we might as well use up some of this—"

"Tell them to go home," said Olive.

"Why? What on earth's the harm? These fellows came all the way down from Cambridge—"

"It simply isn't dignified."

"But they don't care, Olive. One fellow's sister did the same thing—only she did it the day after instead of the day before. Lots of people do it nowadays."

"Send the music home, Harold," said Olive firmly, "or I'll go to your father."

Obviously he felt that no family could be disgraced by an episode on such a magnificent scale, but he reluctantly yielded. The abysmally depressed butler saw to the removal of the champagne, and the young people, somewhat insulted, moved nonchalantly out into the more tolerant night. Alone with the shadow—Emily's shadow—that hung over the house, Olive sat down in the drawing-room to think. Simultaneously the butler appeared in the doorway.

"It's Mr. Blair, Miss Olive."

She jumped tensely to her feet.

"Who does he want to see?"

"He didn't say. He just walked in."

"Tell him I'm in here."

He entered with an air of abstraction rather than depression, nodded to Olive and sat down on a piano stool. She wanted to say, "Come here. Lay your head here, poor man. Never mind." But she wanted to cry, too, and so she said nothing.

"In three hours," he remarked quietly, "we'll be able to get the morning papers. There's a shop on 59th Street."

"That's foolish—" she began.

"I am not a superficial man"—he interrupted her—"nevertheless, my chief feeling now is for the morning papers. Later there will be a politely silent gauntlet of relatives, friends and business acquaintances. About the actual affair I surprise myself by not caring at all."

"I shouldn't care about any of it."

"I'm rather grateful that she did it in time."

"Why don't you go away?" Olive leaned forward earnestly. "Go to Europe until it all blows over."

"Blows over." He laughed. "Things like this don't ever blow over. A little snicker is going to follow me around the rest of my life." He groaned. "Uncle Hamilton started right for Park Row to make the rounds of the newspaper offices. He's a Virginian and he was unwise enough to use the old-fashioned word 'horsewhip' to one editor. I can hardly wait to see *that* paper." He broke off. "How is Mr. Castleton?"

"He'll appreciate your coming to inquire."

"I didn't come about that." He hesitated. "I came to ask you a question. I want to know if you'll marry me in Greenwich tomorrow morning."

For a minute Olive fell precipitately through space; she made a strange little sound; her mouth dropped ajar.

"I know you like me," he went on quickly. "In fact, I once imagined you loved me a little bit, if you'll excuse the presumption. Anyhow, you're very like a girl that once did love me, so maybe you would—" His face was pink with embarrassment, but he struggled grimly on; "anyhow, I like you enormously and whatever feeling I may have had for Emily has, I might say, flown."

The clangor and alarm inside her was so loud that it seemed he must hear it.

"The favor you'll be doing me will be very great," he continued. "My heavens, I know it sounds a little crazy, but what could be crazier than the whole afternoon? You see, if you married me the papers would carry quite a different story; they'd think that Emily went off to get out of our way, and the joke would be on her after all."

Tears of indignation came to Olive's eyes.

"I suppose I ought to allow for your wounded egotism, but do you realize you're making me an insulting proposition?"

His face fell.

"I'm sorry," he said after a moment. "I guess I was an awful fool even to think of it, but a man hates to lose the whole dignity of his life for a girl's whim. I see it would be impossible. I'm sorry."

He got up and picked up his cane.

Now he was moving toward the door, and Olive's heart came into her throat and a great, irresistible wave of self-preservation swept over her—swept over all her scruples and her pride. His steps sounded in the hall.

"Brevoort!" she called. She jumped to her feet and ran to the door. He turned. "Brevoort, what was the name of that paper—the one your uncle went to?"

"Why?"

"Because it's not too late for them to change their story if I telephone now! I'll say we were married tonight!"

III

There is a society in Paris which is merely a heterogeneous prolongation of American society. People moving in are connected by a hundred threads to the motherland, and their entertainments, eccentricities and ups and downs are an open book to friends and relatives at Southampton, Lake Forest or Back Bay. So during her previous European sojourn Emily's whereabouts, as she followed the shifting Continental seasons, were publicly advertised; but from the day, one month after the unsolemnized wedding, when she sailed from New York, she dropped completely from sight. There was an occasional letter for her father, an occasional rumor that she was in Cairo, Constantinople or the less frequented Riviera—that was all.

Once, after a year, Mr. Castleton saw her in Paris, but, as he told Olive, the meeting only served to make him uncomfortable.

"There was something about her," he said vaguely, "as if—well, as if she had a lot of things in the back of her mind I couldn't reach. She was nice enough, but it was all automatic and formal. She asked about you."

Despite her solid background of a three-month-old baby and a beautiful apartment on Park Avenue, Olive felt her heart falter uncertainly.

"What did she say?"

"She was delighted about you and Brevoort." And he added to himself, with a disappointment he could not conceal: "Even though you picked up the best match in New York when she threw it away." . . .

. . . It was more than a year after this that his secretary's voice on the telephone asked Olive if Mr. Castleton could see them that night. They found the old man walking his library in a state of agitation.

"Well, it's come," he declared vehemently. "People won't stand still; nobody stands still. You go up or down in this world. Emily chose to go down. She seems to be somewhere near the bottom.

Did you ever hear of a man described to me as a"—he referred to a letter in his hand—"dissipated ne'er-do-well named Petrocobesco? He calls himself Prince Gabriel Petrocobesco, apparently from—from nowhere. This letter is from Hallam, my European man, and it incloses a clipping from the Paris *Matin*. It seems that this gentleman was invited by the police to leave Paris, and among the small entourage who left with him was an American girl, Miss Castleton, 'rumored to be the daughter of a millionaire.' The party was escorted to the station by gendarmes." He handed clipping and letter to Brevoort Blair with trembling fingers. "What do you make of it? Emily come to that!"

"It's not so good," said Brevoort, frowning.

"It's the end. I thought her drafts were big recently, but I never suspected that she was supporting—"

"It may be a mistake," Olive suggested. "Perhaps it's another Miss Castleton."

"It's Emily all right. Hallam looked up the matter. It's Emily, who was afraid ever to dive into the nice clean stream of life and ends up now by swimming around in the sewers."

Shocked, Olive had a sudden sharp taste of fate in its ultimate diversity. She with a mansion building in Westbury Hills, and Emily was mixed up with a deported adventurer in disgraceful scandal.

"I've got no right to ask you this," continued Mr. Castleton. "Certainly no right to ask Brevoort anything in connection with Emily. But I'm seventy-two and Fraser says if I put off the cure another fortnight he won't be responsible, and then Emily will be alone for good. I want you to set your trip abroad forward by two months and go over and bring her back."

"But do you think we'd have the necessary influence?" Brevoort asked. "I've no reason for thinking that she'd listen to me."

"There's no one else. If you can't go I'll have to."

"Oh, no," said Brevoort quickly. "We'll do what we can, won't we, Olive?"

"Of course."

"Bring her back—it doesn't matter how—but bring her back. Go before a court if necessary and swear she's crazy."

"Very well. We'll do what we can."

* * *

Just ten days after this interview the Brevoort Blairs called on Mr. Castleton's agent in Paris to glean what details were available. They were plentiful but unsatisfactory. Hallam had seen Petrocobesco in various restaurants—a fat little fellow with an attractive leer and a quenchless thirst. He was of some obscure nationality and had been moving around Europe for several years, living heaven knew how—probably on Americans, though Hallam understood that of late even the most outlying circles of international society were closed to him. About Emily, Hallam knew very little. They had been reported last week in Berlin and yesterday in Budapest. It was probably that such an undesirable as Petrocobesco was required to register with the police everywhere, and this was the line he recommended the Blairs to follow.

Forty-eight hours later, accompanied by the American vice consul, they called upon the prefect of police in Budapest. The officer talked in rapid Hungarian to the vice consul, who presently announced the gist of his remarks—the Blairs were too late.

"Where have they gone?"

"He doesn't know. He received orders to move them on and they left last night."

Suddenly the prefect wrote something on a piece of paper and handed it, with a terse remark, to the vice consul.

"He says try there."

Brevoort looked at the paper.

"Sturmdorp—where's that?"

Another rapid conversation in Hungarian.

"Five hours from here on a local train that leaves Tuesdays and Fridays. This is Saturday."

"We'll get a car at the hotel," said Brevoort.

They set out after dinner. It was a rough journey through the night across the still Hungarian plain. Olive awoke once from a worried doze to find Brevoort and the chauffeur changing a tire; then again as they stopped at a muddy little river, beyond which glowed the scattered lights of a town. Two soldiers in an unfamiliar uniform glanced into the car; they crossed a bridge and followed a narrow, warped main street to Sturmdorp's single inn; the roosters were already crowing as they tumbled down on the mean beds.

Olive awoke with a sudden sure feeling that they had caught up with Emily; and with it came that old sense of helplessness in the face of Emily's moods; for a moment the long past, and Emily dominant in it, swept back over her, and it seemed almost a presumption to be here. But Brevoort's singleness of purpose reassured her and confidence had returned when they went downstairs, to find a landlord who spoke fluent American, acquired in Chicago before the war.

"You are not in Hungary now," he explained. "You have crossed the border into Czjeck-Hansa. But it is only a little country with two towns, this one and the capital. We don't ask the visa from Americans."

"That's probably why they came here," Olive thought.

"Perhaps you could give us some information about strangers?" asked Brevoort. "We're looking for an American lady—" He described Emily, without mentioning her probable companion; as he proceeded a curious change came over the innkeeper's face.

"Let me see your passports," he said. Then: "And why you want to see her?"

"This lady is her cousin."

The innkeeper hesitated momentarily.

"I think perhaps I be able to find her for you," he said.

He called the porter; there were rapid instructions in an unintelligible patois. Then: "Follow this boy—he take you there."

They were conducted through filthy streets to a tumbledown house on the edge of town. A man with a hunting rifle, lounging outside, straightened up and spoke sharply to the porter, but after an exchange of phrases they passed, mounted the stairs and knocked at a door. When it opened a head peered around the corner; the porter spoke again and they went in.

They were in a large dirty room which might have belonged to a poor boarding house in any quarter of the Western world—faded walls, split upholstery, a shapeless bed and an air, despite its bareness, of being overcrowded by the ghostly furniture, indicated by dust rings and worn spots, of the last decade. In the middle of the room stood a small stout man with hammock eyes and a peering nose over a sweet, spoiled little mouth, who stared intently at them as they opened the door, and then with a single disgusted "*Chut!*" turned impatiently away. There were several other people in the room, but Brevoort and Olive saw only Emily, who reclined in a chaise longue with half-closed eyes.

At the sight of them the eyes opened in mild astonishment; she made a move as though to jump up, but instead held out her hand, smiled and spoke their names in a clear polite voice, less as a greeting than as a sort of explanation to the others of their presence here. At their names a grudging amenity replaced the sullenness on the little man's face.

The girls kissed.

"Tutu!" said Emily, as if calling him to attention—"Prince Petrocobesco, let me present my cousin Mrs. Blair, and Mr. Blair."

"*Plaisir*," said Petrocobesco. He and Emily exchanged a quick glance, whereupon he said, "Won't you sit down?" and immediately seated himself in the only available chair, as if they were playing Going to Jerusalem.

"*Plaisir*," he repeated. Olive sat down on the foot of Emily's chaise longue and Brevoort took a stool from against the wall, meanwhile noting the other occupants of the room. There was a very fierce young man in a cape who stood, with arms folded and teeth gleaming, by the door, and two ragged, bearded men, one holding a revolver, the other with his head sunk dejectedly on his chest, who sat side by side in the corner.

"You come here long?" the prince asked.

"Just arrived this morning."

For a moment Olive could not resist comparing the two, the tall fair-featured American and the unprepossessing South European, scarcely a likely candidate for Ellis Island. Then she looked at Emily—the same thick bright hair with sunshine in it, the eyes with the hint of vivid seas. Her face was faintly drawn, there were slight new lines around her mouth, but she was the Emily of old—dominant, shining, large of scale. It seemed shameful for all that beauty and personality to have arrived in a cheap boarding house at the world's end.

The man in the cape answered a knock at the door and handed a note to Petrocobesco, who read it, cried *"Chut!"* and passed it to Emily.

"You see, there are no carriages," he said tragically in French. "The carriages were destroyed—all except one, which is in a museum. Anyhow, I prefer a horse."

"No," said Emily.

"Yes, yes, yes!" he cried. "Whose business is it how I go?"

"Don't let's have a scene, Tutu."

"Scene!" he fumed. "Scene!"

Emily turned to Olive: "You came by automobile?"

"Yes."

"A big de luxe car? With a back that opens?"

"Yes."

"There," said Emily to the prince. "We can have the arms painted on the side of that."

"Hold on," said Brevoort. "This car belongs to a hotel in Budapest."

Apparently Emily didn't hear.

"Janierka could do it," she continued thoughtfully.

At this point there was another interruption. The dejected man in the corner suddenly sprang to his feet and made as though to run to the door, whereupon the other man raised his revolver and brought the butt down on his head. The man faltered and would have collapsed had not his assailant hauled him back to the chair, where he sat comatose, a slow stream of blood trickling over his forehead.

"Dirty townsman! Filthy, dirty spy!" shouted Petrocobesco between clenched teeth.

"Now that's just the kind of remark you're not to make!" said Emily sharply.

"Then why we don't hear?" he cried. "Are we going to sit here in this pigsty forever?"

Disregarding him, Emily turned to Olive and began to question her conventionally about New York. Was prohibition any more successful? What were the new plays? Olive tried to answer and simultaneously to catch Brevoort's eye. The sooner their purpose was broached, the sooner they could get Emily away.

"Can we see you alone, Emily?" demanded Brevoort abruptly.

"Why, for the moment we haven't got another room."

Petrocobesco had engaged the man with the cape in agitated conversation, and taking advantage of this, Brevoort spoke hurriedly to Emily in a lowered voice:

"Emily, your father's getting old; he needs you at home. He wants you to give up this crazy life and come back to America. He sent us because he couldn't come himself and no one else knew you well enough—"

She laughed. "You mean, knew the enormities I was capable of."

"No," put in Olive quickly. "Cared for you as we do. I can't tell you how awful it is to see you wandering over the face of the earth."

"But we're not wandering now," explained Emily. "This is Tutu's native country."

"Where's your pride, Emily?" said Olive impatiently. "Do you know that affair in Paris was in the papers? What do you suppose people think back home?"

"That affair in Paris was an outrage." Emily's blue eyes flashed around her. "Someone will pay for that affair in Paris."

"It'll be the same everywhere. Just sinking lower and lower, dragged in the mire, and one day deserted—"

"Stop, please!" Emily's voice was cold as ice. "I don't think you quite understand—"

Emily broke off as Petrocobesco came back, threw himself into his chair and buried his face in his hands.

"I can't stand it," he whispered. "Would you mind taking my pulse? I think it's bad. Have you got the thermometer in your purse?"

She held his wrist in silence for a moment.

"It's all right, Tutu." Her voice was soft now, almost crooning. "Sit up. Be a man."

"All right."

He crossed his legs as if nothing had happened and turned abruptly to Brevoort:

"How are financial conditions in New York?" he demanded.

But Brevoort was in no humor to prolong the absurd scene. The memory of a certain terrible hour three years before swept over him. He was no man to be made a fool of twice, and his jaw set as he rose to his feet.

"Emily, get your things together," he said tersely. "We're going home."

Emily did not move; an expression of astonishment, melting to amusement, spread over her face. Olive put her arm around her shoulder.

"Come, dear. Let's get out of this nightmare." Then:

"We're waiting," Brevoort said.

Petrocobesco spoke suddenly to the man in the cape, who approached and seized Brevoort's arm. Brevoort shook him off angrily, whereupon the man stepped back, his hand searching his belt.

"No!" cried Emily imperatively.

Once again there was an interruption. The door opened without a knock and two stout men in frock coats and silk hats rushed in and up to Petrocobesco. They grinned and patted him on the back chattering in a strange language, and presently he grinned and patted them on the back and they kissed all around; then, turning to Emily, Petrocobesco spoke to her in French.

"It's all right," he said excitedly. "They did not even argue the matter. I am to have the title of king."

With a long sigh Emily sank back in her chair and her lips parted in a relaxed, tranquil smile.

"Very well, Tutu. We'll get married."

"Oh, heavens, how happy!" He clasped his hands and gazed up ecstatically at the faded ceiling. "How extremely happy!" He fell on his knees beside her and kissed her inside arm.

"What's all this about kings?" Brevoort demanded. "Is this—is he a king?"

"He's a king. Aren't you, Tutu?" Emily's hand gently stroked his oiled hair and Olive saw that her eyes were unusually bright.

"I am your husband," cried Tutu weepily. "The most happy man alive."

"His uncle was Prince of Czjeck-Hansa before the war," explained Emily, her voice singing her content. "Since then there's been a republic, but the peasant party wanted a change and Tutu was next in line. Only I wouldn't marry him unless he insisted on being king instead of prince."

Brevoort passed his hand over his wet forehead.

"Do you mean that this is actually a fact?"

Emily nodded. "The assembly voted it this morning. And if you'll lend us this de luxe limousine of yours we'll make our official entrance into the capital this afternoon."

IV

Over two years later Mr. and Mrs. Brevoort Blair and their two children stood upon a balcony of the Carlton Hotel in London, a situation recommended by the management for watching royal processions pass. This one began with a fanfare of trumpets down by the Strand, and presently a scarlet line of horse guards came into sight.

"But, mummy," the little boy demanded, "is Aunt Emily Queen of England?"

"No, dear; she's queen of a little tiny country, but when she visits here she rides in the queen's carriage."

"Oh."

"Thanks to the magnesium deposits," said Brevoort dryly.

"Was she a princess before she got to be queen?" the little girl asked.

"No, dear; she was an American girl and then she got to be a queen."

"Why?"

"Because nothing else was good enough for her," said her father. "Just think, one time she could have married me. Which would you rather do, baby—marry me or be a queen?"

The little girl hesitated.

"Marry you," she said politely, but without conviction.

"That'll do, Brevoort," said her mother. "Here they come."

"I see them!" the little boy cried.

The cavalcade swept down the crowded street. There were more horse guards, a company of dragoons, outriders, then Olive found herself holding her breath and squeezing the balcony rail as, between a double line of beefeaters, a pair of great gilt-and-crimson coaches rolled past. In the first were the royal sovereigns, their uniforms gleaming with ribbons, crosses and stars, and in the second their two royal consorts, one old, the other young. There was about the scene the glamour shed always by the old empire of half the world, by her ships and ceremonies, her pomps and symbols; and the crowd felt it, and a slow murmur rolled along before the carriage, rising to a strong steady cheer. The two ladies bowed to left and right, and though few knew who the second queen was, she was cheered too. In a moment the gorgeous panoply had rolled below the balcony and on out of sight.

When Olive turned away from the window there were tears in her eyes.

"I wonder if she likes it, Brevoort. I wonder if she's really happy with that terrible little man."

"Well, she got what she wanted, didn't she? And that's something."

Olive drew a long breath.

"Oh, she's so wonderful," she cried—"so wonderful! She could always move me like that, even when I was angriest at her."

"It's all so silly," Brevoort said.

"I suppose so," answered Olive's lips. But her heart, winged with helpless adoration, was following her cousin through the palace gates half a mile away.

FAMILY IN THE WIND

The two men drove up the hill toward the blood-red sun. The cotton fields bordering the road were thin and withered, and no breeze stirred in the pines.

"When I am totally sober," the doctor was saying—"I mean when I am *totally* sober—I don't see the same world that you do. I'm like a friend of mine who had one good eye and got glasses made to correct his bad eye; the result was that he kept seeing elliptical suns and falling off tilted curbs, until he had to throw the glasses away. Granted that I am thoroughly anæsthetized the greater part of the day—well, I only undertake work that I know I can do when I am in that condition."

"Yeah," agreed his brother Gene uncomfortably. The doctor was a little tight at the moment and Gene could find no opening for what he had to say. Like so many Southerners of the humbler classes, he had a deep-seated courtesy, characteristic of all violent and passionate lands—he could not change the subject until there was a moment's silence, and Forrest would not shut up.

"I'm very happy," he continued, "or very miserable. I chuckle or I weep alcoholically and, as I continue to slow up, life accommodatingly goes faster, so that the less there is of myself inside, the more diverting becomes the moving picture without. I have cut myself off from the respect of my fellow man, but I am aware of a compensatory cirrhosis of the emotions. And because my sensitivity, my pity, no longer has direction, but fixes itself on whatever is at hand, I have become an exceptionally good fellow—much more so than when I was a good doctor."

As the road straightened after the next bend and Gene saw his house in the distance, he remembered his wife's face as she had made him promise, and he could wait no longer: "Forrest, I got a thing—"

But at that moment the doctor brought his car to a sudden stop in front of a small house just beyond a grove of pines. On the front steps a girl of eight was playing with a grey cat.

"This is the sweetest little kid I ever saw," the doctor said to Gene, and then to the child, in a grave voice: "Helen, do you need any pills for kitty?"

The little girl laughed.

"Well, I don't know," she said doubtfully. She was playing another game with the cat now and this came as rather an interruption.

"Because kitty telephoned me this morning," the doctor continued, "and said her mother was neglecting her and couldn't I get her a trained nurse from Montgomery."

"She did not." The little girl grabbed the cat close indignantly; the doctor took a nickel from his pocket and tossed it to the steps.

"I recommend a good dose of milk," he said as he put the car into gear. "Good-night, Helen."

"Good-night, doctor."

As they drove off, Gene tried again: "Listen, stop," he said. "Stop here a little way down. . . . Here."

The doctor stopped the car and the brothers faced each other. They were alike as to robustness of figure and a certain asceticism of feature and they were both in their middle forties; they were unlike in that the doctor's glasses failed to conceal the veined, weeping eyes of a soak, and that he wore corrugated city wrinkles; Gene's wrinkles bounded fields, followed the lines of rooftrees, of poles propping up sheds. His eyes were a fine, furry blue. But the sharpest contrast lay in the fact that Gene Janney was a country man while Dr. Forrest Janney was obviously a man of education.

"Well?" the doctor asked.

"You know Pinky's at home," Gene said, looking down the road.

"So I hear," the doctor answered noncommittally.

"He got in a row in Birmingham and somebody shot him in the head." Gene hesitated. "We got Doc Behrer because we thought maybe you wouldn't—maybe you wouldn't—"

"I wouldn't," agreed Doctor Janney blandly.

"But look, Forrest, here's the thing," Gene insisted. "You know how it is—you often say Doc Behrer doesn't know nothing. Shucks, I never thought he was much either. He says the bullet's pressing on the—pressing on the brain, and he can't take it out without causin' a hemmering, and he says he doesn't know whether we could get him to Birmingham or Montgomery, or not, he's so low. Doc wasn't no help. What we want—"

"No," said his brother, shaking his head. "No."

"I just want you to look at him and tell us what to do," Gene begged. "He's unconscious, Forrest. He wouldn't know you; you'd hardly know him. Thing is his mother's about crazy."

"She's in the grip of a purely animal instinct." The doctor took from his hip a flask containing half water and half Alabama corn, and drank. "You and I know that boy ought to been drowned the day he was born."

Gene flinched. "He's bad," he admitted, "but I don't know—You see him lying there—"

As the liquor spread over the doctor's insides he felt an instinct to do something, not to violate his prejudices but simply to make some gesture, to assert his own moribund but still struggling will to power.

"All right, I'll see him," he said. "I'll do nothing myself to help him, because he ought to be dead. And even his death wouldn't make up for what he did to Mary Decker."

Gene Janney pursed his lips. "Forrest, you sure about that?"

"Sure about it!" exclaimed the doctor. "Of course I'm sure. She died of starvation; she hadn't had more than a couple cups of coffee in a week. And if you looked at her shoes, you could see she'd walked for miles.

"Doc Behrer says—"

"What does he know? I performed the autopsy the day they found her on the Birmingham Highway. There was nothing the matter with her but starvation. That—that"—his voice shook with feeling—"that Pinky got tired of her and turned her out, and she was trying to get home. It suits me fine that he was invalided home himself a couple of weeks later."

As he talked, the doctor had plunged the car savagely into gear and let the clutch out with a jump; in a moment they drew up before Gene Janney's home.

It was a square frame house with a brick foundation and a well-kept lawn blocked off from the farm, a house rather superior to the buildings that composed the town of Bending and the surrounding agricultural area, yet not essentially different in type or in its interior economy. The last of the plantation houses in this section of Alabama had long disappeared, the proud pillars yielding to poverty, rot and rain.

Gene's wife, Rose, got up from her rocking-chair on the porch.

"Hello, doc." She greeted him a little nervously and without meeting his eyes. "You been a stranger here lately."

The doctor met her eyes for several seconds. "How do you do, Rose," he said. "Hi, Edith.... Hi, Eugene"—this to the little boy and girl who stood beside their mother; and then: "Hi, Butch!" to the stocky youth of nineteen who came around the corner of the house hugging a round stone.

"Goin to have a sort of low wall along the front here—kind of neater," Gene explained.

All of them had a lingering respect for the doctor. They felt reproachful toward him because they could no longer refer to him as their celebrated relative—"one of the bess surgeons up in Montgomery, yes, suh"—but there was his learning and the position he had once occupied in the larger world, before he had committed professional suicide by taking to cynicism and drink. He had come home to Bending and bought a half interest in the local drug store two years ago, keeping up his license, but practising only when sorely needed.

"Rose," said Gene, "doc says he'll take a look at Pinky."

Pinky Janney, his lips curved mean and white under a new beard, lay in bed in a darkened room. When the doctor removed the bandage from his head, his breath blew into a low groan, but his paunchy body did not move. After a few minutes, the doctor replaced the bandage and, with Gene and Rose, returned to the porch.

"Behrer wouldn't operate?" he asked.

"No."

"Why didn't they operate in Birmingham?"

"I don't know."

"H'm." The doctor put on his hat. "That bullet ought to come out, and soon. It's pressing against the carotid sheath. That's the—anyhow, you can't get him to Montgomery with that pulse."

"What'll we do?" Gene's question carried a little tail of silence as he sucked his breath back.

"Get Behrer to think it over. Or else get somebody in Montgomery. There's about a twenty-five per cent chance that the operation would save him—without the operation he hasn't any chance at all."

"Who'll we get in Montgomery?" asked Gene.

"Any good surgeon would do it. Even Behrer could do it if he had any nerve."

Suddenly Rose Janney came close to him, her eyes straining and burning with an animal maternalism. She seized his coat where it hung open.

"Doc, you do it! You can do it. You know you were as good a surgeon as any of 'em once. Please, doc, you go on do it."

He stepped back a little so that her hands fell from his coat, and held out his own hands in front of him.

"See how they tremble?" he said with elaborate irony. "Look close and you'll see. I wouldn't dare operate."

"You could do it all right," said Gene hastily, "with a drink to stiffen you up."

The doctor shook his head and said, looking at Rose: "No. You see, my decisions are not reliable, and if anything went wrong, it would seem to be my fault." He was acting a little now—he chose his words carefully. "I hear that when I found that Mary Decker died of starvation, my opinion was questioned on the ground that I was a drunkard."

"I didn't say that," lied Rose breathlessly.

"Certainly not. I just mention it to show how careful I've got to be." He moved down the steps. "Well, my advice is to see Behrer again, or, failing that, get somebody from the city. Good-night."

But before he had reached the gate, Rose came tearing after him, her eyes white with fury.

"I did say you were a drunkard!" she cried. "When you said Mary Decker died of starvation, you made it out as if it was Pinky's fault—you, swilling yourself full of corn all day! How can anybody tell whether you know what you're doing or not? Why did you think so much about Mary Decker, anyhow—a girl half your age? Everybody saw how she used to come in your drug store and talk to you—"

Gene, who had followed, seized her arms. "Shut up now, Rose.... Drive along, Forrest."

Forrest drove along, stopping at the next bend to drink from his flask. Across the fallow cotton fields he could see the house where Mary Decker had lived, and had it been six months before, he might have detoured to ask her why she hadn't come into the store that day for her free soda, or to delight her with a sample cosmetic left by a salesman that morning. He had not told Mary Decker how he felt about her; never intended to—she was seventeen, he was forty-five, and he no longer dealt in futures—but only after she ran away to Birmingham with Pinky Janney, did he realize how much his love for her had counted in his lonely life.

His thoughts went back to his brother's house.

"Now, if I were a gentleman," he thought, "I wouldn't have done like that. And another person might have been sacrificed to that dirty dog, because if he died afterward Rose would say I killed him."

Yet he felt pretty bad as he put his car away; not that he could have acted differently, but just that it was all so ugly.

He had been home scarcely ten minutes when a car creaked to rest outside and Butch Janney came in. His mouth was set tight and his eyes were narrowed as though to permit of no escape to the temper that possessed him until it should be unleashed upon its proper objective.

"Hi, Butch."

"I want to tell you, Uncle Forrest, you can't talk to my mother thataway. By God, I'll kill you, you talk to my mother like that!"

"Now shut up, Butch, and sit down," said the doctor sharply.

"She's already bout sick on account of Pinky, and you come over and talk to her like that."

"Your mother did all the insulting that was done, Butch. I just took it."

"She doesn't know what she's saying and you ought to understand that."

The doctor thought a minute. "Butch, what do *you* think of Pinky?"

Butch hesitated uncomfortably. "Well, I can't say I ever thought so much of him"—his tone changed defiantly—"but after all, he's my own brother—"

"Wait a minute, Butch. What do you think of the way he treated Mary Decker?"

But Butch had shaken himself free, and now he let go the artillery of his rage:

"That ain't the point; the point is anybody that doesn't do right to my mother has me to answer to. It's only fair when you got all the education—"

"I got my education myself, Butch."

"I don't care. We're going to try again to get Doc Behrer to operate or get us some fellow from the city. But if we can't, I'm coming and get you, and you're going to take that bullet out if I have to hold a gun to you while you do it." He nodded, panting a little; then he turned and went out and drove away.

"Something tells me," said the doctor to himself, "that there's no more peace for me in Chilton County." He called to his colored boy to put supper on the table. Then he rolled himself a cigarette and went out on the back stoop.

The weather had changed. The sky was now overcast and the grass stirred restlessly and there was a sudden flurry of drops without a sequel. A minute ago it had been warm, but now the moisture on his forehead was suddenly cool, and he wiped it away with his handkerchief. There was a buzzing in his ears and he swallowed and shook his head. For a moment he thought he must be sick; then suddenly the buzzing detached itself from him, grew into a swelling sound, louder and ever nearer, that might have been the roar of an approaching train.

II

Butch Janney was halfway home when he saw it—a huge, black, approaching cloud whose lower edge bumped the ground. Even as he stared at it vaguely, it seemed to spread until it included the whole southern sky, and he saw pale electric fire in it and heard an increasing roar. He was in a strong wind now; blown debris, bits of broken branches, splinters, larger objects unidentifiable in the growing darkness, flew by him. Instinctively he got out of his car and, by now hardly able to stand against the wind, ran for a bank, or rather found himself thrown and pinned against a bank. Then for a minute, two minutes, he was in the black center of pandemonium.

First there was the sound, and he was part of the sound, so engulfed in it and possessed by it that he had no existence apart from it. It was not a collection of sounds, it was just Sound itself, a great screeching bow drawn across the chords of the universe. The sound and force were inseparable. The sound as well as the force held him to what he felt was the bank like a man crucified. Somewhere in this first moment his face, pinned sideways, saw his automobile make a little jump, spin halfway around and then go bobbing off over a field in a series of great helpless leaps. Then began the bombardment, the sound dividing its sustained cannon note into the cracks of a gigantic machine gun. He was only half-conscious as he felt himself become part of one of those cracks, felt himself lifted away from the bank to tear through space, through a blinding, lacerating mass of twigs and branches, and then, for an incalculable time, he knew nothing at all.

His body hurt him. He was lying between two branches in the top of a tree; the air was full of dust and rain, and he could hear nothing; it was a long time before he realized that the tree he was in had been blown down and that his involuntary perch among the pine needles was only five feet from the ground.

"Say, man!" he cried aloud, outraged. "Say, man! Say, what a wind! Say, *man!*"

Made acute by pain and fear, he guessed that he had been standing on the tree's root and had been catapulted by the terrific wrench as the big pine was torn from the earth. Feeling over himself, he found that his left ear was caked full of dirt, as if someone had wanted to take an impression of the inside. His clothes were in rags, his coat had torn on the back seam, and he could feel where, as some stray gust tried to undress him, it had cut into him under the arms.

Reaching the ground, he set off in the direction of his father's house, but it was a new and unfamiliar landscape he traversed. The Thing—he did not know it was a tornado—had cut a path a quarter of a mile wide, and he was confused, as the dust slowly settled, by vistas he had never seen before. It was unreal that Bending church tower should be visible from here; there had been groves of trees between.

But where was here? For he should be close to the Baldwin house; only as he tripped over great piles of boards, like a carelessly kept lumber yard, did Butch realize that there was no more Baldwin house, and then, looking around wildly, that there was no Necrawney house on the hill, no Peltzer house below it. There was not a light, not a sound, save the rain falling on the fallen trees.

He broke into a run. When he saw the bulk of his father's house in the distance, he gave a "Hey!" of relief, but coming closer, he realized that something was missing. There were no outhouses and the built-on wing that held Pinky's room had been sheared completely away.

"Mother!" he called. "Dad!" There was no answer; a dog bounded out of the yard and licked his hand. . . .

. . . It was full dark twenty minutes later when Doc Janney stopped his car in front of his own drug store in Bending. The electric lights had gone out, but there were men with lanterns in the street, and in a minute a small crowd had collected around him. He unlocked the door hurriedly.

"Somebody break open the old Wiggins Hospital." He pointed across the street. "I've got six badly injured in my car. I want some fellows to carry 'em in. Is Doc Behrer here?"

"Here he is," offered eager voices out of the darkness as the doctor, case in hand, came through the crowd. The two men stood face to face by lantern light, forgetting that they disliked each other.

"God knows how many more there's going to be," said Doc Janney. "I'm getting dressing and disinfectant. There'll be a lot of fractures—" He raised his voice, "Somebody bring me a barrel!"

"I'll get started over there," said Doc Behrer. "There's about half a dozen more crawled in."

"What's been done?" demanded Doc Janney of the men who followed him into the drug store. "Have they called Birmingham and Montgomery?"

"The telephone wires are down, but the telegraph got through."

"Well, somebody get Doctor Cohen from Wettala, and tell any people who have automobiles to go up the Willard Pike and cut across toward Corsica and all through those roads there. There's not a house left at the crossroads by the nigger store. I passed a lot of folks walking in, all of them hurt, but I didn't have room for anybody else." As he talked he was throwing bandages, disinfectant and drugs into a blanket. "God, I thought I had a lot more stuff than this in stock! And wait!" he called. "Somebody drive out and look down in that hollow where the Wooleys live. Drive right across the fields—the road's blocked.... Now, you with the cap—Ed Jenks, ain't it?"

"Yes, doc."

"You see what I got here? You collect everything in the store that looks like this and bring it across the way, understand?"

"Yes, doc."

As the doctor went out into the street, the victims were streaming into town—a woman on foot with a badly injured child, a buckboard full of groaning Negroes, frantic men gasping terrible stories. Everywhere confusion and hysteria mounted in the dimly illumined darkness. A mud-covered reporter from Birmingham drove up in a sidecar, the wheels crossing the fallen wires and brushwood that clogged the street, and there was the siren of a police car from Cooper, thirty miles away.

Already a crowd pressed around the doors of the hospital, closed these three months for lack of patients. The doctor squeezed past the mêlée of white faces and established himself in the nearest ward, grateful for the waiting row of old iron beds. Doctor Behrer was already at work across the hall.

"Get me half a dozen lanterns," he ordered.

"Doctor Behrer wants iodine and adhesive."

"All right, there it is.... Here, you, Shinkey, stand by the door and keep everybody out except cases that can't walk. Somebody run over and see if there ain't some candles in the grocery store."

The street outside was full of sound now—the cries of women, the contrary directions of volunteer gangs trying to clear the highway, the tense staccato of people rising to an emergency. A little before midnight arrived the first unit of the Red Cross. But the three doctors, presently joined by two others from nearby villages, had lost track of time long before that. The dead began to be brought in by ten o'clock; there were twenty, twenty-five, thirty, forty—the list grew. Having no more needs, these waited, as became simple husbandmen, in a garage behind, while the stream of injured—hundreds of them—flowed through the old hospital built to house only a score. The storm had dealt out fractures of the leg, collar bone, ribs and hip, lacerations of the back, elbows, ears, eyelids, nose; there were wounds from flying planks, and odd splinters in odd places, and a scalped man, who would recover to grow a new head of hair. Living or dead, Doc Janney knew every face, almost every name.

"Don't you fret now. Billy's all right. Hold still and let me tie this. People are drifting in every minute, but it's so consarned dark they can't find 'em— All right, Mrs. Oakey. That's nothing. Ev here'll touch it with iodine.... Now let's see this man."

Two o'clock. The old doctor from Wettala gave out, but now there were fresh men from Montgomery to take his place. Upon the air of the room, heavy with disinfectant, floated the ceaseless babble of human speech reaching the doctor dimly through layer after layer of increasing fatigue:

"... Over and over—just rolled me over and over. Got hold of a bush and the bush came along too."

"*Left! Where's Left?*"

"... I bet that pig sailed a hundred yards—"

"—just stopped the train in time. All the passengers got out and helped pull the poles—"

"*Where's Left?*"

"He says, 'Let's get down cellar,' and I says, 'We ain't got no cellar'—"

"—If there's no more stretchers, find some light doors."

" . . . Five seconds? Say, it was more like five minutes!"

At some time he heard that Gene and Rose had been seen with their two youngest children. He had passed their house on the way in and, seeing it standing, hurried on. The Janney family had been lucky; the doctor's own house was outside the sweep of the storm.

Only as he saw the electric lights go on suddenly in the streets and glimpsed the crowd waiting for hot coffee in front of the Red Cross did the doctor realize how tired he was.

"You better go rest," a young man was saying. "I'll take this side of the room. I've got two nurses with me."

"All right—all right. I'll finish this row."

The injured were being evacuated to the cities by train as fast as their wounds were dressed, and their places taken by others. He had only two beds to go—in the first one he found Pinky Janney.

He put his stethoscope to the heart. It was beating feebly. That he, so weak, so nearly gone, had survived this storm at all was remarkable. How he had got there, who had found him and carried him, was a mystery in itself. The doctor went over the body; there were small contusions and lacerations, two broken fingers, the dirt-filled ears that marked every case—nothing else. For a moment the doctor hesitated, but even when he closed his eyes, the image of Mary Decker seemed to have receded, eluding him. Something purely professional that had nothing to do with human sensibilities had been set in motion inside him, and he was powerless to head it off. He held out his hands before him; they were trembling slightly.

"Hell's bells!" he muttered.

He went out of the room and around the corner of the hall, where he drew from his pocket the flask containing the last of the corn and water he had had in the afternoon. He emptied it. Returning to the ward, he disinfected two instruments and applied a local anæsthetic to a square section at the base of Pinky's skull where the wound had healed over the bullet. He called a nurse to his side and then, scalpel in hand, knelt on one knee beside his nephew's bed.

III

Two days later the doctor drove slowly around the mournful countryside. He had withdrawn from the emergency work after the first desperate night, feeling that his status as a pharmacist might embarrass his collaborators. But there was much to be done in bringing the damage to outlying sections under the ægis of the Red Cross, and he devoted himself to that.

The path of the demon was easy to follow. It had pursued an irregular course on its seven-league boots, cutting cross country, through woods, or even urbanely keeping to roads until they curved, when it went off on its own again. Sometimes the trail could be traced by cotton fields, apparently in full bloom, but this cotton came from the insides of hundreds of quilts and mattresses redistributed in the fields by the storm.

At a lumber pile that had lately been a Negro cabin, he stopped a moment to listen to a dialogue between two reporters and two shy pickaninnies. The old grandmother, her head bandaged, sat among the ruins, gnawing some vague meat and moving her rocker ceaselessly.

"But where *is* the river you were blown across?" one of the reporters demanded.

"There."

"Where?"

The pickaninnies looked to their grandmother for aid.

"Right there behind you-all," spoke up the old woman.

The newspapermen looked disgustedly at a muddy stream four yards wide.

"That's no river."

"That's a Menada River, we always calls it ever since I was a gull. Yes, suh, that's a Menada River. An them two boys was blowed right across it an set down on the othah side just as pretty, 'thout any hurt at all. Chimney fell on me," she concluded, feeling her head.

"Do you mean to say that's all it was?" demanded the younger reporter indignantly. "*That's* the river they were blown across! And one hundred and twenty million people have been led to believe—"

"That's all right, boys," interrupted Doc Janney. "That's a right good river for these parts. And it'll get bigger as those little fellahs get older."

He tossed a quarter to the old woman and drove on.

Passing a country church, he stopped and counted the new brown mounds that marred the graveyard. He was nearing the center of the holocaust now. There was the Howden house where three had been killed; there remained a gaunt chimney, a rubbish heap and a scarecrow surviving ironically in the kitchen garden. In the ruins of the house across the way a rooster strutted on top of a piano, reigning vociferously over an estate of trunks, boots, cans, books, calendars, rugs, chairs and window frames, a twisted radio and a legless sewing machine. Everywhere there was bedding—blankets, mattresses, bent springs, shredded padding—he had not realized how much of people's lives was spent in bed. Here and there, cows and horses, often stained with disinfectant, were grazing again in the fields. At intervals there were Red Cross tents, and sitting by one of these, with the grey cat in her arms, the doctor came upon little Helen Kilrain. The usual lumber pile, like a child's building game knocked down in a fit of temper, told the story.

"Hello, dear," he greeted her, his heart sinking. "How did kitty like the tornado?"

"She didn't."

"What did she do?"

"She meowed."

"Oh."

"She wanted to get away, but I hanged on to her and she scratched me—see?"

He glanced at the Red Cross tent.

"Who's taking care of you?"

"The lady from the Red Cross and Mrs. Wells," she answered. "My father got hurt. He stood over me so it wouldn't fall on me, and I stood over kitty. He's in the hospital in Birmingham. When he comes back, I guess he'll build our house again."

The doctor winced. He knew that her father would build no more houses; he had died that morning. She was alone, and she did not know she was alone. Around her stretched the dark universe, impersonal, inconscient. Her lovely little face looked up at him confidently as he asked: "You got any kin anywhere, Helen?"

"I don't know."

"You've got kitty, anyhow, haven't you?"

"It's just a cat," she admitted calmly, but anguished by her own betrayal of her love, she hugged it closer.

"Taking care of a cat must be pretty hard."

"Oh, no," she said hurriedly. "It isn't any trouble at all. It doesn't eat hardly anything."

He put his hand in his pocket, and then changed his mind suddenly.

"Dear, I'm coming back and see you later—later today. You take good care of kitty now, won't you?"

"Oh, yes," she answered lightly.

The doctor drove on. He stopped next at a house that had escaped damage. Walt Cupps, the owner, was cleaning a shotgun on his front porch.

"What's that, Walt? Going to shoot up the next tornado?"

"Ain't going to be a next tornado."

"You can't tell. Just take a look at that sky now. It's getting mighty dark."

Walt laughed and slapped his gun. "Not for a hundred years, anyhow. This here is for looters. There's a lot of 'em around, and not all black either. Wish when you go to town that you'd tell 'em to scatter some militia out here."

"I'll tell 'em now. You come out all right?"

"I did, thank God. With six of us in the house. It took off one hen, and probably it's still carrying it around somewhere."

The doctor drove on toward town, overcome by a feeling of uneasiness he could not define.

"It's the weather," he thought. "It's the same kind of feel in the air there was last Saturday."

For a month the doctor had felt an urge to go away permanently. Once this countryside had seemed to promise peace. When the impetus that had lifted him temporarily out of tired old stock was exhausted, he had come back here to rest, to watch the earth put forth, and live on simple, pleasant terms with his neighbors.

Peace! He knew that the present family quarrel would never heal, nothing would ever be the same; it would all be bitter forever. And he had seen the placid countryside turned into a land of mourning. There was no peace here. Move on!

On the road he overtook Butch Janney walking to town.

"I was coming to see you," said Butch, frowning. "You operated on Pinky after all, didn't you?"

"Jump in.... Yes, I did. How did you know?"

"Doc Behrer told us." He shot a quick look at the doctor, who did not miss the quality of suspicion in it. "They don't think he'll last out the day."

"I'm sorry for your mother."

Butch laughed unpleasantly. "Yes, you are."

"I said I'm sorry for your mother," said the doctor sharply.

"I heard you."

They drove for a moment in silence.

"Did you find your automobile?"

"Did I?" Butch laughed ruefully. "I found something—I don't know whether you'd call it a car any more. And, you know, I could of had tornado insurance for twenty-five cents." His voice trembled indignantly: "Twenty-five cents—but who would ever of thought of getting tornado insurance?"

It was growing darker; there was a thin crackle of thunder far to the southward.

"Well, all I hope," said Butch with narrowed glance, "is that you hadn't been drinking anything when you operated on Pinky."

"You know, Butch," the doctor said slowly, "that was a pretty dirty trick of mine to bring that tornado here."

He had not expected the sarcasm to hit home, but he expected a retort—when suddenly he caught sight of Butch's face. It was fish-white, the mouth was open, the eyes fixed and staring, and from the throat came a mewling sound. Limply he raised one hand before him, and then the doctor saw.

Less than a mile away, an enormous, top-shaped black cloud filled the sky and bore toward them, dipping and swirling, and in front of it sailed already a heavy, singing wind.

"Christ!" the doctor yelled. "It's come back."

Fifty yards ahead of them was the old iron bridge spanning Bilby Creek. He stepped hard on the accelerator and drove for it. The fields were full of running figures headed in the same direction. Reaching the bridge, he jumped out and yanked Butch's arm.

"Get out, you fool! Get out!"

A nerveless mass stumbled from the car; in a moment they were in a group of half a dozen, huddled in the triangular space that the bridge made with the shore.

"Is it coming here?"

"No, it's turning!"

"Oh, God, we had to leave grampa!"

"Oh, save me, save me! Jesus save me! Help me!"

"Jesus save my soul!"

There was a quick rush of wind outside, sending little tentacles under the bridge with a curious tension in them that made the doctor's skin crawl. Then immediately there was a vacuum, with no more wind, but a sudden thresh of rain. The doctor crawled to the edge of the bridge and put his head up cautiously.

"It's passed," he said. "We only felt the edge; the center went way to the right of us."

He could see it plainly; for a second he could even distinguish objects in it—shrubbery and small trees, planks and loose earth. Crawling farther out, he produced his watch and tried to time it, but the thick curtain of rain blotted it from sight.

Soaked to the skin, he crawled back underneath. Butch lay shivering in the farthest corner, and the doctor shook him.

"It went in the direction of your house!" the doctor cried. "Pull yourself together! Who's there?"

"No one," Butch groaned. "They're all down with Pinky."

The rain had changed to hail now; first small pellets, then larger ones, and larger, until the sound of their fall upon the iron bridge was an ear-splitting tattoo.

The spared wretches under the bridge were slowly recovering, and in the relief there were titters of hysterical laughter. After a certain point of strain, the nervous system makes its transitions without dignity or reason. Even the doctor felt the contagion.

"This is worse than a calamity," he said dryly. "It's getting to be a nuisance."

IV

There were to be no more tornadoes in Alabama that spring. The second one—it was popularly thought to be the first one come back, for to the people of Chilton County it had become a personified force, definite as a pagan god—took a dozen houses, Gene Janney's among them, and injured about thirty people. But this time—perhaps because everyone had developed some scheme of self-protection—there were no fatalities. It made its last dramatic bow by sailing down the main street of Bending, prostrating the telephone poles and crushing in the fronts of three shops, including Doc Janney's drug store.

At the end of a week, houses were going up again, made of the old boards; and before the end of the long, lush Alabama summer the grass would be green again on all the graves. But it would be years before the people of the county ceased to reckon events as happening "before the tornado" or "after the tornado,"—and for many families things would never be the same.

Doctor Janney decided that this was as good a time to leave as any. He sold the remains of his drug store, gutted alike by charity and catastrophe, and turned over his house to his brother until Gene could rebuild his own. He was going up to the city by train, for his car had been rammed against a tree and couldn't be counted on for much more than the trip to the station.

Several times on the way in he stopped by the roadside to say good-bye—once it was to Walter Cupps.

"So it hit you, after all," he said, looking at the melancholy back house which alone marked the site.

"It's pretty bad," Walter answered. "But just think; they was six of us in or about the house and not one was injured. I'm content to give thanks to God for that."

"You were lucky there, Walt," the doctor agreed. "Do you happen to have heard whether the Red Cross took little Helen Kilrain to Montgomery or to Birmingham?"

"To Montgomery. Say, I was there when she came into town with that cat, tryin' to get somebody to bandage up its paw. She must of walked miles through that rain and hail, but all that mattered to her was her kitty. Bad as I felt, I couldn't help laughin' at how spunky she was."

The doctor was silent for a moment. "Do you happen to recollect if she has any people left?"

"I don't, suh," Walter replied, "but I think as not."

At his brother's place, the doctor made his last stop. They were all there, even the youngest, working among the ruins; already Butch had a shed erected to house the salvage of their goods. Save for this the most orderly thing surviving was the pattern of round white stone which was to have inclosed the garden.

The doctor took a hundred dollars in bills from his pocket and handed it to Gene.

"You can pay it back sometime, but don't strain yourself," he said. "It's money I got from the store." He cut off Gene's thanks: "Pack up my books carefully when I send for 'em."

"You reckon to practice medicine up there, Forrest?"

"I'll maybe try it."

The brothers held on to each other's hands for a moment; the two youngest children came up to say good-bye. Rose stood in the background in an old blue dress—she had no money to wear black for her eldest son.

"Good-bye, Rose," said the doctor.

"Good-bye," she responded, and then added in a dead voice, "Good luck to you, Forrest."

For a moment he was tempted to say something conciliatory, but he saw it was no use. He was up against the maternal instinct, the same force that had sent little Helen through the storm with her injured cat.

At the station he bought a one-way ticket to Montgomery. The village was drab under the sky of a retarded spring, and as the train pulled out, it was odd to think that six months ago it had seemed to him as good a place as any other.

He was alone in the white section of the day coach; presently he felt for a bottle on his hip and drew it forth. "After all, a man of forty-five is entitled to more artificial courage when he starts over again." He began thinking of Helen. "She hasn't got any kin. I guess she's my little girl now."

He patted the bottle, then looked down at it as if in surprise.

"Well, we'll have to put you aside for awhile, old friend. Any cat that's worth all that trouble and care is going to need a lot of grade-B milk."

He settled down in his seat, looking out the window. In his memory of that terrible week the winds still sailed about him, came in as draughts through the corridor of the car—winds of the world—cyclones, hurricane, tornadoes—grey and black, expected or unforeseen, some from the sky, some from the caves of hell.

But he would not let them touch Helen again—if he could help it.

He dozed momentarily, but a haunting dream woke him: "*Daddy stood over me and I stood over Kitty.*"

"All right, Helen," he said aloud, for he often talked to himself, "I guess the old brig can keep afloat a little longer—in any wind."

A SHORT TRIP HOME

I was near her, for I had lingered behind in order to get the short walk with her from the living room to the front door. That was a lot, for she had flowered suddenly and I, being a man and only a year older, hadn't flowered at all, had scarcely dared to come near her in the week we'd been home. Nor was I going to say anything in that walk of ten feet, or touch her; but I had a vague hope she'd do something, give a gay little performance of some sort, personal only in so far as we were alone together.

She had bewitchment suddenly in the twinkle of short hairs on her neck, in the sure, clear confidence that at about eighteen begins to deepen and sing in attractive American girls. The lamp light shopped in the yellow strands of her hair.

Already she was sliding into another world—the world of Joe Jelke and Jim Cathcart waiting for us now in the car. In another year she would pass beyond me forever.

As I waited, feeling the others outside in the snowy night, feeling the excitement of Christmas week and the excitement of Ellen here, blooming away, filling the room with "sex appeal"—a wretched phrase to express a quality that isn't like that at all—a maid came in from the dining room, spoke to Ellen quietly and handed her a note. Ellen read it and her eyes faded down, as when the current grows weak on rural circuits, and smouldered off into space. Then she gave me an odd look—in which I probably didn't show—and, without a word, followed the maid into the dining room and beyond. I sat turning over the pages of a magazine for a quarter of an hour.

Joe Jelke came in, red-faced from the cold, his white silk muffler gleaming at the neck of his fur coat. He was a senior at New Haven, I was a sophomore. He was prominent, a member of Scroll and Key, and, in my eyes, very distinguished and handsome.

"Isn't Ellen coming?"

"I don't know," I answered discreetly. "She was all ready."

"Ellen!" he called. "Ellen!"

He had left the front door open behind him and a great cloud of frosty air rolled in from outside. He went halfway up the stairs—he was a familiar in the house—and called again, till Mrs. Baker came to the banister and said that Ellen was below. Then the maid, a little excited, appeared in the dining-room door.

"Mr. Jelke," she called in a low voice.

Joe's face fell as he turned toward her, sensing bad news.

"Miss Ellen says for you to go on to the party. She'll come later."

"What's the matter?"

"She can't come now. She'll come later."

He hesitated, confused. It was the last big dance of vacation, and he was mad about Ellen. He had tried to give her a ring for Christmas, and failing that, got her to accept a gold mesh bag that must have cost two hundred dollars. He wasn't the only one—there were three or four in the same wild condition, and all in the ten days she'd been home—but his chance came first, for he was rich and gracious and at that moment the "desirable" boy of St. Paul. To me it seemed impossible that she could prefer another, but the rumor was she'd described Joe as much too perfect. I suppose he lacked mystery for her, and when a man is up against that with a young girl who isn't thinking of the practical side of marriage yet—well—

"She's in the kitchen," Joe said angrily.

"No, she's not." The maid was defiant and a little scared.

"She is."

"She went out the back way, Mr. Jelke."

"I'm going to see."

I followed him. The Swedish servants washing dishes looked up sideways at our approach and an interested crashing of pans marked our passage through. The storm door, unbolted, was flapping in the wind and as we walked out into the snowy yard we saw the tail-light of a car turn the corner at the end of the back alley.

"I'm going after her," Joe said slowly. "I don't understand this at all."

I was too awed by the calamity to argue. We hurried to his car and drove in a fruitless, despairing zigzag all over the residence section, peering into every machine on the streets. It was half an hour before the futility of the affair began to dawn upon him—St. Paul is a city of almost three hundred thousand people—and Jim Cathcart reminded him that we had another girl to stop for. Like a wounded animal he sank into a melancholy mass of fur in the corner, from which position he jerked upright every few minutes and waved himself backward and forward a little in protest and despair.

Jim's girl was ready and impatient, but after what had happened her impatience didn't seem important. She looked lovely though. That's one thing about Christmas vacation—the excitement of growth and change and adventure in foreign parts transforming the people you've known all your life. Joe Jelke was polite to her in a daze—he indulged in one burst of short, loud, harsh laughter by way of conversation—and we drove to the hotel.

The chauffeur approached it on the wrong side—the side on which the line of cars was not putting forth guests—and because of that we came suddenly upon Ellen Baker just getting out of a small coupé. Even before we came to a stop, Joe Jelke had jumped excitedly from the car.

Ellen turned toward us, a faintly distracted look—perhaps of surprise, but certainly not of alarm—in her face; in fact, she didn't seem very aware of us. Joe approached her with a stern, dignified, injured and, I thought, just exactly correct reproof in his expression. I followed.

Seated in the coupé—he had not dismounted to help Ellen out—was a hard thin-faced man of about thirty-five with an air of being scarred, and a slight sinister smile. His eyes were a sort of taunt to the whole human family—they were the eyes of an animal, sleepy and quiescent in the presence of another species. They were helpless yet brutal, unhopeful yet confident. It was as if they felt themselves powerless to originate activity, but infinitely capable of profiting by a single gesture of weakness in another.

Vaguely I placed him as one of the sort of men whom I had been conscious of from my earliest youth as "hanging around"—leaning with one elbow on the counters of tobacco stores, watching, through heaven knows what small chink of the mind, the people who hurried in and out. Intimate to garages, where he had vague business conducted in undertones, to barber shops and to the lobbies of theatres—in such places, anyhow, I placed the type, if type it was, that he reminded me of. Sometimes his face bobbed up in one of Tad's more savage cartoons, and I had always from earliest boyhood thrown a nervous glance toward the dim borderland where he stood, and seen him watching me and despising me. Once, in a dream, he had taken a few steps toward me, jerking his head back and muttering: "Say, kid" in what was intended to be a reassuring voice, and I had broken for the door in terror. This was that sort of man.

Joe and Ellen faced each other silently; she seemed, as I have said, to be in a daze. It was cold, but she didn't notice that her coat had blown open; Joe reached out and pulled it together, and automatically she clutched it with her hand.

Suddenly the man in the coupé, who had been watching them silently, laughed. It was a bare laugh, done with the breath—just a noisy jerk of the head—but it was an insult if I had ever heard one; definite and not to be passed over. I wasn't surprised when Joe, who was quick-tempered, turned to him angrily and said:

"What's your trouble?"

The man waited a moment, his eyes shifting and yet staring, and always seeing. Then he laughed again in the same way. Ellen stirred uneasily.

"Who is this—this—" Joe's voice trembled with annoyance.

"Look out now," said the man slowly.

Joe turned to me.

"Eddie, take Ellen and Catherine in, will you?" he said quickly. . . . "Ellen, go with Eddie."

"Look out now," the man repeated.

Ellen made a little sound with her tongue and teeth, but she didn't resist when I took her arm and moved her toward the side door of the hotel. It struck me as odd that she should be so helpless, even to the point of acquiescing by her silence in this imminent trouble.

"Let it go, Joe!" I called back over my shoulder. "Come inside!"

Ellen, pulling against my arm, hurried us on. As we were caught up into the swinging doors I had the impression that the man was getting out of his coupé.

Ten minutes later, as I waited for the girls outside the women's dressing-room, Joe Jelke and Jim Cathcart stepped out of the elevator. Joe was very white, his eyes were heavy and glazed, there was a trickle of dark blood on his forehead and on his white muffler. Jim had both their hats in his hand.

"He hit Joe with brass knuckles," Jim said in a low voice. "Joe was out cold for a minute or so. I wish you'd send a bell boy for some witch-hazel and court-plaster."

It was late and the hall was deserted; brassy fragments of the dance below reached us as if heavy curtains were being blown aside and dropping back into place. When Ellen came out I took her directly downstairs. We avoided the receiving line and went into a dim room set with scraggly hotel palms where couples sometimes sat out during the dance; there I told her what had happened.

"It was Joe's own fault," she said, surprisingly. "I told him not to interfere."

This wasn't true. She had said nothing, only uttered one curious little click of impatience.

"You ran out the back door and disappeared for almost an hour," I protested. "Then you turned up with a hard-looking customer who laughed in Joe's face."

"A hard-looking customer," she repeated, as if tasting the sound of the words.

"Well, wasn't he? Where on earth did you get hold of him, Ellen?"

"On the train," she answered. Immediately she seemed to regret this admission. "You'd better stay out of things that aren't your business, Eddie. You see what happened to Joe."

Literally I gasped. To watch her, seated beside me, immaculately glowing, her body giving off wave after wave of freshness and delicacy—and to hear her talk like that.

"But that man's a thug!" I cried. "No girl could be safe with him. He used brass knuckles on Joe—brass knuckles!"

"Is that pretty bad?"

She asked this as she might have asked such a question a few years ago. She looked at me at last and really wanted an answer; for a moment it was as if she were trying to recapture an attitude that had almost departed; then she hardened again. I say "hardened," for I began to notice that when she was concerned with this man her eyelids fell a little, shutting other things—everything else—out of view.

That was a moment I might have said something, I suppose, but in spite of everything, I couldn't light into her. I was too much under the spell of her beauty and its success. I even began to find excuses for her—perhaps that man wasn't what he appeared to be; or perhaps—more romantically—she was involved with him against her will to shield someone else. At this point people began to drift into the room and come up to speak to us. We couldn't talk any more, so we went in and bowed to the chaperones. Then I gave her up to the bright restless sea of the dance, where she moved in an eddy of her own among the pleasant islands of colored favors set out on tables and the south winds from the brasses moaning across the hall. After awhile I saw Joe Jelke sitting in a corner with a strip of court-plaster on his forehead watching Ellen as if she herself had struck him down, but I didn't go up to him. I felt queer myself—like I feel when I wake up after sleeping through an afternoon, strange and portentous, as if something had gone on in the interval that changed the values of everything and that I didn't see.

The night slipped on through successive phases of cardboard horns, amateur tableaux and flashlights for the morning papers. Then was the grand march and supper, and about two o'clock some of the committee dressed up as revenue agents pinched the party, and a facetious newspaper was distributed, burlesquing the events of the evening. And all the time out of the corner of my eye I watched the shining orchid on Ellen's shoulder as it moved like Stuart's plume about the room. I watched it with a definite foreboding until the last sleepy groups had crowded into the elevators, and then, bundled to the eyes in great shapeless fur coats, drifted out into the clear dry Minnesota night.

II

There is a sloping mid-section of our city which lies between the residence quarter on the hill and the business district on the level of the river. It is a vague part of town, broken by its climb into triangles and odd shapes—there are names like Seven Corners—and I don't believe a dozen people could draw an accurate map of it, though everyone traversed it by trolley, auto or shoe leather twice a day. And though it was a busy section, it would be hard for me to name the business that comprised its activity. There were always long lines of trolley cars waiting to start somewhere; there was a big movie theatre and many small ones with posters of Hoot Gibson and Wonder Dogs and Wonder Horses outside; there were small stores with "Old King Brady" and "The Liberty Boys of '76" in the windows, and marbles, cigarettes and candy inside; and—one definite place at least—a fancy costumer whom we all visited at least once a year. Sometime during boyhood I became aware that on one side of a certain obscure street there were bawdy houses, and all through the district were pawnshops, cheap jewellers, small athletic clubs and gymnasiums and somewhat too blatantly run-down saloons.

The morning after the Cotillion Club party, I woke up late and lazy, with the happy feeling that for a day or two more there was no chapel, no classes—nothing to do but wait for another party tonight. It was crisp and bright—one of those days when you forget how cold it is until your cheek freezes—and the events of the evening before seemed dim and far away. After luncheon I started downtown on foot through a light, pleasant snow of small flakes that would probably fall all afternoon, and I was about half through that halfway section of town—so far as I know, there's no inclusive name for it—when suddenly whatever idle thought was in my head blew away like a hat and I began thinking hard of Ellen Baker. I began worrying about her as I'd never worried about anything outside myself before. I began to loiter, with an instinct to go up on the hill again and find her and talk to her; then I remembered that she was at a tea, and I went on again, but still thinking of her, and harder than ever. Right then the affair opened up again.

It was snowing, I said, and it was four o'clock on a December afternoon, when there is a promise of darkness in the air and the street lamps are just going on. I passed a combination pool parlor and restaurant, with a stove loaded with hot-dogs in the window, and a few loungers hanging around the door. The lights were on inside—not bright lights but just a few pale yellow high up on the ceiling—and the glow they threw out into the frosty dusk wasn't bright enough to tempt you to stare inside. As I went past, thinking hard of Ellen all this time, I took in the quartet of loafers out of the corner of my eye. I hadn't gone half a dozen steps down the street when one of them called to me, not by name but in a way clearly intended for my ear. I thought it was a tribute to my raccoon coat and paid no attention, but a moment later whoever it was called to me again in a peremptory voice. I was annoyed and turned around. There, standing in the group not ten feet away and looking at me with the half-sneer on his face with which he'd looked at Joe Jelke, was the scarred, thin-faced man of the night before.

He had on a black fancy-cut coat, buttoned up to his neck as if he were cold. His hands were deep in his pockets and he wore a derby and high-button shoes. I was startled, and for a moment I hesitated, but I was most of all angry, and knowing that I was quicker with my hands than Joe Jelke, I took a tentative step back toward him. The other men weren't looking at me—I don't think they saw me at all—but I knew that this one recognized me; there was nothing casual about his look, no mistake.

"Here I am. What are you going to do about it?" his eyes seemed to say.

I took another step toward him and he laughed soundlessly, but with active contempt, and drew back into the group. I followed. I was going to speak to him—I wasn't sure what I was going to say—but when I came up he had either changed his mind and backed off, or else he wanted me to follow him inside, for he had slipped off and the three men watched my intent approach without curiosity. They were the same kind—sporty, but, unlike him, smooth rather than truculent; I didn't find any personal malice in their collective glance.

"Did he go inside?" I asked.

They looked at one another in that cagy way; a wink passed between them, and after a perceptible pause, one said:

"Who go inside?"

"I don't know his name."

There was another wink. Annoyed and determined, I walked past them and into the pool room. There were a few people at a lunch counter along one side and a few more playing billiards, but he was not among them.

Again I hesitated. If his idea was to lead me into any blind part of the establishment—there were some half-open doors farther back—I wanted more support. I went up to the man at the desk.

"What became of the fellow who just walked in here?"

Was he on his guard immediately, or was that my imagination?

"What fellow?"

"Thin face—derby hat."

"How long ago?"

"Oh—a minute."

He shook his head again. "Didn't see him," he said.

I waited. The three men from outside had come in and were lined up beside me at the counter. I felt that all of them were looking at me in a peculiar way. Feeling helpless and increasingly uneasy, I turned suddenly and went out. A little way down the street I turned again and took a good look at the place, so I'd know it and could find it again. On the next corner I broke impulsively into a run, found a taxi-cab in front of the hotel and drove back up the hill.

Ellen wasn't home. Mrs. Baker came downstairs and talked to me. She seemed entirely cheerful and proud of Ellen's beauty, and ignorant of anything being amiss or of anything unusual having taken place the night before. She was glad that vacation was almost over—it was a strain and Ellen wasn't very strong. Then she said something that relieved my mind enormously. She was glad that I had come in, for of course Ellen would want to see me, and the time was so short. She was going back at half-past eight tonight.

"Tonight!" I exclaimed. "I thought it was the day after tomorrow."

"She's going to visit the Brokaws in Chicago," Mrs. Baker said. "They want her for some party. We just decided it today. She's leaving with the Ingersoll girls tonight."

I was so glad I could barely restrain myself from shaking her hand. Ellen was safe. It had been nothing all along but a moment of the most casual adventure. I felt like an idiot, but I realized how much I cared about Ellen and how little I could endure anything terrible happening to her.

"She'll be in soon?"

"Any minute now. She just phoned from the University Club."

I said I'd be over later—I lived almost next door and I wanted to be alone. Outside I remembered I didn't have a key, so I started up the Bakers' driveway to take the old cut we used in childhood through the intervening yard. It was still snowing, but the flakes were bigger now against the darkness, and trying to locate the buried walk I noticed that the Bakers' back door was ajar.

I scarcely know why I turned and walked into that kitchen. There was a time when I would have known the Bakers' servants by name. That wasn't true now, but they knew me, and I was aware of a sudden suspension as I came in—not only a suspension of talk but of some mood or expectation that had filled them. They began to go to work too quickly; they made unnecessary movements and clamor—those three. The parlor maid looked at me in a frightened way and I suddenly guessed she was waiting to deliver another message. I beckoned her into the pantry.

"I know all about this," I said. "It's a very serious business. Shall I go to Mrs. Baker now, or will you shut and lock that back door?"

"Don't tell Mrs. Baker, Mr. Stinson!"

"Then I don't want Miss Ellen disturbed. If she is—and if she is I'll know of it—" I delivered some outrageous threat about going to all the employment agencies and seeing she never got another job in the city. She was thoroughly intimidated when I went out; it wasn't a minute before the back door was locked and bolted behind me.

Simultaneously I heard a big car drive up in front, chains crunching on the soft snow; it was bringing Ellen home, and I went in to say good-bye.

Joe Jelke and two other boys were along, and none of the three could manage to take their eyes off her, even to say hello to me. She had one of those exquisite rose skins frequent in our part of the country, and beautiful until the little veins begin to break at about forty; now, flushed with the cold, it was a riot of lovely delicate pinks like many carnations. She and Joe had reached some sort of reconciliation, or at least he was too far gone in love to remember last night; but I saw that though she laughed a lot she wasn't really paying any attention to him or any of them. She wanted them to go, so that there'd be a message from the kitchen, but I knew that the message wasn't coming—that she was safe. There was talk of the Pump and Slipper dance at New Haven and of the Princeton Prom, and then, in various moods, we four left and separated quickly outside. I walked home with a certain depression of spirit and lay for an hour in a hot bath thinking that vacation was all over for me now that she was gone; feeling, even more deeply than I had yesterday, that she was out of my life.

And something eluded me, some one more thing to do, something that I had lost amid the events of the afternoon, promising myself to go back and pick it up, only to find that it had escaped me. I associated it vaguely with Mrs. Baker, and now I seemed to recall that it had poked up its head somewhere in the stream of conversation with her. In my relief about Ellen I had forgotten to ask her a question regarding something she had said.

The Brokaws—that was it—where Ellen was to visit. I knew Bill Brokaw well; he was in my class at Yale. Then I remembered and sat bolt upright in the tub—the Brokaws weren't in Chicago this Christmas; they were at Palm Beach!

Dripping I sprang out of the tub, threw an insufficient union suit around my shoulders and sprang for the phone in my room. I got the connection quick, but Miss Ellen had already started for the train.

Luckily our car was in, and while I squirmed, still damp, into my clothes, the chauffeur brought it around to the door. The night was cold and dry, and we made good time to the station through the hard, crusty snow. I felt queer and insecure starting out this way, but somehow more confident as the station loomed up bright and new against the dark, cold air. For fifty years my family had owned the land on which it was built and that made my temerity seem all right somehow. There was always a possibility that I was rushing in where angels feared to tread, but that sense of having a solid foothold in the past made me willing to make a fool of myself. This business was all wrong—terribly wrong. Any idea I had entertained that it was harmless dropped away now; between Ellen and some vague overwhelming catastrophe there stood me, or else the police and a scandal. I'm no moralist—there was another element here, dark and frightening, and I didn't want Ellen to go through it alone.

There are three competing trains from St. Paul to Chicago that all leave within a few minutes of half-past eight. Hers was the Burlington, and as I ran across the station I saw the grating being pulled over and the light above it go out. I knew, though, that she had a drawing-room with the Ingersoll girls, because her mother had mentioned buying the ticket, so she was, literally speaking, tucked in until tomorrow.

The C., M. & St. P. gate was down at the other end and I raced for it and made it. I had forgotten one thing, though, and that was enough to keep me awake and worried half the night. This train got into Chicago ten minutes after the other. Ellen had that much time to disappear into one of the largest cities in the world.

I gave the porter a wire to my family to send from Milwaukee, and at eight o'clock next morning I pushed violently by a whole line of passengers, clamoring over their bags parked in the vestibule, and shot out of the door with a sort of scramble over the porter's back. For a moment the confusion of a great station, the voluminous sounds and echoes and cross-currents of bells and smoke struck me helpless. Then I dashed for the exit and toward the only chance I knew of finding her.

I had guessed right. She was standing at the telegraph counter, sending off heaven knows what black lie to her mother, and her expression when she saw me had a sort of terror mixed up with its surprise. There was cunning in it too. She was thinking quickly—she would have liked to walk away from me as if I weren't there, and go about her own business, but she couldn't. I was too matter-of-fact a thing in her life. So we stood silently watching each other and each thinking hard.

"The Brokaws are in Florida," I said after a minute.

"It was nice of you to take such a long trip to tell me that."

"Since you've found it out, don't you think you'd better go on to school?"

"Please let me alone, Eddie," she said.

"I'll go as far as New York with you. I've decided to go back early myself."

"You'd better let me alone." Her lovely eyes narrowed and her face took on a look of dumb-animal-like resistance. She made a visible effort, the cunning flickered back into it, then both were gone, and in their stead was a cheerful reassuring smile that all but convinced me.

"Eddie, you silly child, don't you think I'm old enough to take care of myself?" I didn't answer. "I'm going to meet a man, you understand. I just want to see him today. I've got my ticket East on the five o'clock train. If you don't believe it, here it is in my bag."

"I believe you."

"The man isn't anybody that you know and—frankly, I think you're being awfully fresh and impossible."

"I know who the man is."

Again she lost control of her face. That terrible expression came back into it and she spoke with almost a snarl:

"You'd better let me alone."

I took the blank out of her hand and wrote out an explanatory telegram to her mother. Then I turned to Ellen and said a little roughly:

"We'll take the five o'clock train East together. Meanwhile you're going to spend the day with me."

The mere sound of my own voice saying this so emphatically encouraged me, and I think it impressed her too; at any rate, she submitted—at least temporarily—and came along without protest while I bought my ticket.

When I start to piece together the fragments of that day a sort of confusion begins, as if my memory didn't want to yield up any of it, or my consciousness let any of it pass through. There was a bright, fierce morning during which we rode about in a taxi-cab and went to a department store where Ellen said she wanted to buy something and then tried to slip away from me by a back way. I had the feeling, for an hour, that someone was following us along Lake Shore Drive in a taxi-cab, and I would try to catch them by turning quickly or looking suddenly into the chauffeur's mirror; but I could find no one, and when I turned back I could see that Ellen's face was contorted with mirthless, unnatural laughter.

All morning there was a raw, bleak wind off the lake, but when we went to the Blackstone for lunch a light snow came down past the windows and we talked almost naturally about our friends, and about casual things. Suddenly her tone changed; she grew serious and looked me in the eye, straight and sincere.

"Eddie, you're the oldest friend I have," she said, "and you oughtn't to find it too hard to trust me. If I promise you faithfully on my word of honor to catch that five o'clock train, will you let me alone a few hours this afternoon?"

"Why?"

"Well"—she hesitated and hung her head a little—"I guess everybody has a right to say—good-bye."

"You want to say good-bye to that—"

"Yes, yes," she said hastily; "just a few hours, Eddie, and I promise faithfully that I'll be on that train."

"Well, I suppose no great harm could be done in two hours. If you really want to say good-bye—"

I looked up suddenly, and surprised a look of such tense cunning in her face that I winced before it. Her lip was curled up and her eyes were slits again; there wasn't the faintest touch of fairness and sincerity in her whole face.

We argued. The argument was vague on her part and somewhat hard and reticent on mine. I wasn't going to be cajoled again into any weakness or be infected with any—and there was a contagion of evil in the air. She kept trying to imply, without any convincing evidence to bring forward, that everything was all right. Yet she was too full of the thing itself—whatever it was—to build up a real story, and she wanted to catch at any credulous and acquiescent train of thought that might start in my head, and work that for all it was worth. After every reassuring suggestion she threw out, she stared at me eagerly, as if she hoped I'd launch into a comfortable moral lecture with the customary sweet at the end—which in this case would be her liberty. But I was wearing her away a little. Two or three times it needed just a touch of pressure to bring her to the point of tears—which, of course, was what I wanted—but I couldn't seem to manage it. Almost I had her—almost possessed her interior attention—then she would slip away.

I bullied her remorselessly into a taxi about four o'clock and started for the station. The wind was raw again, with a sting of snow in it, and the people in the streets, waiting for buses and street cars too small to take them all in, looked cold and disturbed and unhappy. I tried to think how lucky we were to be comfortably off and taken care of, but all the warm, respectable world I had been part of yesterday had dropped away from me. There was something we carried with us now that was the enemy and the opposite of all that; it was in the cabs beside us, the streets we passed through. With a touch of panic, I wondered if I wasn't slipping almost imperceptibly into Ellen's attitude of mind. The column of passengers waiting to go aboard the train were as remote from me as people from another world, but it was I that was drifting away and leaving them behind.

My lower was in the same car with her compartment. It was an old-fashioned car, its lights somewhat dim, its carpets and upholstery full of the dust of another generation. There were half a dozen other travellers, but they made no special impression on me, except that they shared the unreality that I was beginning to feel everywhere around me. We went into Ellen's compartment, shut the door and sat down.

Suddenly I put my arms around her and drew her over to me, just as tenderly as I knew how—as if she were a little girl—as she was. She resisted a little, but after a moment she submitted and lay tense and rigid in my arms.

"Ellen," I said helplessly, "you asked me to trust you. You have much more reason to trust me. Wouldn't it help to get rid of all this, if you told me a little?"

"I can't," she said, very low—"I mean, there's nothing to tell."

"You met this man on the train coming home and you fell in love with him, isn't that true?"

"I don't know."

"Tell me, Ellen. You fell in love with him?"

"I don't know. Please let me alone."

"Call it anything you want," I went on, "he has some sort of hold over you. He's trying to use you; he's trying to get something from you. He's not in love with you."

"What does that matter?" she said in a weak voice.

"It does matter. Instead of trying to fight this—this thing—you're trying to fight me. And I love you, Ellen. Do you hear? I'm telling you all of a sudden, but it isn't new with me. I love you."

She looked at me with a sneer on her gentle face; it was an expression I had seen on men who were tight and didn't want to be taken home. But it was human. I was reaching her, faintly and from far away, but more than before.

"Ellen, I want you to answer me one question. Is he going to be on this train?"

She hesitated; then, an instant too late, she shook her head.

"Be careful, Ellen. Now I'm going to ask you one thing more, and I wish you'd try very hard to answer. Coming West, when did this man get on the train?"

"I don't know," she said with an effort.

Just at that moment I became aware, with the unquestionable knowledge reserved for facts, that he was just outside the door. She knew it, too; the blood left her face and that expression of low-animal perspicacity came creeping back. I lowered my face into my hands and tried to think.

We must have sat there, with scarcely a word, for well over an hour. I was conscious that the lights of Chicago, then of Englewood and of endless suburbs, were moving by, and then there were no more lights and we were out on the dark flatness of Illinois. The train seemed to draw in upon itself; it took on an air of being alone. The porter knocked at the door and asked if he could make up the berth, but I said no and he went away.

After awhile I convinced myself that the struggle inevitably coming wasn't beyond what remained of my sanity, my faith in the essential all-rightness of things and people. That this person's purpose was what we call "criminal," I took for granted, but there was no need of ascribing to him an intelligence that belonged to a higher plane of human, or inhuman, endeavor. It was still as a man that I considered him, and tried to get at his essence, his self-interest—what took the place in him of a comprehensible heart—but I suppose I more than half knew what I would find when I opened the door.

When I stood up Ellen didn't seem to see me at all. She was hunched into the corner staring straight ahead with a sort of film over her eyes, as if she were in a state of suspended animation of body and mind. I lifted her and put two pillows under her head and threw my fur coat over her knees. Then I knelt beside her and kissed her two hands, opened the door and went out into the hall.

I closed the door behind me and stood with my back against it for a minute. The car was dark save for the corridor lights at each end. There was no sound except the groaning of the couplers, the even click-a-click of the rails and someone's loud sleeping breath farther down the car. I became aware after a moment that the figure of a man was standing by the water cooler just outside the men's smoking room, his derby hat on his head, his coat collar turned up around his neck as if he were cold, his hands in his coat pockets. When I saw him, he turned and went into the smoking room, and I followed. He was sitting in the far corner of the long leather bench; I took the single armchair beside the door.

As I went in I nodded to him and he acknowledged my presence with one of those terrible soundless laughs of his. But this time it was prolonged, it seemed to go on forever, and mostly to cut it short, I asked: "Where are you from?" in a voice I tried to make casual.

He stopped laughing and looked at me narrowly, wondering what my game was. When he decided to answer, his voice was muffled as though he were speaking through a silk scarf, and it seemed to come from a long way off.

"I'm from St. Paul, Jack."

"Been making a trip home?"

He nodded. Then he took a long breath and spoke in a hard, menacing voice:

"You better get off at Fort Wayne, Jack."

He was dead. He was dead as hell—he had been dead all along, but what force had flowed through him, like blood in his veins, out to St. Paul and back, was leaving him now. A new outline—the outline of him dead—was coming through the palpable figure that had knocked down Joe Jelke.

He spoke again, with a sort of jerking effort:

"You get off at Fort Wayne, Jack, or I'm going to wipe you out." He moved his hand in his coat pocket and showed me the outline of a revolver.

I shook my head. "You can't touch me," I answered. "You see, I know." His terrible eyes shifted over me quickly, trying to determine whether or not I did know. Then he gave a snarl and made as though he were going to jump to his feet.

"You climb off here or else I'm going to get you, Jack!" he cried hoarsely. The train was slowing up for Fort Wayne and his voice rang loud in the comparative quiet, but he didn't move from his chair—he was too weak, I think—and we sat staring at each other while workmen passed up and down outside the window banging the brakes and wheels, and the engine gave out loud mournful pants up ahead. No one got into our car. After awhile the porter closed the vestibule door and passed back along the corridor, and we slid out of the murky yellow station light and into the long darkness.

What I remember next must have extended over a space of five or six hours, though it comes back to me as something without any existence in time—something that might have taken five minutes or a year. There began a slow, calculated assault on me, wordless and terrible. I felt what I can only call a strangeness stealing over me—akin to the strangeness I had felt all afternoon, but deeper and more intensified. It was like nothing so much as the sensation of drifting away, and I gripped the arms of the chair convulsively, as if to hang onto a piece in the living world. Sometimes I felt myself going out with a rush. There would be almost a warm relief about it, a sense of not caring; then, with a violent wrench of the will, I'd pull myself back into the room.

Suddenly I realized that from awhile back I had stopped hating him, stopped feeling violently alien to him, and with the realization,

I went cold and sweat broke out all over my head. He was getting around my abhorrence, as he had got around Ellen coming West on the train; and it was just that strength he drew from preying on people that had brought him up to the point of concrete violence in St. Paul, and that, fading and flickering out, still kept him fighting now.

He must have seen that faltering in my heart, for he spoke at once, in a low, even, almost gentle voice: "You better go now."

"Oh, I'm not going," I forced myself to say.

"Suit yourself, Jack."

He was my friend, he implied. He knew how it was with me and he wanted to help. He pitied me. I'd better go away before it was too late. The rhythm of his attack was soothing as a song: I'd better go away—*and let him get at Ellen.* With a little cry I sat bolt upright.

"What do you want of this girl?" I said, my voice shaking. "To make a sort of walking hell of her."

His glance held a quality of dumb surprise, as if I were punishing an animal for a fault of which he was not conscious. For an instant I faltered; then I went on blindly:

"You've lost her; she's put her trust in me."

His countenance went suddenly black with evil, and he cried: "You're a liar!" in a voice that was like cold hands.

"She trusts me," I said. "You can't touch her. She's safe!"

He controlled himself. His face grew bland, and I felt that curious weakness and indifference begin again inside me. What was the use of all this? What was the use?

"You haven't got much time left," I forced myself to say, and then, in a flash of intuition, I jumped at the truth. "You died, or you were killed, not far from here!"—Then I saw what I had not seen before—that his forehead was drilled with a small round hole like a larger picture nail leaves when it's pulled from a plaster wall. "And now you're sinking. You've only got a few hours. The trip home is over!"

His face contorted, lost all semblance of humanity, living or dead. Simultaneously the room was full of cold air and with a noise that was something between a paroxysm of coughing and a burst of horrible laughter, he was on his feet, reeking of shame and blasphemy.

"Come and look!" he cried. "I'll show you—"

He took a step toward me, then another and it was exactly as if a door stood open behind him, a door yawning out to an inconceivable abyss of darkness and corruption. There was a scream of mortal agony, from him or from somewhere behind, and abruptly the strength went out of him in a long husky sigh and he wilted to the floor. . . .

How long I sat there, dazed with terror and exhaustion, I don't know. The next thing I remember is the sleepy porter shining shoes across the room from me, and outside the window the steel fires of Pittsburgh breaking the flat perspective of the night. There was something extended on the bench also—something too faint for a man, too heavy for a shadow. Even as I perceived it it faded off and away.

Some minutes later I opened the door of Ellen's compartment. She was asleep where I had left her. Her lovely cheeks were white and wan, but she lay naturally—her hands relaxed and her breathing regular and clear. What had possessed her had gone out of her, leaving her exhausted but her own dear self again.

I made her a little more comfortable, tucked a blanket around her, extinguished the light and went out.

III

When I came home for Easter vacation, almost my first act was to go down to the billiard parlor near Seven Corners. The man at the cash register quite naturally didn't remember my hurried visit of three months before.

"I'm trying to locate a certain party who, I think, came here a lot some time ago."

I described the man rather accurately, and when I had finished, the cashier called to a little jockeylike fellow who was sitting near with an air of having something very important to do that he couldn't quite remember.

"Hey, Shorty, talk to this guy, will you? I think he's looking for Joe Varland."

The little man gave me a tribal look of suspicion. I went and sat near him.

"Joe Varland's dead, fella," he said grudgingly. "He died last winter."

I described him again—his overcoat, his laugh, the habitual expression of his eyes.

"That's Joe Varland you're looking for all right, but he's dead."

"I want to find out something about him."

"What you want to find out?"

"What did he do, for instance?"

"How should I know?"

"Look here! I'm not a policeman. I just want some kind of information about his habits. He's dead now and it can't hurt him. And it won't go beyond me."

"Well"—he hesitated, looking me over—"he was a great one for travelling. He got in a row in the station in Pittsburgh and a dick got him."

I nodded. Broken pieces of the puzzle began to assemble in my head.

"Why was he a lot on trains?"

"How should I know, fella?"

"If you can use ten dollars, I'd like to know anything you may have heard on the subject."

"Well," said Shorty reluctantly, "all I know is they used to say he worked the trains."

"Worked the trains?"

"He had some racket of his own he'd never loosen up about. He used to work the girls travelling alone on the trains. Nobody ever knew much about it—he was a pretty smooth guy—but sometimes he'd turn up here with a lot of dough and he let 'em know it was the janes he got it off of."

I thanked him and gave him the ten dollars and went out, very thoughtful, without mentioning that part of Joe Varland had made a last trip home.

Ellen wasn't West for Easter, and even if she had been I wouldn't have gone to her with the information, either—at least I've seen her almost every day this summer and we've managed to talk about everything else. Sometimes, though, she gets silent about nothing and wants to be very close to me, and I know what's in her mind.

Of course she's coming out this fall, and I have two more years at New Haven; still, things don't look so impossible as they did a few months ago. She belongs to me in a way—even if I lose her she belongs to me. Who knows? Anyhow, I'll always be there.

ONE INTERNE

Traditionally, the Coccidian Club show is given on the hottest night of spring, and that year was no exception. Two hundred doctors and students sweltered in the reception rooms of the old narrow house and another two hundred students pressed in at the doors, effectually sealing out any breezes from the Maryland night. The entertainment reached these latter clients only dimly, but refreshment was relayed back to them by a busy bucket brigade. Down cellar, the janitor made his annual guess that the sagging floors would hold up one more time.

Bill Tulliver was the coolest man in the hall. For no special reason he wore a light tunic and carried a crook during the only number in which he took part, the rendition of the witty, scurrilous and interminable song which described the failings and eccentricities of the medical faculty. He sat in comparative comfort on the platform and looked out over the hot sea of faces. The most important doctors were in front—Doctor Ruff, the ophthalmologist; Doctor Lane, the brain surgeon; Doctor Georgi, the stomach specialist; Doctor Barnett, the alchemist of internal medicine; and on the end of the row, with his saintlike face undisturbed by the rivulets of perspiration that poured down the long dome of his head, Doctor Norton, the diagnostician.

Like most young men who had sat under Norton, Bill Tulliver followed him with the intuition of the belly, but with a difference. He knelt to him selfishly as a sort of great giver of life. He wanted less to win his approval than to compel it. Engrossed in his own career, which would begin in earnest when he entered the hospital as an interne in July, his whole life was pointed toward the day when his own guess would be right and Doctor Norton's would be wrong. In that moment he would emancipate himself—need not base himself upon that human mixture of adding machines and St. Francis of Assisi any longer.

Bill Tulliver had not arrived unprovoked at this pitch of egotism. He was the fifth in an unbroken series of Dr. William Tullivers who had practised with distinction in the city. His father died last winter; it was not unnatural that even from the womb of school this last scion of a medical tradition should clamor for "self-expression."

The faculty song, immemorially popular, went on and on. There was a verse about the sanguinary Doctor Lane, about the new names Doctor Brune made up for the new diseases he invented, about the personal idiosyncrasies of Doctor Schwartze and the domestic embroilments of Doctor Gillespie. Doctor Norton, as one of the most popular men on the staff, got off easy. There were some new verses—several that Bill had written himself:

"*Herpes Zigler, sad and tired,*
Will flunk you out or kill ya,
If you forget Alfonso wired
For dope on hœmophilia.
Bum*tiddy-bum-bum,*
Tiddy-bum-bum.
Three thousand years ago,
Three thousand years ago."

He watched Doctor Zigler and saw the wince that puckered up under the laugh. Bill wondered how soon there would be a verse about him, Bill Tulliver, and he tentatively composed one as the chorus thundered on.

After the show the older men departed, the floors were sloshed with beer and the traditional roughhouse usurped the evening. But Bill had fallen solemn and, donning his linen suit, he watched for ten minutes and then left the hot hall. There was a group on the front steps, breathing the sparse air, and another group singing around the lamppost at the corner. Across the street arose the great bulk of the hospital about which his life revolved. Between the Michael Clinic and the Ward Dispensary arose a round full moon.

The girl—she was hurrying—reached the loiterers at the lamp-post at the same moment as Bill. She wore a dark dress and a dark, flopping hat, but Bill got an impression that there was a gayety of cut, if not of color, about her clothes. The whole thing happened in less than a minute; the man turning about—Bill saw that he was not a member of the grand confraternity—was simply hurling himself into her arms, like a child at its mother.

The girl staggered backward with a frightened cry; and everyone in the group acted at once.

"Are you sure you're all right?"

"Oh, yes," she gasped. "I think he just passed out and didn't realize he was grabbing at a girl."

"We'll take him over to the emergency ward and see if he can swallow a stomach pump."

Bill Tulliver found himself walking along beside the girl.

"Are you sure you're all right?"

"Oh, yes." She was still breathing hard; her bosom rose, putting out its eternal promises, as if the breath she had taken in were the last breath left in the world. "Oh, things like that happen whenever there are a lot of men together. I realized right away that they were students. I shouldn't have gone by there tonight."

Her hair, dark and drawn back of her ears, brushed her shoulders. She laughed uncontrollably.

"He was so helpless," she said. "Lord knows I've seen men helpless—hundreds of them just helpless—but I'll never forget the expression in his face when he decided to—to lean on me."

Her dark eyes shone with mirth and Bill saw that she was really self-reliant. He stared at her, and the impression of her beauty grew until, uncommitted by a word, by even a formal introduction, he felt himself going out toward her, watching the turn of her lips and the shifting of her cheeks when she smiled...

All this was in the three or four minutes that he walked beside her; not till afterward did he realize how profound the impression had been.

As they passed the church-like bulk of the administration building, an open cabriolet slowed down beside them and a man of about thirty-five jumped out. The girl ran toward him.

"Howard!" she cried with excited gayety. "I was attacked. There were some students in front of the Coccidian Club building—"

The man swung sharply and menacingly toward Bill Tulliver.

"Is this one of them?" he demanded.

"No, no; he's all right."

Simultaneously Bill recognized him—it was Dr. Howard Durfee, brilliant among the younger surgeons, heartbreaker and swashbuckler of the staff.

"You haven't been bothering Miss—"

She stopped him, but not before Bill had answered angrily:

"I don't bother people."

Unappeased, as if Bill were in some way responsible, Doctor Durfee got into his car; the girl got in beside him.

"So long," she said. "And thanks." Her eyes shone at Bill with friendly interest, and then, just before the car shot away, she did something else with them—narrowed them a little and then widened them, recognizing by this sign the uniqueness of their relationship. "I see you," it seemed to say. "You registered. Everything's possible."

With the faint fanfare of a new motor, she vanished back into the spring night.

II

Bill was to enter the hospital in July with the first contingent of newly created doctors. He passed the intervening months at Martha's Vineyard, swimming and fishing with Schoatze, his classmate, and returned tense with health and enthusiasm to begin his work.

The red square broiled under the Maryland sun. Bill went in through the administration building where a gigantic Christ gestured in marble pity over the entrance hall. It was by this same portal that Bill's father had entered on his interneship thirty years before.

Suddenly Bill was in a condition of shock, his tranquillity was rent asunder, he could not have given a rational account as to why he was where he was. A dark-haired girl with great, luminous eyes had started up from the very shadow of the statue, stared at him just long enough to effect this damage, and then with an explosive "Hel*lo!*" vanished into one of the offices.

He was still gazing after her, stricken, haywire, scattered and dissolved—when Doctor Norton hailed him:

"I believe I'm addressing William Tulliver the fifth—" Bill was glad to be reminded who he was.

"—looking somewhat interested in Doctor Durfee's girl," continued Norton.

"Is she?" Bill asked sharply. Then: "Oh, howdedo, Doctor?"

Dr. Norton decided to exercise his wit, of which he had plenty. "In fact we know they spend their days together, and gossip adds the evenings."

"Their days? I should think he'd be too busy."

"He is. As a matter of fact, Miss Singleton induces the state of coma during which he performs his internal sculpture. She's an anæsthetist."

"I see. Then they are—thrown together all day."

"If you regard that as a romantic situation." Doctor Norton looked at him closely. "Are you settled yet? Can you do something for me right now?"

"Yes, indeed."

"I know you don't go on the ward till tomorrow, but I'd like you to go to East Michael and take a P. E. and a history."

"Certainly."

"Room 312. I've put your methodical friend Schoatze on the trail of another mystery next door."

Bill hurried to his room on the top of Michael, jumped into a new white uniform, equipped himself with instruments. In his haste he forgot that this was the first time he had performed an inquisition unaided. Outside the door he smoothed himself into a calm, serious manner. He was almost a white apostle when we walked into the room; at least he tried to be.

A paunchy, sallow man of forty was smoking a cigarette in bed.

"Good morning," Bill said heartily. "How are you this morning?"

"Rotten," the man said. "That's why I'm here."

Bill set down his satchel and approached him like a young cat after its first sparrow.

"What seems to be the trouble?"

"Everything. My head aches, my bones ache, I can't sleep, I don't eat, I've got fever. My chauffeur ran over me, I mean ran over me,

I mean ran me, if you know what I mean. I mean from Washington this morning. I can't stand those Washington doctors; they don't talk about anything but politics."

Bill clapped a thermometer in the man's mouth and took his pulse. Then he made the routine examination of chest, stomach, throat and the rest. The reflexes were sluggish to the little rubber hammer. Bill sat down beside the bed.

"I'd trade hearts with you any day," he promised.

"They all say I've got a good heart," agreed the man. "What did you think of Hoover's speech?"

"I thought you were tired of politics."

"That's true, but I got thinking of Hoover while you went over me."

"About Hoover?"

"About me. What did you find out?"

"We'll want to make some tests. But you seem pretty sound really."

"I'm not sound," the patient snapped. "I'm not sound. I'm a sick man."

Bill took out a P. E. form and a fountain pen.

"What's your name?" he began.

"Paul B. Van Schaik."

"Your nearest relative?"

There was nothing in the case history on which to form any opinion. Mr. Van Schaik had had several children's diseases. Yesterday morning he was unable to get out of bed and his valet had taken his temperature and found fever.

Bill's thermometer registered no fever.

"Now we're going to make just a little prick in your thumb," he said, preparing glass slides, and when this had been accomplished to the tune of a short, dismal howl from the patient, he added: "We want just a little specimen from your upper arm."

"You want everything but my tears," protested the patient.

"We have to investigate all the possibilities," said Bill sternly, plunging the syringe into the soft upper arm, inspiring more explosive protests from Mr. Van Schaik.

Reflectively Bill replaced his instruments. He had obtained no clue as to what was the matter and he eyed the patient reproachfully. On a chance, he looked for enlarged cervical glands, and asked him if his parents were alive, and took a last look at throat and teeth.

"Eyes normally prominent," he wrote down, with a feeling of futility. "Pupils round and equal."

"That's all for the moment," he said. "Try and get some rest."

"Rest!" cried Mr. Van Schaik indignantly. "That's just the trouble. I haven't been able to sleep for three days. I feel worse every minute."

As Bill went out into the hall, George Schoatze was just emerging from the room next door. His eyes were uncertain and there was sweat upon his brow.

"Finished?" Bill asked.

"Why, yes, in a way. Did Doctor Norton set you a job too?"

"Yeah. Kind of puzzling case in here—contradictory symptoms," he lied.

"Same here," said George, wiping his brow. "I'd rather have started out on something more clearly defined, like the ones Robinson gave us in class last year—you know, where there were two possibilities and one probability."

"Unobliging lot of patients," agreed Bill.

A student nurse approached him.

"You were just in 312," she said in a low voice. "I better tell you. I unpacked for the patient, and there was one empty bottle of whisky and one half empty. He asked me to pour him a drink, but I didn't like to do that without asking a doctor."

"Quite right," said Bill stiffly, but he wanted to kiss her hand in gratitude.

Dispatching the specimens to the laboratory, the two internes went in search of Doctor Norton, whom they found in his office.

"Through already? What luck, Tulliver?"

"He's been on a bust and he's got a hangover," Bill blurted out. "I haven't got the laboratory reports yet, but my opinion is that's all."

"I agree with you," said Doctor Norton. "All right, Schoatze; how about the lady in 314?"

"Well, unless it's too deep for me, there's nothing the matter with her at all."

"Right you are," agreed Doctor Norton. "Nerves—and not even enough of them for the Ward clinic. What'll we do with them?"

"Throw 'em out," said Bill promptly.

"Let them stay," corrected Doctor Norton. "They can afford it. They come to us for protection they don't need, so let them pay for a couple of really sick people over in the free wards. We're not crowded."

Outside the office, Bill and George fastened eyes.

"Humbling us a little," said Bill rather resentfully. "Let's go up to the operating rooms; I want to convince myself all over again that this is a serious profession." He swore. "I suppose for the next few months we'll be feeling the bellies of four-flushers and taking the case histories of women who aren't cases."

"Never mind," said George cautiously. "I was just as glad to start with something simple like—like—"

"Like what?"

"Why, like nothing."

"You're easily pleased," Bill commented.

Ascertaining from a bulletin board that Dr. Howard Durfee was at work in No. 4, they took the elevator to the operating rooms. As they slipped on the gowns, caps, and then the masks, Bill realized how quickly he was breathing.

He saw HER before he saw anything else in the room, except the bright vermilion spot of the operation itself, breaking the universal whiteness of the scene. There was a sway of eyes toward the two internes as they came into the gallery, and Bill picked out her eyes, darker than ever in contrast with the snowy cap and mask, as she sat working the gas machine at the patient's invisible head. The room was small. The platform on which they stood was raised about four feet, and by leaning out on a glass screen like a windshield, they brought their eyes to within two yards of the surgeon's busy hands.

"It's a neat appendix—not a cut in the muscle," George whispered. "That guy can play lacrosse tomorrow."

Doctor Durfee, busy with catgut, heard him.

"Not this patient," he said. "Too many adhesions."

His hands, tying the catgut, were sure and firm, the fine hands of a pianist, the tough hands of a pitcher combined. Bill thought how insecure, precariously involved, the patient would seem to a layman, and yet how safe he was with those sure hands in an atmosphere made safe from time itself. Time had stopped at the door of the operating room, too profane to enter here.

Thea Singleton guarded the door of the patient's consciousness, a hand on a pulse, another turning the wheels of the gas machine, as if they were the stops on a silent organ.

There were others in attendance—an assisting surgeon, a nurse who passed instruments, a nurse who made liaison between the table and the supplies—but Bill was absorbed in what subtle relationship there was between Howard Durfee and Thea Singleton; he felt a wild jealousy toward the mask with the brilliant, agile hands.

"I'm going," he said to George.

He saw her that afternoon, and again it was in the shadow of the great stone Christ in the entrance hall. She was in street clothes, and she looked slick and fresh and tantalizingly excitable.

"Of course. You're the man the night of the Coccidian show. And now you're an interne. Wasn't it you who came into Room 4 this morning?"

"Yes. How did it go?"

"Fine. It was Doctor Durfee."

"Yes," he said with emphasis. "I know it was Doctor Durfee."

He met her by accident or contrivance half a dozen times in the next fortnight, before he judged he could ask her for a date.

"Why, I suppose so." She seemed a little surprised. "Let's see. How about next week—either Tuesday or Wednesday?"

"How about tonight?"

"Oh, not possibly."

When he called Tuesday at the little apartment she shared with a woman musician from the Peabody Institute, he said:

"What would you like to do? See a picture?"

"No," she answered emphatically. "If I knew you better I'd say let's drive about a thousand miles into the country and go swimming in some quarry." She looked at him quizzically. "You're not one of those very impulsive internes, are you, that just sweep poor nurses off their feet?"

"On the contrary, I'm scared to death of you," Bill admitted.

It was a hot night, but the white roads were cool. They found out a little about each other: She was the daughter of an Army officer and had grown up in the Philippines, and in the black-and-silver water of the abandoned quarry she surprised him with such diving as he had never seen a girl do. It was ghostly inside of the black shadow that ringed the glaring moonlight, and their voices echoed loud when they called to each other.

Afterward, with their heads wet and their bodies stung alive, they sat for awhile, unwilling to start back. Suddenly she smiled, and then looked at him without speaking, her lips just barely parted. There was the starlight set upon the brilliant darkness; and there were her pale cool cheeks, and Bill let himself be lost in love for her, as he had so wanted to do.

"We must go," she said presently.

"Not yet."

"Oh, *yet—very* yet—exceedingly yet."

"Because," he said after a moment, "you're Doctor Durfee's girl?"

"Yes," she admitted after a moment, "I suppose I'm Doctor Durfee's girl."

"Why are you?" he cried.

"Are you in love with me?"

"I suppose I am. Are you in love with Durfee?"

She shook her head. "No, I'm not in love with anybody. I'm just—his girl."

So the evening that had been at first ecstatic was finally unsatisfactory. This feeling deepened when he found that for his date he had to thank the fact that Durfee was out of town for a few days.

With August and the departure of more doctors on vacation, he found himself very busy. During four years he had dreamed of such work as he was doing, and now it was all disturbed by the ubiquity of "Durfee's girl." In vain he searched among the girls in the city, on those Sundays when he could go into the city, for some who would soften the hurt of his unreciprocated emotion. But the city seemed empty of girls, and in the hospital the little probationers in short cuffs had no appeal for him. The truth of his situation was that his initial idealism which had been centered in Doctor Norton had transferred itself to Thea. Instead of a God, it was now a Goddess who symbolized for him the glory and the devotion of his profession; and that she was caught up in an entanglement that bound her away from him, played havoc with his peace of mind.

Diagnosis had become a workaday matter—almost. He had made a few nice guesses and Doctor Norton had given him full credit.

"Nine times out of ten I'll be right," Norton said. "The rare thing is so rare that I'm out of the habit of looking for it. That's where you young men come in; you're cocked for the rare thing and that one time in ten you find it."

"It's a great feeling," said Bill. "I got a big kick out of that actinomycosis business."

"You look tired for your age," said Doctor Norton suddenly. "At twenty-five you shouldn't be existing entirely on nervous energy, Bill, and that's what you're doing. The people you grew up with say they never see you. Why not take a couple of hours a week away from the hospital, if only for the sake of your patients? You took so many chemistry tests of Mr. Doremus that we almost had to give him blood transfusions to build him up again."

"I was right," said Bill eagerly.

"But a little brutal. Everything would have developed in a day or two. Take it gently, like your friend Schoatze. You're going to know a lot about internal medicine someday, but you're trying to rush things."

But Bill was a man driven; he tried more Sunday afternoons with current debutantes, but in the middle of a conversation he would find his mind drifting back to those great red building blocks of an Idea, where alone he could feel the pulse of life.

The news that a famous character in politics was leaving the Coast and coming to the hospital for the diagnosis of some obscure malady had the effect of giving him a sudden interest in politics. He looked up the record of the man and followed his journey east, which occupied half a column daily in the newspapers; party issues depended on his survival and eventual recovery.

Then one August afternoon there was an item in the society column which announced the engagement of Helen, debutante daughter of Mrs. Truby Ponsonby Day, to Dr. Howard Durfee. Bill's reconciled world turned upside down. After an amount of very real suffering, he had accepted the fact that Thea was the mistress of a brilliant surgeon, but that Dr. Durfee should suddenly cut loose from her was simply incredible.

Immediately he went in search of her, found her issuing from the nurses' ward in street clothes. Her lovely face, with the eyes that held for him all the mystery of people trying, all the splendor of a goal, all reward, all purpose, all satisfaction, was harried with annoyance; she had been stared at and pitied.

"If you like," she answered, when he asked if he could run her home, and then: "Heaven help women! The amount of groaning over my body that took place this afternoon would have been plenty for a war."

"I'm going to help you," he said. "If that guy has let you down—"

"Oh, shut up! Up to a few weeks ago I could have married Howard Durfee by nodding my head—that's just what I wouldn't tell those women this afternoon. I think you've got discretion, and that'll help you a lot when you're a doctor."

"I am a doctor," he said somewhat stiffly.

"No, you're just an interne."

He was indignant and they drove in silence. Then, softening, she turned toward him and touched his arm.

"You happen to be a gentleman," she said, "which is nice sometimes—though I prefer a touch of genius."

"I've got that," Bill said doggedly. "I've got everything, except you."

"Come up to the apartment and I'll tell you something that no one else in this city knows."

It was a modest apartment but it told him that at some time she had lived in a more spacious world. It was all reduced, as if she had hung on to several cherished things, a Duncan Phyfe table, a brass by Brancusi, two oil portraits of the '50s.

"I was engaged to John Gresham," she said. "Do you know who he was?"

"Of course," he said. "I took up the subscription for the bronze tablet to him."

John Gresham had died by inches from radium poisoning, got by his own experiments.

"I was with him till the end," Thea went on quickly, "and just before he died he wagged his last finger at me and said, 'I forbid you to go to pieces. That doesn't do any good.' So, like a good little girl, I didn't go to pieces, but I toughened up instead. Anyhow, that's why I never could love Howard Durfee the way he wanted to be loved, in spite of his nice swagger and his fine hands."

"I see." Overwhelmed by the revelation, Bill tried to adjust himself to it. "I knew there was something far off about you, some sort of—oh, dedication to something I didn't know about."

"I'm pretty hard." She got up impatiently. "Anyhow, I've lost a good friend today and I'm cross, so go before I show it. Kiss me good-bye if you like."

"It wouldn't mean anything at this moment."

"Yes, it would," she insisted. "I like to be close to you. I like your clothes."

Obediently he kissed her, but he felt far off from her and very rebuffed and young as he went out the door.

He awoke next morning with the sense of something important hanging over him; then he remembered. Senator Billings, relayed by crack trains, airplanes and ambulances, was due to arrive during the morning, and the ponderous body which had housed and expelled so much nonsense in thirty years was to be at the mercy of the rational at last.

"I'll diagnose the old boy," he thought grimly, "if I have to invent a new disease."

He went about his routine work with a sense of fatigue that morning. Perhaps Doctor Norton would keep this plum to himself and Bill wouldn't have a chance at him. But at eleven o'clock he met his senior in a corridor.

"The senator's come," he said. "I've formed a tentative opinion. You might go in and get his history. Go over him quickly and give him the usual laboratory work-up."

"All right," said Bill, but there was no eagerness in his voice. He seemed to have lost all his enthusiasm. With his instruments and a block of history paper, he repaired to the senator's room.

"Good morning," he began. "Feeling a little tired after your trip?"

The big barrel of a man rolled toward him.

"Exhausted," he squeaked unexpectedly. "All in."

Bill didn't wonder; he felt rather that way himself, as if he had travelled thousands of miles in all sorts of conveyances until his insides, including his brains, were all shaken up together.

He took the case history.

"What's your profession?"

"Legislator."

"Do you use any alcohol?"

The senator raised himself on one arm and thundered, "See here, young man; I'm not going to be heckled! As long as the Eighteenth Amendment—" He subsided.

"Do you use any alcohol?" Bill asked again patiently.

"Why, yes."

"How much?"

"A few drinks every day. I don't count them. Say, if you look in my suitcase you'll find an X-ray of my lungs, taken a few years ago."

Bill found it and stared at it with a sudden feeling that everything was getting a little crazy.

"This is an X-ray of a woman's stomach," he said.

"Oh—well, it must have got mixed up," said the senator. "It must be my wife's."

Bill went into the bathroom to wash his thermometer. When he came back he took the senator's pulse, and was puzzled to find himself regarded in a curious way.

"What's the idea?" the senator demanded. "Are you the patient or am I?" He jerked his hand angrily away from Bill. "Your hand's like ice. And you've put the thermometer in your own mouth."

Only then did Bill realize how sick he was. He pressed the nurse's bell and staggered back to a chair with wave after wave of pain chasing across his abdomen.

III

He awoke with a sense that he had been in bed for many hours. There was fever bumping in his brain, a pervasive weakness in his body, and what had wakened him was a new series of pains in his stomach. Across the room in an armchair sat Dr. George Schoatze, and on his knee was the familiar case-history pad.

"What the hell," Bill said weakly. "What the hell's the matter with me? What happened?"

"You're all right," said George. "You just lie quiet."

Bill tried to sit upright, but found he was too weak.

"Lie quiet!" he repeated incredulously. "What do you think I am—some dumb patient? I asked you what's the matter with me?"

"That's exactly what we're trying to find out. Say, what is your exact age?"

"My age!" Bill cried. "A hundred and ten in the shade! My name's Al Capone and I'm an old hophead. Stick that on your God damn paper and mail it to Santa Claus. I asked you what's the matter with me."

"And I say that's what we're trying to find out," said George, staunch, but a little nervous. "Now, you take it easy."

"Take it easy!" cried Bill. "When I'm burning up with fever and a half-wit interne sits there and asks me how many fillings I've got in my teeth! You take my temperature, and take it right away!"

"All right—all right," said George conciliatingly. "I was just going to."

He put the thermometer in Bill's mouth and felt for the pulse, but Bill mumbled, "I'll shake my ode pulse," and pulled his hand away. After two minutes George deftly extracted the thermometer and walked with it to the window, an act of treachery that brought Bill's legs out of bed.

"I want to read that thermometer!" he cried. "Now, you look here! I want to know what's on that thermometer!"

George shook it down quickly and put it in its case.

"That isn't the way we do things here," he said.

"Oh, isn't it? Well, then, I'll go somewhere where they've got some sense."

George prepared a syringe and two small plates of glass.

Bill groaned. "Do you think for a moment I'm going to let you do that? I taught you everything you know about blood chemistry. By God, I used to do your lessons for you, and you come here to make some clumsy stab into my arm!"

Perspiring fluently, as was his wont under strain, George rang for a nurse, with the hope that a female presence would have a calming effect on Bill. But it was not the right female.

"Another nitwit!" Bill cried as she came in. "Do you think I'm going to lie here and stand more of this nonsense? Why doesn't somebody take care of me? Why doesn't somebody do something? Where's Doctor Norton?"

"He'll be here this afternoon."

"This afternoon! I'll probably be dead by this afternoon. Why isn't he here this morning? Off on some social bat and I lie here surrounded by morons who've lost their heads and don't know what to do about it. What are you writing there—that my 'tongue protrudes in mid-line without tremor'? Give me my slippers and bathrobe. I'm going to report you two as specimens for the nerve clinic."

They pressed him down in bed, whence he looked up at George with infinite reproach.

"You, that I explained a whole book of toxicology to, you're presuming to diagnose *me*. Well, then, *do* it! What have I got? Why is my stomach burning up? Is it appendicitis? What's the white count?"

"How can I find out the white count when—"

With a sigh of infinite despair at the stupidity of mankind, Bill relaxed, exhausted.

Doctor Norton arrived at two o'clock. His presence should have been reassuring, but by this time the patient was too far gone in nervous tension.

"Look here, Bill," he said sternly. "What's all this about not letting George look into your mouth?"

"Because he deliberately gagged me with that stick," Bill cried. "When I get out of this I'm going to stick a plank down that ugly trap of his."

"Now, that'll do. Do you know little Miss Cary has been crying? She says she's going to give up nursing. She says she's never been so disillusioned in her life."

"The same with me. Tell her I'm going to give it up too. After this, I'm going to kill people instead of curing them. Now when I need it nobody has even tried to cure *me.*"

An hour later Doctor Norton stood up.

"Well, Bill, we're going to take you at your word and tell you what's what. I'm laying my cards on the table when I say we don't know what's the matter with you. We've just got the X-rays from this morning, and it's pretty certain it's not the gall bladder. There's a possibility of acute food poisoning or mesenteric thrombosis, or it may be something we haven't thought of yet. Give us a chance, Bill."

With an effort and with the help of a sedative, Bill got himself in comparative control; only to go to pieces again in the morning, when George Schoatze arrived to give him a hypodermoclysis.

"But I can't stand it," he raged. "I never could stand being pricked, and you have as much right with a needle as a year-old baby with a machine gun."

"Doctor Norton has ordered that you get nothing by mouth."

"Then give it intravenously."

"This is best."

"What I'll do to you when I get well! I'll inject stuff into you until you're as big as a barrel! I will! I'll hire somebody to hold you down!"

Forty-eight hours later, Doctor Norton and Doctor Schoatze had a conference in the former's office.

"So there we are," George was saying gloomily. "He just flatly refuses to submit to the operation."

"H'm." Doctor Norton considered. "That's bad."

"There's certainly danger of a perforation."

"And you say that his chief objection—"

"—that it was my diagnosis. He says I remembered the word 'volvulus' from some lecture and I'm trying to wish it on him." George added uncomfortably: "He always was domineering, but I never saw anything like *this*. Today he claims it's acute pancreatitis, but he doesn't have any convincing reasons."

"Does he know I agree with your opinion?"

"He doesn't seem to believe in *any*body," said George uncomfortably. "He keeps fretting about his father; he keeps thinking he could help him if he was alive."

"I wish that there was someone outside the hospital he had some faith in," Norton said. An idea came to him: "I wonder—" He picked up the telephone and said to the operator: "I wish you'd locate Miss Singleton, Doctor Durfee's anæsthetist. And when she's free, ask her to come and see me."

Bill opened his eyes wearily when Thea came into his room at eight that night.

"Oh, it's you," he murmured.

She sat on the side of his bed and put her hand on his arm.

"H'lo, Bill," she said.

"H'lo."

Suddenly he turned in bed and put both his arms around her arm. Her free hand touched his hair.

"You've been bad," she said.

"I can't help it."

She sat with him silently for half an hour; then she changed her position so that her arm was under his head. Stooping over him, she kissed him on the brow. He said:

"Being close to you is the first rest I've had in four days."

After awhile she said: "Three months ago Doctor Durfee did an operation for volvulus and it was entirely successful."

"But it isn't volvulus!" he cried. "Volvulus is when a loop of the intestine gets twisted on itself. It's a crazy idea of Schoatze's! He wants to make a trick diagnosis and get a lot of credit."

"Doctor Norton agrees with him. You must give in, Bill. I'll be right beside you, as close as I am now."

Her soft voice was a sedative; he felt his resistance growing weaker; two long tears rolled from his eyes. "I feel so helpless," he admitted. "How do I know whether George Schoatze has any sense?"

"That's just childish," she answered gently. "You'll profit more by submitting to this than Doctor Schoatze will from his lucky guess."

He clung to her suddenly. "Afterward, will you be my girl?"

She laughed. "The selfishness! The bargainer! You wouldn't be very cheerful company if you went around with a twisted intestine."

He was silent for a moment. "Yesterday I made my will," he said. "I divided what I have between an old aunt and you."

She put her face against his. "You'll make me weep, and it really isn't that serious at all."

"All right then." His white, pinched face relaxed. "Get it over with."

Bill was wheeled upstairs an hour later. Once the matter was decided, all nervousness left him, and he remembered how the hands of Doctor Durfee had given him such a sense of surety last July, and remembered who would be at his head watching over him. His last thought as the gas began was a sudden jealousy that Thea and Howard Durfee would be awake and near each other while he was asleep . . .

. . . When he awoke he was being wheeled down a corridor to his room. Doctor Norton and Doctor Schoatze, seeming very cheerful, were by his side.

"H'lo, hello," cried Bill in a daze. "Say, what did they finally discover about Senator Billings?"

"It was only a common cold, Bill," said Doctor Norton. "They've shipped him back west—by dirigible, helicopter and freight elevator."

"Oh," said Bill; and then, after a moment, "I feel terrible."

"You're not terrible," Doctor Norton assured him. "You'll be up on deck in a week. George here is certainly a swell guesser."

"It was a beautiful operation," said George modestly. "That loop would have perforated in another six hours."

"Good anæsthesia job, too," said Doctor Norton, winking at George. "Like a lullaby."

Thea slipped in to see Bill next morning, when he was rested and the soreness was eased and he felt weak but himself again. She sat beside him on the bed.

"I made an awful fool of myself," he confessed.

"A lot of doctors do when they get sick the first time. They go neurotic."

"I guess everybody's off me."

"Not at all. You'll be in for some kidding probably. Some bright young one wrote this for the Coccidian Club show." She read from a scrap of paper:

> *"Interne Tulliver, chloroformed,*
> *Had dreams above his station;*
> *He woke up thinking he'd performed*
> *His own li'l' operation."*

"I guess I can stand it," said Bill. "I can stand anything when you're around; I'm so in love with you. But I suppose after this you'll always see me as about high-school age."

"If you'd had your first sickness at forty you'd have acted the same way."

"I hear your friend Durfee did a brilliant job, as usual," he said resentfully.

"Yes," she agreed; after a minute she added: "He wants to break his engagement and marry me on my own terms."

His heart stopped beating. "And what did you say?"

"I said No."

Life resumed itself again.

"Come closer," he whispered. "Where's your hand? Will you, anyhow, go swimming with me every night all the rest of September?"

"Every other night."

"Every night."

"Well, every hot night," she compromised.

Thea stood up.

He saw her eyes fix momentarily on some distant spot, linger there for a moment as if she were drawing support from it; then she leaned over him and kissed his hungry lips good-bye, and faded back into her own mystery, into those woods where she hunted, with an old suffering and with a memory he could not share.

But what was valuable in it she had distilled; she knew how to pass it along so that it would not disappear. For the moment Bill had had more than his share, and reluctantly he relinquished her.

"This has been my biggest case so far," he thought sleepily.

The verse to the Coccidian Club song passed through his mind, and the chorus echoed on, singing him into deep sleep:

Bumtiddy, bum-bum,
Tiddy-bum-bum.
Three thousand years ago,
Three thousand years ago.

THE FIEND

On June 3, 1895, on a country road near Stillwater, Minnesota, Mrs. Crenshaw Engels and her seven-year-old son, Mark, were waylaid and murdered by a fiend, under circumstances so atrocious that, fortunately, it is not necessary to set them down here.

Crenshaw Engels, the husband and father, was a photographer in Stillwater. He was a great reader and considered "a little unsafe," for he had spoken his mind frankly about the railroad-agrarian struggles of the time—but no one denied that he was a devoted family man, and the catastrophe visited upon him hung over the little town for many weeks. There was a move to lynch the perpetrator of the horror, for Minnesota did not permit the capital punishment he deserved, but the instigators were foiled by the big stone penitentiary close at hand.

The cloud hung over Engels' home so that folks went there only in moods of penitence, of fear or guilt, hoping that they would be visited in turn should their lives ever chance to trek under a black sky. The photography studio suffered also: the routine of being posed, the necessary silences and pauses in the process, permitted the clients too much time to regard the prematurely aged face of Crenshaw Engels, and high-school students, newly married couples, mothers of new babies, were always glad to escape from the place into the open air. So Crenshaw's business fell off and he went through a time of hardship—finally liquidating the lease, the apparatus and the good will, and wearing out the money obtained. He sold his house for a little more than its two mortgages, went to board and took a position clerking in Radamacher's Department Store.

In the sight of his neighbors he had become a man ruined by adversity, a man *manqué*, a man emptied. But in the last opinion they were wrong—he was empty of all save one thing. His memory was long as a Jew's, and though his heart was in the grave he was sane as when his wife and son had started on their last walk that summer morning. At the first trial he lost control and got at the Fiend, seizing him by the necktie—and then had been dragged off with the Fiend's tie in such a knot that the man was nearly garroted.

At the second trial Crenshaw cried aloud once. Afterwards he went to all the members of the state legislature in the county and handed them a bill he had written himself for the introduction of capital punishment in the state—the bill to be retroactive on criminals condemned to life imprisonment. The bill fell through; it was on the day Crenshaw heard this that he got inside the penitentiary by a ruse and was only apprehended in time to be prevented from shooting the Fiend in his cell.

Crenshaw was given a suspended sentence and for some months it was assumed that the agony was fading gradually from his mind. In fact when he presented himself to the Warden in another role a year after the crime, the official was sympathetic to his statement that he had had a change of heart and felt he could only emerge from the valley of the shadow by forgiveness, that he wanted to help the Fiend, show him the True Path by means of good books and appeals to his buried better nature. So, after being carefully searched, Crenshaw was permitted to sit for half an hour in the corridor outside the Fiend's cell.

But had the Warden suspected the truth he would not have permitted the visit—for, far from forgiving, Crenshaw's plan was to wreak upon the Fiend a mental revenge to replace the physical one of which he was subducted.

When he faced the Fiend, Crenshaw felt his scalp tingle. From behind the bars a roly-poly man, who somehow made his convict's uniform resemble a business suit, a man with thick brown-rimmed glasses and the trim air of an insurance salesman, looked at him uncertainly. Feeling faint Crenshaw sat down in the chair that had been brought for him.

"The air around you stinks!" he cried suddenly. "This whole corridor, this whole prison."

"I suppose it does," admitted the Fiend. "I noticed it too."

"You'll have time to notice it," Crenshaw muttered. "All your life you'll pace up and down stinking in that little cell, with everything getting blacker and blacker. And after that there'll be hell waiting for you. For all eternity you'll be shut in a little space, but in hell it'll be so small that you can't stand up or stretch out."

"*Will* it now?" asked the Fiend concerned.

"It will!" said Crenshaw. "You'll be alone with your own vile thoughts in that little space, forever and ever and ever. You'll itch with corruption so that you can never sleep, and you'll always be thirsty, with water just out of reach."

"*Will* I now?" repeated the Fiend, even more concerned. "I remember once—"

"All the time you'll be full of horror," Crenshaw interrupted. "You'll be like a person just about to go crazy but can't go crazy. All the time you'll be thinking that it's forever and ever."

"That's bad," said the Fiend, shaking his head gloomily. "That's real bad."

"Now listen here to me," went on Crenshaw. "I've brought you some books you're going to read. It's arranged that you get no books or papers except what I bring you."

As a beginning Crenshaw had brought half a dozen books which his vagarious curiosity had collected over as many years. They comprised a German doctor's thousand case histories of sexual abnormality—cases with no cures, no hopes, no prognoses, cases listed cold; a series of sermons by a New England Divine of the Great Revival which pictured the tortures of the damned in hell; a collection of horror stories; and a volume of erotic pieces from each of which the last two pages, containing the consummations, had been torn out; a volume of detective stories mutilated in the same manner. A tome of the Newgate Calendar completed the batch. These Crenshaw handed through the bars—the Fiend took them and put them on his iron cot.

This was the first of Crenshaw's long series of fortnightly visits. Always he brought with him something somber and menacing to say, something dark and terrible to read—save that once when the Fiend had had nothing to read for a long time he brought him four inspiringly titled books—that proved to have nothing but blank paper inside. Another time, pretending to concede a point, he promised to bring newspapers—he brought ten copies of the yellowed journal that had reported the crime and the arrest. Sometimes he obtained medical books that showed in color the red and blue and green ravages of leprosy and skin disease, the mounds of shattered cells, the verminous tissue and brown corrupted blood.

And there was no sewer of the publishing world from which he did not obtain records of all that was gross and vile in man.

Crenshaw could not keep this up indefinitely both because of the expense and because of the exhaustibility of such books. When five years had passed he leaned toward another form of torture. He built up false hopes in the Fiend with protests of his own change of heart and maneuvers for a pardon, and then dashed the hopes to pieces. Or else he pretended to have a pistol with him, or an inflammatory substance that would make the cell a raging Inferno and consume the Fiend in two minutes—once he threw a dummy bottle into the cell and listened in delight to the screams as the Fiend ran back and forth waiting for the explosion. At other times he would pretend grimly that the legislature had passed a new law which provided that the Fiend would be executed in a few hours.

A decade passed. Crenshaw was grey at forty—he was white at fifty when the alternating routine of his fortnightly visits to the graves of his loved ones and to the penitentiary had become the only part of his life—the long days at Radamacher's were only a weary dream. Sometimes he went and sat outside the Fiend's cell, with no word said during the half hour he was allowed to be there. The Fiend too had grown white in twenty years. He was very respectable-looking with his horn-rimmed glasses and his white hair. He seemed to have a great respect for Crenshaw and even when the latter, in a renewal of diminishing vitality, promised him one day that on his very next visit he was going to bring a revolver and end the matter, he nodded gravely as if in agreement, said, "I suppose so. Yes, I suppose you're perfectly right," and did not mention the matter to the guards. On the occasion of the next visit he was waiting with his hands on the bars of the cell looking at Crenshaw both hopefully and desperately. At certain tensions and strains death takes on, indeed, the quality of a great adventure as any soldier can testify.

Years passed. Crenshaw was promoted to floor manager at Radamacher's—there were new generations now that did not know of his tragedy and regarded him as an austere nonentity. He came into a little legacy and bought new stones for the graves of his wife and son. He knew he would soon be retired and while a third decade lapsed through the white winters, the short sweet smoky summers, it became more and more plain to him that the time had come to put an end to the Fiend, to avoid any mischance by which the other would survive him.

The moment he fixed upon came at the exact end of thirty years. Crenshaw had long owned the pistol with which it would be accomplished; he had fingered the shells lovingly and calculated the lodgement of each in the Fiend's body, so that death would be sure but lingering—he studied the tales of abdominal wounds in the war news and delighted in the agony that made victims pray to be killed.

After that, what happened to *him* did not matter.

When the day came he had no trouble in smuggling the pistol into the penitentiary. But to his surprise he found the Fiend scrunched up upon his iron cot, instead of waiting for him avidly by the bars.

"I'm sick," the Fiend said. "My stomach's been burning me up all morning. They gave me a physic but now it's worse and nobody comes."

Crenshaw fancied momentarily that this was a premonition in the man's bowels of a bullet that would shortly ride ragged through that spot.

"Come up to the bars," he said mildly.

"I can't move."

"Yes you can."

"I'm doubled up. All doubled up."

"Come doubled up then."

With an effort the Fiend moved himself, only to fall on his side on the cement floor. He groaned and then lay quiet for a minute, after which, still bent in two, he began to drag himself a foot at a time toward the bars.

Suddenly Crenshaw set off at a run toward the end of the corridor.

"I want the prison doctor," he demanded of the guard. "That man's sick—*sick*, I tell you."

"The doctor has—"

"Get him—get him now!"

The guard hesitated, but Crenshaw had become a tolerated, even privileged person around the prison, and in a moment the guard took down his phone and called the infirmary.

All that afternoon Crenshaw waited in the bare area inside the gates, walking up and down with his hands behind his back. From time to time he went to the front entrance and demanded of the guard:

"Any news?"

"Nothing yet. They'll call me when there's anything."

Late in the afternoon the Warden appeared at the door, looked about and spotted Crenshaw. The latter, all alert, hastened over.

"He's dead," the Warden said. "His appendix burst. They did everything they could."

"Dead," Crenshaw repeated.

"I'm sorry to bring you this news. I know how—"

"It's all right," said Crenshaw, and licking his lips. "So he's dead."

The Warden lit a cigarette.

"While you're here, Mr. Engels, I wonder if you can let me have that pass that was issued to you—I can turn it in to the office. That is—I suppose you won't need it anymore."

Crenshaw took the blue card from his wallet and handed it over. The Warden shook hands with him.

"One thing more," Crenshaw demanded as the Warden turned away. "Which is the—the window of the infirmary?"

"It's on the interior court, you can't see it from here."

"Oh."

When the Warden had gone Crenshaw still stood there a long time, the tears running out down his face. He could not collect his thoughts and he began by trying to remember what day it was; Saturday, the day, every other week, on which he came to see the Fiend.

He would not see the Fiend two weeks from now.

In a misery of solitude and despair he muttered aloud: "So he is dead. He has left me." And then with a long sigh of mingled grief and fear, "So I have lost him—my only friend—now I am alone."

He was still saying that to himself as he passed through the outer gate, and as his coat caught in the great swing of the outer door the guard opened up to release it, he heard a reiteration of the words:

"I'm alone. At last—at last I am alone."

Once more he called on the Fiend, after many weeks.

"But he's dead," the Warden told him kindly.

"Oh, yes," Crenshaw said. "I guess I must have forgotten."

And he set off back home, his boots sinking deep into the white diamond surface of the flats.

BABYLON REVISITED

"And where's Mr. Campbell?" Charlie asked.

"Gone to Switzerland. Mr. Campbell's a pretty sick man, Mr. Wales."

"I'm sorry to hear that. And George Hardt?" Charlie inquired.

"Back in America, gone to work."

"And where is the Snow Bird?"

"He was in here last week. Anyway his friend Mr. Schaeffer is in Paris."

Two familiar names from the long list of a year and a half ago. Charlie scribbled an address in his notebook and tore out the page.

"If you see Mr. Schaeffer, give him this," he said. "It's my brother-in-law's address. I haven't settled on a hotel yet."

He was not really disappointed to find Paris was so empty. But the stillness in the Ritz bar was strange and portentous. It was not an American bar any more—he felt polite in it, and not as if he owned it. It had gone back into France. He felt the stillness from the moment he got out of the taxi and saw the doorman, usually in a frenzy of activity at this hour, gossiping with a *chasseur* by the servants' entrance.

Passing through the corridor, he heard only a single, bored voice in the once-clamorous women's room. When he turned into the bar he travelled the twenty feet of green carpet with his eyes fixed straight ahead by old habit, and then with his foot firmly on the rail he turned and surveyed the room—encountering only a single pair of eyes that fluttered up from a newspaper in the corner. Charlie asked for the head barman, Paul, who in the latter days of the bull market had come to work in his own custom-built car—disembarking, however, with due nicety at the nearest corner. But Paul was at his country house today and Alix was giving him information.

"No, no more," Charlie said, "I'm going slow these days."

Alix congratulated him: "You were going pretty strong couple of years ago."

"I'll stick to it all right," Charlie assured him. "I've stuck to it for over a year and a half now."

"How do you find conditions in America?"

"I haven't been to America for months. I'm in business in Prague, representing a couple of concerns there. They don't know about me down there."

Alix smiled.

"Remember the night of George Hardt's bachelor dinner here?" said Charlie. "By the way, what's become of Claude Fessenden?"

Alix lowered his voice confidentially: "He's in Paris, but he doesn't come here anymore. Paul doesn't allow it. He ran up a bill of thirty thousand francs, charging all his drinks and his lunches, and usually his dinner, for more than a year. And when Paul finally told him he had to pay, he gave him a bad check."

Alix shook his head sadly.

"I don't understand it, such a dandy fellow. Now he's all bloated up—" He made a plump apple of his hands.

Charlie watched a group of strident queens installing themselves in a corner.

"Nothing affects them," he thought. "Stocks rise and fall, people loaf or work, but they go on forever." The place oppressed him. He called for the dice and shook with Alix for the drink.

"Here for long, Mr. Wales?"

"I'm here for four or five days to see my little girl."

"Oh-h! You have a little girl?"

Charlie directed his taxi to the Avenue de l'Opera, which was out of his way. But he wanted to see the blue hour spread over the magnificent façade, and imagine that the cab horns, playing endlessly the first few bars of "La Plus que Lente," were the trumpets of the Second Empire. They were closing the iron grill in front of Brentano's bookstore, and people were already at dinner behind the trim little bourgeois hedge of Duval's. He had never eaten at a really cheap restaurant in Paris. Five-course dinner, four francs fifty, eighteen cents, wine included. For some odd reason he wished that he had.

As they rolled onto the Left Bank and he felt its sudden provincialism, he thought, "I spoiled this city for myself. I didn't realize it, but the days came along one after another, and then two years were gone, and everything was gone, and I was gone."

He was thirty-five, and good to look at. The Irish mobility of his face was sobered by a deep wrinkle between his eyes. As he rang his brother-in-law's bell in the Rue Palatine, the wrinkle deepened till it pulled down his brows; he felt a cramping sensation in his belly. From behind the maid who opened the door darted a lovely little girl of nine who shrieked "Daddy!" and flew up, struggling like a fish, into his arms. She pulled his head around by one ear and set her cheek against his.

"My old pie," he said.

"Oh, daddy, daddy, daddy, daddy, dads, dads, dads!"

She drew him into the salon where the family waited, a boy and girl his daughter's age, his sister-in-law and her husband. He greeted Marion with his voice pitched carefully to avoid either feigned enthusiasm or dislike, but her response was more frankly tepid, though she minimized her expression of unalterable distrust by directing her regard toward his child. The two men clasped hands in a friendly way and Lincoln Peters rested his for a moment on Charlie's shoulder.

The room was warm and comfortably American. The three children moved intimately about, playing through the yellow oblongs that led to other rooms; the cheer of six o'clock spoke in the eager smacks of the fire and the sounds of French activity in the kitchen. But Charlie did not relax—his heart sat up rigidly in his body and he drew confidence from his daughter, who from time to time came close to him, holding in her arms the doll he had brought.

"Really extremely well," he declared in answer to Lincoln's question. "There's a lot of business there that isn't moving at all, but we're doing even better than ever. In fact, damn well. I'm bringing my sister over from America next month to keep house for me. My income last year was bigger than it was when I had money. You see, the Czechs—"

His boasting was for a specific purpose; but after a moment, seeing a faint restiveness in Lincoln's eye, he changed the subject.

"Those are fine children of yours, well brought up, good manners."

"We think Honoria's a great little girl too."

Marion Peters came back from the kitchen. She was a tall woman with worried eyes who had once possessed a fresh American loveliness. Charlie had never been sensitive to it and was always surprised when people spoke of how pretty she had been. From the first there had been an instinctive antipathy between them.

"Well, how do you find Honoria?" she asked.

"Wonderful. I was astonished how much she's grown in ten months. All the children are looking well."

"We haven't had a doctor for a year. How do you like being back in Paris?"

"It seems very funny to see so few Americans around."

"I'm delighted," Marion said vehemently. "Now at least you can go into a store without their assuming you're a millionaire. We've suffered like everybody, but on the whole it's a good deal pleasanter."

"But it was nice while it lasted," Charlie said. "We were a sort of royalty, almost infallible, with a sort of magic around us. In the bar this afternoon"—he stumbled, seeing his mistake—"there wasn't a man I knew."

She looked at him keenly. "I should think you'd have had enough of bars."

"I only stayed a minute. I take one drink every afternoon and no more."

"Don't you want a cocktail before dinner?" Lincoln asked.

"I take only one drink every afternoon, and I've had that."

"I hope you keep to it," said Marion.

Her dislike was evident in the coldness with which she spoke, but Charlie only smiled—he had larger plans. Her very aggressiveness gave him an advantage, and he knew enough to wait. He wanted them to initiate the discussion of what they knew had brought him to Paris.

At dinner he couldn't decide whether Honoria was most like him or her mother. Fortunate if she didn't combine the traits of both that had brought them to disaster. A great wave of protectiveness went over him. He thought he knew what to do for her. He believed in character; he wanted to jump back a whole generation and trust in character again as the eternally valuable element. Everything wore out.

He left soon after dinner, but not to go home. He was curious to see Paris by night with clearer and more judicious eyes than those of other days. He bought a *strapontin* for the Casino and watched Josephine Baker go through her chocolate arabesques.

After an hour he left and strolled toward Montmartre, up the Rue Pigalle into the Place Blanche. The rain had stopped and there were a few people in evening clothes disembarking from taxis in front of cabarets, and *cocottes* prowling singly or in pairs, and many Negroes. He passed a lighted door from which issued music, and stopped with the sense of familiarity—it was Bricktop's, where he had parted with so many hours and so much money. A few doors farther on he found another ancient rendezvous and incautiously put his head inside. Immediately an eager orchestra burst into sound, a pair of professional dancers leaped to their feet and a *maître d'hôtel* swooped toward him, crying, "Crowd just arriving, sir!" But he withdrew quickly.

"You have to be damn drunk," he thought.

Zelli's was closed; the bleak and sinister cheap hotels surrounding it were dark; up in the Rue Blanche there was more light and a local colloquial French crowd. The Poet's Cave had disappeared, but the two great mouths of the Café of Heaven and the Café of Hell still yawned—even devoured, as he watched, the meagre contents of a tourist bus—a German, a Japanese, and an American couple who glanced at him with frightened eyes.

So much for the effort and ingenuity of Montmartre. All the catering to vice and waste was on an utterly childish scale, and he suddenly realized the meaning of the word "dissipate"—to dissipate into thin air; to make nothing out of something. In the little hours of the night every move from place to place was an enormous human jump, an increase of paying for the privilege of slower and slower motion.

He remembered thousand-franc notes given to an orchestra for playing a single number, hundred-franc notes tossed to a doorman for calling a cab.

But it hadn't been given for nothing.

It had been given, even the most wildly squandered sum, as an offering to destiny that he might not remember the things most worth remembering, the things that now he would always remember—his child taken from his control, his wife escaped to a grave in Vermont.

In the glare of a *brasserie* a woman spoke to him. He bought her some eggs and coffee and then, eluding her encouraging stare, gave her a twenty-franc note and took a taxi to his hotel.

II

He woke upon a fine fall day—football weather. The depression of yesterday was gone and he liked the people on the streets. At noon he sat opposite Honoria at Le Grand-Vatel, the only restaurant he could think of not reminiscent of champagne dinners and long luncheons that began at two and ended in a blurred and vague twilight.

"Now, how about vegetables? Oughtn't you to have some vegetables?"

"Well, yes."

"Here's *épinards* and *chou-fleur* and carrots and *haricots*."

"I'd like *chou-fleur*."

"Wouldn't you like to have two vegetables?"

"I usually only have one at lunch."

The waiter was pretending to be inordinately fond of children. "*Qu'elle est mignonne la petite? Elle parle exactement comme une française.*"

"How about dessert? Shall we wait and see?"

The waiter disappeared. Honoria looked at her father expectantly.

"What are we going to do?"

"First we're going to that toy store in the Rue Saint-Honoré and buy you anything you like. And then we're going to the vaudeville at the Empire."

She hesitated. "I like it about the vaudeville, but not the toy store."

"Why not?"

"Well, you brought me this doll." She had it with her. "And I've got lots of things. And we're not rich anymore, are we?"

"We never were. But today you are to have anything you want."

"All right," she agreed resignedly.

When there had been her mother and a French nurse he had been inclined to be strict; now he extended himself, reached out for a new tolerance; he must be both parents to her and not shut any of her out of communication.

"I want to get to know you," he said gravely. "First let me introduce myself. My name is Charles J. Wales, of Prague."

"Oh, *daddy!*" her voice cracked with laughter.

"And who are you, please?" he persisted, and she accepted a role immediately: "Honoria Wales, Rue Palatine, Paris."

"Married or single?"

"No, not married. Single."

He indicated the doll. "But I see you have a child, madame."

Unwilling to disinherit it, she took it to her heart and thought quickly: "Yes, I've been married, but I'm not married now. My husband is dead."

He went on quickly, "And the child's name?"

"Simone. That's after my best friend at school."

"I'm very pleased that you're doing so well at school."

"I'm third this month," she boasted. "Elsie"—that was her cousin—"is only about eighteenth, and Richard is about at the bottom."

"You like Richard and Elsie, don't you?"

"Oh, yes. I like Richard *quite* well and I like her all right."

Cautiously and casually he asked: "And Aunt Marion and Uncle Lincoln—which do you like best?"

"Oh, Uncle Lincoln, I guess."

He was increasingly aware of her presence. As they came in, a murmur of "... *adorable*" followed them, and now the people at the next table bent all their silences upon her, staring as if she were something no more conscious than a flower.

"Why don't I live with you?" she asked suddenly. "Because mamma's dead?"

"You must stay here and learn more French. It would have been hard for daddy to take care of you so well."

"I don't really need much taking care of anymore. I do everything for myself."

Going out of the restaurant, a man and a woman unexpectedly hailed him.

"Well, the old Wales!"

"Hello there, Lorraine ... Dunc."

Sudden ghosts out of the past—Duncan Schaeffer, a friend from college. Lorraine Quarrles, a lovely pale blonde of thirty; one of a crowd who had helped them make months into days in the lavish times of three years ago.

"My husband couldn't come this year," she said, in answer to his question. "We're poor as hell. So he gave me two hundred a month and told me I could do my worst on that.... This your little girl?"

"What about coming back and sitting down?" Duncan asked.

"Can't do it." He was glad for an excuse. As always, he felt Lorraine's passionate, provocative attraction, but his own rhythm was different now.

"Well, how about dinner?" she asked.

"I'm not free. Give me your address and let me call you."

"Charlie, I believe you're sober," she said judicially. "I honestly believe he's sober, Dunc. Pinch him and see if he's sober."

Charlie indicated Honoria with his head. They both laughed.

"What's your address?" said Duncan skeptically.

He hesitated, unwilling to give the name of his hotel.

"I'm not settled yet. I'd better call you. We're going to see the vaudeville at the Empire."

"There! That's what I want to do," Lorraine said. "I want to see some clowns and acrobats and jugglers. That's just what we'll do, Dunc."

"We've got to do an errand first," said Charlie. "Perhaps we'll see you there."

"All right, you snob.... Good-bye, beautiful little girl."

"Good-bye."

Honoria bobbed politely.

Somehow an unwelcome encounter. They liked him because he was functioning, because he was serious; they wanted to see him because he was stronger than they were now, because they wanted to draw a certain sustenance from his strength.

At the Empire, Honoria proudly refused to sit upon her father's folded coat. She was already an individual with a code of her own, and Charlie was more and more absorbed by the desire of putting a little of himself into her before she crystallized utterly. It was hopeless to try to know her in so short a time.

Between the acts they came upon Duncan and Lorraine in the lobby where the band was playing.

"Have a drink?"

"All right, but not up at the bar. We'll take a table."

"The perfect father."

Listening abstractedly to Lorraine, Charlie watched Honoria's eyes leave their table, and he followed them wistfully about the room, wondering what they saw. He met her glance and she smiled.

"I liked that lemonade," she said.

What had she said? What had he expected? Going home in a taxi afterward, he pulled her over until her head rested against his chest.

"Darling, do you ever think about your mother?"

"Yes, sometimes," she answered vaguely.

"I don't want you to forget her. Have you got a picture of her?"

"Yes, I think so. Anyhow, Aunt Marion has. Why don't you want me to forget her?"

"She loved you very much."

"I loved her too."

They were silent for a moment.

"Daddy, I want to come and live with you," she said suddenly.

His heart leaped—he had wanted it to come like this.

"Aren't you perfectly happy?"

"Yes, but I love you better than anybody. And you love me better than anybody, don't you, now that mummy's dead?"

"Of course I do. But you won't always like me best, honey. You'll grow up and meet somebody your own age and go marry him and forget you ever had a daddy."

"Yes, that's true," she agreed tranquilly.

He didn't go in. He was coming back at nine o'clock and he wanted to keep himself fresh and new for the thing he must say then.

"When you're safe inside, just show yourself in that window."

"All right. Good-bye dads dads dads dads."

He waited in the dark street until she appeared, all warm and glowing, in the window above and kissed her fingers out into the night.

III

They were waiting. Marion sat behind the coffee service in a dignified black dinner dress that just faintly suggested mourning. Lincoln was walking up and down with the animation of one who had already been talking. They were as anxious as he was to get into the question. He opened it almost immediately:

"I suppose you know what I want to see you about—why I really came to Paris."

Marion played with the black stars on her necklace and frowned.

"I'm awfully anxious to have a home," he continued. "And I'm awfully anxious to have Honoria in it. I appreciate your taking in Honoria for her mother's sake, but things have changed now"—he hesitated and then continued more forcibly—"changed radically with me, and I want to ask you to reconsider the matter. It would be silly for me to deny that about three years ago I was acting badly—"

Marion looked up at him with hard eyes.

"—but all that's over. As I told you, I haven't had more than a drink a day for over a year, and I take that drink deliberately, so that the idea of alcohol won't get too big in my imagination. You see the idea?"

"No," said Marion succinctly.

"It's a sort of stunt I set myself. It keeps the matter in proportion—"

"I get you," said Lincoln. "You don't want to admit it's got any attraction for you."

"Something like that. Sometimes I forget and don't take it. But I try to take it. Anyhow I couldn't afford to drink in my position. The people I represent are more than satisfied with what I've done, and I'm bringing my sister over from Burlington to keep house for me—and I want awfully to have Honoria too. You know that even when her mother and I weren't getting along well we never let anything that happened touch Honoria. I know she's fond of me and I know I'm able to take care of her and—well, there you are. How do you feel about it?"

He knew that now he would have to take a beating. It would last an hour or two hours, and it would be difficult, but if he modulated his inevitable resentment to the chastened attitude of the reformed sinner, he might win his point in the end.

Keep your temper, he told himself. You don't want to be justified. You want Honoria.

Lincoln spoke first. "We've been talking it over ever since we got your letter last month. We're happy to have Honoria here. She's a dear little thing, and we're glad to be able to help her, but of course that isn't the question—"

Marion interrupted suddenly. "How long are you going to stay sober, Charlie?" she asked.

"Permanently, I hope."

"How can anybody count on that?"

"You know I never did drink heavily until I gave up business and came over here with nothing to do. Then Helen and I began to run around with—"

"Please leave Helen out of it. I can't bear to hear you talk about her like that."

He stared at her grimly—he had never been certain how fond of each other the sisters were in life.

"My drinking only lasted about a year and a half—from the time we came over until I—collapsed."

"It was time enough."

"It was time enough," he agreed.

"My duty is entirely to Helen," she said. "I try to think what she would have wanted me to do. Frankly, from the night you did that terrible thing you haven't really existed for me. I can't help that. She was my sister."

"Yes."

"When she was dying she asked me to look out for Honoria. If you hadn't been in a sanitarium then, it might have helped matters."

He had no answer.

"I'll never in my life be able to forget the morning when Helen knocked at my door, soaked to the skin and shivering, and said you'd locked her out."

Charlie gripped the sides of the chair. This was more difficult than he expected—he wanted to launch out into a long expostulation and explanation, but he only said: "The night I locked her out—" and she interrupted, "I don't feel up to going over that again."

After a moment's silence Lincoln said: "We're getting off the subject. You want Marion to set aside her legal guardianship and give you Honoria. I think the main point for her is whether she has confidence in you or not."

"I don't blame Marion," Charlie said slowly, "but I think she can have entire confidence in me. I had a good record up to three years ago. Of course it's within human possibilities I might go wrong any time. But if we wait much longer I'll lose Honoria's childhood and my chance for a home." He shook his head, "I'll simply lose her, don't you see?"

"Yes, I see," said Lincoln.

"Why didn't you think of all this before?" Marion asked.

"I suppose I did, from time to time—but Helen and I were getting along badly. When I consented to the guardianship, I was flat on my back in a sanitarium and the market had cleaned me out. I knew I'd acted badly, and I thought if it would bring any peace to Helen, I'd agree to anything. But now it's different. I'm functioning, I'm behaving damn well, so far as—"

"Please don't swear at me," Marion said.

He looked at her, startled. With each remark the force of her dislike became more and more apparent. She had built up all her fear of life into one wall and faced it toward him. This trivial reproof was possibly the result of some trouble with the cook several hours before. Charlie became increasingly alarmed at leaving Honoria in this atmosphere of hostility against himself—sooner or later it would come out, in a word here, a shake of the head there, and some of that distrust would be irrevocably implanted in Honoria. But he pulled his temper down out of his face and shut it up inside him; he had won a point, for Lincoln realized the absurdity of Marion's remark and asked her lightly since when she had objected to the word "damn."

"Another thing," Charlie said: "I'm able to give her certain advantages now. I'm going to take a French governess to Prague with me. I've got a lease on a new apartment—"

He stopped, realizing that he was blundering. They couldn't be expected to accept with equanimity the fact that his income was again twice as large as their own.

"I suppose you can give her more luxuries than we can," said Marion. "When you were throwing away money we were living along watching every ten francs.... I suppose you'll start doing it again."

"Oh, no," he said. "I've learned. I worked hard for ten years, you know—until I got lucky in the market, like so many people. Terribly lucky. It didn't seem any use working any more, so I quit. It won't happen again."

There was a long silence. All of them felt their nerves straining, and for the first time in a year Charlie wanted a drink. He was sure now that Lincoln Peters wanted him to have his child.

Marion shuddered suddenly; part of her saw that Charlie's feet were planted on the earth now, and her own maternal feeling recognized the naturalness of his desire; but she had lived for a long time with a prejudice—a prejudice founded on a curious disbelief in her sister's happiness, and which, in the shock of one terrible night, had turned to hatred for him. It had all happened at a point in her life where the discouragement of ill health and adverse circumstances made it necessary for her to believe in tangible villainy and a tangible villain.

"I can't help what I think!" she cried out suddenly. "How much you were responsible for Helen's death, I don't know. It's something you'll have to square with your own conscience."

An electric current of agony surged through him; for a moment he was almost on his feet, an unuttered sound echoing in his throat. He hung on to himself for a moment, another moment.

"Hold on there," said Lincoln uncomfortably. "I never thought you were responsible for that."

"Helen died of heart trouble," Charlie said dully.

"Yes, heart trouble." Marion spoke as if the phrase had another meaning for her.

Then, in the flatness that followed her outburst, she saw him plainly and she knew he had somehow arrived at control over the situation. Glancing at her husband, she found no help from him, and as abruptly as if it were a matter of no importance, she threw up the sponge.

"Do what you like!" she cried, springing up from her chair. "She's your child. I'm not the person to stand in your way. I think if it were my child I'd rather see her—"She managed to check herself. "You two decide it. I can't stand this. I'm sick. I'm going to bed."

She hurried from the room; after a moment Lincoln said:

"This has been a hard day for her. You know how strongly she feels—" His voice was almost apologetic. "When a woman gets an idea in her head."

"Of course."

"It's going to be all right. I think she sees now that you—can provide for the child, and so we can't very well stand in your way or Honoria's way."

"Thank you, Lincoln."

"I'd better go along and see how she is."

"I'm going."

He was still trembling when he reached the street, but a walk down the Rue Bonaparte to the quais set him up, and as he crossed the Seine, fresh and new by the quai lamps, he felt exultant. But back in his room he couldn't sleep. The image of Helen haunted him. Helen whom he had loved so until they had senselessly begun to abuse each other's love, tear it into shreds. On that terrible February night that Marion remembered so vividly, a slow quarrel had gone on for hours. There was a scene at the Florida, and then he attempted to take her home, and then she kissed young Webb at a table; after that there was what she had hysterically said. When he arrived home alone he turned the key in the lock in wild anger. How could he know she would arrive an hour later alone, that there would be a snowstorm in which she wandered about in slippers, too confused to find a taxi? Then the aftermath, her escaping pneumonia by a miracle, and all the attendant horror. They were "reconciled," but that was the beginning of the end, and Marion, who had seen with her own eyes and who imagined it to be one of many scenes from her sister's martyrdom, never forgot.

Going over it again brought Helen nearer, and in the white soft light that steals upon half sleep near morning he found himself talking to her again. She said that he was perfectly right about Honoria and that she wanted Honoria to be with him. She said she was glad he was being good and doing better. She said a lot of other things—very friendly things—but she was in a swing in a white dress and swinging faster and faster all the time so that at the end he could not hear clearly all that she said.

IV

He woke up feeling happy. The door of the world was open again. He made plans, vistas, futures for Honoria and himself, but suddenly he grew sad, remembering all the plans he and Helen had made. She had not planned to die. The present was the thing—work to do and someone to love. But not to love too much, for he knew the injury that a father can do to a daughter or a mother to a son by attaching them too closely. Afterward, out in the world, the child would seek in the marriage partner the same blind tenderness and, failing probably to find it, turn against love and life.

It was another bright crisp day. He called Lincoln Peters at the bank where he worked and asked if he could count on taking Honoria when he left for Prague. Lincoln agreed that there was no reason for delay. One thing—the legal guardianship. Marion wanted to retain that awhile longer. She was upset by the whole matter, and it would oil things if she felt that the situation was still in her control for another year. Charlie agreed, wanting only the tangible, visible child.

Then the question of a governess. Charlie sat in a gloomy agency and talked to a cross Béarnaise and to a buxom Breton peasant, neither of whom he could have endured. There were others whom he would see tomorrow.

He lunched with Lincoln Peters at Griffons, trying to keep down his exultation.

"There's nothing quite like your own child," Lincoln said. "But you understand how Marion feels too."

"She's forgotten how hard I worked for seven years there," Charlie said. "She just remembers one night."

"There's another thing." Lincoln hesitated. "While you and Helen were tearing around Europe throwing money away, we were just getting along. I didn't touch any of the prosperity because I never got ahead enough to carry anything but my insurance. I think Marion felt there was some kind of injustice in it—you not even working toward the end, and getting richer and richer."

"It went just as quick as it came," said Charlie.

"Yes, a lot of it stayed in the hands of *chasseurs* and saxophone players and *maîtres d'hôtel*—well, the big party's over now. I just said that to explain Marion's feeling about those crazy years. If you drop in about six o'clock tonight before Marion's too tired, we'll settle the details on the spot."

Back at his hotel, Charlie found a *pneumatique* that had been redirected from the Ritz bar where Charlie had left his address for the purpose of finding a certain man.

DEAR CHARLIE:
You were so strange when we saw you the other day that I wondered if I did something to offend you. If so, I'm not conscious of it. In fact, I have thought about you too much for the last year, and it's always been in the back of my mind that I might see you if I came over here. We *did* have such good times that crazy spring, like the night you and I stole the butcher's tricycle, and the time we tried to call on the president and you had the old derby rim and the wire cane. Everybody seems so old lately, but I don't feel old a bit. Couldn't we get together some time today for old time's sake? I've got a vile hangover for the moment, but will be feeling better this afternoon and will look for you about five in the sweat-shop at the Ritz.

Always devotedly,

LORRAINE.

His first feeling was one of awe that he had actually, in his mature years, stolen a tricycle and pedalled Lorraine all over the Étoile between the small hours and dawn. In retrospect it was a nightmare. Locking out Helen didn't fit in with any other act of his life, but the tricycle incident did—it was one of many. How many weeks or months of dissipation to arrive at that condition of utter irresponsibility?

He tried to picture how Lorraine had appeared to him then—very attractive; Helen was unhappy about it, though she said nothing. Yesterday, in the restaurant, Lorraine had seemed trite, blurred, worn away. He emphatically did not want to see her, and he was glad Alix had not given away his hotel address. It was a relief to think, instead, of Honoria, to think of Sundays spent with her and of saying good morning to her and of knowing she was there in his house at night, drawing her breath in the darkness.

At five he took a taxi and bought presents for all the Peters—a piquant cloth doll, a box of Roman soldiers, flowers for Marion, big linen handkerchiefs for Lincoln.

He saw when he arrived in the apartment that Marion had accepted the inevitable. She greeted him now as though he were a recalcitrant member of the family, rather than a menacing outsider. Honoria had been told she was going; Charlie was glad to see that her tact made her conceal her excessive happiness. Only on his lap did she whisper her delight and the question "When?" before she slipped away with the other children.

He and Marion were alone for a minute in the room, and on an impulse he spoke out boldly:

"Family quarrels are bitter things. They don't go according to any rules. They're not like aches or wounds; they're more like splits in the skin that won't heal because there's not enough material. I wish you and I could be on better terms."

"Some things are hard to forget," she answered. "It's a question of confidence." There was no answer to this and presently she asked, "When do you propose to take her?"

"As soon as I can get a governess. I hoped the day after tomorrow."

"That's impossible. I've got to get her things in shape. Not before Saturday."

He yielded. Coming back into the room, Lincoln offered him a drink.

"I'll take my daily whiskey," he said.

It was warm here, it was a home, people together by a fire. The children felt very safe and important; the mother and father were serious, watchful. They had things to do for the children more important than his visit here. A spoonful of medicine was after all more important than the strained relations between Marion and himself. They were not dull people, but they were very much in the grip of life and circumstances. He wondered if he couldn't do something to get Lincoln out of his rut at the bank.

A long peal at the doorbell; the *bonne à tout faire* passed through and went down the corridor. The door opened upon another long ring, and then voices, and the three in the salon looked up expectantly; Lincoln moved to bring the corridor within his range of vision, and Marion rose. Then the maid came back along the corridor, closely followed by the voices, which developed under the light into Duncan Schaeffer and Lorraine Quarrles.

They were gay, they were hilarious, they were roaring with laughter. For a moment Charlie was astounded, unable to understand how they ferreted out the Peters' address.

"Ah-h-h!" Duncan wagged his finger roguishly at Charlie. "Ah-h-h!"

They both slid down another cascade of laughter. Anxious and at a loss, Charlie shook hands with them quickly and presented them to Lincoln and Marion. Marion nodded, scarcely speaking. She had drawn back a step toward the fire; her little girl stood beside her, and Marion put an arm about her shoulder.

With growing annoyance at the intrusion, Charlie waited for them to explain themselves. After some concentration Duncan said:

"We came to invite you out to dinner. Lorraine and I insist that all this shishi, cagy business 'bout your address got to stop."

Charlie came closer to them, as if to force them backward down the corridor.

"Sorry, but I can't. Tell me where you'll be and I'll phone you in half an hour."

This made no impression. Lorraine sat down suddenly on the side of a chair, and focussing her eyes on Richard, cried, "Oh, what a nice little boy! Come here, little boy." Richard glanced at his mother, but did not move. With a perceptible shrug of her shoulders, Lorraine turned back to Charlie:

"Come and dine. Sure your cousins won' mine. See you so sel'om. Or solemn."

"I can't," said Charlie sharply. "You two have dinner and I'll phone you."

Her voice became suddenly unpleasant. "All right, we'll go. But I remember once when you hammered on my door at four A.M. I was enough of a good sport to give you a drink. Come on, Dunc."

Still in slow motion, with blurred, angry faces, with uncertain feet, they retired along the corridor.

"Good-night," Charlie said.

"Good-*night!*" responded Lorraine emphatically.

When he went back into the salon Marion had not moved, only now her son was standing in the circle of her other arm. Lincoln was still swinging Honoria back and forth like a pendulum from side to side.

"What an outrage!" Charlie broke out. "What an absolute outrage!"

Neither of them answered. Charlie dropped into an armchair, picked up his drink, set it down again and said:

"People I haven't seen for two years having the colossal nerve—"

He broke off. Marion had made the sound "Oh!" in one swift, furious breath, turned her body from him with a jerk and left the room.

Lincoln set down Honoria carefully.

"You children go in and start your soup," he said, and when they obeyed, he said to Charlie:

"Marion's not well and she can't stand shocks. That kind of people make her really physically sick."

"I didn't tell them to come here. They wormed your name out of somebody. They deliberately—"

"Well, it's too bad. It doesn't help matters. Excuse me a minute."

Left alone, Charlie sat tense in his chair. In the next room he could hear the children eating, talking in monosyllables, already oblivious to the scene between their elders. He heard a murmur of conversation from a farther room and then the ticking bell of a telephone receiver picked up, and in a panic he moved to the other side of the room and out of earshot.

In a minute Lincoln came back. "Look here, Charlie. I think we'd better call off dinner for tonight. Marion's in bad shape."

"Is she angry with me?"

"Sort of," he said, almost roughly. "She's not strong and—"

"You mean she's changed her mind about Honoria?"

"She's pretty bitter right now. I don't know. You phone me at the bank tomorrow."

"I wish you'd explain to her I never dreamed these people would come here. I'm just as sore as you are."

"I couldn't explain anything to her now."

Charlie got up. He took his coat and hat and started down the corridor. Then he opened the door of the dining room and said in a strange voice, "Good-night, children."

Honoria rose and ran around the table to hug him.

"Good-night, sweetheart," he said vaguely, and then trying to make his voice more tender, trying to conciliate something, "Good-night, dear children."

V

Charlie went directly to the Ritz bar with the furious idea of finding Lorraine and Duncan, but they were not there, and he realized that in any case there was nothing he could do. He had not touched his drink at the Peters', and now he ordered a whisky-and-soda. Paul came over to say hello.

"It's a great change," he said sadly. "We do about half the business we did. So many fellows I hear about back in the States lost everything, maybe not in the first crash, but then in the second. Your friend George Hardt lost every cent, I hear. Are you back in the States?"

"No, I'm in business in Prague."

"I heard that you lost a lot in the crash."

"I did," and he added grimly, "but I lost everything I wanted in the boom."

"Selling short."

"Something like that."

Again the memory of those days swept over him like a nightmare—the people they had met travelling; then people who couldn't add a row of figures or speak a coherent sentence. The little man Helen had consented to dance with at the ship's party, who had insulted her ten feet from the table; the women and girls carried screaming with drink or drugs out of public places—

—The men who locked their wives out in the snow, because the snow of twenty-nine wasn't real snow. If you didn't want it to be snow you just paid some money.

He went to the phone and called the Peters' apartment; Lincoln answered.

"I called up because this thing is on my mind. Has Marion said anything definite?"

"Marion's sick," Lincoln answered shortly. "I know this thing isn't altogether your fault, but I can't have her go to pieces about it. I'm afraid we'll have to let it slide for six months; I can't take the chance of working her up to this state again."

"I see."

"I'm sorry, Charlie."

He went back to his table. His whiskey glass was empty, but he shook his head when Alix looked at it questioningly. There wasn't much he could do now except send Honoria some things; he would send her a lot of things tomorrow. He thought rather angrily that this was just money—he had given so many people money....

"No, no more," he said to another waiter. "What do I owe you?"

He would come back some day—they couldn't make him pay forever. But he wanted his child, and nothing was much good now, beside that fact. He wasn't young anymore, with a lot of nice thoughts and dreams to have by himself. He was absolutely sure Helen wouldn't have wanted him to be so alone.

ADDITIONAL STORIES
December 1928–July 1931

OUTSIDE THE CABINET-MAKER'S

The automobile stopped at the corner of 16th and some dingy-looking street. The lady got out. The man and the little girl stayed in the car.

"I'm going to tell him it can't cost more than twenty dollars," said the lady.

"All right. Have you got the plans?"

"Oh, yes"—she reached for her bag in the back seat—"at least I have now."

"Dites qu'il ne faut pas avoir les forts placards," said the man. "Ni le bon bois."

"All right."

"I wish you wouldn't talk French," said the little girl.

"Et il faut avoir un bon 'height.' L'un des Murphys était comme ça."

He held his hand five feet from the ground. The lady went through a door lettered "Cabinet-Maker" and disappeared up a small stairs.

The man and the little girl looked around unexpectantly. The neighborhood was red brick, vague, quiet. There were a few darkies doing something or other up the street and an occasional automobile went by. It was a fine November day.

"Listen," said the man to the little girl, "I love you."

"I love you too," said the little girl, smiling politely.

"Listen," the man continued. "Do you see that house over the way?"

The little girl looked. It was a flat in back of a shop. Curtains masked most of its interior, but there was a faint stir behind them. On one window a loose shutter banged from back to forth every few minutes. Neither the man nor the little girl had ever seen the place before.

"There's a Fairy Princess behind those curtains," said the man. "You can't see her but she's there, kept concealed by an Ogre. Do you know what an Ogre is?"

"Yes."

"Well, this Princess is very beautiful with long golden hair."

They both regarded the house. Part of a yellow dress appeared momentarily in the window.

"That's her," the man said. "The people who live there are guarding her for the Ogre. He's keeping the King and Queen prisoner ten thousand miles below the earth. She can't get out until the Prince finds the three—" He hesitated.

"And what, daddy? The three what?"

"The three—Look! There she is again."

"The three what?"

"The three—the three stones that will release the King and Queen."

He yawned.

"And what then?"

"Then he can come and tap three times on each window and that will set her free."

The lady's head emerged from the upper story of the cabinet-maker's.

"He's busy," she called down. "Gosh, what a nice day!"

"And what, daddy?" asked the little girl. "Why does the Ogre want to keep her there?"

"Because he wasn't invited to the christening. The Prince has already found one stone in President Coolidge's collar-box. He's looking for the second in Iceland. Every time he finds a stone the room where the Princess is kept turns blue. *Gosh!*"

"What, daddy?"

Just as you turned away I could see the room turn blue. That means he's found the second stone."

"Gosh!" said the little girl. "Look! It turned blue again, that means he's found the third stone."

Aroused by the competition the man looked around cautiously and his voice grew tense.

"Do you see what I see?" he demanded. "Coming up the street—there's the Ogre himself, disguised—you know: transformed, like Mombi in 'The Land of Oz.'"

"I know."

They both watched. The small boy, extraordinarily small and taking very long steps, went to the door of the flat and knocked; no one answered but he didn't seem to expect it or to be greatly disappointed. He took some chalk from his pocket and began drawing pictures under the doorbell.

"He's making magic signs," whispered the man. "He wants to be sure that the Princess doesn't get out this door. He must know that the Prince has set the King and Queen free and will be along for her pretty soon."

The small boy lingered for a moment; then he went to a window and called an unintelligible word. After awhile a woman threw the window open and made an answer that the crisp wind blew away.

"She says she's got the Princess locked up," explained the man.

"Look at the Ogre," said the little girl. "He's making magic signs under the window too. And on the sidewalk. Why?"

"He wants to keep her from getting out, of course. That's why he's dancing. That's a charm too—it's a magic dance."

The Ogre went away, taking very big steps. Two men crossed the street ahead and passed out of sight.

"Who are they, daddy?"

"They're two of the King's soldiers. I think the army must be gathering over on Market Street to surround the house. Do you know what 'surround' means?"

"Yes. Are those men soldiers too?"

"Those too. And I believe that the old one just behind is the King himself. He's keeping bent down low like that so that the Ogre's people won't recognize him."

"Who is the lady?"

"She's a Witch, a friend of the Ogre's."

The shutter blew closed with a bang and then slowly opened again.

"That's done by the good and bad fairies," the man explained. "They're invisible, but the bad fairies want to close the shutter so nobody can see in and the good ones want to open it."

"The good fairies are winning now."

"Yes." He looked at the little girl. "You're my good fairy."

"Yes. Look, daddy! What is that man?"

"He's in the King's army too." The clerk of Mr. Miller, the jeweler, went by with a somewhat unmartial aspect. "Hear the whistle? That means they're gathering. And listen—there goes the drum."

"There's the Queen, daddy. Look at there. Is that the Queen?"

"No, that's a girl called Miss Television." He yawned. He began to think of something pleasant that had happened yesterday. He went into a trance. Then he looked at the little girl and saw that she was quite happy. She was six and lovely to look at. He kissed her.

"That man carrying the cake of ice is also one of the King's soldiers," he said. "He's going to put the ice on the Ogre's head and freeze his brains so he can't do any more harm."

Her eyes followed the man down the street. Other men passed. A darky in a yellow darky's overcoat drove by with a cart marked The Del Upholstery Co. The shutter banged again and then slowly opened.

"See, daddy, the good fairies are winning again."

The man was old enough to know that he would look back to that time—the tranquil street and the pleasant weather and the mystery playing before the child's eyes, mystery which he had created, but whose luster and texture he could never see or touch any more himself. Again he touched his daughter's cheek instead and in payment fitted another small boy and limping man into the story.

"Oh, I love you," he said.

"I know, daddy," she answered, abstractedly. She was staring at the house. For a moment he closed his eyes and tried to see with her but he couldn't see—those ragged blinds were drawn against him forever. There were only the occasional darkies and the small boys and the weather that reminded him of more glamorous mornings in the past.

The lady came out of the cabinet-maker's shop.

"How did it go?" he asked.

"Good. Il dit qu'il a fait les maisons de poupée pour les Du Ponts. Il va le faire."

"Combien?"

"Vingt-cinq. I'm sorry I was so long."

"Look, daddy, there go a lot more soldiers!"

They drove off. When they had gone a few miles the man turned around and said, "We saw the most remarkable thing while you were there." He summarized the episode. "It's too bad we couldn't wait and see the rescue."

"But we did," the child cried. "They had the rescue in the next street. And there's the Ogre's body in that yard there. The King and Queen and Prince were killed and now the Princess is queen."

He had liked his King and Queen and felt that they had been too summarily disposed of.

"You had to have a heroine," he said rather impatiently.

"She'll marry somebody and make him Prince."

They rode on abstractedly. The lady thought about the doll's house, for she had been poor and had never had one as a child; the man thought how he had almost a million dollars and the little girl thought about the odd doings on the dingy street that they had left behind.

THE ROUGH CROSSING

Once on the long covered piers you have come into a ghostly country that is no longer Here and not yet There. Especially at night. There is a hazy yellow vault full of shouting echoing voices. There is the rumble of trucks and the clump of trunks, the strident chatter of a crane and the first salt smell of the sea. You hurry through, even though there's time. The past, the continent, is behind you—the future is that glowing mouth in the side of the ship—this dim turbulent alley is too confusedly the present.

Up the gangplank and the vision of the world adjusts itself, narrows. One is a citizen of a commonwealth smaller than Andorra. One is no longer so sure of anything. Curiously unmoved the men at the purser's desk, cell-like the cabin, disdainful the eyes of voyagers and their friends, solemn the officer who stands on the deserted promenade deck thinking something of his own as he stares at the crowd below. A last odd idea that one didn't really have to come—then the loud mournful whistles, and the thing, certainly not a boat, but rather a human idea, a frame of mind, pushes forth into the big dark night.

Adrian Smith, one of the celebrities on board—not a very great celebrity but important enough to be bathed in flash light by a photographer who had been given his name but wasn't sure what his subject "did"—Adrian Smith and his blonde wife, Eva, went up to the promenade deck, passed the melancholy ship's officer, and finding a quiet aerie put their elbows on the rail.

"We're going!" he cried presently, and they both laughed in ecstasy. "We've escaped. They can't get us now."

"Who?"

He waved his hand vaguely at the civic tiara.

"All those people out there. They'll come with their posses and their warrants and list of crimes we've committed, and ring the bell at 288 Park Avenue and ask for the Adrian Smiths, but what ho! the Adrian Smiths and their children and nurse are off for France."

"You make me think we really have committed crimes."

"They can't have you," he said, frowning. "That's one thing they're after me about—they know I haven't got any right to a person like you, and they're furious. That's one reason I'm glad to get away."

"Darling," said Eva.

She was twenty-six—five years younger than he. She was something precious to everyone who knew her.

"I like this boat better than the *Majestic* or the *Aquitania*," she remarked, unfaithful to the ships that had served their honeymoon.

"It's much smaller."

"But it's very slick and it has all those little shops and things along the corridors. And I think the staterooms are bigger."

"The people are very formal—did you notice?—as if they thought everyone else was a card sharp. And in about four days half of them will be calling the other half by their first names."

Four of the people came by now—a quartet of young girls abreast, making a circuit of the deck. Their eight eyes swept momentarily toward Adrian and Eva and then swept automatically back, save for one pair which lingered for an instant with a little start. They belonged to one of the girls in the middle, who was, indeed, the only passenger of the four. She was not more than eighteen—a dark little beauty with the fine crystal gloss over her that, in brunettes, takes the place of a blonde's bright glow.

"Now, who's that?" wondered Adrian. "I've seen her before."

"She's pretty," said Eva.

"Yes." He kept wondering, and Eva deferred momentarily to his distraction; then, smiling up at him, she drew him back into their privacy.

"Tell me more," she said.

"About what?"

"About us—what a good time we'll have, and how we'll be much better and happier, and very close always."

"How could we be any closer?" His arm pulled her to him.

"But I mean never even quarrel anymore about silly things. You know, I made up my mind when you gave me my birthday present last week"—her fingers caressed the fine seed pearls at her throat—"that I'd try never to say a mean thing to you again."

"You never have, my precious."

Yet even as he strained her against his side she knew that the moment of utter isolation had passed almost before it had begun. His antennæ were already out, feeling over this new world.

"Most of the people look rather awful," he said—"little and swarthy and ugly. Americans didn't use to look like that."

"They look dreary," she agreed. "Let's not get to know anybody, but just stay together."

A gong was beating now, and stewards were shouting down the decks, "Visitors ashore, please!" and voices rose to a strident chorus. For awhile the gangplanks were thronged; then they were empty, and the jostling crowd behind the barrier waved and called unintelligible things, and kept up a grin of good will. As the stevedores began to work at the ropes, a flat-faced, somewhat befuddled young man arrived in a great hurry and was assisted up the gangplank by a porter and a taxi-driver. The ship having swallowed him as impassively as though he were a missionary for Beirut, a low portentous vibration began. The pier with its faces commenced to slide by, and for a moment the boat was just a piece accidentally split off from it; then the faces became remote, voiceless, and the pier was one among many yellow blurs along the water front. Now the harbor flowed swiftly toward the sea.

On a northern parallel of latitude a hurricane was forming and moving south by southeast preceded by a strong west wind. On its course it was destined to swamp the *Peter I. Eudim* of Amsterdam, with a crew of sixty-six, to break a boom on the largest boat in the world, and to bring grief and want to the wives of several hundred seamen. This liner, leaving New York Sunday evening, would enter the zone of the storm Tuesday, and of the hurricane late Wednesday night.

II

Tuesday afternoon Adrian and Eva paid their first visit to the smoking room. This was not in accord with their intentions—they had "never wanted to see a cocktail again" after leaving America—but they had forgotten the staccato loneliness of ships, and such activity as existed centered about the bar. So they went in for just a minute.

It was full. There were those who had been there since lunch, and those who would be there until dinner, not to mention a faithful few who had been there since nine this morning. It was a prosperous assembly, taking its recreation at bridge, solitaire, detective stories, alcohol, argument and love. Up to this point you could have matched it in the club or casino life of any country, but over it all played a repressed nervous energy, a barely disguised impatience that extended to old and young alike. The cruise had begun, and they had enjoyed the beginning, but the show was not varied enough to last six days, and already they wanted it to be over.

At a table near them Adrian saw the pretty girl who had stared at him on the deck the first night. Again he was fascinated by her loveliness; there was no mist upon the brilliant gloss that gleamed through the smoky confusion of the room. He and Eva had decided from the passenger list that she was probably "Miss Elizabeth D'Amido and maid," and he had heard her called Betsy as he walked past a deck-tennis game. Among the young people with her was the flat-nosed youth who had been "poured on board" the night of their departure; yesterday he had walked the deck morosely, but he was apparently reviving. Miss D'Amido whispered something to him, and he looked over at the Smiths with curious eyes. Adrian was new enough at being a celebrity to turn self-consciously away.

"There's a little roll. Do you feel it?" Eva demanded.

"Perhaps we'd better split a pint of champagne."

While he gave the order a short colloquy was taking place at the other table; presently a young man rose and came over to them.

"Isn't this Mr. Adrian Smith?"

"Yes."

"We wondered if we couldn't put you down for the deck-tennis tournament. We're going to have a deck-tennis tournament."

"Why—" Adrian hesitated.

"My name's Stacomb," burst out the young man. "We all know your—your plays or whatever it is, and all that and we wondered if you wouldn't like to come over to our table."

Somewhat overwhelmed, Adrian laughed: Mr. Stacomb, glib, soft, slouching, waited; evidently under the impression that he had delivered himself of a graceful compliment.

Adrian, understanding that too, replied: "Thanks, but perhaps you'd better come over here."

"We've got a bigger table."

"But we're older and more—more settled."

The young man laughed kindly, as if to say, "That's all right."

"Put me down," said Adrian. "How much do I owe you?"

"One buck. Call me Stac."

"Why?" asked Adrian, startled.

"It's shorter."

When he had gone they smiled broadly.

"Heavens," Eva gasped, "I believe they are coming over."

They were. With a great draining of glasses, calling of waiters, shuffling of chairs, three boys and two girls moved to the Smiths' table. If there was any diffidence, it was confined to the hosts; for the new additions gathered around them eagerly, eying Adrian with respect—too much respect—as if to say: "This was probably a mistake and won't be amusing, but maybe we'll get something out of it to help us in our afterlife, like at school."

In a moment Miss D'Amido changed seats with one of the men and placed her radiant self at Adrian's side, looking at him with manifest admiration.

"I fell in love with you the minute I saw you," she said, audibly and without self-consciousness, "so I'll take all the blame for butting in. I've seen your play four times."

Adrian called a waiter to take their orders.

"You see," continued Miss D'Amido, "we're going into a storm, and you might be prostrated the rest of the trip, so I couldn't take any chances."

He saw that there was no undertone or innuendo in what she said, nor the need of any. The words themselves were enough, and the deference with which she neglected the young men and bent her politeness on him was somehow very touching. A little glow went over him—he was having rather more than a pleasant time.

Eva was less entertained; but the flat-nosed young man, whose name was Butterworth, knew people that she did, and that seemed to make the affair less careless and casual. She did not like meeting new people unless they had "something to contribute," and she was often bored by the great streams of them, of all types and conditions and classes, that passed through Adrian's life. She herself "had everything"—which is to say that she was well endowed with talents and with charm—and the mere novelty of people did not seem a sufficient reason for eternally offering everything up to them.

Half an hour later when she rose to go and see the children, she was content that the episode was over. It was colder on deck, with a damp that was almost rain, and there was a perceptible motion. Opening the door of her stateroom she was surprised to find the cabin steward sitting languidly on her bed, his head slumped upon the upright pillow. He looked at her listlessly as she came in but made no move to get up.

"When you've finished your nap you can fetch me a new pillow-case," she said briskly.

Still the man didn't move. She perceived then that his face was green.

"You can't be seasick in here," she announced firmly. "You go and lie down in your own quarters."

"It's me side," he said faintly. He tried to rise, gave out a little rasping sound of pain and sank back again. Eva rang for the stewardess.

A steady pitch—toss—roll had begun in earnest and she felt no sympathy for the steward, but only wanted to get him out as quick as possible. It was outrageous for a member of the crew to be seasick. When the stewardess came in Eva tried to explain this, but now her own head was whirring, and throwing herself on the bed, she covered her eyes.

"It's his fault," she groaned when the man was assisted from the room. "I was all right and it made me sick to look at him. I wish he'd die."

In a few minutes Adrian came in.

"Oh, but I'm sick!" she cried.

"Why, you poor baby." He leaned over and took her in his arms. "Why didn't you tell me?"

"I was all right upstairs, but there was a steward— Oh, I'm too sick to talk."

"You'd better have dinner in bed."

"Dinner! Oh, my heavens!"

He waited solicitously, but she wanted to hear his voice, to have it drown out the complaining sound of the beams.

"Where've you been?"

"Helping to sign up people for the tournament."

"Will they have it if it's like this? Because if they do I'll just lose for you."

He didn't answer; opening her eyes, she saw that he was frowning.

"I didn't know you were going in the doubles," he said.

"Why, that's the only fun."

"I told the D'Amido girl I'd play with her."

"Oh."

"I didn't think. You know I'd much rather play with you."

"Why didn't you, then?" she asked coolly.

"It never occurred to me."

She remembered that on their honeymoon they had been in the finals and won a prize. Years passed. But Adrian never frowned in this regretful way unless he felt a little guilty. He stumbled about, getting his dinner clothes out of the trunk, and she shut her eyes.

When a particularly violent lurch startled her awake again he was dressed and tying his tie. He looked healthy and fresh, and his eyes were bright.

"Well, how about it?" he inquired. "Can you make it, or no?"

"No."

"Can I do anything for you before I go?"

"Where are you going?"

"Meeting those kids in the bar for cocktails. Can I do anything for you?"

"No."

"Darling, I hate to leave you like this."

"Don't be silly. I just want to sleep."

That solicitous frown—when she knew he was crazy to be out and away from the close cabin. She was glad when the door closed. The thing to do was to sleep, sleep...

Up—down—sideways. *Hey* there, not so far! Pull her round the corner there! Now roll her, right—left—*crea-eak! wrench!* swoop!

Some hours later, Eva was dimly conscious of Adrian bending over her. She wanted him to put his arms around her and draw her up out of this dizzy lethargy, but by the time she was fully awake the cabin was empty. He had looked in and gone. When she awoke next the cabin was dark and he was in bed.

The morning was fresh and cool, and the sea was just enough calmer to make Eva think she could get up. They breakfasted in the cabin and with Adrian's help she accomplished an unsatisfactory makeshift toilet and they went up on the boat deck. The tennis tournament had already begun and was furnishing action for a dozen amateur movie cameras, but the majority of passengers were represented by lifeless bundles in deck chairs beside untasted trays.

Adrian and Miss D'Amido played their first match. She was deft and graceful—blatantly well. There was even more warmth behind her ivory skin than there had been the day before. The strolling first officer stopped and talked to her; half a dozen men whom she couldn't have known three days ago called her Betsy. She was already the pretty girl of the voyage, the cynosure of starved ship's eyes.

But after awhile Eva preferred to watch the gulls in the wireless masts and the slow slide of the roll-top sky. Most of the passengers looked silly with their movie cameras that they had all rushed to get and now didn't know what to use for, but the sailors painting the lifeboat stanchions were quiet and beaten and sympathetic, and probably wished, as she did, that the voyage was over.

Butterworth sat down on the deck beside her chair.

"They're operating on one of the stewards this morning. Must be terrible in this sea."

"Operating? What for?" she asked listlessly.

"Appendicitis. They have to operate now because we're going into worse weather. That's why they're having the ship's party tonight."

"Oh, the poor man!" she cried, realizing it must be her steward.

Adrian was showing off now by being very courteous and thoughtful in the game.

"Sorry. Did you hurt yourself?... No, it was my fault.... You better put on your coat right away, pardner, or you'll catch cold."

The match was over and they had won. Flushed and hearty, he came up to Eva's chair.

"How do you feel?"

"Terrible."

"Winners are buying a drink in the bar," he said apologetically.

"I'm coming too," Eva said, but an immediate dizziness made her sink back in her chair.

"You'd better stay here. I'll send you up something."

She felt that his public manner had hardened toward her slightly.

"You'll come back?"

"Oh, right away."

She was alone on the boat deck, save for a solitary ship's officer who slanted obliquely as he paced the bridge. When the cocktail arrived she forced herself to drink it, and felt better. Trying to distract her mind with pleasant things, she reached back to the sanguine talks that she and Adrian had had before sailing. There was the little villa in Brittany, the children learning French—that was all she could think of now—the little villa in Brittany, the children learning French—so she repeated the words over and over to herself until they became as meaningless as the wide white sky. The why of their being here had suddenly eluded her; she felt unmotivated, accidental, and she wanted Adrian to come back quick, all responsive and tender, to reassure her. It was in the hope that there was some secret of graceful living, some real compensation for the lost careless confidence of twenty-one, that they were going to spend a year in France.

The day passed darkly, with fewer people around and a wet sky falling. Suddenly it was five o'clock, and they were all in the bar again, and Mr. Butterworth was telling her about his past. She took a good deal of champagne, but she was seasick dimly through it, as if the illness was her soul trying to struggle up through some thickening incrustation of abnormal life.

"You're my idea of a Greek goddess, physically," Butterworth was saying.

It was pleasant to be Mr. Butterworth's idea of a Greek goddess physically, but where was Adrian? He and Miss D'Amido had gone out on a forward deck to feel the spray. Eva heard herself promising to get out her colors and paint the Eiffel Tower on Butterworth's shirt front for the party tonight.

When Adrian and Betsy D'Amido, soaked with spray, opened the door with difficulty against the driving wind and came into the now-covered security of the promenade deck, they stopped and turned toward each other.

"Well?" she said. But he only stood with his back to the rail, looking at her, afraid to speak. She was silent, too, because she wanted him to be first; so for a moment nothing happened. Then she made a step toward him, and he took her in his arms and kissed her forehead.

"You're just sorry for me, that's all." She began to cry a little. "You're just being kind."

"I feel terribly about it." His voice was taut and trembling.

"Then kiss me."

The deck was empty. He bent over her swiftly.

"No, really kiss me."

He could not remember when anything had felt so young and fresh as her lips. The rain lay like tears shed for him upon the softly shining porcelain cheeks. She was all new and immaculate, and her eyes were wild.

"I love you," she whispered. "I can't help loving you, can I? When I first saw you—oh, not on the boat, but over a year ago—Grace Heally took me to a rehearsal and suddenly you jumped up in the second row and began telling them what to do. I wrote you a letter and tore it up."

"We've got to go."

She was weeping as they walked along the deck. Once more, imprudently, she held up her face to him at the door of her cabin. His blood was beating through him in wild tumult as he walked on to the bar.

He was thankful that Eva scarcely seemed to notice him or to know that he had been gone. After a moment he pretended an interest in what she was doing.

"What's that?"

"She's painting the Eiffel Tower on my shirt front for tonight," explained Butterworth.

"There." Eva laid away her brush and wiped her hands. "How's that?"

"A *chef-d'œuvre*."

Her eyes swept around the watching group, lingered casually upon Adrian.

"You're wet. Go and change."

"You come too."

"I want another champagne cocktail."

"You've had enough. It's time to dress for the party."

Unwilling, she closed her paints and preceded him.

"Stacomb's got a table for nine," he remarked as they walked along the corridor.

"The younger set," she said with unnecessary bitterness. "Oh, the younger set. And you just having the time of your life—with a child."

"You're tight."

"No, I'm not—nor feeble-minded either. What's more I don't think I want to go to the party."

They had a long discussion in the cabin, unpleasant on her part and evasive on his, which ended when the ship gave a sudden gigantic heave, and Eva, the edge worn off her champagne, felt ill again. There was nothing to do but to have a cocktail in the cabin, and after that they decided to go to the party—she believed him now, or she didn't care.

Adrian was ready first—he never wore fancy dress.

"I'll go on up. Don't be long."

"Wait for me, please—it's rocking so."

He sat down on a bed, concealing his impatience.

"You don't mind waiting, do you? I don't want to parade up there all alone."

She was taking a tuck in an oriental costume rented from the barber.

"Ships make people feel crazy," she said. "I think they're awful."

"Yes," he muttered absently.

"When it gets very bad I pretend I'm in the top of a tree, rocking to and fro. But finally I get pretending everything, and finally I have to pretend I'm sane when I know I'm not."

"If you get thinking that way you will go crazy."

"Look, Adrian." She held up the string of pearls before clasping them on. "Aren't they lovely?"

In Adrian's impatience she seemed to move around the cabin like a figure in a slow-motion picture. After a moment he demanded:

"Are you going to be long? It's stifling in here."

"You go on!" she fired up.

"I don't want—"

"Go on. Please! You just make me nervous trying to hurry me."

With a show of reluctance he left her. After a moment's hesitation he went down a flight to a deck below and knocked at a door.

"Betsy."

"Just a minute."

She came out in the corridor attired in a red pea-jacket and trousers borrowed from the elevator boy.

"Do elevator boys have fleas?" she demanded. "I've got everything in the world on under this as a precaution."

"I had to see you," he said quickly.

"Careful," she whispered. "Mrs. Worden, who's supposed to be chaperoning me, is across the way. She's sick."

"I'm sick for you."

They kissed suddenly, clung close together in the narrow corridor, swaying to and fro with the motion of the ship.

"Don't go away," she murmured.

"I've got to. I've—"

Her youth seemed to flow into him, bearing him up into a delicate romantic ecstasy that transcended passion. He couldn't relinquish it—he had discovered something that he had thought was lost with his own youth forever. As he walked along the passage he knew that he had stopped thinking, no longer dared to think.

He met Eva going into the bar.

"Where've you been?" she asked with a strained smile.

"To see about the table."

She was lovely—her cool distinction conquered the trite costume and filled him with a resurgence of approval and pride. They sat down at a table.

The gale was rising hour by hour and the mere traversing of a passage had become a rough matter. In every stateroom trunks were lashed to the washstands, and the *Vestris* disaster was being reviewed in detail by nervous ladies, tossing ill and wretched upon their beds. In the smoking room a stout gentleman had been hurled backward and suffered a badly cut head; and now the lighter chairs and tables were stacked and roped against the wall.

The crowd who had donned fancy dress and were dining together had swollen to about sixteen. The only remaining qualification for membership was the ability to reach the smoking room. They ranged from a Groton-Harvard lawyer to an ungrammatical curb broker they had nicknamed Gyp the Blood, but distinctions had disappeared. For the moment they were samurai, chosen from several hundred for their triumphant resistance to the storm.

The gala dinner, overhung sardonically with lanterns and streamers, was interrupted by great communal slides across the room, precipitate retirements and spilt wine, while the ship roared and complained that under the panoply of a palace it was a ship after all. Upstairs afterward a dozen couples tried to dance, shuffling and galloping here and there in a crazy fandango, thrust around fantastically by a will alien to their own. In view of the condition of tortured hundreds below, there grew to be something indecent about it, like a revel in a house of mourning, and presently there was an egress of the ever-dwindling survivors toward the only haven, the bar.

As the evening passed, Eva's feeling of unreality increased. Adrian had disappeared—presumably with Miss D'Amido—and her mind, distorted by illness and champagne, began to enlarge upon the fact. Annoyance changed slowly to dark and brooding anger, grief to desperation. She had never tried to bind Adrian, never needed to, for they were serious people, with all sorts of mutual interests, and satisfied with each other—but this was a breach of the contract, this was cruel. How could he think that she didn't know?

It seemed several hours later that he leaned over her chair in the bar where she was giving some woman an impassioned lecture upon babies, and said:

"Eva, we'd better turn in."

Her lip curled.

"So that you can leave me there and then come back to your eighteen-year—"

"Be quiet."

"I won't come to bed."

"Very well. Good-night."

More time passed and the people at the table changed. The stewards wanted to close up the room, and thinking of Adrian, her Adrian, off somewhere saying tender things to someone fresh and lovely, Eva began to cry.

"But he's gone to bed," her last attendants assured her. "We saw him go."

She shook her head. She knew better. Adrian was lost. The long seven-year dream was broken. Probably she was punished for something she had done; as this thought occurred to her the shrieking timbers overhead began to mutter that she had guessed at last. This was for the selfishness to her mother, who hadn't wanted her to marry Adrian; for her reluctance to have their second child; for all the sins and omissions of her life. She stood up, saying she must go out and get some air.

The deck was dark and drenched with wind and rain. The ship pounded through valleys, fleeing from black mountains of water that roared toward it. Looking out at the night, Eva saw that there was no chance for them unless she could make atonement, propitiate the storm. It was Adrian's love that was demanded of her. Deliberately she unclasped her pearl necklace, lifted it to her lips—for she knew that with it went the freshest, fairest part of her life—and flung it out into the gale.

III

When Adrian awoke it was lunchtime, but he knew that some heavier sound than the bugle had called him up from his deep sleep. Then he realized that the trunk had broken loose from its lashings and was being thrown back and forth between a wardrobe and Eva's bed. With an exclamation he jumped up, but she was unharmed—still in costume and stretched out in deep sleep. When the steward had helped him secure the trunk, Eva opened a single eye.

"How are you?" he demanded, sitting on the side of her bed.

She closed the eye, opened it again.

"We're in a hurricane now," he told her. "The steward says it's the worst he's seen in twenty years."

"My head," she muttered. "Hold my head."

"How?"

"In front. My eyes are going out. I think I'm dying."

"Nonsense. Do you want the doctor?"

She gave a funny little gasp that frightened him; he rang and sent the steward for the doctor.

The young doctor was pale and tired. There was a stubble of beard upon his face. He bowed curtly as he came in and, turning to Adrian, said with scant ceremony:

"What's the matter?"

"My wife doesn't feel well."

"Well, what is it you want—a bromide?"

A little annoyed by his shortness, Adrian said, "You'd better examine her and see what she needs."

"She needs a bromide," said the doctor. "I've given orders that she is not to have any more to drink on this ship."

"Why not?" demanded Adrian in astonishment.

"Don't you know what happened last night?"

"Why, no—I was asleep."

"Mrs. Smith wandered around the boat for an hour, not knowing what she was doing. A sailor was set to follow her, and then the medical stewardess tried to get her to bed, and your wife insulted her."

"How?" Adrian gasped.

"Some rot about herself being the Duchess of Rutland and the nurse being the rubber heel of the British Empire."

"Oh, my heavens!" cried Eva faintly.

"The nurse and I had both been up all night with Steward Carton, who died this morning." He picked up his case. "I'll send down a bromide for Mrs. Smith. Good-bye."

For a few minutes there was silence in the cabin. Then Adrian put his arm around her quickly.

"Never mind," he said. "We'll straighten it out."

"I remember now." Her voice was an awed whisper. "My pearls. I threw them overboard."

"Threw them overboard!"

"Then I began looking for you."

"But I was here in bed."

"I didn't believe it—I thought you were with that girl."

"She collapsed during dinner. I was taking a nap down here."

Frowning, he rang the bell and asked the steward for lunch and a bottle of beer.

"Sorry, but we can't serve any beer to your cabin, sir."

When he went out Adrian exploded: "This is an outrage. You were simply crazy from that storm and they can't be so high-handed. I'll see the captain."

"Isn't that awful?" Eva murmured. "The poor man died."

She turned over and began to sob into her pillow. There was a knock at the door.

"Can I come in?"

The assiduous Mr. Butterworth, surprisingly healthy and immaculate, came into the crazily tipping cabin.

"Well, how's the mystic?" he demanded of Eva. "Do you remember praying to the elements in the bar last night?"

"I don't want to remember anything about last night."

They told him about the stewardess, and with the telling the situation lightened; they all laughed together.

"I'm going to get you some beer to have with your luncheon," Butterworth said. "You ought to get up on deck."

"Don't go," Eva said. "You look so cheerful and nice."

"Just for ten minutes."

When he had gone, Adrian rang for two baths.

"The thing is to put on our best clothes and walk proudly three times around the deck," he said.

"Yes." After a moment she added abstractedly: "I like that young man. He was awfully nice to me last night—when you'd disappeared."

The bath steward appeared with the information that bathing was too dangerous today. They were in the midst of the wildest hurricane on the North Atlantic in ten years—there were two broken arms this morning from attempts to take baths. An elderly lady had been thrown down a staircase and was not expected to live. Furthermore they had received the S O S signal from several boats this morning.

"Will we go to help them?"

"They're all behind us, sir, so we have to leave them to the *Mauretania*. If we tried to turn in this sea the portholes would be smashed."

This array of calamities minimized their own troubles. Having eaten a sort of lunch and drunk the beer provided by Butterworth, they dressed and went on deck.

Despite the fact that it was only possible to progress step by step, holding to rope or rail, more people were abroad than on the day before. Fear had driven them from their cabins, where the trunks bumped and the waves pounded the portholes and they awaited momentarily the call to the boats. Indeed, as Adrian and Eva stood on the transverse deck above the second class, there was a bugle call, followed by a gathering of stewards and stewardesses on the deck below. But the boat was sound; it had outlasted one of its cargo—Steward James Carton was being buried at sea.

It was very British and sad. There were the rows of stiff disciplined men and women standing in the driving rain, and there was a shape covered by the flag of the Empire that owned and lived by the sea. The chief purser read the service, a hymn was sung, the body slid off into the hurricane. With Eva's burst of wild weeping for this humble end, some last string snapped within her. Now she really didn't care. She responded eagerly when Butterworth suggested that he get some champagne to their cabin. Her mood worried Adrian—she wasn't used to so much drinking and he wondered what he ought to do. At his suggestion that they sleep instead, she merely laughed, and the bromide the doctor had sent stood untouched on the washstand. Pretending to listen to the insipidities of several Mr. Stacombs, he watched her. To his surprise and discomfort she seemed on intimate and even sentimental terms with Butterworth, and he wondered if this was a form of revenge for his attention to Betsy D'Amido.

The cabin was full of smoke, the voices went on incessantly, the suspension of activity, the waiting for the storm's end, was getting on his nerves. They had been at sea only four days. It was like a year.

The two Mr. Stacombs left finally, but Butterworth remained. Eva was urging him to go for another bottle of champagne.

"We've had enough," objected Adrian. "We ought to go to bed."

"I won't go to bed!" she burst out. "You must be crazy! You play around all you want and then when I find somebody I—I like, you want to put me to bed."

"You're hysterical."

"On the contrary, I've never been so sane."

"I think you'd better leave us, Butterworth," Adrian said. "Eva doesn't know what she's saying."

"He won't go. I won't let him go." She clasped Butterworth's hand passionately. "He's the only person that's been half decent to me. I'm in love with him—"

"You'd better go, Butterworth," repeated Adrian.

The young man looked at him uncertainly.

"It seems to me you're being unjust to your wife," he ventured.

"My wife isn't herself."

"That's no reason for bullying her."

Adrian lost his temper. "You get out of here!" he cried.

The two men looked at each other for a moment in silence. Then Butterworth turned to Eva, said, "I'll be back later," and left the cabin.

"Eva, you've got to pull yourself together," said Adrian when the door closed.

She didn't answer, looked at him from sullen half-closed eyes.

"I'll order dinner here for us both and then we'll try to get some sleep."

"I want to go up and send a wireless."

"Who to?"

"Some Paris lawyer. I want a divorce."

In spite of his annoyance, he laughed. "Don't be silly."

"Then I want to see the children."

"Well, go and see them. I'll order dinner."

He waited for her in the cabin twenty minutes. Then impatiently he opened the door across the corridor; the nurse told him that Mrs. Smith had not been there.

With a sudden prescience of disaster he ran upstairs, glanced in the bar, the salons, even knocked at Butterworth's door. Then a quick round of the decks, feeling his way through the black spray and rain. A sailor stopped him at a network of ropes.

"Orders are no one goes by, sir. A wave has gone over the wireless room."

"Have you seen a lady?"

"There was a young lady here—" He stopped and glanced around. "Hello, she's gone."

"She went up the stairs!" Adrian said anxiously. "Up to the wireless room!"

The sailor ran up to the boat deck; stumbling and slipping, Adrian followed. As he cleared the protected sides of the companionway, a tremendous body struck the boat a staggering blow and, as she keeled over to an angle of forty-five degrees, he was thrown in a helpless roll down the drenched deck, to bring up dizzy and bruised against a stanchion.

"Eva!" he called. His voice was soundless in the black storm. Against the faint light of the wireless-room window he saw the sailor making his way forward.

"Eva!"

The wind blew him like a sail up against a lifeboat. Then there was another shuddering crash, and high over his head, over the very boat, he saw a gigantic, glittering white wave, and in the split second that it balanced there he became conscious of Eva, standing beside a ventilator twenty feet away. Pushing out from the stanchion, he lunged desperately toward her, just as the wave broke with a smashing roar. For a moment the rushing water was five feet deep, sweeping with enormous force toward the side, and then a human body was washed against him, and frantically he clutched it and was swept with it back toward the rail. He felt his body bump against it, but desperately he held on to his burden. Then, as the ship rocked slowly back, the two of them, still joined by his fierce grip, were rolled out exhausted on the wet planks. For a moment he knew no more.

IV

Two days later, as the boat train moved tranquilly south toward Paris, Adrian tried to persuade his children to look out the window at the Norman countryside.

"It's beautiful," he assured them. "All the little farms like toys. Why, in heaven's name, won't you look?"

"I like the boat better," said Estelle.

Her parents exchanged an infanticidal glance.

"The boat is still rocking for me," Eva said with a shiver. "Is it for you?"

"No. Somehow, it all seems a long way off. Even the passengers looked unfamiliar going through the customs."

"Most of them hadn't appeared above ground before."

He hesitated. "By the way, I cashed Butterworth's check for him."

"You're a fool. You'll never see the money again."

"He must have needed it pretty badly or he would not have come to me."

A pale and wan girl, passing along the corridor, recognized them and put her head through the doorway.

"How do you feel?"

"Awful."

"Me too," agreed Miss D'Amido. "I'm vainly hoping my fiancé will recognize me at the Gare du Nord. Do you know two waves went over the wireless room?"

"So we heard," Adrian answered dryly.

She passed gracefully along the corridor and out of their life.

"The real truth is that none of it happened," said Adrian after a moment. "It was a nightmare—an incredibly awful nightmare."

"Then, where are my pearls?"

"Darling, there are better pearls in Paris. I'll take the responsibility for those pearls. My real belief is that you saved the boat."

"Adrian, let's never get to know anyone else, but just stay together always—just we two."

He tucked her arm under his and they sat close. "Who do you suppose those Adrian Smiths on the boat were?" he demanded. "It certainly wasn't me."

"Nor me."

"It was two other people," he said, nodding to himself. "There are so many Smiths in this world."

AT YOUR AGE

Tom Squires came into the drug store to buy a toothbrush, a can of talcum, a gargle, Castile soap, Epsom salts and a box of cigars. Having lived alone for many years, he was methodical, and while waiting to be served he held the list in his hand. It was Christmas week and Minneapolis was under two feet of exhilarating, constantly refreshed snow; with his cane Tom knocked two clean crusts of it from his overshoes. Then, looking up, he saw the blonde girl.

She was a rare blonde, even in that Promised Land of Scandinavians, where pretty blondes are not rare. There was warm color in her cheeks, lips and pink little hands that folded powders into papers; her hair, in long braids twisted about her head, was shining and alive. She seemed to Tom suddenly the cleanest person he knew of, and he caught his breath as he stepped forward and looked into her grey eyes.

"A can of talcum."

"What kind?"

"Any kind. . . . That's fine."

She looked back at him apparently without self-consciousness, and, as the list melted away, his heart raced with it wildly.

"I am not old," he wanted to say. "At fifty I'm younger than most men of forty. Don't I interest you at all?"

But she only said, "What kind of gargle?"

And he answered, "What can you recommend? . . . That's fine."

Almost painfully he took his eyes from her, went out and got into his coupé.

"If that young idiot only knew what an old imbecile like me could do for her," he thought humorously—"what worlds I could open out to her!"

As he drove away into the winter twilight he followed this train of thought to a totally unprecedented conclusion. Perhaps the time of day was the responsible stimulant, for the shop windows glowing into the cold, the tinkling bells of a delivery sleigh, the white gloss left by shovels on the sidewalks, the enormous distance of the stars, brought back the feel of other nights thirty years ago. For an instant the girls he had known then slipped like phantoms out of their dull matronly selves of today and fluttered past him with frosty, seductive laughter, until a pleasant shiver crawled up his spine.

"Youth! Youth! Youth!" he apostrophized with conscious lack of originality, and, as a somewhat ruthless and domineering man of no morals whatsoever, he considered going back to the drug store to seek the blonde girl's address. It was not his sort of thing, so the half-formed intention passed; the idea remained.

"Youth, by heaven—youth!" he repeated under his breath. "I want it near me, all around me, just once more before I'm too old to care."

He was tall, lean and handsome, with the ruddy, bronzed face of a sportsman and a just faintly greying mustache. Once he had been among the city's best beaus, organizer of cotillions and charity balls, popular with men and women, and with several generations of them. After the war he had suddenly felt poor, gone into business, and in ten years accumulated nearly a million dollars. Tom Squires was not introspective, but he perceived now that the wheel of his life had revolved again, bringing up forgotten, yet familiar, dreams and yearnings. Entering his house, he turned suddenly to a pile of disregarded invitations to see whether or not he had been bidden to a dance tonight.

Throughout his dinner, which he ate alone at the Downtown Club, his eyes were half closed and on his face was a faint smile. He was practicing so that he would be able to laugh at himself painlessly, if necessary.

"I don't even know what they talk about," he admitted. "They pet—prominent broker goes to petting party with debutante. What is a petting party? Do they serve refreshments? Will I have to learn to play a saxophone?"

These matters, lately as remote as China in a newsreel, came alive to him. They were serious questions. At ten o'clock he walked up the steps of the College Club to a private dance with the same sense of entering a new world as when he had gone into a training camp back in '17. He spoke to a hostess of his generation and to her daughter, overwhelmingly of another, and sat down in a corner to acclimate himself.

He was not alone long. A silly young man named Leland Jaques, who lived across the street from Tom, remarked him kindly and came over to brighten his life. He was such an exceedingly fatuous young man that, for a moment, Tom was annoyed, but he perceived craftily that he might be of service.

"Hello, Mr. Squires. How are you, sir?"

"Fine, thanks, Leland. Quite a dance."

As one man of the world with another, Mr. Jaques sat, or lay, down on the couch and lit—or so it seemed to Tom—three or four cigarettes at once.

"You should of been here last night, Mr. Squires. Oh, boy, that was a party and a half! The Caulkins. Hap-past five!"

"Who's that girl who changes partners every minute?" Tom asked. . . . "No, the one in white passing the door."

"That's Annie Lorry."

"Arthur Lorry's daughter?"

"Yes."

"She seems popular."

"About the most popular girl in town—anyway, at a dance."

"Not popular except at dances?"

"Oh, sure, but she hangs around with Randy Cambell all the time."

"What Cambell?"

"D. B."

There were new names in town in the last decade.

"It's a boy-and-girl affair." Pleased with this phrase, Jaques tried to repeat it: "One of those boy-and-girls affair—boys-and-girl affairs—" He gave it up and lit several more cigarettes, crushing out the first series on Tom's lap.

"Does she drink?"

"Not especially. At least I never saw her passed out. . . . That's Randy Cambell just cut in on her now."

They were a nice couple. Her beauty sparkled bright against his strong, tall form, and they floated hoveringly, delicately, like two people in a nice, amusing dream. They came near and Tom admired the faint dust of powder over her freshness, the guarded sweetness of her smile, the fragility of her body calculated by Nature to a millimeter to suggest a bud, yet guarantee a flower. Her innocent, passionate eyes were brown, perhaps; but almost violet in the silver light.

"Is she out this year?"

"Who?"

"Miss Lorry."

"Yes."

Although the girl's loveliness interested Tom, he was unable to picture himself as one of the attentive, grateful queue that pursued her around the room. Better meet her when the holidays were over and most of these young men were back in college "where they belonged." Tom Squires was old enough to wait.

He waited a fortnight while the city sank into the endless northern mid-winter, where grey skies were friendlier than metallic blue skies, and dusk, whose lights were a reassuring glimpse into the continuity of human cheer, was warmer than the afternoons of bloodless sunshine. The coat of snow lost its press and became soiled and shabby, and ruts froze in the street; some of the big houses on Crest Avenue began to close as their occupants went South. In those cold days Tom asked Annie and her parents to go as his guests to the last Bachelors' Ball.

The Lorrys were an old family in Minneapolis, grown a little harassed and poor since the war. Mrs. Lorry, a contemporary of Tom's, was not surprised that he should send mother and daughter orchids and dine them luxuriously in his apartment on fresh caviar, quail and champagne. Annie saw him only dimly—he lacked vividness, as the old do for the young—but she perceived his interest in her and performed for him the traditional ritual of young beauty—smiles, polite, wide-eyed attention, a profile held obligingly in this light or in that. At the ball he danced with her twice, and, though she was teased about it, she was flattered that such a man of the world—he had become that instead of a mere old man—had singled her out. She accepted his invitation to the symphony the following week, with the idea that it would be uncouth to refuse.

There were several "nice invitations" like that. Sitting beside him, she dozed in the warm shadow of Brahms and thought of Randy Cambell and other romantic nebulosities who might appear tomorrow. Feeling casually mellow one afternoon, she deliberately provoked Tom to kiss her on the way home, but she wanted to laugh when he took her hands and told her fervently he was falling in love.

"But how could you?" she protested. "Really, you musn't say such crazy things. I won't go out with you anymore, and then you'll be sorry."

A few days later her mother spoke to her as Tom waited outside in his car:

"Who's that, Annie?"

"Mr. Squires."

"Shut the door a minute. You're seeing him quite a bit."

"Why not?"

"Well, dear, he's fifty years old."

"But, mother, there's hardly anybody else in town."

"But you musn't get any silly ideas about him."

"Don't worry. Actually, he bores me to extinction most of the time." She came to a sudden decision: "I'm not going to see him anymore. I just couldn't get out of going with him this afternoon."

And that night, as she stood by her door in the circle of Randy Cambell's arm, Tom and his single kiss had no existence for her.

"Oh, I do love you so," Randy whispered. "Kiss me once more."

Their cool cheeks and warm lips met in the crisp darkness, and, watching the icy moon over his shoulder, Annie knew that she was his surely and, pulling his face down, kissed him again, trembling with emotion.

"When'll you marry me then?" he whispered.

"When can you—we afford it?"

"Couldn't you announce our engagement? If you knew the misery of having you out with somebody else and then making love to you."

"Oh, Randy, you ask so much."

"It's so awful to say good-night. Can't I come in for a minute?"

"Yes."

Sitting close together in a trance before the flickering, lessening fire, they were oblivious that their common fate was being coolly weighed by a man of fifty who lay in a hot bath some blocks away.

II

Tom Squires had guessed from Annie's extremely kind and detached manner of the afternoon that he had failed to interest her. He had promised himself that in such an eventuality he would drop the matter, but now he found himself in no such humor. He did not want to marry her; he simply wanted to see her and be with her a little; and up to the moment of her sweetly casual, half passionate, yet wholly unemotional kiss, giving her up would have been easy, for he was past the romantic age; but since that kiss the thought of her made his heart move up a few inches in his chest and beat there steady and fast.

"But this is the time to get out," he said to himself. "My age; no possible right to force myself into her life."

He rubbed himself dry, brushed his hair before the mirror, and, as he laid down the comb, said decisively: "That is that." And after reading for an hour he turned out the lamp with a snap and repeated aloud: "That is that."

In other words, that was not that at all, and the click of material things did not finish off Annie Lorry as a business decision might be settled by the tap of a pencil on the table.

"I'm going to carry this matter a little further," he said to himself about half-past four; on that acknowledgment he turned over and found sleep.

In the morning she had receded somewhat, but by four o'clock in the afternoon she was all around him—the phone was for calling her, a woman's footfalls passing his office were her footfalls, the snow outside the window was blowing, perhaps, against her rosy face.

"There is always the little plan I thought of last night," he said to himself. "In ten years I'll be sixty, and then no youth, no beauty for me ever anymore."

In a sort of panic he took a sheet of note paper and composed a carefully phrased letter to Annie's mother, asking permission to pay court to her daughter. He took it himself into the hall, but before the letter slide he tore it up and dropped the pieces in a cuspidor.

"I couldn't do such an underhand trick," he told himself, "at my age." But this self-congratulation was premature, for he rewrote the letter and mailed it before he left his office that night.

Next day the reply he had counted on arrived—he could have guessed its very words in advance. It was a curt and indignant refusal.

It ended:

I think it best that you and my daughter meet no more.

Very Sincerely Yours,

MABLE TOLLMAN LORRY.

"And now," Tom thought coolly, "we'll see what the girl says to that." He wrote a note to Annie. Her mother's letter had surprised him, it said, but perhaps it was best that they should meet no more, in view of her mother's attitude.

By return post came Annie's defiant answer to her mother's fiat: "This isn't the Dark Ages. I'll see you whenever I like." She named a rendezvous for the following afternoon. Her mother's shortsightedness brought about what he had failed to achieve directly; for where Annie had been on the point of dropping him, she was now determined to do nothing of the sort. And the secrecy engendered by disapproval at home simply contributed the missing excitement. As February hardened into deep, solemn, interminable winter, she met him frequently and on a new basis. Sometimes they drove over to St. Paul to see a picture or to have dinner; sometimes they parked far out on a boulevard in his coupé, while the bitter sleet glazed the windshield to opacity and furred his lamps with ermine. Often he brought along something special to drink—enough to make her gay, but, carefully, never more; for mingled with his other emotions about her was something paternally concerned.

Laying his cards on the table, he told her that it was her mother who had unwittingly pushed her toward him, but Annie only laughed at his duplicity.

She was having a better time with him than with anyone else she had ever known. In place of the selfish exigency of a younger man, he showed her a never-failing consideration. What if his eyes were tired, his cheeks a little leathery and veined, if his will was masculine and strong. Moreover, his experience was a window looking out upon a wider, richer world; and with Randy Cambell next day she would feel less taken care of, less valued, less rare.

It was Tom now who was vaguely discontented. He had what he wanted—her youth at his side—and he felt that anything further would be a mistake. His liberty was precious to him and he could offer her only a dozen years before he would be old, but she had become something precious to him and he perceived that drifting wasn't fair. Then one day late in February the matter was decided out of hand.

They had ridden home from St. Paul and dropped into the College Club for tea, breaking together through the drifts that masked the walk and rimmed the door. It was a revolving door; a young man came around in it, and stepping into his space, they smelt onions and whisky. The door revolved again after them, and he was back within, facing them. It was Randy Cambell; his face was flushed, his eyes dull and hard.

"Hello, beautiful," he said, approaching Annie.

"Don't come so close," she protested lightly. "You smell of onions."

"You're particular all of a sudden."

"Always. I'm always particular." Annie made a slight movement back toward Tom.

"Not always," said Randy unpleasantly. Then, with increased emphasis and a fractional glance at Tom: "Not always." With his remark he seemed to join the hostile world outside. "And I'll just give you a tip," he continued: "Your mother's inside."

The jealous ill-temper of another generation reached Tom only faintly, like the protest of a child, but at this impertinent warning he bristled with annoyance.

"Come on, Annie," he said brusquely. "We'll go in."

With her glance uneasily averted from Randy, Annie followed Tom into the big room.

It was sparsely populated; three middle-aged women sat near the fire. Momentarily Annie drew back, then she walked toward them.

"Hello, mother... Mrs. Trumble ... Aunt Caroline."

The two latter responded; Mrs. Trumble even nodded faintly at Tom. But Annie's mother got to her feet without a word, her eyes frozen, her mouth drawn. For a moment she stood staring at her daughter; then she turned abruptly and left the room.

Tom and Annie found a table across the room.

"Wasn't she terrible?" said Annie, breathing aloud. He didn't answer.

"For three days she hasn't spoken to me." Suddenly she broke out: "Oh, people can be so small! I was going to sing the leading part in the Junior League show, and yesterday Cousin Mary Betts, the president, came to me and said I couldn't."

"Why not?"

"Because a representative Junior League girl mustn't defy her mother. As if I were a naughty child!"

Tom stared on at a row of cups on the mantelpiece—two or three of them bore his name. "Perhaps she was right," he said suddenly. "When I begin to do harm to you it's time to stop."

"What do you mean?"

At her shocked voice his heart poured a warm liquid forth into his body, but he answered quietly: "You remember I told you I was going South? Well, I'm going tomorrow."

There was an argument, but he had made up his mind. At the station next evening she wept and clung to him.

"Thank you for the happiest month I've had in years," he said.

"But you'll come back, Tom."

"I'll be two months in Mexico; then I'm going East for a few weeks."

He tried to sound fortunate, but the frozen city he was leaving seemed to be in blossom. Her frozen breath was a flower on the air, and his heart sank as he realized that some young man was waiting outside to take her home in a car hung with blooms.

"Good-bye, Annie. Good-bye, sweet!"

Two days later he spent the morning in Houston with Hal Meigs, a classmate at Yale.

"You're in luck for such an old fella," said Meigs at luncheon, "because I'm going to introduce you to the cutest little travelling companion you ever saw, who's going all the way to Mexico City."

The lady in question was frankly pleased to learn at the station that she was not returning alone. She and Tom dined together on the train and later played rummy for an hour; but when, at ten o'clock, standing in the door of the stateroom, she turned back to him suddenly with a certain look, frank and unmistakable, and stood there holding that look for a long moment, Tom Squires was suddenly in the grip of an emotion that was not the one in question. He wanted desperately to see Annie, call her for a second on the phone, and then fall asleep, knowing she was young and pure as a star, and safe in bed.

"Good-night," he said, trying to keep any repulsion out of his voice.

"Oh! Good-night."

Arriving in El Paso next day, he drove over the border to Juarez. It was bright and hot, and after leaving his bags at the station he went into a bar for an iced drink; as he sipped it a girl's voice addressed him thickly from the table behind:

"You'n American?"

He had noticed her slumped forward on her elbows as he came in; now, turning, he faced a young girl of about seventeen, obviously drunk, yet with gentility in her unsteady, sprawling voice. The American bartender leaned confidentially forward.

"I don't know what to do about her," he said. "She come in about three o'clock with two young fellows—one of them her sweetie. They had a fight and the men went off, and this one's been here ever since."

A spasm of distaste passed over Tom—the rules of his generation were outraged and defied. That an American girl should be drunk and deserted in a tough foreign town—that such things happened, might happen to Annie. He looked at his watch, hesitated.

"Has she got a bill?" he asked.

"She owes for five gins. But suppose her boyfriends come back?"

"Tell them she's at the Roosevelt Hotel in El Paso."

Approaching, he put his hand on her shoulder. She looked up.

"You look like Santa Claus," she said vaguely. "You couldn't possibly be Santa Claus, could you?"

"I'm going to take you to El Paso."

"Well," she considered, "you look perfectly safe to me."

She was so young—a drenched little rose. He could have wept for her wretched unconsciousness of the old facts, the old penalties of life. Jousting at nothing in an empty tilt yard with a shaking spear. The taxi moved too slowly through the suddenly poisonous night.

Having explained things to a reluctant night clerk, he went out and found a telegraph office.

"Have given up Mexican trip," he wired. "Leaving here tonight. Please meet train in the St. Paul station at three o'clock and ride with me to Minneapolis, as I can't spare you for another minute. All my love."

He could at least keep an eye on her, advise her, see what she did with her life. That silly mother of hers!

On the train, as the baked tropical lands and green fields fell away and the North swept near again with patches of snow, then fields of it, fierce winds in the vestibule and bleak, hibernating farms, he paced the corridors with intolerable restlessness. When they drew into the St. Paul station he swung himself off like a young man and searched the platform eagerly, but his eyes failed to find her. He had counted on those few minutes between the cities; they had become a symbol of her fidelity to their friendship, and as the train started again he searched it desperately from smoker to observation car. But he could not find her, and now he knew that he was mad for her; at the thought that she had taken his advice and plunged into affairs with other men, he grew weak with fear.

Drawing into Minneapolis, his hands fumbled so that he must call the porter to fasten his baggage. Then there was an interminable wait in the corridor while the baggage was taken off and he was pressed up against a girl in a squirrel-trimmed coat.

"Tom!"

"Well, I'll be—"

Her arms went up around his neck. "But, Tom," she cried, "I've been right here in this car since St. Paul!"

His cane fell in the corridor, he drew her very tenderly close and their lips met like starved hearts.

III

The new intimacy of their definite engagement brought Tom a feeling of young happiness. He awoke on winter mornings with the sense of undeserved joy hovering in the room; meeting young men, he found himself matching the vigor of his mind and body against theirs. Suddenly his life had a purpose and a background; he felt rounded and complete. On grey March afternoons when she wandered familiarly in his apartment, the warm sureties of his youth flooded back—ecstasy and poignancy, the mortal and the eternal posed in their immemorially tragic juxtaposition and, a little astounded, he found himself relishing the very terminology of young romance. But he was more thoughtful than a younger lover; and to Annie he seemed to "know everything," to stand holding open the gates for her passage into the truly golden world.

"We'll go to Europe first," he said.

"Oh, we'll go there a lot, won't we? Let's spend our winters in Italy and the spring in Paris."

"But, little Annie, there's business."

"Well, we'll stay away as much as we can anyhow. I hate Minneapolis."

"Oh, no." He was a little shocked. "Minneapolis is all right."

"When you're here it's all right."

Mrs. Lorry yielded at length to the inevitable. With ill grace she acknowledged the engagement, asking only that the marriage should not take place until fall.

"Such a long time," Annie sighed.

"After all, I'm your mother. It's so little to ask."

It was a long winter, even in a land of long winters. March was full of billowy drifts, and when it seemed at last as though the cold must be defeated, there was a series of blizzards, desperate as last stands. The people waited; their first energy to resist was spent, and man, like weather, simply hung on. There was less to do now and the general restlessness was expressed by surliness in daily contacts. Then, early in April, with a long sigh the ice cracked, the snow ran into the ground and the green, eager spring broke up through.

One day, riding along a slushy road in a fresh, damp breeze with a little starved, smothered grass in it, Annie began to cry. Sometimes she cried for nothing, but this time Tom suddenly stopped the car and put his arm around her.

"Why do you cry like that? Are you unhappy?"

"Oh, no, no!" she protested.

"But you cried yesterday the same way. And you wouldn't tell me why. You must always tell me."

"Nothing, except the spring. It smells so good, and it always has so many sad thoughts and memories in it."

"It's our spring, my sweetheart," he said. "Annie, don't let's wait. Let's be married in June."

"I promised mother, but if you like we can announce our engagement in June."

The spring came fast now. The sidewalks were damp, then dry, and the children roller-skated on them and boys played baseball in the soft, vacant lots. Tom got up elaborate picnics of Annie's contemporaries and encouraged her to play golf and tennis with them. Abruptly, with a final, triumphant lurch of Nature, it was full summer.

On a lovely May evening Tom came up the Lorrys' walk and sat down beside Annie's mother on the porch.

"It's so pleasant," he said, "I thought Annie and I would walk instead of driving this evening. I want to show her the funny old house I was born in."

"On Chambers Street, wasn't it? Annie'll be home in a few minutes. She went riding with some young people after dinner."

"Yes, on Chambers Street."

He looked at his watch presently, hoping Annie would come while it was still light enough to see. Quarter of nine. He frowned. She had kept him waiting the night before, kept him waiting an hour yesterday afternoon.

"If I was twenty-one," he said to himself, "I'd make scenes and we'd both be miserable."

He and Mrs. Lorry talked; the warmth of the night precipitated the vague evening lassitude of the fifties and softened them both, and for the first time since his attentions to Annie began, there was no unfriendliness between them. By and by long silences fell, broken only by the scratch of a match or the creak of her swinging settee. When Mr. Lorry came home Tom threw away his second cigar in surprise and looked at his watch; it was after ten.

"Annie's late," Mrs. Lorry said.

"I hope there's nothing wrong," said Tom anxiously. "Who is she with?"

"There were four when they started out. Randy Cambell and another couple—I didn't notice who. They were only going for a soda."

"I hope there hasn't been any trouble. Perhaps—Do you think I ought to go and see?"

"Ten isn't late nowadays. You'll find—" Remembering that Tom Squires was marrying Annie, not adopting her, she kept herself from adding: "You'll get used to it."

Her husband excused himself and went up to bed, and the conversation became more forced and desultory. When the church clock over the way struck eleven they both broke off and listened to the beats. Twenty minutes later, just as Tom impatiently crushed out his last cigar, an automobile drifted down the street and came to rest in front of the door.

For a minute no one moved on the porch or in the auto. Then Annie, with a hat in her hand, got out and came quickly up the walk. Defying the tranquil night, the car snorted away.

"Oh, hello!" she cried. "I'm so sorry! What time is it? Am I terribly late?"

Tom didn't answer. The street lamp threw wine color upon her face and expressed with a shadow the heightened flush of her cheek. Her dress was crushed, her hair was in brief, expressive disarray. But it was the strange little break in her voice that made him afraid to speak, made him turn his eyes aside.

"What happened?" Mrs. Lorry asked casually.

"Oh, a blow-out and something wrong with the engine—and we lost our way. Is it terribly late?"

And then, as she stood before them, her hat still in her hand, her breast rising and falling a little, her eyes wide and bright, Tom realized with a shock that he and her mother were people of the same age looking at a person of another. Try as he might, he could not separate himself from Mrs. Lorry. When she excused herself he suppressed a frantic tendency to say, "But why should you go now? After sitting here all evening?"

They were alone. Annie came up to him and pressed his hand. He had never been so conscious of her beauty; her damp hands were touched with dew.

"You were out with young Cambell," he said.

"Yes. Oh, don't be mad. I feel—I feel so upset tonight."

"Upset?"

She sat down, whimpering a little.

"I couldn't help it. Please don't be mad. He wanted so for me to take a ride with him and it was such a wonderful night, so I went just for an hour. And we began talking and I didn't realize the time. I felt so sorry for him."

"How do you think I felt?" He scorned himself, but it was said now.

"Don't, Tom. I told you I was terribly upset. I want to go to bed."

"I understand. Good-night, Annie."

"Oh, please don't act that way, Tom. Can't you understand?"

But he could, and that was just the trouble. With the courteous bow of another generation, he walked down the steps and off into the obliterating moonlight. In a moment he was just a shadow passing the street lamps and then a faint footfall up the street.

IV

All through that summer he often walked abroad in the evenings. He liked to stand for a minute in front of the house where he was born, and then in front of another house where he had been a little boy. On his customary routes there were other sharp landmarks of the nineties, converted habitats of gayeties that no longer existed—the shell of Jansen's Livery Stables and the old Nushka Rink, where every winter his father had curled on the well-kept ice.

"And it's a darn pity," he would mutter. "A darn pity."

He had a tendency, too, to walk past the lights of a certain drug store, because it seemed to him that it had contained the seed of another and nearer branch of the past. Once he went in, and inquiring casually about the blonde clerk, found that she had married and departed several months before. He obtained her name and on an impulse sent her a wedding present "from a dumb admirer," for he felt he owed something to her for his happiness and pain. He had lost the battle against youth and spring, and with his grief paid the penalty for age's unforgivable sin—refusing to die. But he could not have walked down wasted into the darkness without being used up a little; what he had wanted, after all, was only to break his strong old heart. Conflict itself has a value beyond victory and defeat, and those three months—he had them forever.

THE SWIMMERS

In the Place Benoît, a suspended mass of gasoline exhaust cooked slowly in the June sun. It was a terrible thing, for, unlike pure heat, it held no promise of rural escape, but suggested only roads choked with the same foul asthma. In the offices of The Promissory Trust Company, Paris Branch, facing the square, an American man of thirty-five inhaled it, and it became the odor of the thing he must presently do. A black horror suddenly descended upon him, and he went up to the washroom, where he stood, trembling a little, just inside the door.

Through the washroom window his eyes fell upon a sign—100,000 Chemises. The shirts in question filled the shop window, piled, cravated and stuffed, or else draped with shoddy grace on the show-case floor. 100,000 Chemises—Count them! To the left he read Papeterie, Pâtisserie, Solde, Réclame, and Constance Talmadge in *Déjeuner de Soleil*; and his eye, escaping to the right, met yet more somber announcements: Vêtements Ecclésiastiques, Déclaration de Décès, and Pompes Funèbres. Life and Death.

Henry Marston's trembling became a shaking; it would be pleasant if this were the end and nothing more need be done, he thought, and with a certain hope he sat down on a stool. But it is seldom really the end, and after awhile, as he became too exhausted to care, the shaking stopped and he was better. Going downstairs, looking as alert and self-possessed as any other officer of the bank, he spoke to two clients he knew, and set his face grimly toward noon.

"Well, Henry Clay Marston!" A handsome old man shook hands with him and took the chair beside his desk.

"Henry, I want to see you in regard to what we talked about the other night. How about lunch? In that green little place with all the trees."

"Not lunch, Judge Waterbury; I've got an engagement."

"I'll talk now, then; because I'm leaving this afternoon. What do these plutocrats give you for looking important around here?"

Henry Marston knew what was coming.

"Ten thousand and certain expense money," he answered.

"How would you like to come back to Richmond at about double that? You've been over here eight years and you don't know the opportunities you're missing. Why both my boys—"

Henry listened appreciatively, but this morning he couldn't concentrate on the matter. He spoke vaguely about being able to live more comfortably in Paris and restrained himself from stating his frank opinion upon existence at home.

Judge Waterbury beckoned to a tall pale man who stood at the mail desk.

"This is Mr. Wiese," he said. "Mr. Wiese's from downstate; he's a halfway partner of mine."

"Glad to meet you, suh." Mr. Wiese's voice was rather too deliberately Southern. "Understand the judge is makin' you a proposition."

"Yes," Henry answered briefly. He recognized and detested the type—the prosperous sweater, presumably evolved from a cross between carpetbagger and poor white. When Wiese moved away, the judge said almost apologetically:

"He's one of the richest men in the South, Henry." Then, after a pause: "Come home, boy."

"I'll think it over, judge." For a moment the grey and ruddy head seemed so kind; then it faded back into something one-dimensional, machine-finished, blandly and bleakly un-European. Henry Marston respected that open kindness—in the bank he touched it with daily appreciation, as a curator in a museum might touch a precious object removed in time and space; but there was no help in it for him; the questions which Henry Marston's life propounded could be answered only in France. His seven generations of Virginia ancestors were definitely behind him every day at noon when he turned home.

Home was a fine high-ceiling apartment hewn from the palace of a Renaissance cardinal in the Rue Monsieur—the sort of thing Henry could not have afforded in America. Choupette, with something more than the rigid traditionalism of a French bourgeois taste, had made it beautiful, and moved through gracefully with their children. She was a frail Latin blonde with fine large features and vividly sad French eyes that had first fascinated Henry in a Grenoble *pension* in 1918. The two boys took their looks from Henry, voted the handsomest man at the University of Virginia a few years before the war.

Climbing the two broad flights of stairs, Henry stood panting a moment in the outside hall. It was quiet and cool here, and yet it was vaguely like the terrible thing that was going to happen. He heard a clock inside his apartment strike one, and inserted his key in the door.

The maid who had been in Choupette's family for thirty years stood before him, her mouth open in the utterance of a truncated sigh.

"*Bonjour*, Louise."

"Monsieur!" He threw his hat on a chair. "But, monsieur—but I thought monsieur said on the phone he was going to Tours for the children!"

"I changed my mind, Louise."

He had taken a step forward, his last doubt melting away at the constricted terror in the woman's face.

"Is madame home?"

Simultaneously he perceived a man's hat and stick on the hall table and for the first time in his life he *heard* silence—a loud, singing silence, oppressive as heavy guns or thunder. Then, as the endless moment was broken by the maid's terrified little cry, he pushed through the *portières* into the next room.

An hour later Doctor Derocco, *de la Faculté de Médecine*, rang the apartment bell. Choupette Marston, her face a little drawn and rigid, answered the door. For a moment they went through French forms; then:

"My husband has been feeling unwell for some weeks," she said concisely. "Nevertheless, he did not complain in a way to make me uneasy. He has suddenly collapsed; he cannot articulate or move his limbs. All this, I must say, might have been precipitated by a certain indiscretion of mine—in all events, there was a violent scene, a discussion, and sometimes when he is agitated, my husband cannot comprehend well in French."

"I will see him," said the doctor, thinking: "Some things are comprehended instantly in all languages."

During the next four weeks several people listened to strange speeches about one hundred thousand chemises, and heard how all the population of Paris was becoming etherized by cheap gasoline—there was a consulting psychiatrist, not inclined to believe in any underlying mental trouble; there was a nurse from the American Hospital, and there was Choupette, frightened, defiant and, after her fashion, deeply sorry. A month later, when Henry awoke to his familiar room, lit with a dimmed lamp, he found her sitting beside his bed and reached out for her hand.

"I still love you," he said—"that's the odd thing."

"Sleep, male cabbage."

"At all costs," he continued with a certain feeble irony, "you can count on me to adopt the Continental attitude."

"Please! You tear at my heart."

When he was sitting up in bed they were ostensibly close together again—closer than they had been for months.

"Now you're going to have another holiday," said Henry to the two boys, back from the country. "Papa has got to go to the seashore and get really well."

"Will we swim?"

"And get drowned, my darlings?" Choupette cried. "But fancy, at your age. Not at all!"

So, at St-Jean-de-Luz they sat on the shore instead, and watched the English and Americans and a few hardy French pioneers of *le sport* voyage between raft and diving tower, motorboat and sand. There were passing ships, and bright islands to look at, and mountains reaching into cold zones, and red and yellow villas, called Fleur des Bois, Mon Nid, or Sans-Souci; and farther back, tired French villages of baked cement and grey stone.

Choupette sat at Henry's side, holding a parasol to shelter her peach-bloom skin from the sun.

"Look!" she would say, at the sight of tanned American girls. "Is that lovely? Skin that will be leather at thirty—a sort of brown veil to hide all blemishes, so that everyone will look alike. And women of a hundred kilos in such bathing suits! Weren't clothes intended to hide Nature's mistakes?"

Henry Clay Marston was a Virginian of the kind who are prouder of being Virginians than of being Americans. That mighty word printed across a continent was less to him than the memory of his grandfather, who freed his slaves in '58, fought from Manassas to Appomattox, knew Huxley and Spencer as light reading, and believed in caste only when it expressed the best of race.

To Choupette all this was vague. Her more specific criticisms of his compatriots were directed against the women.

"How would you place them?" she exclaimed. "Great ladies, bourgeoises, adventuresses—they are all the same. Look! Where would I be if I tried to act like your friend, Madame de Richepin? My father was a professor in a provincial university, and I have certain things I wouldn't do because they wouldn't please my class, my family. Madame de Richepin has other things she wouldn't do because of her class, her family." Suddenly she pointed to an American girl going into the water: "But that young lady may be a stenographer and yet be compelled to warp herself, dressing and acting as if she had all the money in the world."

"Perhaps she will have, some day."

"That's the story they are told—it happens to one, not to the ninety-nine. That's why all their faces over thirty are discontented and unhappy."

Though Henry was in general agreement, he could not help being amused at Choupette's choice of target this afternoon. The girl, she was perhaps eighteen, was obviously acting like nothing but herself—she was what his father would have called a thoroughbred. A deep, thoughtful face that was pretty only because of the irrepressible determination of the perfect features to be recognized, a face that could have done without them and not yielded up its poise and distinction.

In her grace, at once exquisite and hardy, she was that perfect type of American girl that makes one wonder if the male is not being sacrificed to it, much as, in the last century, the lower strata in England were sacrificed to produce the governing class.

The two young men, coming out of the water as she went in, had large shoulders and empty faces. She had a smile for them that was no more than they deserved, that must do until she chose one to be the father of her children and gave herself up to destiny. Until then—Henry Marston was glad about her as her arms, like flying fish, clipped the water in a crawl, as her body spread in a swan dive or doubled in a jackknife from the springboard and her head appeared from the depth, jauntily flipping the damp hair away.

The two young men passed near.

"They push water," Choupette said, "then they go elsewhere and push other water. They pass months in France and they couldn't tell you the name of the President. They are parasites such as Europe has not known in a hundred years."

But Henry had stood up abruptly, and now all the people on the beach were suddenly standing up. Something had happened out there in the fifty yards between the deserted raft and the shore. The bright head showed upon the surface; it did not flip water now, but called: "*Au secours!* Help!" in a feeble and frightened voice.

"Henry!" Choupette cried. "Stop! Henry!"

The beach was almost deserted at noon, but Henry and several others were sprinting toward the sea; the two young Americans heard, turned and sprinted after them. There was a frantic little time with half a dozen bobbing heads in the water. Choupette, still clinging to her parasol, but managing to wring her hands at the same time, ran up and down the beach crying: "Henry! Henry!"

Now there were more helping hands, and then two swelling groups around prostrate figures on the shore. The young fellow who pulled in the girl brought her around in a minute or so, but they had more trouble getting the water out of Henry, who had never learned to swim.

II

"This is the man who didn't know whether he could swim, because he'd never tried."

Henry got up from his sun chair, grinning. It was next morning, and the saved girl had just appeared on the beach with her brother.

She smiled back at Henry, brightly casual, appreciative rather than grateful.

"At the very least, I owe it to you to teach you how," she said.

"I'd like it. I decided that in the water yesterday, just before I went down the tenth time."

"You can trust me. I'll never again eat chocolate ice cream before going in."

As she went on into the water, Choupette asked: "How long do you think we'll stay here? After all, this life wearies one."

"We'll stay till I can swim. And the boys too."

"Very well. I saw a nice bathing suit in two shades of blue for fifty francs that I will buy you this afternoon."

Feeling a little paunchy and unhealthily white, Henry, holding his sons by the hand, took his body into the water. The breakers leaped at him, staggering him, while the boys yelled with ecstasy; the returning water curled threateningly around his feet as it hurried back to sea. Farther out, he stood waist-deep with other intimidated souls, watching the people dive from the raft tower, hoping the girl would come to fulfill her promise, and somewhat embarrassed when she did.

"I'll start with your eldest. You watch and then try it by yourself."

He floundered in the water. It went into his nose and started a raw stinging; it blinded him; it lingered afterward in his ears, rattling back and forth like pebbles for hours. The sun discovered him, too, peeling long strips of parchment from his shoulders, blistering his back so that he lay in a feverish agony for several nights. After a week he swam, painfully, pantingly, and not very far. The girl taught him a sort of crawl, for he saw that the breast stroke was an obsolete device that lingered on with the inept and the old. Choupette caught him regarding his tanned face in the mirror with a sort of fascination, and the youngest boy contracted some sort of mild skin infection in the sand that retired him from competition. But one day Henry battled his way desperately to the float and drew himself up on it with his last breath.

"That being settled," he told the girl, when he could speak, "I can leave St-Jean tomorrow."

"I'm sorry."

"What will you do now?"

"My brother and I are going to Antibes; there's swimming there all through October. Then Florida."

"And swim?" he asked with some amusement.

"Why, yes. We'll swim."

"Why do you swim?"

"To get clean," she answered surprisingly.

"Clean from what?"

She frowned. "I don't know why I said that. But it feels clean in the sea."

"Americans are too particular about that," he commented.

"How could anyone be?"

"I mean we've got too fastidious to even clean up our messes."

"I don't know."

"But tell me why you—" He stopped himself in surprise. He had been about to ask her to explain a lot of other things—to say what was clean and unclean, what was worth knowing and what was only words—to open up a new gate to life. Looking for a last time into her eyes, full of cool secrets, he realized how much he was going to miss these mornings, without knowing whether it was the girl who interested him or what she represented of his ever-new, ever-changing country.

"All right," he told Choupette that night. "We'll leave tomorrow."

"For Paris?"

"For America."

"You mean I'm to go too? And the children?"

"Yes."

"But that's absurd," she protested. "Last time it cost more than we spend in six months here. And then there were only three of us. Now that we've managed to get ahead at last—"

"That's just it. I'm tired of getting ahead on your skimping and saving and going without dresses. I've got to make more money. American men are incomplete without money."

"You mean we'll stay?"

"It's very possible."

They looked at each other and against her will Choupette understood. For eight years, by a process of ceaseless adaptation, he had lived her life, substituting for the moral confusion of his own country the tradition, the wisdom, the sophistication of France. After that matter in Paris, it had seemed the bigger part to understand and to forgive, to cling to the home as something apart from the vagaries of love. Only now, glowing with a good health that he had not experienced for years, did he discover his true reaction. It had released him. For all his sense of loss, he possessed again the masculine self he had handed over to the keeping of a wise little Provençal girl eight years ago.

She struggled on for a moment.

"You've got a good position and we really have plenty of money. You know we can live cheaper here."

"The boys are growing up now, and I'm not sure I want to educate them in France."

"But that's all decided," she wailed. "You admit yourself that education in America is superficial and full of silly fads. Do you want them to be like those two dummies on the beach?"

"Perhaps I was thinking more of myself, Choupette. Men just out of college who brought their letters of credit into the bank eight years ago travel about with ten-thousand-dollar cars now. I didn't used to care. I used to tell myself that I had a better place to escape to, just because we knew that lobster American was really lobster *Amoricaine*. Perhaps I haven't that feeling any more."

She stiffened. "If that's it—"

"It's up to you. We'll make a new start."

Choupette thought for a moment. "Of course my sister can take over the apartment."

"Of course." He waxed enthusiastic. "And there are sure to be things that'll tickle you—we'll have a nice car, for instance, and one of those electric ice boxes, and all sorts of funny machines to take the place of servants. It won't be bad. You'll learn to play golf and talk about children all day. Then there are the movies."

Choupette groaned.

"It's going to be pretty awful at first," he admitted, "but there are still a few good nigger cooks, and we'll probably have two bathrooms."

"I am unable to use more than one at a time."

"You'll learn."

A month afterward, when the beautiful white island floated toward them in the Narrows, Henry's throat grew constricted with the rest and he wanted to cry out to Choupette and all foreigners, "Now, you see!"

III

Almost three years later, Henry Marston walked out of his office in the Calumet Tobacco Company and along the hall to Judge Waterbury's suite. His face was older, with a suspicion of grimness, and a slight irrepressible heaviness of body was not concealed by his white linen suit.

"Busy, judge?"

"Come in, Henry."

"I'm going to the shore tomorrow to swim off this weight. I wanted to talk to you before I go."

"Children going too?"

"Oh, sure."

"Choupette'll go abroad, I suppose."

"Not this year. I think she's—coming with me, if she doesn't stay here in Richmond."

The judge thought: "There isn't a doubt but what he knows everything." He waited.

"I wanted to tell you, judge, that I'm resigning the end of September."

The judge's chair creaked backward as he brought his feet to the floor.

"You're quitting, Henry?"

"Not exactly. Walter Ross wants to come home; let me take his place in France."

"Boy, do you know what we pay Walter Ross?"

"Seven thousand."

"And you're getting twenty-five."

"You've probably heard I've made something in the market," said Henry deprecatingly.

"I've heard everything between a hundred thousand and half a million."

"Somewhere in between."

"Then why a seven-thousand-dollar job? Is Choupette homesick?"

"No, I think Choupette likes it over here. She's adapted herself amazingly."

"He knows," the judge thought. "He wants to get away."

After Henry had gone, he looked up at the portrait of his grandfather on the wall. In those days the matter would have been simpler. Dueling pistols in the old Wharton meadow at dawn. It would be to Henry's advantage if things were like that today.

Henry's chauffeur dropped him in front of a Georgian house in a new suburban section. Leaving his hat in the hall, he went directly out on the side verandah.

From the swaying canvas swing Choupette looked up with a polite smile. Save for a certain alertness of feature and a certain indefinable knack of putting things on, she might have passed for an American. Southernisms overlay her French accent with a quaint charm; there were still college boys who rushed her like a debutante at the Christmas dances.

Henry nodded at Mr. Charles Wiese, who occupied a wicker chair, with a gin fizz at his elbow.

"I want to talk to you," he said, sitting down.

Wiese's glance and Choupette's crossed quickly before coming to rest on him.

"You're free, Wiese," Henry said. "Why don't you and Choupette get married?"

Choupette sat up, her eyes flashing.

"Now wait." Henry turned back to Wiese. "I've been letting this thing drift for about a year now, while I got my financial affairs in shape. But this last brilliant idea of yours makes me feel a little uncomfortable, a little sordid, and I don't want to feel that way."

"Just what do you mean?" Wiese inquired.

"On my last trip to New York you had me shadowed. I presume it was with the intention of getting divorce evidence against me. It wasn't a success."

"I don't know where you got such an idea in your head, Marston; you—"

"Don't lie!"

"Suh—" Wiese began, but Henry interrupted impatiently:

"Now don't 'Suh' me, and don't try to whip yourself up into a temper. You're not talking to a scared picker full of hookworm. I don't want a scene; my emotions aren't sufficiently involved. I want to arrange a divorce."

"Why do you bring it up like this?" Choupette cried, breaking into French. "Couldn't we talk of it alone, if you think you have so much against me?"

"Wait a minute; this might as well be settled now," Wiese said. "Choupette does want a divorce. Her life with you is unsatisfactory, and the only reason she has kept on is because she's an idealist. You don't seem to appreciate that fact, but it's true; she couldn't bring herself to break up her home."

"Very touching." Henry looked at Choupette with bitter amusement. "But let's come down to facts. I'd like to close up this matter before I go back to France."

Again Wiese and Choupette exchanged a look.

"It ought to be simple," Wiese said. "Choupette doesn't want a cent of your money."

"I know. What she wants is the children. The answer is, You can't have the children."

"How perfectly outrageous!" Choupette cried. "Do you imagine for a minute I'm going to give up my children?"

"What's your idea, Marston?" demanded Wiese. "To take them back to France and make them expatriates like yourself?"

"Hardly that. They're entered for St. Regis School and then for Yale. And I haven't any idea of not letting them see their mother whenever she so desires—judging from the past two years, it won't be often. But I intend to have their entire legal custody."

"Why?" they demanded together.

"Because of the home."

"What the devil do you mean?"

"I'd rather apprentice them to a trade than have them brought up in the sort of home yours and Choupette's is going to be."

There was a moment's silence. Suddenly Choupette picked up her glass, dashed the contents at Henry and collapsed on the settee, passionately sobbing.

Henry dabbed his face with his handkerchief and stood up.

"I was afraid of that," he said, "but I think I've made my position clear."

He went up to his room and lay down on the bed. In a thousand wakeful hours during the past year he had fought over in his mind the problem of keeping his boys without taking those legal measures against Choupette that he could not bring himself to take. He knew that she wanted the children only because without them she would be suspect, even *déclassée*, to her family in France; but with that quality of detachment peculiar to old stock, Henry recognized this as a perfectly legitimate motive. Furthermore, no public scandal must touch the mother of his sons—it was this that had rendered his challenge so ineffectual this afternoon.

When difficulties became insurmountable, inevitable, Henry sought surcease in exercise. For three years, swimming had been a sort of refuge, and he turned to it as one man to music or another to drink. There was a point when he would resolutely stop thinking and go to the Virginia coast for a week to wash his mind in the water. Far out past the breakers he could survey the green-and-brown line of the Old Dominion with the pleasant impersonality of a porpoise. The burden of his wretched marriage fell away with the buoyant tumble of his body among the swells, and he would begin to move in a child's dream of space. Sometimes remembered playmates of his youth swam with him; sometimes, with his two sons beside him, he seemed to be setting off along the bright pathway to the moon. Americans, he liked to say, should be born with fins, and perhaps they were—perhaps money was a form of fin. In England property begot a strong place sense, but Americans, restless and with shallow roots, needed fins and wings. There was even a recurrent idea in America about an education that would leave out history and the past, that should be a sort of equipment for aerial adventure, weighed down by none of the stowaways of inheritance or tradition.

Thinking of this in the water the next afternoon brought Henry's mind to the children; he turned and at a slow trudgen started back toward shore. Out of condition, he rested, panting, at the raft, and glancing up, he saw familiar eyes. In a moment he was talking with the girl he had tried to rescue four years ago.

He was overjoyed. He had not realized how vividly he remembered her. She was a Virginian—he might have guessed it abroad—the laziness, the apparent casualness that masked an unfailing courtesy and attention; a good form devoid of forms was based on kindness and consideration. Hearing her name for the first time, he recognized it—an Eastern Shore name, "good" as his own.

Lying in the sun, they talked like old friends, not about races and manners and the things that Henry brooded over with Choupette, but rather as if they naturally agreed about those things; they talked about what they liked themselves and about what was fun. She showed him a sitting-down, standing-up dive from the high springboard, and he emulated her inexpertly—that was fun. They talked about eating soft-shelled crabs, and she told him how, because of the curious acoustics of the water, one could lie here and be diverted by conversations on the hotel porch. They tried it and heard two ladies over their tea say:

"Now, at the Lido—"

"Now, at Asbury Park—"

"Oh, my dear, he just scratched and scratched all night; he just scratched and scratched—"

"My dear, at Deauville—"

"—scratched and scratched all night."

After awhile the sea got to be that very blue color of four o'clock, and the girl told him how, at nineteen, she had been divorced from a Spaniard who locked her in the hotel suite when he went out at night.

"It was one of those things," she said lightly. "But speaking more cheerfully, how's your beautiful wife? And the boys—did they learn to float? Why can't you all dine with me tonight?"

"I'm afraid I won't be able to," he said, after a moment's hesitation. He must do nothing, however trivial, to furnish Choupette weapons, and with a feeling of disgust, it occurred to him that he was possibly being watched this afternoon. Nevertheless, he was glad of his caution when she unexpectedly arrived at the hotel for dinner that night.

After the boys had gone to bed, they faced each other over coffee on the hotel verandah.

"Will you kindly explain why I'm not entitled to a half share in my own children?" Choupette began. "It is not like you to be vindictive, Henry."

It was hard for Henry to explain. He told her again that she could have the children when she wanted them, but that he must exercise entire control over them because of certain old-fashioned convictions—watching her face grow harder, minute by minute, he saw there was no use, and broke off. She made a scornful sound.

"I wanted to give you a chance to be reasonable before Charles arrives."

Henry sat up. "Is he coming here this evening?"

"Happily. And I think perhaps your selfishness is going to have a jolt, Henry. You're not dealing with a woman now."

When Wiese walked out on the porch an hour later, Henry saw that his pale lips were like chalk; there was a deep flush on his forehead and hard confidence in his eyes. He was cleared for action and he wasted no time. "We've got something to say to each other, suh, and since I've got a motorboat here, perhaps that'd be the quietest place to say it."

Henry nodded coolly; five minutes later the three of them were headed out into Hampton Roads on the wide fairway of the moonlight. It was a tranquil evening, and half a mile from shore Wiese cut down the engine to a mild throbbing, so that they seemed to drift without will or direction through the bright water. His voice broke the stillness abruptly:

"Marston, I'm going to talk to you straight from the shoulder. I love Choupette and I'm not apologizing for it. These things have happened before in this world. I guess you understand that. The only difficulty is this matter of the custody of Choupette's children. You seem determined to try and take them away from the mother that bore them and raised them"—Wiese's words became more clearly articulated, as if they came from a wider mouth—"but you left one thing out of your calculations, and that's me. Do you happen to realize that at this moment I'm one of the richest men in Virginia?"

"I've heard as much."

"Well, money is power, Marston. I repeat, suh, money is power."

"I've heard that too. In fact, you're a bore, Wiese." Even by the moon Henry could see the crimson deepen on his brow.

"You'll hear it again, suh. Yesterday you took us by surprise and I was unprepared for your brutality to Choupette. But this morning I received a letter from Paris that puts the matter in a new light. It is a statement by a specialist in mental diseases, declaring you to be of unsound mind, and unfit to have the custody of children. The specialist is the one who attended you in your nervous breakdown four years ago."

Henry laughed incredulously, and looked at Choupette, half expecting her to laugh, too, but she had turned her face away, breathing quickly through parted lips. Suddenly he realized that Wiese was telling the truth—that by some extraordinary bribe he had obtained such a document and fully intended to use it.

For a moment Henry reeled as if from a material blow. He listened to his own voice saying, "That's the most ridiculous thing I ever heard," and to Wiese's answer: "They don't always tell people when they have mental troubles."

Suddenly Henry wanted to laugh, and the terrible instant when he had wondered if there could be some shred of truth in the allegation passed. He turned to Choupette, but again she avoided his eyes.

"How could you, Choupette?"

"I want my children," she began, but Wiese broke in quickly:

"If you'd been halfway fair, Marston, we wouldn't have resorted to this step."

"Are you trying to pretend you arranged this scurvy trick since yesterday afternoon?"

"I believe in being prepared, but if you had been reasonable; in fact, if you will be reasonable, this opinion needn't be used." His voice became suddenly almost paternal, almost kind: "Be wise, Marston. On your side there's an obstinate prejudice; on mine there are forty million dollars. Don't fool yourself. Let me repeat, Marston, that money is power. You were abroad so long that perhaps you're inclined to forget that fact. Money made this country, built its great and glorious cities, created its industries, covered it with an iron network of railroads. It's money that harnesses the forces of Nature, creates the machine and makes it go when money says go, and stop when money says stop."

As though interpreting this as a command, the engine gave forth a sudden hoarse sound and came to rest.

"What is it?" demanded Choupette.

"It's nothing." Wiese pressed the self-starter with his foot. "I repeat, Marston, that money—The battery is dry. One minute while I spin the wheel."

He spun it for the best part of fifteen minutes while the boat meandered about in a placid little circle.

"Choupette, open that drawer behind you and see if there isn't a rocket."

A touch of panic had crept into her voice when she answered that there was no rocket. Wiese eyed the shore tentatively.

"There's no use in yelling; we must be half a mile out. We'll just have to wait here until someone comes along."

"We won't wait here," Henry remarked.

"Why not?"

"We're moving toward the bay. Can't you tell? We're moving out with the tide."

"That's impossible!" said Choupette sharply.

"Look at those two lights on shore—one passing the other now. Do you see?"

"Do something!" she wailed, and then, in a burst of French: "*Ah, c'est épouvantable! N'est-ce pas qu'il y a quelque chose qu'on peut faire?*"

The tide was running fast now, and the boat was drifting down the Roads with it toward the sea. The vague blots of two ships passed them, but at a distance, and there was no answer to their hail. Against the western sky a lighthouse blinked, but it was impossible to guess how near to it they would pass.

"It looks as if all our difficulties would be solved for us," Henry said.

"What difficulties?" Choupette demanded. "Do you mean there's nothing to be done? Can you sit there and just float away like this?"

"It may be easier on the children, after all." He winced as Choupette began to sob bitterly, but he said nothing. A ghostly idea was taking shape in his mind.

"Look here, Marston. Can you swim?" demanded Wiese, frowning.

"Yes, but Choupette can't."

"I can't either—I didn't mean that. If you could swim in and get to a telephone, the coast-guard people would send for us."

Henry surveyed the dark, receding shore.

"It's too far," he said.

"You can try!" said Choupette.

Henry shook his head.

"Too risky. Besides, there's an outside chance that we'll be picked up."

The lighthouse passed them, far to the left and out of earshot. Another one, the last, loomed up half a mile away.

"We might drift to France like that man Gerbault," Henry remarked. "But then, of course, we'd be expatriates—and Wiese wouldn't like that, would you, Wiese?"

Wiese, fussing frantically with the engine, looked up.

"See what you can do with this," he said.

"I don't know anything about mechanics," Henry answered. "Besides, this solution of our difficulties grows on me. Just suppose you were dirty dog enough to use that statement and got the children because of it—in that case I wouldn't have much impetus to go on living. We're all failures—I as head of my household, Choupette as a wife and a mother, and you, Wiese, as a human being. It's just as well that we go out of life together."

"This is no time for a speech, Marston."

"Oh, yes, it's a fine time. How about a little more house-organ oratory about money being power?"

Choupette sat rigid in the bow; Wiese stood over the engine, biting nervously at his lips.

"We're not going to pass that lighthouse very close." An idea suddenly occurred to him. "Couldn't you swim to that, Marston?"

"Of course he could!" Choupette cried.

Henry looked at it tentatively.

"I might. But I won't."

"You've got to!"

Again he flinched at Choupette's weeping; simultaneously he saw the time had come.

"Everything depends on one small point," he said rapidly. "Wiese, have you got a fountain pen?"

"Yes. What for?"

"If you'll write and sign about two hundred words at my dictation, I'll swim to the lighthouse and get help. Otherwise, so help me God, we'll drift out to sea! And you better decide in about one minute."

"Oh, anything!" Choupette broke out frantically. "Do what he says, Charles; he means it. He always means what he says. Oh, please don't wait!"

"I'll do what you want"—Wiese's voice was shaking—"only, for God's sake, go on. What is it you want—an agreement about the children? I'll give you my personal word of honor—"

"There's no time for humor," said Henry savagely. "Take this piece of paper and write."

The two pages that Wiese wrote at Henry's dictation relinquished all lien on the children thence and forever for himself and Choupette. When they had affixed trembling signatures Wiese cried:

"Now go, for God's sake, before it's too late!"

"Just one thing more: The certificate from the doctor."

"I haven't it here."

"You lie."

Wiese took it from his pocket.

"Write across the bottom that you paid so much for it, and sign your name to that."

A minute later, stripped to his underwear, and with the papers in an oiled-silk tobacco pouch suspended from his neck, Henry dived from the side of the boat and struck out toward the light.

The waters leapt up at him for an instant, but after the first shock it was all warm and friendly, and the small murmur of the waves was an encouragement. It was the longest swim he had ever tried, and he was straight from the city, but the happiness in his heart buoyed him up. Safe now, and free. Each stroke was stronger for knowing that his two sons, sleeping back in the hotel, were safe from what he dreaded. Divorced from her own country, Choupette had picked the things out of American life that pandered best to her own self-indulgence. That, backed by a court decree, she should be permitted to hand on this preposterous moral farrago to his sons was unendurable. He would have lost them forever.

Turning on his back, he saw that already the motorboat was far away, the blinding light was nearer. He was very tired. If one let go—and, in the relaxation from strain, he felt an alarming impulse to let go—one died very quickly and painlessly, and all these problems of hate and bitterness disappeared. But he felt the fate of his sons in the oiled-silk pouch about his neck, and with a convulsive effort he turned over again and concentrated all his energies on his goal.

Twenty minutes later he stood shivering and dripping in the signal room while it was broadcast out to the coast patrol that a launch was drifting in the bay.

"There's not much danger without a storm," the keeper said. "By now they've probably struck a cross current from the river and drifted into Peyton Harbor."

"Yes," said Henry, who had come to this coast for three summers. "I knew that too."

IV

In October Henry left his sons in school and embarked on the *Majestic* for Europe. He had come home as to a generous mother and had been profusely given more than he asked—money, release from an intolerable situation, and the fresh strength to fight for his own. Watching the fading city, the fading shore, from the deck of the *Majestic*, he had a sense of overwhelming gratitude and of gladness that America was there, that under the ugly debris of industry the rich land still pushed up, incorrigibly lavish and fertile, and that in the heart of the leaderless people the old generosities and devotions fought on, breaking out sometimes in fanaticism and excess, but indomitable and undefeated. There was a lost generation in the saddle at the moment, but it seemed to him that the men coming on, the men of the war, were better; and all his old feeling that

America was a bizarre accident, a sort of historical sport, had gone forever. The best of America was the best of the world.

Going down to the purser's office, he waited until a fellow passenger was through at the window. When she turned, they both started, and he saw it was the girl.

"Oh, hello!" she cried. "I'm glad you're going! I was just asking when the pool opened. The great thing about this ship is that you can always get a swim."

"Why do you like to swim?" he demanded.

"You always ask me that." She laughed.

"Perhaps you'd tell me if we had dinner together tonight."

But when, in a moment, he left her he knew that she could never tell him—she or another. France was a land, England was a people, but America, having about it still that quality of the idea, was harder to utter—it was the graves at Shiloh and the tired, drawn, nervous faces of its great men, and the country boys dying in the Argonne for a phrase that was empty before their bodies withered. It was a willingness of the heart.

THE BRIDAL PARTY

There was the usual insincere little note saying: "I wanted you to be the first to know." It was a double shock to Michael, announcing, as it did, both the engagement and the imminent marriage—which moreover was to be held, not in New York, decently and far away, but here in Paris under his very nose, if that could be said to extend over the Cathedral Church of the Holy Trinity, Avenue George V. The date was two weeks off, early in June.

At first Michael was afraid and his stomach felt hollow. When he left the hotel that morning, the *femme de chambre*, who was in love with his fine sharp profile and his pleasant buoyancy, scented the hard abstraction that had settled over him. He walked in a daze to his bank, he bought a detective story at Smith's on the Rue de Rivoli, he sympathetically stared for awhile at a faded panorama of the battlefields in a tourist-office window and cursed a Greek tout who followed him with a half-displayed packet of innocuous post cards warranted to be very dirty indeed.

But the fear stayed with him, and after awhile he recognized it as the fear that now he would never be happy. He had met Caroline Dandy when she was seventeen, possessed her young heart all through her first season in New York and then lost her, slowly, tragically, uselessly, because he had no money and could make no money; because with all the energy and good will in the world he could not find himself; because, loving him still, Caroline had lost faith and begun to see him as something pathetic, futile and shabby, outside the great shining stream of life toward which she was inevitably drawn.

Since his only support was that she loved him, he leaned weakly on that; the support broke, but still he held on to it and was carried out to sea and washed up on the French coast with its broken pieces still in his hands. He carried them around with him in the form of photographs and packets of correspondence and a liking for a maudlin popular song called "Among My Souvenirs." He kept clear of other girls, as if Caroline would somehow know it and reciprocate with a faithful heart. Her note informed him that he had lost her forever.

It was a fine morning. In front of the shops in the Rue de Castiglione, proprietors and patrons were on the sidewalk gazing upward, for the Graf Zeppelin, shining and glorious, symbol of escape and destruction—of escape, if necessary, through destruction—glided in the Paris sky. He heard a woman say in French that it would not her astonish if that commenced to let fall the bombs. Then he heard another voice, full of husky laughter, and the void in his stomach froze. Jerking about, he was face to face with Caroline Dandy and her fiancé.

"Why, *Michael!* Why, we were wondering where you were. I asked at the Guaranty Trust, and Morgan and Company, and finally sent a note to the National City—"

Why didn't they back away? Why didn't they back right up, walking backward down the Rue de Castiglione, across the Rue de Rivoli, through the Tuileries Gardens, still walking backward as fast as they could till they grew vague and faded out across the river?

"This is Hamilton Rutherford, my fiancé."

"We've met before."

"At Pat's, wasn't it?"

"And last spring in the Ritz bar."

"*Michael*, where *have* you been keeping yourself?"

"Around here." This agony. Previews of Hamilton Rutherford flashed before his eyes—a quick series of pictures, sentences. He remembered hearing that he had bought a seat in 1920 for a hundred and twenty-five thousand of borrowed money, and just before the break sold it for more than half a million. Not handsome like Michael, but vitally attractive, confident, authoritative, just the right height over Caroline there—Michael had always been too short for Caroline when they danced.

Rutherford was saying: "No, I'd like it very much if you'd come to the bachelor dinner. I'm taking the Ritz bar from nine o'clock on.

Then right after the wedding there'll be a reception and breakfast at the Hôtel George V."

"And, Michael, George Packman is giving a party day after tomorrow at Chez Victor, and I want you to be sure and come. And also to tea Friday at Jebby West's—she'd want to have you if she knew where you were. What's your hotel, so we can send you an invitation? You see, the reason we decided to have it over here is because mother has been sick in a nursing home here and the whole clan is in Paris. Then Hamilton's mother's being here too—"

The entire clan; they had always hated him, except her mother; always discouraged his courtship. What a little counter he was in this game of families and money! Under his hat his brow sweated with the humiliation of the fact that for all his misery he was worth just exactly so many invitations. Frantically he began to mumble something about going away.

Then it happened—Caroline saw deep into him, and Michael knew that she saw. She saw through to his profound woundedness, and something quivered inside her, died out along the curve of her mouth and in her eyes. He had moved her. All the unforgettable impulses of first love had surged up once more; their hearts had in some way touched across two feet of Paris sunlight. She took her fiancé's arm suddenly, as if to steady herself with the feel of it.

They parted. Michael walked quickly for a minute; then he stopped, pretending to look in a window, and saw them farther up the street, walking fast into the Place Vendôme, people with much to do.

He had things to do also—he had to get his laundry.

"Nothing will ever be the same again," he said to himself. "She will never be happy in her marriage and I will never be happy at all anymore."

The two vivid years of his love for Caroline moved back around him like years in Einstein's physics. Intolerable memories arose—of rides in the Long Island moonlight; of a happy time at Lake Placid with her cheeks so cold there, but warm just underneath the surface; of a despairing afternoon in a little café on 48th Street in the last sad months when their marriage had come to seem impossible, where if drinking made nothing better it adorned their grief with an ecstasy of sentiment. . . .

"Come in," he said aloud.

The concierge with a telegram; brusque because Mr. Curly's clothes were a little shabby. Mr. Curly gave few tips; Mr. Curly was obviously a *petit client.*

Michael read the telegram.

"An answer?" the concierge asked.

"No," said Michael, and then, on an impulse: "Look."

"Too bad—too bad," said the concierge. "Your grandfather is dead."

"Not too bad," said Michael. "It means that I come into a quarter of a million dollars."

Too late by a single month—after the first flush of the news his misery was deeper than ever. Lying awake in bed that night, he listened endlessly to the long caravan of a circus moving through the street from one Paris fair to another.

When the last van had rumbled out of hearing and the corners of the furniture were pastel blue with the dawn, he was still thinking of the look in Caroline's eyes that morning, the look that seemed to say: "Oh, why couldn't you have done something about it? Why couldn't you have been stronger, made me marry you? Don't you see how sad I am?"

Michael's fists clenched.

"Well, by God, I won't give up till the last moment," he whispered. "I've had all the bad luck so far, and maybe it's turned at last. One takes what one can get, up to the limit of one's strength, and if I can't have her, at least she'll go into this marriage with some of me in her heart."

II

Accordingly he went to the party at Chez Victor two days later, upstairs and into the little salon off the bar where the party was to assemble for cocktails. He was early; the only other occupant was a tall lean man of fifty. They spoke.

"You waiting for George Packman's party?"

"Yes. My name's Michael Curly."

"My name's—"

Michael failed to catch the name. They ordered a drink, and Michael supposed that the bride and groom were having a gay time.

"Too much so," the other agreed, frowning. "I don't see how they stand it. We all crossed on the boat together; five days of that crazy life and then two weeks of Paris. You"—he hesitated, smiling faintly—"you'll excuse me for saying that your generation drinks too much."

"Not Caroline."

"No, not Caroline. She seems to take only a cocktail and a glass of champagne, and then she's had enough, thank God. But Hamilton drinks too much and all this crowd of young people drink too much. Do you live in Paris?"

"For the moment," said Michael.

"I don't like Paris. My wife—that is to say, my ex-wife, Hamilton's mother—lives in Paris."

"You're Hamilton Rutherford's father?"

"I have that honor. And I'm not denying that I'm proud of what he's done—it was just a general comment."

"Of course."

Michael glanced up nervously as four people came in. He felt suddenly that his dinner coat was old and shiny; he had ordered a new one that morning. The people who had come in were rich and at home in their richness with one another—a dark lovely girl with a hysterical little laugh whom he had met before; two confident men whose jokes referred invariably to last night's scandal and tonight's potentialities, as if they had important roles in a play that extended indefinitely into the past and the future. When Caroline arrived, Michael had scarcely a moment of her, but it was enough to note that, like all the others, she was strained and tired. She was pale beneath her rouge; there were shadows under her eyes. With a mixture of relief and wounded vanity, he found himself placed far from her and at another table; he needed a moment to adjust himself to his surroundings. This was not like the immature set in which he and Caroline had moved; the men were more than thirty and had an air of sharing the best of this world's goods. Next to him was Jebby West, whom he knew; and on the other side a jovial man who immediately began to talk to Michael about a stunt for the bachelor dinner: They were going to hire a French girl to appear with an actual baby in her arms, crying: "Hamilton, you can't desert me now!" The idea seemed stale and unamusing to Michael, but its originator shook with anticipatory laughter.

Farther up the table there was talk of the market—another drop today, the most appreciable since the crash; people were kidding Rutherford about it: "Too bad, old man. You better not get married, after all."

Michael asked the man on his left, "Has he lost a lot?"

"Nobody knows. He's heavily involved, but he's one of the smartest young men in Wall Street. Anyhow, nobody ever tells you the truth."

It was a champagne dinner from the start, and toward the end it reached a pleasant level of conviviality, but Michael saw that all these people were too weary to be exhilarated by any ordinary stimulant; for weeks they had drunk cocktails before meals like Americans, wines and brandies like Frenchmen, beer like Germans, whisky-and-soda like the English, and as they were no longer in the twenties, this preposterous *mélange*, that was like some gigantic cocktail in a nightmare, served only to make them temporarily less conscious of the mistakes of the night before. Which is to say that it was not really a gay party; what gayety existed was displayed in the few who drank nothing at all.

But Michael was not tired, and the champagne stimulated him and made his misery less acute. He had been away from New York for more than eight months and most of the dance music was unfamiliar to him, but at the first bars of the "Painted Doll," to which he and Caroline had moved through so much happiness and despair the previous summer, he crossed to Caroline's table and asked her to dance.

She was lovely in a dress of thin ethereal blue, and the proximity of her crackly yellow hair, of her cool and tender grey eyes, turned his body clumsy and rigid; he stumbled with their first step on the floor. For a moment it seemed that there was nothing to say; he wanted to tell her about his inheritance, but the idea seemed abrupt, unprepared for.

"Michael, it's so nice to be dancing with you again."

He smiled grimly.

"I'm so happy you came," she continued. "I was afraid maybe you'd be silly and stay away. Now we can be just good friends and natural together. Michael, I want you and Hamilton to like each other."

The engagement was making her stupid; he had never heard her make such a series of obvious remarks before.

"I could kill him without a qualm," he said pleasantly, "but he looks like a good man. He's fine. What I want to know is, what happens to people like me who aren't able to forget?"

As he said this he could not prevent his mouth from dropping suddenly, and glancing up Caroline saw and her heart quivered violently as it had the other morning.

"Do you mind so much, Michael?"

"God, yes."

For a second as he said this, in a voice that seemed to have come up from his shoes, they were not dancing; they were simply clinging together. Then she leaned away from him and twisted her mouth into a lovely smile.

"I didn't know what to do at first, Michael. I told Hamilton about you—that I'd cared for you an awful lot—but it didn't worry him, and he was right. Because I'm over you now—yes, I am. And you'll wake up some sunny morning and be over me just like that."

He shook his head stubbornly.

"Oh, yes. We weren't for each other. I'm pretty flighty, and I need somebody like Hamilton to decide things. It was that more than the question of—of—"

"Of money." Again he was on the point of telling her what had happened, but again something told him it was not the time.

"Then how do you account for what happened when we met the other day," he demanded helplessly—"what happened just now? When we just *pour* toward each other like we used to—as if we were one person, as if the same blood was flowing through both of us?"

"Oh, don't," she begged him. "You mustn't talk like that; everything's decided now. I love Hamilton with all my heart. It's just that I remember certain things in the past and I feel sorry for you—for us—for the way we were."

Over her shoulder, Michael saw a man come toward them to cut in. In a panic he danced her away, but inevitably the man came on.

"I've got to see you alone, if only for a minute," Michael said quickly. "When can I?"

"I'll be at Jebby West's tea tomorrow," she whispered as a hand fell politely upon Michael's shoulder.

But he did not talk to her at Jebby West's tea. Rutherford stood next to her, and each brought the other into all conversations. They left early. The next morning the wedding cards arrived in the first mail.

Then Michael, grown desperate with pacing up and down his room, determined on a bold stroke; he wrote to Hamilton Rutherford, asking him for a rendezvous the following afternoon. In a short telephone communication Rutherford agreed, but for a day later than Michael had asked. And the wedding was only six days away.

They were to meet in the bar of the Hôtel Jena. Michael knew what he would say: "See here, Rutherford, do you realize the responsibility you're taking in going through with this marriage? Do you realize the harvest of trouble and regret you're sowing in persuading a girl into something contrary to the instincts of her heart?" He would explain that the barrier between Caroline and himself had been an artificial one and was now removed, and demand that the matter be put up to Caroline frankly before it was too late.

Rutherford would be angry, conceivably there would be a scene, but Michael felt that he was fighting for his life now.

He found Rutherford in conversation with an older man, whom Michael had met at several of the wedding parties.

"I saw what happened to most of my friends," Rutherford was saying, "and I decided it wasn't going to happen to me. It isn't so difficult—if you take a girl with common sense, and tell her what's what, and do your stuff damn well, and play decently square with her, it's a marriage. If you stand for any nonsense at the beginning, it's one of these arrangements—within five years the man gets out, or else the girl gobbles him up and you have the usual mess."

"Right!" agreed his companion enthusiastically. "Hamilton, boy, you're right."

Michael's blood boiled slowly.

"Doesn't it strike you," he inquired coldly, "that your attitude went out of fashion about a hundred years ago?"

"No, it didn't," said Rutherford pleasantly, but impatiently. "I'm as modern as anybody. I'd get married in an aeroplane next Saturday if it'd please my girl."

"I don't mean that way of being modern. You can't take a sensitive woman—"

"Sensitive? Women aren't so darn sensitive. It's fellows like you who are sensitive; it's fellows like you they exploit—all your devotion and kindness and all that. They read a couple of books and see a few pictures because they haven't got anything else to do, and then they say they're finer in grain than you are, and to prove it they take the bit in their teeth and tear off for a fare-you-well—just about as sensitive as a fire horse."

"Caroline happens to be sensitive," said Michael in a clipped voice.

At this point the other man got up to go; when the dispute about the check had been settled and they were alone, Rutherford leaned back to Michael as if a question had been asked him.

"Caroline's more than sensitive," he said. "She's got sense."

His combative eyes, meeting Michael's, flickered with a grey light. "This all sounds pretty crude to you, Mr. Curly, but it seems to me that the average man nowadays just asks to be made a monkey of by some woman who doesn't even get any fun out of reducing him to that level. There are darn few men who possess their wives anymore, but I am going to be one of them."

To Michael it seemed time to bring the talk back to the actual situation: "Do you realize the responsibility you're taking?"

"I certainly do," interrupted Rutherford. "I'm not afraid of responsibility. I'll make the decisions—fairly, I hope, but anyhow they'll be final."

"What if you didn't start right?" said Michael impetuously. "What if your marriage isn't founded on mutual love?"

"I think I see what you mean," Rutherford said, still pleasant. "And since you've brought it up, let me say that if you and Caroline had married, it wouldn't have lasted three years. Do you know what your affair was founded on? On sorrow. You got sorry for each other. Sorrow's a lot of fun for most women and for some men, but it seems to me that a marriage ought to be based on hope." He looked at his watch and stood up.

"I've got to meet Caroline. Remember, you're coming to the bachelor dinner day after tomorrow."

Michael felt the moment slipping away. "Then Caroline's personal feelings don't count with you?" he demanded fiercely.

"Caroline's tired and upset. But she has what she wants, and that's the main thing."

"Are you referring to yourself?" demanded Michael incredulously.

"Yes."

"May I ask how long she's wanted you?"

"About two years." Before Michael could answer, he was gone.

During the next two days Michael floated in an abyss of helplessness. The idea haunted him that he had left something undone that would sever this knot drawn tighter under his eyes. He phoned Caroline, but she insisted that it was physically impossible for her to see him until the day before the wedding, for which day she granted him a tentative rendezvous. Then he went to the bachelor dinner, partly in fear of an evening alone at his hotel, partly from a feeling that by his presence at that function he was somehow nearer to Caroline, keeping her in sight.

The Ritz bar had been prepared for the occasion by French and American banners and by a great canvas covering one wall, against which the guests were invited to concentrate their proclivities in breaking glasses.

At the first cocktail, taken at the bar, there were many slight spillings from many trembling hands, but later, with the champagne, there was a rising tide of laughter and occasional bursts of song.

Michael was surprised to find what a difference his new dinner coat, his new silk hat, his new, proud linen made in his estimate of himself; he felt less resentment toward all these people for being so rich and assured. For the first time since he had left college he felt rich and assured himself; he felt that he was part of all this, and even entered into the scheme of Johnson, the practical joker, for the appearance of the woman betrayed, now waiting tranquilly in the room across the hall.

"We don't want to go too heavy," Johnson said, "because I imagine Ham's had a pretty anxious day already. Did you see Fullman Oil's sixteen points off this morning?"

"Will that matter to him?" Michael asked, trying to keep the interest out of his voice.

"Naturally. He's in heavily; he's always in everything heavily. So far he's has luck; anyhow, up to a month ago."

The glasses were filled and emptied faster now, and men were shouting at one another across the narrow table. Against the bar a group of ushers was being photographed, and the flash light surged through the room in a stifling cloud.

"Now's the time," Johnson said. "You're to stand by the door, remember, and we're both to try and keep her from coming in—just till we get everybody's attention."

He went on out into the corridor, and Michael waited obediently by the door. Several minutes passed. Then Johnson reappeared with a curious expression on his face.

"There's something funny about this."

"Isn't the girl there?"

"She's there all right, but—there's another woman there too, and it's nobody we engaged either. She wants to see Hamilton Rutherford, and she looks as if she had something on her mind."

They went out into the hall. Planted firmly in a chair near the door sat an American girl a little the worse for liquor, but with a determined expression on her face. She looked up at them with a jerk of her head.

"Well, j'tell him?" she demanded. "The name is Marjorie Collins, and he'll know it. I've come a long way, and I want to see him now and quick, or there's going to be more trouble than you ever saw." She rose unsteadily to her feet.

"You go in and tell Ham," whispered Johnson to Michael. "Maybe he'd better get out. I'll keep her here."

Back at the table, Michael leaned close to Rutherford's ear and, with a certain grimness, whispered:

"A girl outside named Marjorie Collins says she wants to see you. She looks as if she wanted to make trouble."

Hamilton Rutherford blinked and his mouth fell ajar; then slowly the lips came together in a straight line and he said in a crisp voice:

"Please keep her there. And send the head barman to me right away."

Michael spoke to the barman, and then, without returning to the table, asked quietly for his coat and hat. Out in the hall again, he passed Johnson and the girl without speaking and went out into the Rue Cambon. Calling a cab, he gave the address of Caroline's hotel.

His place was beside her now. Not to bring bad news, but simply to be with her when her house of cards came falling around her head.

Rutherford had implied that he was soft—well, he was hard enough not to give up the girl he loved without taking advantage of every chance within the pale of honor. Should she turn away from Rutherford, she would find him there.

She was in—she was surprised when he called, but she was still dressed and would be down immediately. Presently she appeared in a dinner gown, holding two blue telegrams in her hand. They sat down in armchairs in the deserted lobby.

"But, Michael, is the dinner over?"

"I wanted to see you, so I came away."

"I'm glad." Her voice was friendly, but matter-of-fact. "Because I'd just phoned your hotel that I had fittings and rehearsals all day tomorrow. Now we can have our talk after all."

"You're tired," he guessed. "Perhaps I shouldn't have come."

"No. I was waiting up for Hamilton. Telegrams that may be important. He said he might go on somewhere, and that may mean any hour, so I'm glad I have someone to talk to."

Michael winced at the impersonality in the last phrase.

"Don't you care when he gets home?"

"Naturally," she said, laughing, "but I haven't got much say about it, have I?"

"Why not?"

"I couldn't start by telling him what he could and couldn't do."

"Why not?"

"He wouldn't stand for it."

"He seems to want merely a housekeeper," said Michael ironically.

"Tell me about your plans, Michael," she asked quickly.

"My plans? I can't see any future after the day after tomorrow. The only real plan I ever had was to love you."

Their eyes brushed past each other's, and the look he knew so well was staring out at him from hers. Words flowed quickly from his heart:

"Let me tell you just once more how well I've loved you, never wavering for a moment, never thinking of another girl. And now when I think of all the years ahead without you, without any hope, I don't want to live, Caroline darling. I used to dream about our home, our children, about holding you in my arms and touching your face and hands and hair that used to belong to me, and now I just can't wake up."

Caroline was crying softly. "Poor Michael—poor Michael." Her hand reached out and her fingers brushed the lapel of his dinner coat. "I was so sorry for you the other night. You looked so thin, and as if you needed a new suit and somebody to take care of you." She sniffled and looked more closely at his coat. "Why, you've got a new suit! And a new silk hat! Why, Michael, how *swell!*" She laughed, suddenly cheerful through her tears. "You must have come into money, Michael; I never saw you so well turned out."

For a moment, at her reaction, he hated his new clothes.

"I have come into money," he said. "My grandfather left me about a quarter of a million dollars."

"Why, Michael," she cried, "how perfectly swell! I can't tell you how glad I am. I've always thought you were the sort of person who ought to have money."

"Yes, just too late to make a difference."

The revolving door from the street groaned around and Hamilton Rutherford came into the lobby. His face was flushed, his eyes were restless and impatient.

"Hello, darling; hello, Mr. Curly." He bent and kissed Caroline. "I broke away for a minute to find out if I had any telegrams. I see you've got them there." Taking them from her, he remarked to Curly, "That was an odd business there in the bar, wasn't it? Especially as I understand some of you had a joke fixed up in the same line." He opened one of the telegrams, closed it and turned to Caroline with the divided expression of a man carrying two things in his head at once.

"A girl I haven't seen for two years turned up," he said. "It seemed to be some clumsy form of blackmail, for I haven't and never have had any sort of obligation toward her whatever."

"What happened?"

"The head barman had a *Sûreté nationale* man there in ten minutes and it was settled in the hall. The French blackmail laws make ours look like a sweet wish, and I gather they threw a scare into her that she'll remember. But it seems wiser to tell you."

"Are you implying that I mentioned the matter?" said Michael stiffly.

"No," Rutherford said slowly. "No, you were just going to be on hand. And since you're here, I'll tell you some news that will interest you even more."

He handed Michael one telegram and opened the other.

"This is in code," Michael said.

"So is this. But I've got to know all the words pretty well this last week. The two of them together mean that I'm due to start life all over."

Michael saw Caroline's face grow a shade paler, but she sat quiet as a mouse.

"It was a mistake and I stuck to it too long," continued Rutherford. "So you see I don't have all the luck, Mr. Curly. By the way, they tell me you've come into money."

"Yes," said Michael.

"There we are, then." Rutherford turned to Caroline. "You understand, darling, that I'm not joking or exaggerating. I've lost almost every cent I had and I'm starting life over."

Two pairs of eyes were regarding her—Rutherford's noncommittal and unrequiring, Michael's hungry, tragic, pleading. In a minute she had raised herself from the chair and with a little cry thrown herself into Hamilton Rutherford's arms.

"Oh, darling," she cried, "what does it matter! It's better; I like it better, honestly I do! I want to start that way; I want to! Oh, please don't worry or be sad even for a minute!"

"All right, baby," said Rutherford. His hand stroked her hair gently for a moment; then he took his arm from around her.

"I promised to join the party for an hour," he said. "So I'll say good-night, and I want you to go to bed soon and get a good sleep. Good-night, Mr. Curly. I'm sorry to have let you in for all these financial matters."

But Michael had already picked up his hat and cane. "I'll go along with you," he said.

III

It was such a fine morning. Michael's cutaway hadn't been delivered, so he felt rather uncomfortable passing before the cameras and moving-picture machines in front of the little church on the Avenue George V.

It was such a clean new church that it seemed unforgivable not to be dressed properly, and Michael, white and shaky after a sleepless night, decided to stand in the rear. From there he looked at the back of Hamilton Rutherford, and the lacy filmy back of Caroline, and the fat back of George Packman, which looked unsteady, as if it wanted to lean against the bride and groom.

The ceremony went on for a long time under the gay flags and pennons overhead, under the thick beams of June sunlight slanting down through the tall windows upon the well-dressed people.

As the procession, headed by the bride and groom, started down the aisle, Michael realized with alarm he was just where everyone would dispense with their parade stiffness, become informal and speak to him.

So it turned out. Rutherford and Caroline spoke first to him; Rutherford grim with the strain of being married, and Caroline lovelier than he had ever seen her, floating all softly down through the friends and relatives of her youth, down through the past and forward to the future by the sunlit door.

Michael managed to murmur, "Beautiful, simply beautiful," and then other people passed and spoke to him—old Mrs. Dandy, straight from her sickbed and looking remarkably well, or carrying it off like the very fine old lady she was; and Rutherford's father and mother, ten years divorced, but walking side by side and looking made for each other and proud. Then all Caroline's sisters and their husbands and her little nephews in Eton suits, and then a long parade, all speaking to Michael because he was still standing paralyzed just at that point where the procession broke.

He wondered what would happen now. Cards had been issued for a reception at the George V; an expensive enough place, heaven knew. Would Rutherford try to go through with that on top of those disastrous telegrams? Evidently, for the procession outside was streaming up there through the June morning, three by three and four by four. On the corner the long dresses of girls, five abreast, fluttered many-colored in the wind. Girls had become gossamer again, perambulatory flora—such lovely fluttering dresses in the bright noon wind.

Michael needed a drink—he couldn't face that reception line without a drink. Diving into a side doorway of the hotel, he asked for the bar, whither a *chasseur* led him through half a kilometer of new American-looking passages.

But—how did it happen?—the bar was full. There were ten—fifteen men and two—four girls, all from the wedding, all needing a drink. There were cocktails and champagne in the bar; Rutherford's cocktails and champagne, as it turned out, for he had engaged the whole bar and the ballroom and the two great reception rooms and all the stairways leading up and down, and windows looking out over the whole square block of Paris. By and by Michael went and joined the long, slow drift of the receiving line. Through a flowery mist of "Such a lovely wedding," "My dear, you were simply lovely," "You're a lucky man, Rutherford" he passed down the line. When Michael came to Caroline, she took a single step forward and kissed him on the lips, but he felt no contact in the kiss; it was unreal and he floated on away from it. Old Mrs. Dandy, who had always liked him, held his hand for a minute and thanked him for the flowers he had sent when he heard she was ill.

"I'm so sorry not to have written; you know, we old ladies are grateful for—" The flowers, the fact that she had not written, the wedding—Michael saw that they all had the same relative importance to her now; she had married off five other children and seen two of the marriages go to pieces, and this scene, so poignant, so confusing to Michael, appeared to her simply a familiar charade in which she had played her part before.

A buffet luncheon with champagne was already being served at small tables and there was an orchestra playing in the empty ballroom. Michael sat down with Jebby West; he was still a little embarrassed at not wearing a morning coat, but he perceived now that he was not alone in the omission and felt better. "Wasn't Caroline divine?" Jebby West said. "So entirely self-possessed. I asked her this morning if she wasn't a little nervous at stepping off like this. And she said, 'Why should I be? I've been after him for two years, and now I'm just happy, that's all.'"

"It must be true," said Michael gloomily.

"What?"

"What you just said."

He had been stabbed, but, rather to his distress, he did not feel the wound.

He asked Jebby to dance. Out on the floor, Rutherford's father and mother were dancing together.

"It makes me a little sad, that," she said. "Those two hadn't met for years; both of them were married again and she divorced again. She went to the station to meet him when he came over for Caroline's wedding, and invited him to stay at her house in the Avenue du Bois with a whole lot of other people, perfectly proper, but he was afraid his wife would hear about it and not like it, so he went to a hotel. Don't you think that's sort of sad?"

An hour or so later Michael realized suddenly that it was afternoon. In one corner of the ballroom an arrangement of screens like a moving-picture stage had been set up and photographers were taking official pictures of the bridal party. The bridal party, still as death and pale as wax under the bright lights, appeared to the dancers circling the modulated semidarkness of the ballroom like those jovial or sinister groups that one comes upon in The Old Mill at an amusement park.

After the bridal party had been photographed, there was a group of the ushers; then the bridesmaids, the families, the children. Later, Caroline, active and excited, having long since abandoned the repose implicit in her flowing dress and great bouquet, came and plucked Michael off the floor.

"Now we'll have them take one of just old friends." Her voice implied that this was best, most intimate of all. "Come here, Jebby, George—not you, Hamilton; this is just my friends—Sally—"

A little after that, what remained of formality disappeared and the hours flowed easily down the profuse stream of champagne. In the modern fashion, Hamilton Rutherford sat at the table with his arm about an old girl of his and assured his guests, which included not a few bewildered but enthusiastic Europeans, that the party was not nearly at an end; it was to reassemble at Zelli's after midnight. Michael saw Mrs. Dandy, not quite over her illness, rise to go and become caught in polite group after group, and he spoke of it to one of her daughters, who thereupon forcibly abducted her mother and called her car. Michael felt very considerate and proud of himself after having done this, and drank much more champagne.

"It's amazing," George Packman was telling him enthusiastically. "This show will cost Ham about five thousand dollars, and I understand they'll be just about his last. But did he countermand a bottle of champagne or a flower? Not he! He happens to have it—that young man. Do you know that T. G. Vance offered him a salary of fifty thousand dollars a year ten minutes before the wedding this morning? In another year he'll be back with the millionaires."

The conversation was interrupted by a plan to carry Rutherford out on communal shoulders—a plan which six of them put into effect, and then stood in the four-o'clock sunshine waving good-bye to the bride and groom. But there must have been a mistake somewhere, for five minutes later Michael saw both bride and groom descending the stairway to the reception, each with a glass of champagne held defiantly on high.

"This is our way of doing things," he thought. "Generous and fresh and free—a sort of Virginia-plantation hospitality, but at a different pace now, nervous as a ticker-tape."

Standing unselfconsciously in the middle of the room to see which was the American ambassador, he realized with a start that he hadn't really thought of Caroline for hours. He looked about him with a sort of alarm, and then he saw her across the room, very bright and young, and radiantly happy. He saw Rutherford near her, looking at her as if he could never look long enough, and as Michael watched them they seemed to recede as he had wished them to do that day in the Rue de Castiglione—recede and fade off into joys and griefs of their own, into the years that would take the toll of Rutherford's fine pride and Caroline's young, moving beauty; fade far away, so that now he could scarcely see them, as if they were shrouded in something as misty as her white, billowing dress.

Michael was cured. The ceremonial function, with its pomp and its revelry, had stood for a sort of initiation into a life where even his regret could not follow them. All the bitterness melted out of him suddenly and the world reconstituted itself out of the youth and happiness that was all around him, profligate as the spring sunshine. He was trying to remember which one of the bridesmaids he had made a date to dine with tonight as he walked forward to bid Hamilton and Caroline Rutherford good-bye.

ONE TRIP ABROAD

In the afternoon the air became black with locusts, and some of the women shrieked, sinking to the floor of the motorbus and covering their hair with travelling rugs. The locusts were coming north, eating everything in their path, which was not so much in that part of the world; they were flying silently and in straight lines, flakes of black snow. But none struck the windshield or tumbled into the bus, and presently humorists began holding out their hands, trying to catch some. After ten minutes the cloud thinned out, passed, and the women emerged from the blankets, disheveled and feeling silly. And everyone talked together.

Everyone talked; it would have been absurd not to talk after having been through a swarm of locusts on the edge of the Sahara. The Smyrna-American talked to the British widow going down to Biskra to have one last fling with an as-yet-unencountered sheik. The member of the San Francisco stock exchange talked shyly to the author. "Aren't you an author?" he said. The father and daughter from Wilmington talked to the cockney airman who was going to fly to Timbuctoo. Even the French chauffeur turned about and explained in a loud, clear voice: "Bumblebees," which sent the trained nurse from New York into shriek after shriek of hysterical laughter.

Among the unsubtle rushing together of the travellers there was one interchange more carefully considered. Mr. and Mrs. Liddell Miles, turning as one person, smiled and spoke to the young American couple in the seat behind:

"Didn't catch any in your hair?"

The young couple smiled back politely.

"No. We survived that plague."

They were in their twenties, and there was still a pleasant touch of bride and groom upon them. A handsome couple, the man rather intense and sensitive, the girl arrestingly light of hue in eyes and hair, her face without shadows, its living freshness modulated by a lovely confident calm. Mr. and Mrs. Miles did not fail to notice their air of good breeding, of a specifically "swell" background—expressed both by their unsophistication and by their ingrained reticence that was not stiffness. If they held aloof, it was because they were sufficient to each other, while Mr. and Mrs. Miles' aloofness toward the other passengers was a conscious mask, a social attitude, quite as public an affair in its essence as the ubiquitous advances of the Smyrna-American, who was snubbed by all.

The Mileses had, in fact, decided that the young couple were "possible" and, bored with themselves, were frankly approaching them.

"Have you been to Africa before? It's been so utterly fascinating! Are you going on to Tunis?"

The Mileses, if somewhat worn away inside by fifteen years of a particular set in Paris, had undeniable style, even charm, and before the evening arrival at the little oasis town of Bou Saada they had all four become companionable. They uncovered mutual friends in New York and, meeting for a cocktail in the bar of the Hôtel Transatlantique, decided to have dinner together.

As the young Kellys came downstairs later, Nicole was conscious of a certain regret that they had accepted, realizing that now they were probably committed to seeing a certain amount of their new acquaintances as far as Constantine, where their routes diverged.

In the eight months of their marriage she had been so very happy that it seemed like spoiling something. On the Italian liner that had brought them to Gibraltar they had not joined the groups that leaned desperately on one another in the bar; instead, they seriously studied French, and Nelson worked on business contingent on his recent inheritance of half a million dollars. Also he painted a picture of a smokestack. When one member of the gay crowd in the bar disappeared permanently into the Atlantic just this side of the Azores, the young Kellys were almost glad, for it justified their aloof attitude.

But there was another reason Nicole was sorry they had committed themselves. She spoke to Nelson about it: "I passed that couple in the hall just now."

"Who—the Mileses?"

"No, that young couple—about our age—the ones that were on the other motorbus, that we thought looked so nice, in Bir Rabalou after lunch, in the camel market."

"They did look nice."

"Charming," she said emphatically, "the girl and man, both. I'm almost sure I've met the girl somewhere before."

The couple referred to were sitting across the room at dinner, and Nicole found her eyes drawn irresistibly toward them. They, too, now had companions, and again Nicole, who had not talked to a girl her own age for two months, felt a faint regret. The Mileses, being formally sophisticated and frankly snobbish, were a different matter. They had been to an alarming number of places and seemed to know all the flashing phantoms of the newspapers.

They dined on the hotel verandah under a sky that was low and full of the presence of a strange and watchful god; around the corners of the hotel the night already stirred with the sounds of which they had so often read but that were, even so, hysterically unfamiliar—drums from Senegal, a native flute, the selfish, effeminate whine of a camel, the Arabs pattering past in shoes made of old automobile tires, the wail of Magian prayer.

At the desk in the hotel, a fellow passenger was arguing monotonously with the clerk about the rate of exchange, and the inappropriateness added to the detachment which had increased steadily as they went south.

Mrs. Miles was the first to break the lingering silence—with a sort of impatience she pulled them with her, in from the night and up to the table.

"We really should have dressed. Dinner's more amusing if people dress, because they feel differently in formal clothes. The English know that."

"Dress here?" her husband objected. "I'd feel like that man in the ragged dress suit we passed today, driving the flock of sheep."

"I always feel like a tourist if I'm not dressed."

"Well, we are, aren't we?" asked Nelson.

"I don't consider myself a tourist. A tourist is somebody who gets up early and goes to cathedrals and talks about scenery."

Nicole and Nelson, having seen all the official sights from Fez to Algiers, and taken reels of moving pictures and felt improved, confessed themselves, but decided that their experiences on the trip would not interest Mrs. Miles.

"Every place is the same," Mrs. Miles continued. "The only thing that matters is who's there. New scenery is fine for half an hour, but after that you want your own kind to see. That's why some places have a certain vogue, and then the vogue changes and the people move on somewhere else. The place itself really never matters."

"But doesn't somebody first decide that the place is nice?" objected Nelson. "The first ones go there because they like the place."

"Where were you going this spring?" Mrs. Miles asked.

"We thought of San Remo, or maybe Sorrento. We've never been to Europe before."

"My children, I know both Sorrento and San Remo, and you won't stand either of them for a week. They're full of the most awful English, reading the *Daily Mail* and waiting for letters and talking about the most incredibly dull things. You might as well go to Brighton or Bournemouth and buy a white poodle and a sunshade and walk on the pier. How long are you staying in Europe?"

"We don't know; perhaps several years." Nicole hesitated. "Nelson came into a little money, and we wanted a change. When I was young, my father had asthma and I had to live in the most depressing health resorts with him for years; and Nelson was in the fur business in Alaska and he loathed it; so when we were free we came abroad. Nelson's going to paint and I'm going to study singing." She looked triumphantly at her husband. "So far, it's been absolutely gorgeous."

Mrs. Miles decided, from the evidence of the younger woman's clothes, that it was quite a bit of money, and their enthusiasm was infectious.

"You really must go to Biarritz," she advised them. "Or else come to Monte Carlo."

"They tell me there's a great show here," said Miles, ordering champagne. "The Ouled Naïls. The concierge says they're some kind of tribe of girls who come down from the mountains and learn to be dancers, and what not, till they've collected enough gold to go back to their mountains and marry. Well, they give a performance tonight."

Walking over to the café of the Ouled Naïls afterward, Nicole regretted that she and Nelson were not strolling alone through the ever-lower, ever-softer, ever-brighter night. Nelson had reciprocated the bottle of champagne at dinner, and neither of them was accustomed to so much. As they drew near the sad flute she didn't want to go inside, but rather to climb to the top of a low hill where a white mosque shone clear as a planet through the night. Life was better than any show—closing in toward Nelson, she pressed his hand.

The little cave of a café was filled with the passengers from the two busses. The girls—light-brown, flat-nosed Berbers with fine, deep-shaded eyes—were already doing each one her solo on the platform. They wore cotton dresses, faintly reminiscent of Southern mammies—under these their bodies writhed in a slow nautch, culminating in a stomach dance, with silver belts bobbing wildly and their strings of real gold coins tinkling on their necks and arms. The flute player was also a comedian—he danced, burlesquing the girls. The drummer, swathed in goatskins like a witch doctor, was a true black from the Sudan.

Through the smoke of cigarettes each girl went in turn through the finger movement, like piano playing in the air—outwardly facile, yet, after a few moments, so obviously exacting, and then through the very simple, languid, yet equally precise steps of the feet—these were but preparation to the wild sensuality of the culminated dance.

Afterward there was a lull. Though the performance seemed not quite over, most of the audience gradually got up to go, but there was a whispering in the air.

"What is it?" Nicole asked her husband.

"Why, I believe—it appears that for a consideration the Ouled Naïls dance in more or less—ah—Oriental style—in very little except jewelry."

"Oh."

"We're all staying," Mr. Miles assured her jovially. "After all, we're here to see the real customs and manners of the country. We shouldn't let a little prudishness stand in our way."

Most of the men remained, and several of the women. Nicole stood up suddenly.

"I'll wait outside," she said.

"Why not stay, Nicole? After all, Mrs. Miles is staying."

The flute player was making preliminary flourishes. Upon the raised dais two pale brown children of perhaps fourteen were taking off their cotton dresses. For an instant Nicole hesitated, torn between repulsion and the desire not to appear to be a prig. Then she saw another young American woman get up quickly and start for the door. Recognizing the attractive young wife from the other bus, her own decision came quickly and she followed.

Nelson hurried after her. "I'm going if you go," he said, but with evident reluctance.

"Please don't bother. I'll wait with the guide outside."

"Well—" The drum was starting. He compromised: "I'll only stay a minute. I want to see what it's like."

Waiting in the fresh night, she found that the incident had hurt her—Nelson's not coming with her at once, giving it as an argument that Mrs. Miles was staying. From being hurt, she grew angry and made signs to the guide that she wanted to return to the hotel.

Twenty minutes later, Nelson appeared, angry with the anxiety at finding her gone, as well as to hide his guilt at having left her. Incredulous with themselves, they were suddenly in a quarrel.

Much later, when there were no sounds at all in Bou Saada and the nomads in the marketplace were only motionless bundles rolled up in their burnouses, she was asleep upon his shoulder. Life is progressive, no matter what our intentions, but something was harmed, some precedent of possible nonagreement was set. It was a love match, though, and it could stand a great deal. She and Nelson had passed lonely youths, and now they wanted the taste and smell of the living world—for the present they were finding it in each other.

A month later they were in Sorrento, where Nicole took singing lessons and Nelson tried to paint something new into the Bay of

Naples. It was the existence they had planned and often read about. But they found, as so many have found, that the charm of idyllic interludes depends upon one person's "giving the party"—which is to say, furnishing the background, the experience, the patience, against which the other seems to enjoy again the spells of pastoral tranquility recollected from childhood. Nicole and Nelson were at once too old and too young, and too American, to fall into immediate soft agreement with a strange land. Their vitality made them restless, for as yet his painting had no direction and her singing no immediate prospect of becoming serious. They said they were not "getting anywhere"—the evenings were long, so they began to drink a lot of *vin de Capri* at dinner.

The English owned the hotel. They were aged, come South for good weather and tranquility. Nelson and Nicole resented the mild tenor of their days. Could people be content to talk eternally about the weather, promenade the same walks, face the same variant of macaroni at dinner month after month? They grew bored, and Americans bored are already in sight of excitement. Things came to a head all in one night.

Over a flask of wine at dinner they decided to go to Paris, settle in an apartment and work seriously. Paris promised metropolitan diversion, friends of their own age, a general intensity that Italy lacked. Eager with new hopes, they strolled into the salon after dinner, when, for the tenth time, Nelson noticed an ancient and enormous mechanical piano and was moved to try it.

Across the salon sat the only English people with whom they had had any connection—General Sir Evelyn Frazelle and Lady Frazelle. The connection had been brief and unpleasant—seeing them walking out of the hotel in peignoirs to swim, Lady Frazelle had announced, over quite a few yards of floor space, that it was disgusting and shouldn't be allowed.

But that was nothing compared with her response to the first terrific bursts of sound from the electric piano. As the dust of years trembled off the keyboard at the vibration, she shot galvanically forward with the sort of jerk associated with the electric chair. Somewhat stunned himself by the sudden din of "Waiting for the Robert E. Lee," Nelson had scarcely sat down when she projected herself across the room, her train quivering behind her, and, without glancing at the Kellys, turned off the instrument.

It was one of those gestures that are either plainly justified, or else outrageous. For a moment Nelson hesitated uncertainly—then, remembering Lady Frazelle's arrogant remark about his bathing suit, he returned to the instrument in her still-billowing wake and turned it on again.

The incident had become international. The eyes of the entire salon fell eagerly upon the protagonists, watching for the next move. Nicole hurried after Nelson, urging him to let the matter pass, but it was too late. From the outraged English table there arose, joint by joint, General Sir Evelyn Frazelle, faced with perhaps his most crucial situation since the relief of Ladysmith.

"'T'lee outrageous!—'t'lee outrageous!"

"I beg your pardon," said Nelson.

"Here for fifteen years!" screamed Sir Evelyn to himself. "Never heard of anyone doing such a thing before!"

"I gathered that this was put here for the amusement of the guests."

Scorning to answer, Sir Evelyn knelt, reached for the catch, pushed it the wrong way, whereupon the speed and volume of the instrument tripled until they stood in a wild pandemonium of sound, Sir Evelyn livid with military emotions, Nelson on the point of maniacal laughter.

In a moment the firm hand of the hotel manager settled the matter—the instrument gulped and stopped, trembling a little from its unaccustomed outburst, leaving behind it a great silence in which Sir Evelyn turned to the manager.

"Most outrageous affair ever heard of in my life. My wife turned it off once, and *he*"—this was his first acknowledgment of Nelson's identity as distinct from the instrument—"*he* put it on again!"

"This is a public room in a hotel," Nelson protested. "The instrument is apparently here to be used."

"Don't get in an argument," Nicole whispered. "They're old."

But Nelson said, "If there's any apology, it's certainly due to me."

Sir Evelyn's eye was fixed menacingly upon the manager, waiting for him to do his duty. The latter thought of Sir Evelyn's fifteen years of residence, and cringed.

"It is not the habitude to play the instrument in the evening. The clients are each one quiet on his or her table."

"American cheek!" snapped Sir Evelyn.

"Very well," Nelson said. "We'll relieve the hotel of our presence tomorrow."

As a reaction from this incident, as a sort of protest against Sir Evelyn Frazelle, they went not to Paris but to Monte Carlo after all. They were through with being alone.

II

A little more than two years after the Kellys' first visit to Monte Carlo, Nicole woke up one morning into what, though it bore the same name, had become to her a different place altogether.

In spite of hurried months in Paris or Biarritz, it was now home to them. They had a villa, they had a large acquaintance among the spring and summer crowd—a crowd which naturally did not include people on chartered trips or the shore parties from Mediterranean cruises—these latter had become for them "tourists."

They loved the Riviera in full summer with many friends there and the nights open and full of music. Before the maid drew the curtains this morning to shut out the glare, Nicole saw from her window the yacht of T. F. Golding, placid among the swells of the Monacan Bay, as if constantly bound on a romantic voyage not dependent upon actual motion.

The yacht had taken the slow tempo of the coast—it had gone no farther than to Cannes and back all summer, though it might have toured the world. The Kellys were dining on board that night.

Nicole spoke excellent French, she had five new evening dresses and four others that would do, she had her husband, she had two men in love with her, and she felt sad for one of them. She had her pretty face. At ten-thirty she was meeting a third man, who was just beginning to be in love with her "in a harmless way." At one she was having a dozen charming people to luncheon. All that.

"I'm happy," she brooded toward the bright blinds. "I'm young and good-looking, and my name is often in the paper as having been here and there, but really I don't care about shishi. I think it's all awfully silly, but if you do want to see people, you might as well see the chic, amusing ones, and if people call you a snob, it's envy, and they know it and everybody knows it."

She repeated the substance of this to Oscar Dane on the Mont Agel golf course two hours later, and he cursed her quietly.

"Not at all," he said. "You're just getting to be an old snob. Do you call that crowd of drunks you run with amusing people? Why, they're not even very swell. They're so hard that they've shifted down through Europe like nails in a sack of wheat, till they stick out of it a little into the Mediterranean Sea."

Annoyed, Nicole fired a name at him, but he answered: "Class C. A good solid article for beginners."

"The Colbys—anyway, her."

"Third flight."

"Marquis and Marquise de Kalb."

"If she didn't happen to take dope and he didn't have even stranger peculiarities."

"Well then, where are the amusing people?" she demanded impatiently.

"Off by themselves somewhere. They don't hunt in herds, except occasionally."

"How about you? You'd snap up an invitation from every person I named. I've heard stories about you wilder than any you can make up. There's not a man that's known you six months that would take your check for ten dollars. You're a sponge and a parasite and everything—"

"Shut up for a minute," he interrupted. "I don't want to spoil this drive. . . . I just don't like to see you kid yourself," he continued. "What passes with you for international society is just about as hard to enter nowadays as the public rooms at the Casino—and if I can make my living by sponging off it, I'm still giving twenty times more than I get. We dead beats are about the only people in it with any stuff, and we stay with it because we have to."

She laughed, liking him immensely, wondering how angry Nelson would be when he found that Oscar had walked off with his nail scissors and his copy of the *New York Herald* this morning.

"Anyhow," she thought afterward as she drove home toward lunch, "we're getting out of it all soon, and we'll be serious and have a baby. After this last summer."

Stopping for a moment at a florist's, she saw a young woman coming out with an armful of flowers. The young woman glanced at her over the heap of color, and Nicole perceived that she was extremely smart, and then that her face was familiar. It was someone she had known once, but only slightly; the name had escaped her so she did not nod, and forgot the incident until that afternoon.

They were twelve for lunch: the Goldings' party from the yacht, Liddell and Cardine Miles, Mr. Dane—seven different nationalities she counted, among them an exquisite young Frenchwoman, Madame Delauney, whom Nicole referred to lightly as "Nelson's girl." Noel Delauney was perhaps her closest friend; when they made up foursomes for golf or for trips, she paired off with Nelson—but today, as Nicole introduced her to someone as "Nelson's girl," the bantering phrase filled Nicole with distaste.

She said aloud at luncheon: "Nelson and I are going to get away from it all."

Everybody agreed that they, too, were going to get away from it all.

"It's all right for the English," someone said, "because they're doing a sort of dance of death—you know, gayety in the doomed fort, with the Sepoys at the gate. You can see it by their faces when they dance—the intensity. They know it and they want it, and they don't see any future. But you Americans, you're having a rotten time. If you want to wear the green hat or the crushed hat, or whatever it is, you always have to get a little tipsy."

"We're going to get away from it all," Nicole said firmly, but something within her argued: "What a pity—this lovely blue sea, this happy time." What came afterward? Did one just accept a lessening of tension? It was somehow Nelson's business to answer that. His growing discontent that he wasn't getting anywhere ought to explode into a new life for both of them, or rather a new hope and content with life. That secret should be his masculine contribution.

"Well, children, good-bye."

"It was a great luncheon."

"Don't forget about getting away from it all."

"See you when—"

The guests walked down the path toward their cars. Only Oscar, just faintly flushed on liqueurs, stood with Nicole on the verandah, talking on and on about the girl he had invited up to see his stamp collection. Momentarily tired of people, impatient to be alone, Nicole listened for a moment and then, taking a glass vase of flowers from the luncheon table, went through the French windows into the dark, shadowy villa, his voice following her as he talked on and on out there.

It was when she crossed the first salon, still hearing Oscar's monologue on the verandah, that she began to hear another voice in the next room, cutting sharply across Oscar's voice.

"Ah, but kiss me again," it said, stopped; Nicole stopped too, rigid in the silence, now broken only by the voice on the porch.

"Be careful." Nicole recognized the faint French accent of Noel Delauney.

"I'm tired of being careful. Anyhow, they're on the verandah."

"No, better the usual place."

"Darling, sweet darling."

The voice of Oscar Dane on the verandah grew weary and stopped and, as if thereby released from her paralysis, Nicole took a step—forward or backward, she did not know which. At the sound of her heel on the floor, she heard the two people in the next room breaking swiftly apart.

Then she went in. Nelson was lighting a cigarette, Noel with her back turned was apparently hunting for hat or purse on a chair. With blind horror rather than anger, Nicole threw, or rather pushed away from her, the glass vase which she carried. If at anyone, it was at Nelson she threw it, but the force of her feeling had entered the inanimate thing—it flew past him, and Noel Delauney, just turning about, was struck full on the side of her head and face.

"Say there!" Nelson cried. Noel sank slowly into the chair before which she stood, her hand slowly rising to cover the side of her face. The jar rolled unbroken on the thick carpet, scattering its flowers.

"You look out!" Nelson was at Noel's side, trying to take the hand away to see what had happened.

"*C'est liquide*," gasped Noel in a whisper. "*Est-ce que c'est le sang?*"

He forced her hand away, and cried breathlessly, "No, it's just water!" and then to Oscar who had appeared in the doorway: "Get some cognac!" and to Nicole: "You damn fool, you must be crazy!"

Nicole, breathing hard, said nothing. When the brandy arrived, there was a continuing silence, like that of people watching an operation, while Nelson poured a glass down Noel's throat. Nicole signaled to Oscar for a drink, and, as if afraid to break the silence without it, they all had a brandy. Then Noel and Nelson spoke at once:

"If you can find my hat—"

"This is the silliest—"

"—I shall go immediately."

"—thing I ever saw, I—"

They all looked at Nicole, who said: "Have her car drive right up to the door." Oscar departed quickly.

"Are you sure you don't want to see a doctor?" asked Nelson anxiously.

"I want to go."

A minute later when the car had driven away Nelson came in and poured himself another glass of brandy. A wave of subsiding tension flowed over him, showing in his face. Nicole saw it, and saw also his gathering will to make the best he could of it.

"I want to know just why you did that," he demanded. "No, don't go, Oscar." He saw the story starting out into the world. "What possible reason—"

"Oh, shut up!" snapped Nicole.

"If I kissed Noel, there's nothing so terrible about it. It's of absolutely no significance."

She made a contemptuous sound. "I heard what you said to her."

"You're *crazy*."

He said it as if she *were* crazy, and wild rage filled her.

"You liar! All this time pretending to be so square and so particular what I did and all the time behind my back you've been playing around with that little—"

She used a serious word, and as if maddened with the sound of it she sprang toward his chair. In protection against this sudden attack, he flung up his arm quickly, and the knuckles of his open hand struck across the socket of her eye. Covering her face with her hand as Noel had done ten minutes previously, she fell sobbing to the floor.

"For God's sake, hasn't this gone far enough?" Oscar cried.

"Yes," admitted Nelson, "I guess it has."

"You go on out on the verandah and cool off."

Oscar got Nicole to a couch and sat beside her, holding her hand.

"Brace up—brace up, baby," he said, over and over. "What are you—Jack Dempsey? You can't go around hitting French women; they'll sue you."

"He told her he loved her," she gasped hysterically. "She said she'd meet him at the same place. . . . Has he gone there now?"

"He's out on the porch, walking up and down, sorry as the devil that he accidentally hit you, and sorry he ever saw Noel Delauney."

"Oh, yes!"

"You might have heard wrong, and it doesn't prove a thing anyhow."

After twenty minutes, Nelson came in suddenly and sank down on his knees by the side of his wife. Mr. Oscar Dane, reinforced in his idea that he gave much more than he got, backed discreetly and far from unwillingly to the door.

In another hour Nelson and Nicole, arm in arm, emerged from their villa and walked slowly down to the Café de Paris. They walked instead of driving, as if trying to return to the simplicity they had once possessed, as if they were trying to unwind something that had become visibly tangled. Nicole accepted his explanations, not because they were credible, but because she wanted passionately to believe them. They were both very quiet and sorry.

The Café de Paris was pleasant at that hour, with sunset drooping through the yellow awnings and the red parasols as through stained glass. Glancing about, Nicole saw the young woman she had encountered that morning. She was with a man now, and Nelson placed them immediately as the young couple they had seen in Algeria, almost three years ago.

"They've changed," he commented. "I suppose we have, too, but not so much. They're harder-looking and he looks dissipated. Dissipation always shows in light eyes rather than in dark ones. The girl is *tout ce qu'il y a de chic*, as they say, but there's a hard look in her face too."

"I like her."

"Do you want me to go and ask them if they are that same couple?"

"No! That'd be like lonesome tourists do. They have their own friends."

At that moment people were joining them at their table.

"Nelson, how about tonight?" Nicole asked a little later. "Do you think we can appear at the Goldings' after what's happened?"

"We not only can, but we've got to. If the story's around and we're not there, we'll just be handing them a nice juicy subject of conversation .... Hello! What on earth—"

Something strident and violent had happened across the café—a woman screamed and the people at one table were all on their feet, surging back and forth like one person. Then the people at the other tables were standing and crowding forward—for just a moment the Kellys saw the face of the girl they had been watching, pale now and distorted with anger. Panic-stricken, Nicole plucked at Nelson's sleeve.

"I want to get out. I can't stand any more today. Take me home. Is everybody going crazy?"

On the way home Nelson glanced at Nicole's face and perceived with a start that they were not going to dinner on the Goldings' yacht after all. For Nicole had the beginnings of a well-defined and unmistakable black eye—an eye that by eleven o'clock would be beyond the aid of all the cosmetics in the principality. His heart sank and he decided to say nothing about it until they reached home.

III

There is some wise advice in the catechism about avoiding the occasions of sin, and when the Kellys went up to Paris a month later they made a conscientious list of the places they wouldn't visit anymore and the people they didn't want to see again. The places included several famous bars, all the night clubs except one or two that were highly decorous, all the early-morning clubs of every description, and all summer resorts that made whoopee for its own sake, whoopee triumphant and unrestrained, the main attraction of the season.

The people they were through with included three-fourths of those with whom they had passed the last two years. They did this not in snobbishness but for self-preservation—and not without a certain fear in their hearts that they were cutting themselves off from human contacts forever.

But the world is always curious, and people become valuable merely for their inaccessibility. They found that there were others in Paris who were only interested in those who had separated from the many. The first crowd they had known was largely American, salted with Europeans; the second was largely European, peppered with Americans. This latter crowd was "society," and here and there it touched the ultimate milieu, made up of individuals of high position, of great fortune, very occasionally of genius and always of power. Without being intimate with the great, they made new friends of a more conservative type. Moreover, Nelson began to paint again; he had a studio, and they visited the studios of Brancusi and Léger and Duchamp. It seemed that they were more part of something than before, and when certain gaudy rendezvous were mentioned they felt a contempt for their first two years in Europe, speaking of their former acquaintances as "that crowd" and as "people who waste your time."

So, although they kept their rules, they entertained frequently at home and they went out to the houses of others. They were young and handsome and intelligent, they came to know what did go and what did not go and adapted themselves accordingly. Moreover, they were naturally generous and willing, within the limits of common sense, to pay.

When one went out one generally drank. This meant little to Nicole, who had a horror of losing her *soigné* air, losing a touch of bloom or a ray of admiration, but Nelson, thwarted somewhere, found himself quite as tempted to drink at these small dinners as in the more frankly rowdy world. He was not a drunk, he did nothing conspicuous or sodden—but he was no longer willing to go out socially without the stimulus of liquor. It was with the idea of bringing him to a serious and responsible attitude that Nicole decided, after a year in Paris, that the time had come to have a baby.

This was coincidental with their meeting Count Chiki Sarolai. He was an attractive relic of the Austrian court, with no fortune or pretense to any, but with solid social and financial connections in France. His sister was married to the Marquis de la Clos d'Hirondelle, who, in addition to being of the ancient noblesse, was a successful banker in Paris. Count Chiki roved here and there, frankly sponging, rather like Oscar Dane, but in a different sphere.

His penchant was Americans—he hung on their words with a pathetic eagerness, as if they would sooner or later let slip their mysterious formula for making money. After a casual meeting, his interest gravitated to the Kellys. During Nicole's months of waiting he was in the house continually, tirelessly interested by anything that concerned American crime, slang, finance or manners. He came in for a lunch or dinner when he had no other place to go, and with tacit gratitude he persuaded his sister to call on Nicole, who was immensely flattered.

It was arranged that when Nicole went to the hospital he would stay at the apartment and keep Nelson company—an arrangement of which Nicole didn't approve, since they were inclined to drink together. But the day on which it was decided, he arrived with news of one of his brother-in-law's famous canal-boat parties on the Seine, to which the Kellys were to be invited and which, conveniently enough, was to occur three weeks after the arrival of the baby. So when Nicole moved out to the American Hospital, Count Chiki moved in.

The baby was a boy. For awhile Nicole forgot all about people and their human status, and their value. She even wondered at the fact that she had become such a snob, since everything seemed trivial compared with the new individual that, eight times a day, they carried to her breast.

After two weeks she and the baby went back to the apartment, but Chiki and his valet stayed on. It was understood, with that subtlety the Kellys had only recently begun to appreciate, that he was merely staying until after his brother-in-law's party, but the apartment was crowded and Nicole wished him gone. But her old idea, that if one had to see people they might as well be the best, was carried out in being invited to the De la Clos d'Hirondelles'.

As she lay in her chaise longue the day before the event, Chiki explained the arrangements, in which he had evidently aided.

"Everyone who arrives must drink two cocktails in the American style before they can come aboard. As a ticket of admission."

"But I thought that very fashionable French, Faubourg Saint-Germain and all that, didn't drink cocktails."

"Oh, but my family is very modern. We adopt many American customs."

"Who'll be there?"

"Everyone! Everyone in Paris."

Great names swam before her eyes. Next day she could not resist dragging the affair into conversation with her doctor. But she was rather offended at the look of astonishment and incredulity that came into his eyes.

"Did I understand you aright?" he demanded. "Did I understand you to say that you were going to a ball tomorrow?"

"Why—yes," she faltered. "Why not?"

"My dear lady, you are not going to stir out of the house for two more weeks—you are not going to dance or do anything strenuous for two more after that."

"That's ridiculous!" she cried. "It's been three weeks already! Esther Sherman went to America after—"

"Never mind," he interrupted. "Every case is different. There is a complication which makes it positively necessary for you to follow my orders."

"But the idea is that I'll just go for two hours, because of course I'll have to come home to Sonny—"

"You'll not go for two minutes."

She knew from the seriousness of his tone that he was right—but perversely she did not mention the matter to Nelson. She said instead that she was tired, that possibly she might not go, and lay awake that night measuring her disappointment against her fear. She woke up for Sonny's first feeding, thinking to herself: "But if I just take ten steps from a limousine to a chair and just sit half an hour—"

At the last minute the pale green evening dress from Callets, draped across a chair in her bedroom, decided her. She went.

Somewhere during the shuffle and delay on the gangplank while the guests went aboard and were challenged and drank down their cocktails with attendant gayety, Nicole realized that she had made a mistake. There was, at any rate, no formal receiving line and, after greeting their hosts, Nelson found her a chair on deck, where presently her faintness disappeared.

Then she was glad she had come. The boat was hung with fragile lanterns, which blended with the pastels of the bridges and the reflected stars in the dark Seine, like a child's dream out of the Arabian Nights. A crowd of hungry-eyed spectators were gathered on the banks. Champagne moved past in platoons like a drill of bottles while the music, instead of being loud and obtrusive, drifted down from the upper deck like frosting dripping over a cake. She became aware presently that they were not the only Americans there—across the deck were the Liddell Mileses, whom she had not seen for several years.

Other people from that crowd were present, and she felt a faint disappointment. What if this was not the marquis' best party? She remembered her mother's second days at home. She asked Chiki, who was at her side, to point out celebrities, but when she inquired about several people whom she associated with that set, he replied vaguely that they were away, or were coming later, or could not be there. It seemed to her that she saw across the room the girl who had made the scene in the Café de Paris at Monte Carlo, but she could not be sure, for with the faint almost imperceptible movement of the boat, she realized that she was growing faint again. She sent for Nelson to take her home.

"You can come right back, of course. You needn't wait for me, because I'm going right to bed."

He left her in the hands of the nurse, who helped her upstairs and aided her to undress quickly.

"I'm desperately tired," Nicole said. "Will you put my pearls away?"

"Where?"

"In the jewel box—on the dressing table."

"I don't see it," said the nurse, after a minute.

"Then it's in a drawer."

There was a thorough rummaging of the dressing table, without result.

"But of course it's there." Nicole attempted to rise, but fell back, exhausted. "Look for it, please, again. Everything is in it—all my mother's things and my engagement things."

"I'm sorry, Mrs. Kelly. There's nothing in this room that answers to that description."

"Wake up the maid."

The maid knew nothing; then after a persistent cross-examination she did know something. Count Sarolai's valet had gone out carrying his suitcase half an hour after madame left the house.

Writhing in sharp and sudden pain, with a hastily summoned doctor at her side, it seemed to Nicole hours before Nelson came home. When he arrived, his face was deathly pale and his eyes were wild. He came directly into her room.

"What do you think?" he said savagely. Then he saw the doctor. "Why, what's the matter?"

"Oh, Nelson, I'm sick as a dog and my jewel box is gone—and Chiki's valet has gone. I've told the police.... Perhaps Chiki would know where the man—"

"Chiki will never come in this house again," he said slowly. "Do you know whose party that was? Have you got any idea whose party that was?" He burst into wild laughter. "It was *our* party—*our* party, do you understand? We gave it—we didn't know it, but we did."

"*Maintenant, monsieur, il ne faut pas exciter madame—*" the doctor began.

"I thought it was odd when the marquis went home early, but I didn't suspect till the end. They were just guests—Chiki invited all the people. After it was over, the caterers and musicians began to come up and ask me where to send their bills. And that damn Chiki had the nerve to tell me he thought I knew all the time. He said that all he'd promised was that it would be his brother-in-law's sort of party, and that his sister would be there. He said perhaps I was drunk, or perhaps I didn't understand French—as if we'd ever talked anything but English to him."

"Don't pay!" she said. "I wouldn't think of paying."

"So I said, but they're going to sue—the boat people and the others. They want twelve thousand dollars."

She relaxed suddenly. "Oh, go away!" she cried. "I don't care! I've lost my jewels and I'm sick, sick!"

IV

This is the story of a trip abroad, and the geographical element must not be slighted. Having visited North Africa, Italy, the Riviera, Paris and points in between, it was not surprising that eventually the Kellys should go to Switzerland. Switzerland is a country where very few things begin, but many things end.

While there was an element of choice in their other ports of call, the Kellys went to Switzerland because they had to. They had been married a little more than four years when they arrived one spring day at the lake that is the center of Europe—a placid, smiling spot with pastoral hillsides, a backdrop of mountains and waters of postcard blue, waters that are a little sinister beneath the surface with all the misery that has dragged itself here from every corner of Europe. Weariness to recuperate and death to die. There are schools, too, and young people splashing at the sunny plages; there is Bonivard's dungeon and Calvin's city, and the ghosts of Byron and Shelley still sail the dim shores by night—but the Lake Geneva that Nelson and Nicole came to was the dreary one of sanatoriums and rest hotels.

For, as if by some profound sympathy that had continued to exist beneath the unlucky destiny that had pursued their affairs, health had failed them both at the same time; Nicole lay on the balcony of a hotel coming slowly back to life after two successive operations, while Nelson fought for life against jaundice in a hospital two miles away. Even after the reserve force of twenty-nine years had pulled him through, there were months ahead during which he must live quietly. Often they wondered why, of all those who sought pleasure over the face of Europe, this misfortune should have come to them.

"There've been too many people in our lives," Nelson said. "We've never been able to resist people. We were so happy the first year when there weren't any people."

Nicole agreed. "If we could ever be alone, really alone, we could make up some kind of life for ourselves. We'll try, won't we, Nelson?"

But there were other days when they both wanted company desperately, concealing it from each other. Days when they eyed the obese, the wasted, the crippled and the broken of all nationalities who filled the hotel, seeking for one who might be amusing. It was a new life for them, turning on the daily visits of their two doctors, the arrival of the mail and newspapers from Paris, the little walk into the hillside village or occasionally the descent by funicular to the pale resort on the lake, with its *Kursaal*, its grass beach, its tennis clubs and sight-seeing busses. They read Tauchnitz editions and yellow-jacketed Edgar Wallaces; at a certain hour each day they watched the baby being given its bath; three nights a week there was a tired and patient orchestra in the lounge after dinner, that was all.

And sometimes there was a booming from the vine-covered hills on the other side of the lake, which meant that cannons were shooting at hail-bearing clouds, to save the vineyard from an approaching storm; it came swiftly, first falling from the heavens and then falling again in torrents from the mountains, washing loudly down the roads and stone ditches; it came with a dark, frightening sky and savage filaments of lightning and crashing, world-splitting thunder, while ragged and destroyed clouds fled along before the wind past the hotel. The mountains and the lake disappeared; the hotel crouched alone amid tumult and chaos and darkness.

It was during such a storm, when the mere opening of a door admitted a tornado of rain and wind into the hall, that the Kellys for the first time in months saw someone they knew. Sitting downstairs with other victims of frayed nerves, they became aware of two new arrivals, a man and woman whom they recognized as that couple, first seen in Algiers, who had crossed their path several times since. A single unexpressed thought flashed through Nelson and Nicole. It seemed like destiny that at last here in this desolate place they should know them, and watching, they saw the other couple eying them in the same tentative way. Yet something held the Kellys back. Had they not just been complaining that there were too many people in their lives?

Later when the storm had dozed off into a quiet rain, Nicole found herself near the girl on the glass verandah. Under cover of reading a book, she inspected the face closely. It was an inquisitive face, she saw at once, possibly calculating; the eyes, intelligent enough, but with no peace in them, swept over people in a single quick glance as though estimating their value. "Terrible egoist," Nicole thought with a certain distaste. For the rest, the cheeks were wan, and there were little pouches of ill health under the eyes, these combining with a certain flabbiness of arms and legs to give an impression of unwholesomeness. She was dressed expensively but with a hint of slovenliness, as if she did not consider the people of the hotel important.

On the whole Nicole decided she did not like her; she was glad that they had not spoken, but she was rather surprised that she had not noticed these things when the girl crossed her path before.

Telling Nelson her impression at dinner, he agreed with her.

"I ran into the man in the bar, and I noticed we both took nothing but mineral water, so I started to say something. But I got a good look at his face in the mirror and I decided not to. His face is so weak and self-indulgent that it's almost mean—the kind of face that needs half a dozen drinks really to open the eyes and stiffen the mouth up to normal."

After dinner the rain stopped and the night was fine outside. Eager for the air, the Kellys wandered down into the dark garden; on their way they passed the subjects of their late discussion, who withdrew abruptly down a side path.

"I don't think they want to know us any more than we do them," Nicole laughed.

They loitered among the wild rose bushes and the beds of damp-sweet indistinguishable flowers. Below the hotel, where the terrace fell a thousand feet to the lake, stretched a necklace of lights that was Montreux and Vevey, and then, in a dim pendant, Lausanne; a blurred twinkling across the lake was Evian and France. From somewhere below, probably the *Kursaal*, came the sound of full-bodied dance music—American, they guessed, though now they heard American tunes months late, mere distant echoes of what was happening far away.

Over the Dents du Midi, over a black bank of clouds that was the rearguard of the receding storm, the moon lifted itself and the lake brightened—the music and the far-away lights were like hope, like the enchanted distance from which children see things. In their separate hearts Nelson and Nicole gazed backward to a time when life was all like this. Her arm went through his quietly and drew him close.

"We can have it all again," she whispered. "Can't we try, Nelson?"

She paused as two dark forms came into the shadows nearby and stood looking down at the lake below.

Nelson put his arm around Nicole and pulled her closer.

"It's just that we don't understand what's the matter," she said. "Why did we lose peace and love and health, one after the other? If we knew, if there was anybody to tell us, I believe we could try. I'd try so hard."

The last dark clouds were lifting themselves over the Bernese Alps. Suddenly, with a final intensity, the west flared with pale white lightning. Nelson and Nicole turned—and simultaneously the other couple turned, while for an instant the night was as bright as day.

Then darkness and a last low peal of thunder—and from Nicole a sharp, terrified cry. She flung herself against Nelson; even in the darkness she saw that his face was as white and strained as her own.

"Did you see?" she cried in a whisper. "Did you see them?"

"God, Yes!"

"They're us! They're us! Don't you see?"

Trembling, they clung together. The clouds merged into the dark mass of mountains; looking around after a moment, Nelson and Nicole saw that they were alone together in the tranquil moonlight.

THE HOTEL CHILD

It is a place where one's instinct is to give a reason for being there—"Oh, you see, I'm here because—" Failing that, you are faintly suspect, because this corner of Europe does not draw people; rather, it accepts them without too many inconvenient questions—live and let live. Routes cross here—people bound for private *cliniques* or tuberculosis resorts in the mountains, people who are no longer *persona grata* in Italy or France. And if that were all—

Yet on a gala night at the Hôtel des Trois Mondes a new arrival would scarcely detect the current beneath the surface. Watching the dancing there would be a gallery of Englishwomen of a certain age, with neckbands, dyed hair and faces powdered pinkish grey; a gallery of American women of a certain age, with snowy-white transformations, black dresses and lips of cherry red. And most of them with their eyes swinging right or left from time to time to rest upon the ubiquitous Fifi. The entire hotel had been made aware that Fifi had reached the age of eighteen that night.

Fifi Schwartz. An exquisitely, radiantly beautiful Jewess whose fine high forehead sloped gently up to where her hair, bordering it like an armorial shield, burst into lovelocks and waves and curlicues of soft dark red. Her eyes were bright, big, clear, wet and shining; the color of her cheeks and lips was real, breaking close to the surface from the strong young pump of her heart. Her body was so assertively adequate that one cynic had been heard to remark that she always looked as if she had nothing on underneath her dresses; but he was probably wrong, for Fifi had been as thoroughly equipped for beauty by man as by God. Such dresses—cerise for Chanel, mauve for Molyneux, pink for Patou; dozens of them, tight at the hips, swaying, furling, folding just an eighth of an inch off the dancing floor. Tonight she was a woman of thirty in dazzling black, with long white gloves dripping from her forearms. "Such ghastly taste," the whispers said. "The stage, the shop window, the manikins' parade. What can her mother be thinking? But, then, look at her mother."

Her mother sat apart with a friend and thought about Fifi and Fifi's brother, and about her other daughters, now married, whom she considered to have been even prettier than Fifi. Mrs. Schwartz was a plain woman; she had been a Jewess a long time, and it was a matter of effortless indifference to her what was said by the groups around the room. Another large class who did not care were the young men—dozens of them. They followed Fifi about all day in and out of motorboats, night clubs, inland lakes, automobiles, tea rooms and funiculars, and they said, "Hey, look, Fifi!" and showed off for her, or said, "Kiss me, Fifi," or even, "Kiss me again, Fifi," and abused her and tried to be engaged to her.

Most of them, however, were too young, since this little Swiss city, through some illogical reasoning, is supposed to have an admirable atmosphere as an educational center.

Fifi was not critical, nor was she aware of being criticized herself. Tonight the gallery in the great, crystal, horseshoe room made observations upon her birthday party, being somewhat querulous about Fifi's entrance. The table had been set in the last of a string of dining rooms, each accessible from the central hall. But Fifi, her black dress shouting and halloing for notice, came in by way of the first dining room, followed by a whole platoon of young men of all possible nationalities and crosses, and at a sort of little run that swayed her lovely hips and tossed her lovely head, led them bumpily through the whole vista, while old men choked on fish bones, old women's facial muscles sagged, and the protest rose to a roar in the procession's wake.

They need not have resented her so much. It was a bad party, because Fifi thought she had to entertain everybody and be a dozen people, so she talked to the entire table and broke up every conversation that started, no matter how far away from her. So no one had a good time, and the people in the hotel needn't have minded so much that she was young and terribly happy.

Afterward, in the salon, many of the supernumerary males floated off with a temporary air to other tables. Among these was young Count Stanislas Borowki, with his handsome shining brown eyes of a stuffed deer, and his black hair already dashed with distinguished streaks like the keyboard of a piano. He went to the table of some Kentuckians of position named Taylor and sat down with just a faint sigh, which made them smile.

"Was it ghastly?" he was asked.

The blonde Miss Howard who was travelling with the Taylors was almost as pretty as Fifi and stitched up with more consideration. She had taken pains not to make Miss Schwartz's acquaintance, although she shared several of the same young men. The Taylors were "career" people in the diplomatic service and were now on their way to London, after the League Conference at Geneva. They were presenting Miss Howard at court this season. They were very Europeanized Americans; in fact, they had reached a position where they could hardly be said to belong to any nation at all; certainly not to any great power, but perhaps to a sort of Balkan-like state composed of people like themselves. They considered that Fifi was as much of a gratuitous outrage as a new stripe in the flag.

The tall Englishwoman with the long cigarette holder and the half-paralyzed Pekingese presently got up, announcing to the Taylors that she had an engagement in the bar.

"Most awfully kind of you to ask me for coffee," she strained forth. "I've been so blind drunk ever since I landed here that I haven't remembered to order any."

Lady Capps-Karr strolled away, carrying her paralyzed Pekingese and causing, as she passed, a chilled lull in the seething baby talk that raged around Fifi's table.

About midnight, Mr. Weicker, the assistant manager, looked into the bar, where Fifi's phonograph roared new German tangoes into the smoke and clatter. He had a small face that looked into things quickly, and lately he had taken a cursory glance into the bar every night. But he had not come to admire Fifi—he was engaged in an inquiry as to why matters were not going well at the Hôtel des Trois Mondes this summer.

There was, of course, the continually sagging American Stock Exchange. With so many hotels begging to be filled, the clients had become finicky, exigent, quick to complain, and Mr. Weicker had had many fine decisions to make recently. One large family had departed because of a night-going phonograph belonging to Lady Capps-Karr. Also there was presumably a thief operating in the hotel—there had been complaints about pocketbooks, cigarette cases, watches and rings. Guests sometimes spoke to Mr. Weicker as if they would have liked to search his pockets. There were empty suites that need not have been empty this summer.

His glance fell dourly, in passing, upon Count Borowki, who was playing pool with Fifi. Count Borowki had not paid his bill for three weeks. He had told Mr. Weicker that he was expecting his mother, who would arrange everything. Then there was Fifi, who attracted an undesirable crowd—young students living on pensions who often charged drinks, but never paid for them. Lady Capps-Karr, on the contrary, was a *grande cliente*; one could count three bottles of whisky a day for herself and entourage, and her father in London was good for every drop of it. Mr. Weicker decided to issue an ultimatum about Borowki's bill this very night. And withdrew. His visit had lasted about ten seconds.

Count Borowki put away his cue and came close to Fifi, whispering something. She seized his hand and pulled him to a corner near the phonograph.

"My American dream girl," he said. "We must have you painted in Budapest the way you are tonight. You will hang with the portraits of my ancestors in my castle in Transylvania."

One would suppose that a normal American girl, who had been to an average number of moving pictures, would have detected a vague ring of familiarity in Count Borowki's persistent wooing. But the Hôtel des Trois Mondes was full of people who were actually rich and noble, people who did fine embroidery or took cocaine in closed apartments and meanwhile laid claim to the thrones of France and Brazil and half a dozen mediatized German principalities, and Fifi did not choose to doubt the one who paid court to her beauty. Tonight she was surprised at nothing: not even his precipitate proposal that they get married this very week.

"Mama doesn't want that I should get married for a year. I only said I'd be engaged to you."

"But my mother wants me to marry. She is hard-boiling, as you Americans say; she brings pressure to bear that I marry Princess This and Countess That."

Meanwhile Lady Capps-Karr was having a reunion across the room. A tall stooped Englishman, dusty with travel, had just opened the door of the bar, and Lady Capps-Karr with a caw of "Bopes!" had flung herself upon him.

"Bopes, I *say!*"

"Capps, darling. Hi, there, Rafe—" this to her companion. "Good God, Capps, fancy running into you."

"Bopes! Bopes!"

Their exclamations and laughter filled the room, and the bartender whispered to an inquisitive American that the new arrival was the Marquis Kinkallow.

Bopes stretched himself out in several chairs and a sofa, took a hasheesh tablet from a silver box which he proffered to the other two, and called for the barman. He announced that he had driven from Paris without a stop and was going over the Simplon Pass next morning to meet the only woman he had ever loved, in Milan. He did not look in a condition to meet anyone.

"Oh, Bopes, I've been so blind," said Lady Capps-Karr pathetically. "Day after day after day. I flew here from Cannes, meaning to stay one day, and I ran into Rafe here and some other Americans I knew, and it's been two weeks, and now all my tickets to Malta are void. Stay here and save me! Oh, Bopes! Bopes! Bopes!"

The Marquis Kinkallow glanced with tired eyes about the bar.

"Ah, who is that?" he demanded, surreptitiously feeding a hasheesh tablet to the Pekingese. "The lovely Sheeny. And who is that item with her?"

"She's an American," said the daughter of a hundred earls. "The man is a scoundrel of some sort, but apparently he's a cat of the stripe—he's a great pal of Schenzi, in Vienna. I sat up till five the other night playing two-handed *chemin de fer* with him here in the bar and he owes me a mille Swiss."

"Have to have a word with that wench," said Bopes twenty minutes later. "You arrange it for me, Rafe, that's a good chap."

Ralph Berry had met Miss Schwartz, and, as the opportunity for the introduction now presented itself, he rose obligingly. The opportunity was that a *chasseur* had just requested Count Borowki's presence in the office; he managed to beat two or three young men to her side.

"The Marquis Kinkallow is so anxious to meet you. Can't you come and join us?"

Fifi looked across the room, her fine brow wrinkling a little. Something warned her that her evening was full enough already. Lady Capps-Karr had never spoken to her—Fifi believed she was jealous of her clothes.

"Can't you bring him over here?"

A minute later Bopes sat down beside Fifi with a shadow of fine tolerance settling on his face. This was nothing he could help; in fact, he constantly struggled against it, but it was something that happened to his expression when he met Americans. "The whole thing is too much for me," it seemed to say. "Compare my confidence with your uncertainty, my sophistication with your naïveté, and yet the whole world has slid into your power." Of later years he found that his tone, unless carefully guarded, held a smoldering resentment.

Fifi eyed him brightly and told him about her glamorous future.

"Next I'm going to Paris," she said, announcing the fall of Rome, "to maybe study at the Sorbonne. Then maybe I'll get married, you can't tell. I'm only eighteen. I had eighteen candles on my birthday cake tonight. I wish you could have been here. . . . I've had marvelous offers to go on the stage, but of course a girl on the stage gets talked about so."

"What are you doing tonight?" asked Bopes.

"Oh, lots more boys are coming in later. Stay around and join the party."

"I thought you and I might do something. I'm going over the Simplon Pass tomorrow."

Across the room, Lady Capps-Karr was tense with displeasure at the desertion.

"After all," she protested, "a chep's a chep, and a chum's a chum, but there are certain things that one simply doesn't do. I never saw Bopes in such frightful condition."

She stared at the dialogue across the room.

"Come along to Milan with me," the marquis was saying. "Come to Tibet or Hindustan. We'll see them crown the King of Ethiopia. Anyhow, let's go for a drive right now."

"I got too many guests here. Besides, I don't go out to ride with people the first time I meet them. I'm supposed to be engaged. To a Hungarian count. He'd be furious and would probably challenge you to a duel."

Annoyed at her resistance, Bopes resorted to his usual solution in difficulties, which was another "happy" from the silver case. Whenever an explanation of this peculiarity seemed in order he would make a gloomy reference to the war.

Mrs. Schwartz, with an apologetic expression, came across the room to Fifi.

"John's gone," she announced. "He's up there again."

Fifi gave a yelp of annoyance.

"He gave me his word of honor he would not go."

"Anyhow, he went. I looked in his room and his hat's gone. It was that champagne at dinner." She turned to the marquis. "John is not a vicious boy, but vurry, vurry weak."

"I suppose I'll have to go after him?" said Fifi resignedly.

"I hate to spoil your good time tonight, but I don't know what else. Maybe this gentleman would go with you. You see, Fifi is the only one that can handle him. His father is dead and it really takes a man to handle a boy."

"Quite," said Bopes.

"Can you take me?" Fifi asked. "It's just up in town to the Café Central."

He agreed with alacrity. Out in the September night, with her fragrance seeping through an ermine cape, she explained further:

"Some Russian woman's got hold of him; she claims to be a countess, but she's only got one silver-fox fur that she wears with everything. My brother's just nineteen, so whenever he's had a couple glasses champagne he says he's going to marry her, and mother worries."

Bopes' arm dropped impatiently around her shoulder as they started up the hill to the town.

Fifteen minutes later the car stopped at a point several blocks beyond the Café Central and Fifi stepped out. The marquis' face was now decorated by a long, irregular fingernail scratch that ran diagonally across his cheek, traversed his nose in a few sketchy lines and finished in a sort of grand terminal of tracks upon his lower jaw.

"I don't like to have anybody get so foolish," Fifi explained. "You needn't wait. We can get a taxi."

"Wait!" cried the marquis furiously. "For a common little person like you? They tell me you're the laughingstock of the hotel, and I quite understand why."

Fifi hurried along the street and into the Café Central, pausing in the door until she saw her brother. He was a reproduction of Fifi without her high warmth—at the moment he was sitting quite drunk at a table with a frail exile from the Caucasus and two Serbian consumptives. Fifi waited for her temper to rise to an executive pitch; then she crossed the dance floor, conspicuous as a thunder cloud in her bright black dress.

"Mama sent me after you, John. Get your coat."

"Oh, what's biting her?" he demanded, with a vague eye.

"Mama says you should come along."

He got up unwillingly. The two Serbians rose also; the countess never moved; her eyes, sunk deep in Mongol cheekbones, never left Fifi's face; her head crouched in the silver-fox fur which Fifi knew represented her brother's last month's allowance. As John Schwartz stood there swaying unsteadily the orchestra launched into "*Ich bin von Kopf bis Fuss.*" Diving into the confusion of the table, Fifi emerged with her brother's arm, marched him to the coat-room and then out toward the taxi-stand in the Place Saint-François.

It was late, the evening was over, her birthday was over, and driving back to the hotel, with John slumped against her shoulder, Fifi felt a sudden depression. By virtue of her fine health she had never been a worrier, and certainly the Schwartz family had lived so long against similar backgrounds that Fifi felt no insufficiency in the Hôtel des Trois Mondes as club and community—and yet the evening was suddenly all wrong. Did English lords attack girls like Miss Howard in motor cars? Didn't evenings sometimes end on a high note and not fade out vaguely in bars? After ten o'clock every night she felt she was the only real being in a colony of ghosts, that she was surrounded by utterly intangible figures who retreated whenever she stretched out her hand.

The doorman assisted her brother to the elevator. Stepping in, Fifi saw too late that there were two other people inside. Before she could pull John out again, they had both brushed past her as if in fear of contamination. Fifi heard "Mercy!" from Mrs. Taylor and "How revolting!" from Miss Howard. The elevator mounted. Fifi held her breath until it stopped at her floor.

It was perhaps the impact of this last encounter that caused her to stand very still just inside the door of the dark apartment. Then she had the sense that someone else was there in the blackness ahead of her, and after her brother had stumbled forward and thrown himself on a sofa, she still waited.

"Mama," she called, but there was no answer, only a sound fainter than a rustle, like a shoe scraped along the floor.

A few minutes later, when her mother came upstairs, they called the *valet de chambre* and went through the rooms together, but there was no one. Then they stood side by side in the open door to their balcony and looked out on the lake with the bright cluster of Evian on the French shore and the white caps of snow on the mountains.

"I think we've been here long enough," said Mrs. Schwartz suddenly. "I think I'll take John back to the States this fall."

Fifi was aghast.

"But I thought John and I were going to the Sorbonne in Paris?"

"How can I trust him in Paris? And how could I leave you behind alone there?"

"But—we're used to living in Europe now. Why did I learn to talk French? Why, mama, we don't even know any people in Dayton any more."

"We can always meet people. We always have."

"But you know it's different; everybody is so bigoted there. A girl hasn't the chance to meet the same sort of men, even if there were any. Everybody just watches everything you do."

"So they do here," said her mother. "That Mr. Weicker just stopped me in the hall; he saw you come in with John, and he talked to me about how you must keep out of the bar, you were so young. I told him you only took lemonade, but he said it didn't matter; scenes like tonight made people leave the hotel."

"Oh, how perfectly mean!"

"So I think we better go back home."

The empty word rang desolately in Fifi's ears. She put her arms around her mother's waist, realizing that it was she and not her mother, with her mother's clear grip on the past, who was completely lost in the universe. On the sofa her brother snored, having already entered the world of the weak, of the leaners together, and found its fetid and mercurial warmth sufficient. But Fifi kept looking at the alien sky, knowing that she could pierce it and find her own way through envy and corruption. For the first time she seriously considered marrying Borowki immediately.

"Do you want to go downstairs and say good-night to the boys?" suggested her mother. "There's lots of them still there asking where you are."

But the Furies were after Fifi now—after her childish complacency and her innocence, even after her beauty—out to break it all down and drag it in any convenient mud. When she shook her head and walked sullenly into her bedroom, they had already taken something from her forever.

II

The following morning Mrs. Schwartz went to Mr. Weicker's office to report the loss of two hundred dollars in American money. She had left the sum on her chiffonier upon retiring; when she awoke, it was gone. The door of the apartment had been bolted, but in the morning the bolt was found drawn, and yet neither of her children was awake. Fortunately, she had taken her jewels to bed with her in a chamois sack.

Mr. Weicker decided that the situation must be handled with care. There were not a few guests in the hotel who were in straitened circumstances and inclined to desperate remedies, but he must move slowly. In America one has money or hasn't; in Europe the heir to a fortune may be unable to stand himself a haircut until the collapse of a fifth cousin, yet be a sure risk and not to be lightly offended. Opening the office copy of the *Almanach de Gotha*, Mr. Weicker found Stanislas Karl Joseph Borowki hooked firmly on to the end of a line older than the Crown of St. Stephen. This morning, in riding clothes that were smart as a hussar's uniform, he had gone riding with the utterly correct Miss Howard. On the other hand, there was no doubt as to who had been robbed, and Mr. Weicker's indignation began to concentrate on Fifi and her family, who might have saved him this trouble by taking themselves off some time ago. It was even conceivable that the dissipated son, John, had nipped the money.

In all events, the Schwartzes were going home. For three years they had lived in hotels—in Paris, Florence, Saint-Raphaël, Como, Vichy, La Baule, Lucerne, Baden-Baden and Biarritz. Everywhere there had been schools, always new schools, and both children spoke in perfect French and scrawny fragments of Italian. Fifi had grown from a large-featured child of fourteen to a beauty; John had grown into something rather dismal and lost. Both of them played bridge, and somewhere Fifi had picked up tap-dancing. Mrs. Schwartz felt that it was all somehow unsatisfactory, but she did not know why. So, two days after Fifi's party, she announced that they would pack their trunks, go to Paris for some new fall clothes and then go home.

That same afternoon Fifi came to the bar to get her phonograph, left there the night of her party. She sat up on a high stool and talked to the barman while she drank a ginger ale.

"Mother wants to take me back to America, but I'm not going."

"What will you do?"

"Oh, I've got a little money of my own, and then I may get married." She sipped her ginger ale moodily.

"I hear you had some money stolen," he remarked. "How did it happen?"

"Well, Count Borowki thinks the man got into the apartment early and hid in between the two doors between us and the next apartment. Then, when we were asleep, he took the money and walked out."

"Ha!"

Fifi sighed.

"Well, you probably won't see me in the bar anymore."

"We'll miss you, Miss Schwartz."

Mr. Weicker put his head in the door, withdrew it and then came in slowly.

"Hello," said Fifi coldly.

"A-ha, young lady." He waggled his finger at her with affected facetiousness. "Didn't you know I spoke to your mother about your coming into the bar? It's merely for your own good."

"I'm just having a ginger ale," she said indignantly.

"But no one can tell what you're having. It might be whisky or what not. It is the other guests who complain."

She stared at him indignantly—the picture was so different from her own—of Fifi as the lively center of the hotel, of Fifi in clothes that ravished the eye, standing splendid and unattainable amid groups of adoring men. Suddenly Mr. Weicker's obsequious but hostile face infuriated her.

"We're getting out of this hotel!" she flared up. "I never saw such a narrow-minded bunch of people in my life, always criticizing everybody and making up terrible things about them, no matter what they do themselves. I think it would be a good thing if the hotel caught fire and burned down, with all the nasty cats in it."

Banging down her glass, she seized the phonograph case and stalked out of the bar.

In the lobby a porter sprang to help her, but she shook her head and hurried on through the salon, where she came upon Count Borowki.

"Oh, I'm so furious!" she cried. "I never saw so many old cats! I just told Mr. Weicker what I thought of them!"

"Did someone dare to speak rudely to you?"

"Oh, it doesn't matter. We're going away."

"Going away!" He started. "When?"

"Right away. I don't want to, but mama says we've got to."

"I must talk to you seriously about this," he said. "I just called your room. I have brought you a little engagement present."

Her spirits returned as she took the handsome gold-and-ivory cigarette case engraved with her initials.

"How lovely!"

"Now listen. What you tell me makes it more important that I talk to you immediately. I have just received another letter from my mother. They have chosen a girl for me in Budapest—a lovely girl, rich and beautiful and of my own rank who would be very happy at the match, but I am in love with you. I would never have thought it possible, but I have lost my heart to an American."

"Well, why not?" said Fifi indignantly. "They call girls beautiful here if they have one good feature. And then, if they've got nice eyes or hair, they're usually bow-legged or haven't got nice teeth."

"There is no flaw or fault in you."

"Oh, yes," said Fifi modestly. "I got a sort of big nose. Would you know I was Jewish?"

With a touch of impatience, Borowki came back to his argument: "So they are bringing pressure to bear for me to marry. Questions of inheritance depend on it."

"Besides, my forehead is too high," observed Fifi abstractedly. "It's so high it's got sort of wrinkles in it. I knew an awfully funny boy who used to call me 'the highbrow.'"

"So the sensible thing," pursued Borowki, "is for us to marry immediately. I tell you frankly there are other American girls not far from here who wouldn't hesitate."

Fifi snapped the cigarette case open and shut.

"Mama would be about crazy," Fifi said.

"I've thought about that too," he assured her eagerly. "Don't tell her. In Switzerland we'd have to wait a week according to the law. But if we drove over the border tonight into Liechtenstein we could be married tomorrow morning. Then we come back and you show your mother the little gilt coronets painted on your luggage. My own personal opinion is that she'll be delighted. There you are, off her hands, with social position second to none in Europe. In my opinion, your mother has probably thought of it already, and may be saying to herself: 'Why don't those two young people just take matters into their own hands and save me all the fuss and expense of a wedding?' I think she would like us for being so hard-boiled."

He broke off impatiently as Lady Capps-Karr, emerging from the dining room with her Pekingese, surprised them by stopping at their table. Count Borowki was obliged to introduce them. As he had not known of the Marquis Kinkallow's defection the other evening, nor that His Lordship had taken a wound over the Simplon Pass the following morning, he had no suspicion of what was coming.

"I've noticed Miss Schwartz," said the Englishwoman in a clear, concise voice. "And of course I've noticed Miss Schwartz's clothes."

"Won't you sit down?" said Fifi.

"No, thank you." She turned to Borowki. "Miss Schwartz's clothes make us all appear somewhat drab. I always refuse to dress elaborately in hotels. It seems such rotten taste. Don't you think so?"

"I think people always ought to look nice," said Fifi, flushing.

"Naturally. I merely said that I consider it rotten taste to dress elaborately, save in the houses of one's friends."

She said "Goodby-ee" to Borowki and moved on, emitting a mouthed cloud of smoke and a faint fragrance of whisky.

The insult had been as stinging as the crack of a whip, and as Fifi's pride in her wardrobe was swept away from her, she heard all the comments that she had not heard, in one great resurgent whisper. Then they said that she wore her clothes here because she had nowhere else to wear them. That was why the Howard girl considered her vulgar and did not care to know her. For an instant her anger flamed up against her mother for not telling her, but she saw that her mother did not know either.

"I think she's so dowdy," she forced herself to say aloud, but inside she was quivering. "What is she, anyhow? I mean, how high is her title? Very high?"

"She's the widow of a baronet."

"Is that high?" Fifi's face was rigid. "Higher than a countess?"

"No. A countess is much higher—infinitely higher." He moved his chair closer and began to talk intently.

Half an hour later Fifi got up with indecision on her face.

"At seven you'll let me know definitely," Borowki said. "And I'll be ready with a car at ten."

Fifi nodded. He escorted her across the room and saw her vanish into a dark hall mirror in the direction of the lift. As he turned away, Lady Capps-Karr, sitting alone over her coffee, spoke to him:

"I want a word with you. Did you, by some slip of the tongue, suggest to Weicker that in case of difficulties I would guarantee your bills?"

Borowki flushed.

"I may have said something like that, but—"

"Well, I told him the truth—that I never laid eyes on you until a fortnight ago."

"I naturally turned to a person of equal rank—"

"Equal rank! What cheek! The only titles left are English titles. I must ask you not to make use of my name again."

He bowed.

"Such inconveniences will soon be for me a thing of the past."

"Are you getting off with that vulgar little American?"

"I beg your pardon," he said stiffly.

"Don't be angry. I'll stand you a whisky-and-soda. I'm getting in shape for Bopes Kinkallow, who's just telephoned he's tottering back here. He and his chauffeur and his valet stopped off in Sierre and have been lying there ever since in a stupor. But he's run out of happies so he's arriving tonight."

Meanwhile, upstairs, Mrs. Schwartz was saying to Fifi: "Now that I know we're going away I'm getting excited about it. It will be so nice seeing the Hirsts and Mrs. Bell and Amy and Marjorie and Gladys again, and the new baby. You'll be happy too—you've forgotten how they're like. You and Gladys used to be great friends. And Marjorie—"

"Oh, mama, don't talk about it," cried Fifi miserably. "I can't go back to Dayton."

"We needn't stay in Dayton. If John was in a college like his father wanted we could maybe go to California."

But for Fifi all the romance of life was rolled up into the last three impressionable years in Europe. She remembered the tall guardsmen in Rome and the old Spaniard who had first made her conscious of her beauty at the Villa d'Este at Como, and the French naval aviator at Saint-Raphaël who had dropped her a note from his plane into their garden, and the feeling that she had sometimes, when she danced with Borowki at the Perroquet, that he was dressed in gleaming boots and a white-furred dolman. She had seen many American moving pictures and she knew that the girls there always married the faithful boy from the old home town, and after that there was nothing.

"I won't go," she said aloud.

Her mother turned with a pile of clothes in her arms.

"What talk is that from you, Fifi? You think I could leave you here alone?" As Fifi didn't answer, she continued, with an air of finality: "That talk doesn't sound nice from you. Now you stop fretting and saying such things, and get me this list of things uptown and later we can have tea at Nussneger's."

But Fifi had decided. It was Borowki, then, and the chance of living fully and adventurously. He could go into the diplomatic service, and then one day when they encountered Lady Capps-Karr and Miss Howard at a legation ball, she could make audible the observation that for the moment seemed so necessary to her: "I hate people who always look as if they were going to or from a funeral."

"So run along," her mother continued. "And look in at that Café Central and see if John is up there, and take him to tea."

Fifi accepted the shopping list mechanically. Then she went into her room and wrote a little note to Borowki which she would leave with the concierge on the way out. Coming out, she saw her mother struggling with a trunk, and felt terribly sorry for her. But there were Amy and Gladys in America, and Fifi hardened herself.

She walked out and down the stairs, remembering halfway that in her distraction she had omitted an official glance in the mirror; but there was a large mirror on the wall just outside the grand salon, and she stopped in front of that instead.

She was beautiful—she learned that once more, but now it made her sad. She wondered whether the dress she wore this afternoon was in bad taste, whether it would minister to the superiority of Miss Howard or Lady Capps-Karr. It seemed to her a lovely dress, soft and gentle in cut, but in color a hard, bright, metallic powder blue.

Then a sudden sound broke the stillness of the gloomy hall and Fifi stood suddenly breathless and motionless.

III

At eleven o'clock Mr. Weicker was tired, but the bar was in one of its periodic riots and he was waiting for it to quiet down. There was nothing to do in the stale office or the empty lobby; and the salon, where all day he held long conversations with lonely English and American women, was deserted; so he went out the front door and began to make the circuit of the hotel. Whether due to his circumambient course or to his frequent glances up at the twinkling bedroom lights and into the humble, grilled windows of the kitchen floor, the promenade gave him a sense of being in control of the hotel, of being adequately responsible, as though it were a ship and he was surveying it from a quarterdeck.

He went past a flood of noise and song from the bar, past a window where two bus boys sat on a bunk and played cards over a bottle of Spanish wine. There was a phonograph somewhere above, and a woman's form blocked out a window; then there was the quiet wing, and turning the corner he arrived back at his point of departure. And in front of the hotel, under the dim porte-cochère light, he saw Count Borowki.

Something made him stop and watch, something incongruous—Borowki, who couldn't pay his bill, had a car and a chauffeur. He was giving the chauffeur some sort of detailed instructions, and then Mr. Weicker perceived that there was a bag in the front seat, and came forward into the light.

"You are leaving us, Count Borowki?"

Borowki started at the voice.

"For the night only," he answered. "I'm going to meet my mother."

"I see."

Borowki looked at him reproachfully.

"My trunk and hat box are in my room, you'll discover. Did you think I was running away from my bill?"

"Certainly not. I hope you will have a pleasant journey and find your mother well."

But inside he took the precaution of dispatching a *valet de chambre* to see if the baggage was indeed there, and even to give it a thoughtful heft, lest its kernel were departed.

He dozed—for perhaps an hour. When he woke up, the night concierge was pulling at his arm and there was a strong smell of smoke in the lobby. It was some moments before he could get it through his head that one wing of the hotel was on fire.

Setting the concierge at the alarms, he rushed down the hall to the bar, and through the smoke that poured from the door he caught sight of the burning billiard table and the flames licking along the floor and flaring up in alcoholic ecstasy every time a bottle on the shelves cracked with the heat. As he hastily retreated he met a line of half-dressed *chasseurs* and bus boys already struggling up from the lower depths with buckets of water. The concierge shouted that the fire department was on its way. He put two men at the telephones to awaken the guests, and, as he ran back to form a bucket line at the danger point, he thought for the first time of Fifi.

Blind rage consumed him—with a precocious Indian-like cruelty she had carried out her threat. Ah, he would deal with that later—there was still law in the cantons. Meanwhile a clangor outdoors announced that the engines had arrived, and he made his way back through the lobby, filled now with men in pajamas carrying briefcases, and women in bedclothes carrying jewel boxes and small dogs—the number swelling every minute and the talk rising from a cadence heavy with sleep to the full staccato buzz of an afternoon soirée.

A *chasseur* called Mr. Weicker to the phone, but the manager shook him off impatiently.

"It's the commissaire of police," the boy persisted. "He says you must speak to him."

With an exclamation, Mr. Weicker hurried into the office.

"'Allo!"

"I'm calling from the station. Is this the manager of the Hôtel des Trois Mondes?"

"Yes, but there's a fire here."

"Have you among your guests a man calling himself Count Borowki?"

"Why, yes—"

"We're bringing him there for identification. He was picked up on the road on some information we received."

"But—"

"We picked up a girl with him. We're bringing them both down there immediately."

"I tell you—"

The receiver clicked briskly in his ear and Mr. Weicker hurried back to the lobby, where the smoke was diminishing. The reassuring pumps had been at work for five minutes and the bar was a wet charred ruin. Mr. Weicker began passing here and there among the guests, tranquilizing and persuading; the phone operators began calling the rooms again, advising such guests as had not appeared that it was safe to go back to bed—and then, at the continued demands for an explanation, he thought again of Fifi, and this time of his own accord he hurried to the phone.

Mrs. Schwartz's anxious voice answered—Fifi wasn't there. That was what he wanted to know. He rang off brusquely. There was the story, and he could not have wished for anything more sordidly complete—an incendiary blaze and an attempted elopement with a man wanted by the police. It was time for paying, and all the money of America couldn't make any difference. If the season was ruined, at least Fifi would have no more seasons at all. She would go to a girls' institution where the prescribed uniform was rather plainer than any clothing she had ever worn.

As the last of the guests departed into the elevators, leaving only a few curious rummagers among the soaked débris, another procession came in by the front door. There was a man in civilian clothes and a little wall of policemen with two people behind. The commissaire spoke and the screen of policemen parted.

"I want you to identify these two people. Has this man been staying here under the name of Borowki?"

Mr. Weicker looked. "He has."

"He's been wanted for a year in Italy, France and Spain. And this girl?"

She was half hidden behind Borowki, her head hanging, her face in shadow. Mr. Weicker craned toward her eagerly. He was looking at Miss Howard.

A wave of horror swept over Mr. Weicker. Again he craned his head forward, as if by the intensity of his astonishment he could convert her into Fifi, or look through her and find Fifi. But this would have been difficult, for Fifi was far away. She was in front of the Café Central, assisting the stumbling and reluctant John Schwartz into a taxi. "I should *say* you can't go back. Mother says you should come right home."

IV

Count Borowki took his incarceration with a certain grace, as though, having lived so long by his own wits, there was a certain relief in having his days planned by an external agency. But he resented the lack of intercourse with the outer world, and was overjoyed when, on the fourth day of his imprisonment, he was led forth to find Lady Capps-Karr.

"After all," she said, "a chep's a chep and a chum's a chum, whatever happens. Luckily our consul here is a friend of my father's, or they wouldn't have let me see you. I even tried to get you out on bail, because I told them you went to Oxford for a year and spoke English perfectly, but the brutes wouldn't listen."

"I'm afraid there's no use," said Count Borowki gloomily. "When they've finished trying me I'll have had a free journey all over Europe."

"But that's not the only outrageous thing," she continued. "Those idiots have thrown Bopes and me out of the Trois Mondes, and the authorities are trying to get us to leave Lausanne."

"What for?"

"They're trying to put the full blame of that tiresome fire on us."

"Did you start it?"

"We did set some brandy on fire because we wanted to cook some potato chips in alcohol, and the bartender had gone to bed and left us there. But you'd think, from the way the swine talk, that we'd come there with the sole idea of burning everyone in their beds. The whole thing's an outrage and Bopes is furious. He says he'll never come to Switzerland again. I went to the consulate, and they agreed that the whole affair was perfectly disgraceful, and they've wired the Foreign Office, and I've phoned Sir George Munready at Berne, who happens to be a personal friend of mine."

Borowki considered for a moment.

"If I could be born over again," he said slowly, "I think without any doubt I should choose to be born an Englishman."

"I should choose to be anything but a Swiss—or an American! By the way, the Taylors are not presenting Miss Howard at court because of the disgraceful way the newspapers played up the matter."

"What puzzles me is what made Fifi suspicious," said Borowki.

"Then it was Miss Schwartz who blabbed?"

"Yes. I thought I had convinced her to come with me, and I knew that if she didn't, I had only to snap my fingers to the other girl.... That very afternoon Fifi visited the jeweler's and discovered I'd paid for the cigarette case with a hundred-dollar American note I'd lifted from her mother's chiffonier. She went straight to the police."

"Without coming to you first! After all, a chep's a chep—"

"But what I want to know is what made her suspicious enough to investigate, what turned her against me."

Fifi, at that moment sitting on a high stool in the Meurice Hotel bar in Paris and sipping a lemonade, was answering that very question to an interested bartender.

"I was standing in the hall looking in the mirror," she said, "and I heard him talking to the English lady—the one who set the hotel on fire. And I heard him say, 'After all, my one nightmare is that she'll turn out to look like her mother.'" Fifi's voice blazed with indignation. "Well, you've seen my mother, haven't you?"

"Yes, and a very fine woman she is."

"After that I knew there was something the matter with him, and I wondered how much he'd paid for the cigarette case. So I went up to see. They showed me the bill he paid with."

"And you will go to America now?" the barman asked.

Fifi finished her glass. The straw made a gurgling sound in the sugar at the bottom.

"We've got to go back and testify, and we'll stay a few months anyhow." She stood up. "Bye-bye. I've got a fitting."

They had not got her—not yet. The Furies had withdrawn a little and stood in the background with a certain gnashing of teeth. But there was plenty of time.

Yet, as Fifi tottered out through the lobby, her face gentle with new hopes, her lovely body shining though her clothes—as she went out looking for completion under the impression that she was going to the *couturier*, there was a certain doubt among the eldest and most experienced of the Furies whether they would get her after all.

INDECISION

This one was dressed in a horizon-blue Swiss skiing suit with, however, the unmistakable touch of a Paris shears about it. Above it shone her snow-warm cheeks and her eyes that were less confident than brave. With his hat, Tommy McLane slapped snow from his dark convict-like costume. He was already reflecting that he might have been out with Rosemary, dancing around with Rosemary and the two ickle durls down at the other hotel, amid the gleam of patent Argentine hair, to the soothing whispers of "I'm Getting Myself Ready for You." When he was with Emily he felt always a faint nostalgia for young Rosemary and for the sort of dance that seemed to go on inside and all around Rosemary and the two ickle durls. He knew just how much happened there—not much, just a limited amount of things, just a pleasant lot of little things strung into hours, moving to little melodies hither and thither. But he missed it—it was new to him again after four years, and he missed it. Likewise when he was with Rosemary, making life fun with jokes for her, he thought of Emily, who was twenty-five and carried space around with her, into which he could step and be alone with their two selves, mature and complicated and trusting, and almost in love.

Out the window, the snow on the pine trees was turning lilac in the first dusk; and because the world was round, or for some such reason, there was rosy light still on that big mountain, the Dent de Something. Bundled-up children were splattering back to their hotels for tea as if the outdoors were tired of them and wanted to change its dress in quiet dignity. Down in the valley there were already bright windows and misty glows from the houses and hotels of the town.

He left Emily at her hotel door. She had never seemed so attractive, so good, so tranquil a person, given a half-decent chance. He was annoyed that he was already thinking of Rosemary.

"We'll meet in the bar down there at seven-thirty," he said, "and don't dress."

Putting on his jacket and flat cap, Tommy stepped out into the storm. It was a welcome blizzard and he inhaled damp snowflakes that he could no longer see against the darkening sky. Three flying kids on a sled startled him with a warning in some strange language and he just managed to jump out of their path. He heard them yell at the next bend, and then, a little farther on, he heard sleigh bells coming up the hill in the dark. It was all very pleasant and familiar, yet it did not remind him of Minneapolis, where he was born, because the automobile had spoiled all that side of Northwestern life while he was still a baby. It was pleasant and familiar because these last five days here among alien mountains held some of the happiest moments of his life.

He was twenty-seven; he was assistant manager and slated for manager of a New York bank in Paris, or else he would be offered the option of Chicago next spring at a larger salary. He had come up here to one of the gayest places in Switzerland with the idea that, if he had nothing else to think of for ten days, he might fall in love. He could afford to fall in love, but in Paris the people he saw all knew it, and he had instinctively become analytical and cagy. Here he felt free—the first night he had seen at least a dozen girls and women, "any one of whom"; on the second night there had still been half a dozen; the third night there were three, with one new addition—Emily Elliot from the other hotel. Now, on the day after Christmas, it had narrowed down to two—Emily and Rosemary Merriweather. He had actually written all this down on a blotter as if he were in his office in the Place Vendôme, added them and subtracted them, listed points.

"Two really remarkable girls," he said to himself in a tone not unlike the clumping squeak of his big shoes on the snow. "Two absolutely good ones."

Emily Elliot was divorced and twenty-five. Rosemary was eighteen.

He saw her immediately as he went into his hotel—a blonde, ravishing, Southern beauty like so many that had come before her and so many yet to be born. She was from "Nawlins, 'riginly," but now from "Athens, Joja." He had first spoken to her on Christmas Eve, after an unavailing search for someone to introduce him, some means to pierce the wall of vacationing boys within which she seemed hermetically sealed. She was sitting with another man. He stared at her across the room, admiring her with his eyes, frankly and tauntingly. Presently she spoke to her escort; they crossed the room and sat down at the table next to him, with Rosemary's back just one inch from his. She sent her young man for something—Tommy spoke. The next day, at the risk of both their lives, he took her down the big bob run.

Rosemary saw him now as he came in. She was revolving slowly through the last of the tea hour with a young Levantine whom he disliked. She wore white and her face lighted up white, like an angel under an arc lamp. "Where you been?" her big eyes said.

But Tommy was shrewd, and he merely nodded to her and to the two ickle durls who danced by, and found a seat in a far corner. He knew that a surfeit of admiration such as Rosemary's breeds an appreciation of indifference. And presently she came over to him, dragging her bridling partner by an interlaced little finger.

"Where you been?" she demanded.

"Tell that Spic to go count his piasters and I'll talk turkey with you."

She bestowed upon the puzzled darkling a healing smile.

"You don't mind, honey, if I sit this out? See you later."

When he had departed, Tommy protested, "'Honey'! Do you call him 'honey'? Why don't you call him 'greasy'?"

She laughed sweetly.

"Where you been?"

"Skiing. But every time I go away, that doesn't mean you can go dance with a whole lot of gigolo numbers from Cairo. Why does he hold his hand parallel to the floor when he dances? Does he think he's stilling the waves? Does he think the floor's going to swing up and crack him?"

"He's a Greek, honey."

"That's no reason. And you better get that word 'honey' cleaned and pressed before you use it on me again." He felt very witty. "Let's go to my boudoir," he suggested.

He had a bedroom and bath and a tiny salon. Once inside the door of the latter, he shot the bolt and took her in his arms, but she drew away from him.

"You been up at that other hotel," she said.

"I had to invite a girl to dinner. Did you know you're having dinner with me tonight? God, you're beautiful."

It was true. Her face, flushed with cold and then warmed again with the dance, was a riot of lovely delicate pinks, like many carnations rising in many shades from the white of her nose to the high spot of her cheeks. Her breathing was very young as she came close to him—young and eager and exciting. Her lips were faintly chapped, but soft in the corners.

After a moment she sat with him in a single chair. And just for a second words formed on his lips that it was hard not to utter. He knew she was in love with him and would probably marry him, but the old terror of being held rose in him. He would have to tell this girl so many things. He looked closely at her, holding her face under his, and if she had said one wise or witty thing he might have spoken, but she only looked up with a glaze of childish passion in her eyes and said: "What are you thinking, honey?"

The moment passed. She fell back smoothly into being only a part of the day's pleasure, the day's excitement. She was desirable here, but she was desirable downstairs too. The mountains were bewitching his determinations out of him.

Drawing her close to him, lightly he said: "So you like the Spics, eh? I suppose the boys are all Spics down in New Orleans?"

As she squeezed his face furiously between thumb and finger, his mind was already back with Emily at the other hotel a quarter of a mile away.

II

Tommy's dinner was not to be at his hotel. After meeting in the bar, they sledded down into the village to a large old-fashioned Swiss taproom, a thing of woodwork, clocks, steins, kegs and antlers. There were other parties like their own, bound together by the common plan of eating fondue—a peculiarly indigestible form of

Welsh rarebit—and drinking spiced wine, and then hitching on the backs of sleighs to Doldorp several miles away, where there was a townspeople's ball.

His own party included Emily; her cousin, young Frank Forrester; young Count de Caros Moros, a friend of Rosemary's—she played ping-pong with him and harked to his guitar and to his tales of machine-gunning his discontented fellow countrymen in Andalusia; a Harvard University hockey hero named Harry Whitby; and lastly the two ickle durls—Californians who were up from a Montreux school for the holidays and very anxious to be swept off their feet. Six Americans, two Europeans.

It was a good party. Some grey-haired men of the golden nineties sang ancient glees at the piano, the fondue was fun, the wine was pert and heady, the smoke swirled out of the brown walls and toned the bright costumes into the room. They were all on a ship going somewhere, with the port just ahead; the faces of girls and young men bore the same innocent and unlined expectations of the great possibilities inherent in the situation and the night. The Latins became Americans easily, the English with more effort. Then it was over and one hundred five-pound boots stamped toward the sleighs that waited at the door.

For a moment Tommy lingered, engrossed in conversation with Emily, yet with sudden twinges of conscience about Rosemary. She had been on his left; he had last seen her listening to young Caros Moros perform upon his extremely portable guitar. Outside in the crisp moonlight he saw her tying her sled to one of the sleighs ahead. The sleighs were moving off—he and Emily caught one, and at the crisp-cracking whips the horses pulled, breasting the dark air. Past them figures ran and scrambled, the younger people pushing one another off, landing in a cloud of soft snow, then panting after the horses, to fling themselves exhausted on a sled, or else wail that they were being left behind. On either side the fields were tranquil; the space through which the cavalcade moved was high and limitless. After they were in the country there was less noise—perhaps ears were listening atavistically for wolves howling in the clumps of trees far across the snow.

At Doldorp he stood with Emily in the doorway, watching the others go in.

"Everybody's first husband with everybody's first wife," she remarked. "Who believes in marriage? I do. A plucky girl—takes the count of nine and comes up for more. But not for two years—I'm over here to do some straight thinking."

It occurred to Tommy that two years was a long time, but he knew that girls so frequently didn't mean what they said. He and Emily watched the entrance of Mr. Cola, nicknamed Capone, with his harem, consisting of wife, daughters, wife's friend, and three Siamese. Then they went inside.

The crowd was enormous—peasants, servants from the hotels, shopkeepers, guides, outlanders, cowherders, ski teachers and tourists. They all got seats where they could, and Tommy saw Rosemary with a crowd of young people across the room; she seemed a little tired and pale, sitting back with her lips apart and her eyes fixed and sleepy. When someone waltzed off with Emily, he went over and asked her to dance.

"I don't want to dance. I'm tired."

"Let's go sit where we can hear the yodeling."

"I can hear it here."

"What am I accused of?" he demanded.

"Nothing. I haven't even seen you."

Her current partner smiled at him ingratiatingly, but Tommy was growing annoyed.

"Didn't I explain that this dinner was for a girl who'd been particularly nice to me? I told you I'd have to devote a lot of the evening to her."

"Go on devote it, then. I'm leaving soon."

"Who with?"

"Capone has a sleigh."

"Yes, you're leaving with him! He'll take you for a ride—you'll be on the spot if you don't look out."

He felt a touch of uneasiness. The mystery she had lacked this afternoon was strong in her now. Before he should be so weak as to grant her another advantage, he turned and asked one of the ickle durls to dance.

The ickle durl bored him. She admired him; she was used to clasping her hands together in his wake and heaving audible sighs. When the music stopped he gave her an outrageous compliment to atone for his preoccupation and left her at her table. The night was ruined. He realized that it was Rosemary who moved him most deeply, and his eyes wandered to her across the room. He told himself that she was playing him jealously, but he hated the way she was fooling with young Caros Moros—and he liked it still less when he glanced over a little later and found that the two of them were gone.

He sprang up and dashed out of the door; there was the snow lightly falling, there were the waiting sleighs, the horses patient in their frozen harness, and there was a small excited crowd of Swiss gathered around Mr. Cola's sleigh.

"*Salaud!*" he heard. "*Salaud Français!*"

It appeared that the French courier, long accepted as a member of the Cola ménage, had spent the afternoon tippling with his master; the courier had not survived. Cola had been compelled to assist him outdoors, where he promptly gave tongue to a series of insults directed at the Swiss. They were all Boches. Why hadn't they come in the war? A crowd gathered and, as it included several Swiss who were in the same state as the Frenchman, the matter was growing complicated. The women were uncomfortable, the Siamese were smiling diplomatically among themselves. One of the Swiss was on the runner of the sleigh, leaning over Mrs. Cola and shaking his fist in the courier's face. Mr. Cola stood up in the sleigh and addressed them in hoarse American as to "the big idea?"

"Dirty Frenchmen!" cried the Swiss. "Yes, and during your Revolution did you not cut the Swiss Guards down to the last man?"

"Get the hell out of here!" shouted Cola. "Hey, coachman, drive right over 'em! You guys go easy there! Take your hands off the sleigh. Shut up, you!"—this to the courier, who was still muttering wildly. Cola looked at him as if he contemplated throwing him to the crowd. In a moment Tommy edged himself between the outraged Swiss patriot and the sleigh.

"Ne'mine what they say! Drive on!" cried Cola again. "We got to get these broads out of here!"

Conscious of Rosemary's eyes staring at him out of a bearskin robe, and of Caros Moros next to her, Tommy raised his voice:

"*Ce sont des dames Américaines; il n'y a qu'un Français. Voyons! Qu'est-ce que vous voulez?*"

But the massacre of the Swiss Guards was not to be disposed of so lightly.

Tommy had an inspiration. "But who tried to save the Swiss Guards? Answer me that!" he shouted. "An American—Benjamin Franklin! He almost saved them!"

His preposterous statement rang out strong and true upon the electric air. The protagonist of the martyrs was momentarily baffled.

"An American saved them!" Tommy cried. "Hurray for America and Switzerland!" And he added quickly, to the coachman, "Drive on now—and fast!"

The sleigh started with a lurch. Two men clung to it for a moment and then let go, and the conveyance slid free behind the swiftly trotting horses.

"*Vive l'Amérique! Vive la Suisse!*" Tommy shouted.

"*Vive la Fra—*" began the courier, but Cola put his fur glove in the man's mouth. They drove rapidly for a few minutes.

"Drop me here," Tommy said. "I have to go back to the dance." He looked at Rosemary, but she would not meet his eye. She was a bundle of fur next to Caros Moros, and he saw the latter drop his arm around her till they were one mass of fur together. The sight was horrible—of all people in the world she had become the most desirable, and he wanted every bit of her youth and freshness. He wanted to jerk Caros Moros to his feet and pull him from the sleigh. He saw how stupid it had been to play so long with her innocence and sincerity—until now she scarcely saw him anymore, scarcely knew he was there.

As he swung himself off the sleigh, Rosemary and Caros Moros were singing softly:

> "*. . . I wouldn't stoop*
> *To onion soup;*
> *With corn-beef hash I'm all*
> *through—*"

and the Spaniard winked at Tommy as if to say, "We know how to handle this little girl, don't we?"

The courier struggled and then cried in a blurred voice: "Beeb wa Fwance."

"Keep your glove in his mouth," said Tommy savagely. "Choke him to death."

He walked off down the road, utterly miserable.

III

His first instinct next morning was to phone her immediately; his second was to sulk proudly in his room, hoping against hope that his own phone would ring. After luncheon he went downstairs, where he was addressed by the objectionable Greek who had danced with her at tea yesterday afternoon—ages ago.

"Tell me—you like to play the ping-pong?"

"It depends who with," Tommy answered rudely. Immediately he was so sorry that he went downstairs with the man and batted the white puffballs for half an hour.

At four he skied over to Emily's hotel, resolving to drive the other and more vivid image from his mind. The lobby was filled with children in fancy dress, who had gathered there from many hotels for the children's Christmas ball.

Emily was a long time coming down, and when she did she was hurried and distracted.

"I'm so sorry. I've been costuming my children, and now I've got to get them launched into this orgy, because they're both very shy."

"Sit and get your breath a minute. We'll talk about love."

"Honestly I can't, Tommy. I'll see you later." And she added quickly, "Can't you get your little Southern girl? She seemed to worry you a lot last night."

After half an hour of diffident grand marches Emily came back to him, but Tommy's patience was exhausted and he was on his feet to go. Even now she showed him that he was asking for time and attention out of turn—and, being unavailable, she had again grown as mysterious as Rosemary.

"It's been a hard day in lots of ways," she explained as she walked with him to the door. "Things I can't tell you about."

"Oh yes?" People had so many affairs. You never knew how much space you actually occupied in their lives.

Outdoors he came across her young cousin, Frank Forrester, buckling on his skis. Pushing off together, they drifted slowly down a slushy hill.

"Let me tell you something," Frank burst out. "I'm never going to get married. I've seen too much of it. And if any girl asked my advice, I'd tell her to stay out." He was full of the idea: "There's my mother, for instance. She married a second husband, and what does he do but have her spied on and bribe her maids to open her mail? Then there's Emily. You know what happened to her—one night her husband came home and told her she was acting cold to him, but that he'd fix that up. So he built a bonfire under her bed, made up of shoes and things, and set fire to it. And if the leather hadn't smelled so terrible she'd have been burned to death."

"That's just two marriages."

"Two!" said Frank resentfully. "Isn't that enough? Now we think Emily's husband is having her spied on. There's a man keeps watching us in the dining room."

As Tommy stemmed into the driveway of his hotel, he wondered if he was really attractive to women at all. Yesterday he had been sure of these two, holding them in the hollow of his hand. As he dressed for dinner he realized that he wanted them both. It was an outrage that he couldn't have them both. Wouldn't a girl rather have half of him than all of Harry Whitby—or a whole Spic with a jar of pomade thrown in? Life was so badly arranged—better no women at all than only one woman.

He shouted "Come in!" to a knock at his salon door, and leaning around the corner, his hand on his dress tie, found the two ickle durls.

He started. Had they inherited him from Rosemary? Had he been theirs since the superior pair seemed to have relinquished their claims? Were they really presuming that he might escort them to the fancy-dress ball tonight?

Slipping on his coat, he went into his parlor. They were got up as Arlesienne peasant girls, with high black bonnets and starched aprons.

"We've come about Rosemary," they said directly. "We wanted to see if you won't do something about it. She's been in bed all day and she says she isn't coming to the party tonight. Couldn't you at least call her up?"

"Why should I call her up?"

"You know she's perfectly crazy about you, and last night was the most miserable she ever spent in her life. After she broke Caros Moros' guitar, we couldn't stop her crying."

A contented glow spread over Tommy. His instinct was to telephone at once—but, curiously enough, to telephone Emily, so that he could talk to her with his newborn confidence.

The ickle durls moved toward the door. "You will call her up," they urged him respectfully.

"Right now." He took them each in one arm, like a man in a musical comedy, and kissed the rouge on their cheeks. When they were gone, he telephoned Rosemary. Her "hello" was faint and frightened.

"Are you sorry you were so terrible to me last night, baby?" he demanded. "No real pickaninny would—"

"You were the terrible one."

"Are you coming to the party tonight?"

"Oh, I will if you'll act differently. But I'll be hours—I'm still in bed. I can't get down till after dinner."

With Rosemary safely locked up again in the tranquil cells of his mind, he rang up Emily.

"I'm sorry I was so short with you this afternoon," she said immediately.

"Are you in love with me?"

"Why no, I don't think so."

"Aren't you a little bit in love with me?"

"I like you a lot."

"Dear Emily. What's this about being spied on?"

"Oh, there's a man here who walked into my room—maybe by accident. But he always watches us."

"I can't stand having you annoyed," he said. "Please call on me if anything definite happens. I'd be glad to come up and rub his face in the snow."

There was a pregnant telephone silence.

"I wish I was with you now," he said gently.

After a moment she whispered, "I do too."

He had nothing to complain of; the situation was readjusted; things were back where they had been twenty-four hours ago. Eating dinner alone, he felt that in reality both girls were beside him, one on either hand. The dining room was shimmering with unreality for the fancy-dress party, for tonight was the last big event of the Christmas season. Most of the younger people who gave it its real color would start back to school tomorrow.

And Tommy felt that in the evening somewhere—but in whose company he couldn't say—there would come a moment, perhaps *the* moment. Probably very late, when the orchestra and what remained of the party—the youth and cream of it—would move into the bar, and Abdul, with Oriental delight in obscurity, would manipulate the illumination in a sort of counterpoint whose other tone was the flashing moon from the ice rink, bouncing in the big windows. Tommy had danced with Rosemary in that light a few hours after their first meeting. He remembered the mysterious darkness, with the cigarette points turning green or silver when the lights shone red, the sense of snow outside and the occasional band of white falling across the dancers as a door was opened and shut. He remembered her in his arms and the plaint of the orchestra playing:

"That's why mother made me,
Promise to be true—"

and the other vague faces passing in the darkness.

"She knew I'd meet someone
Exactly like you."

He thought now of Emily. They would have a very long, serious conversation, sitting in the hall. Then they would slip away and talk even more seriously, but this time with her very close to him. Anything might happen—anything.

But he was thinking of the two apart—and tonight they would both be here in full view of each other. There must be no more complications like last evening—he must dovetail the affairs with skill and thought . . .

Emerging from dinner, he strolled down the corridor, already filled with graces and grotesques, conventional clouds of columbines, clowns, peasants, pirates and ladies of Spain. He never wore costume himself and the sight of a man in motley made him sad, but some of the girls were lovelier than in life, and his heart jumped as he caught sight of a snow-white ballet dancer at the end of the corridor, and recognized Rosemary. But almost as he started toward her, another party emerged from the cloakroom, and in it was Emily.

He thought quickly. Neither one had seen him, and to greet one with the other a few yards away was to get off on the wrong foot, for he had invented opening remarks for each one—remarks which must be made alone. With great presence of mind, he dove for the men's washroom and stood there tensely.

Emerging in a few minutes, he hovered cautiously along the hall. Passing the lounge, he saw in a side glance that Caros Moros was with Rosemary and that she was glancing about impatiently. Emily looked up from her table, saw him and beckoned. Without moving a muscle of his face, Tommy stared above her and passed on. He decided to wait in the bar until the dancing actually started—it would be easier when the two were separated in the crowd. In the bar he was hailed gratefully by Mr. Cola—Mr. Cola was killing time there desperately, with his harem waiting outside.

"I'm having them all psychoanalyzed," he said. "I got a guy down from Zurich, and he's doing one a day. I never saw such a gloomy bunch of women—always bellyaching wherever I takem. A man I knew told me he had his wife psychoanalyzed and she was easier to be with afterward."

Tommy heard only vaguely. He had become aware that, as if they had planned it in collusion, Emily and Rosemary had sauntered simultaneously into the bar. Blind-eyed and breathless, he strode out and into the ballroom. One of the ickle durls danced by him and he seized her gratefully.

"Rosemary was looking for you," she told him, turning up the flattered face of seventeen.

Presently he felt silly dancing with her, but, perhaps because of her admirers' deference to his maturer years, three encores passed and no one cut in. He began to feel like a man pushing a baby carriage. He took a dislike to her colonial costume, the wig of which sent gusts of powder up his nose. She even *smelled* young—of very pure baby soap and peppermint candy. Like almost every act he had performed in the last two days, he was unable to realize why he had cut in on her at all.

He saw Rosemary dancing with Caros Moros, then with other partners, and then again with Caros Moros. He had now been a half hour with the ickle durl; his gayety was worn thin and his smile was becoming strained when at last he was cut in on. Feeling ruffled and wilted, he looked around to find that Rosemary and Caros Moros had disappeared. With the discovery, he came to the abrupt decision that he would ask her to marry him.

He went searching—plowing brusquely through crowds like a swimmer in surf. Just as finally he caught sight of the white-pointed cap and escaping yellow curls, he was accosted by Frank Forrester:

"Emily sent me to look for you. Her maid telephoned that somebody tried to get into her room, and we think it's the man who keeps watching her in the dining room."

Tommy stared at him vaguely, and Frank continued:

"Don't you think you and I ought to go up there now and rub his face in the snow?"

"Where?"

"To our hotel."

Tommy's eyes begged around him. There was nothing he wanted less.

"We'd like to find out one way or another." And then, as Tommy still hesitated: "You haven't lost your nerve, have you? About rubbing his face in the snow?"

Evasion was impossible. Tommy threw a last quick glance at Rosemary, who was moving with Caros Moros back toward the dancing floor.

At Emily's hotel the maid waited in the lower hall. It seemed that the bedroom door had opened slowly a little way—then closed again quickly. She had fled downstairs. Silently Tommy and Frank mounted the stairs and approached the room; they breathed quietly at the threshold and flung open the door. The room was empty.

"I think this was a great flight of the imagination," Tommy scolded. "We might as well go back—"

He broke off, as there were light footsteps in the corridor and a man walked coolly into the room.

"*Ach je!*" he exclaimed sharply.

"Aha!" Frank stepped behind him and shut the door. "We got you."

The man looked from one to the other in alarm.

"I must be in the wrong room!" he exclaimed, and then, with an uncomfortable laugh: "*O bei Gott*, I see! My room is just above this and I got the wrong floor again. In my last hotel I was on the third floor, so I got the habit—"

"Why do you always listen to every word we say at table?" demanded Frank.

"I like to look at you because you are such nice, handsome, wealthy American people. I've come to this hotel for years."

"We're wasting time," said Tommy impatiently. "Let's go to the manager."

The intruder was more than willing. He proved to be a coal dealer from Berlin, an old and valued client of the house. They apologized—there was no hard feeling—they must join him in a drink. It was ten minutes before they got away, and Tommy led a furious pace back toward the dance. He was chiefly furious at Emily. Why should people be spied upon? What sort of women were spied upon? He felt as if this were a plan of Emily's to keep him away from Rosemary, who with every instant was dancing farther and farther off with Caros Moros into a youthful Spanish dream. At the drive of the hotel Frank said good-night.

"You're not going back to the dance?"

"It's finished—the ballroom's dark. Everybody's probably gone to Doldorp, because here it always closes early on Sunday night."

Tommy dashed up the drive to the hotel. In the gloomy half light of the office a last couple were struggling into overshoes. The dance was over.

"For you, Mr. McLane." The night concierge handed him a telegram. Tommy stared at it for a moment before he tore it open.

GENEVA SWITZERLAND 2/1/31

H P EASTBY ARRIVED TONIGHT FROM PARIS STOP ABSOLUTELY ESSENTIAL YOU BE HERE FOR EARLY LUNCH MONDAY STOP AFTERWARD ACCOMPANYING HIM TO DIJON

SAGE

For a moment he couldn't understand. When he had grasped the utterly inarguable dictum, he took the concierge by both arms.

"You know Miss Merriweather. Did she go to Doldorp?"

"I think she did."

"Get me a sleigh?"

"Every sleigh in town has gone over there; some with ten people in them. These last people here couldn't get sleighs."

"Any price!" cried Tommy fiercely. "Think!"

He threw down five large silver wheels on the desk.

"There's the station sleigh, but the horses have got to be out at seven in the morning. If you went to the stables and asked Eric—"

Half an hour later the big, glassed-in carryall jingled out on the Doldorp road with a solitary passenger. After a mile a first open sleigh dashed past them on its way home, and Tommy leaned out and glared into the anonymous bundles of fur and called "Rosemary!" in a firm but unavailing voice. When they had gone another mile, sleighs began to pass in increasing numbers. Sometimes a taunting shout drifted back to him; sometimes his voice was drowned in a chorus of "Jingle Bells" or "Merrily We Roll Along." It was hopeless—the sleighs were coming so fast now that he couldn't examine the occupants; and then there were no more sleighs and he sat upright in the great, hearselike vehicle, rocking on toward a town that he knew no longer held what he was after. A last chorus rang in his ears:

"*Good-night, ladies,*
Good-night, ladies,
Good-night, lay-de-es,
I'm going to leave you now."

IV

He was awake at seven with the *valet de chambre* shaking his shoulders. The sun was waving gold, green and white flags on the Wildstrubel as he fumbled clumsily for his razor. The great fiasco of the night before drifted over him, and he could hear even the great blackbirds cawing, "You went away too far," on the white balcony outside.

Desperately he considered telephoning her, wondering if he could explain to a girl still plunged in drowsiness what he would have had trouble in explaining in person. But it was already time to go; he drove off in a crowded sleigh with other faces wan in the white morning.

They were passing the crisp pale green rink where Wiener waltzes blared all day and the blazing colors of many schools flashed against pale blue skies. Then there was the station full of frozen breath . . . he was in the first-class carriage of the train drawing away from the little valley . . . past pink pines and fresh, diamond-strewn snow.

Across from him women were weeping softly for temporarily lost children whom they had left up there for another term at school. And in a compartment farther up he suddenly glimpsed the two ickle durls. He drew back—he couldn't stand that this morning. But he was not to escape so readily. As the train passed Caux, high on its solitary precipice, the ickle durls came along the corridor and spied him.

"Hey, there!" They exchanged glances. "We didn't think you were on the train."

"Do you know," began the older one—the one he had danced with last night—"what we'd like?"

It was something daring evidently, for they went off into spasms of suppressed giggles.

"What we'd like," the ickle durl continued, "is to ask you if—we wondered if you would send us a photo."

"Of what?" asked Tommy.

"Of yourself."

"She's asking for herself," declared the other ickle durl indignantly. "I wouldn't be so darn fresh."

"I haven't had a photo taken for years."

"Even an old one?" pursued the ickle durl timidly.

"And listen," said the other one: "Won't you come up for just a minute and say good-bye to Rosemary. She's still crying her eyes out, and I think she'd like it if you even came up to say good-bye."

He jerked forward as if thrown by the train.

"Rosemary!"

"She cried all the way to Doldorp and all the way back, and then she broke Caros Moros' other guitar that he keeps in reserve; so he feels awful, being up there another month without any guitar—"

But Tommy was gone. As the train began traversing back and forth toward Lake Geneva, the two ickle durls sat down resignedly in his compartment.

"So then—" he was saying at the moment. "No, don't move—I don't mind a bit. I like you like that. Use my handkerchief. . . . Listen. If you've got to go to Paris, can't you possibly come by way of Geneva and Dijon?"

"Oh, I'd love to. I don't want to let you out of my sight—not now anyhow."

At that moment—perhaps out of habit, perhaps because the two girls had become almost indissolubly wedded in his mind—he had a sharp vivid impression of Emily. Wouldn't it be better for him to see them both together before coming to such an important decision?

"Will you marry me?" he cried, quickly, desperately. "Are we engaged? Can't we put it in writing?"

With the sound of his own voice the other image faded from his mind forever.

A NEW LEAF

It was the first day warm enough to eat outdoors in the Bois de Boulogne, while chestnut blossoms slanted down across the tables and dropped impudently into the butter and the wine. Julia Ross ate a few with her bread and listened to the big goldfish rippling in the pool and the sparrows whirring about an abandoned table. You could see everybody again—the waiters with their professional faces, the watchful Frenchwomen all heels and eyes, Phil Hoffman opposite her with his heart balanced on his fork, and the extraordinarily handsome man just coming out on the terrace.

—the purple noon's transparent might.
The breath of the moist air is light
Around each unexpanded bud—

Julia trembled discreetly; she controlled herself; she didn't spring up and call, "Yi-yi-yi-yi! Isn't this grand?" and push the *maître d'hôtel* into the lily pond. She sat there, a well-behaved woman of twenty-one, and discreetly trembled.

Phil was rising, napkin in hand. "Hi there, Dick!"

"Hi, Phil!"

It was the handsome man; Phil took a few steps forward and they talked apart from the table.

"—seen Carter and Kitty in Spain—"

"—poured onto the *Bremen*—"

"—so I was going to—"

The man went on, following the head waiter, and Phil sat down.

"Who is that?" she demanded.

"A friend of mine—Dick Ragland."

"He's without doubt the handsomest man I ever saw in my life."

"Yes, he's handsome," he agreed without enthusiasm.

"Handsome! He's an archangel, he's a mountain lion, he's something to eat. Just why didn't you introduce him?"

"Because he's got the worst reputation of any American in Paris."

"Nonsense. He must be maligned. It's all a dirty frame-up—a lot of jealous husbands whose wives got one look at him. Why, that man's never done anything in his life except lead cavalry charges and save children from drowning."

"The fact remains he's not received anywhere—not for one reason but for a thousand."

"What reasons?"

"Everything. Good Lord—drink, women, jails, scandals, killed somebody with an automobile, lazy, worthless—"

"I don't believe a word of it," said Julia firmly. "I bet he's tremendously attractive. And you spoke to him as if you thought so too."

"Yes," he said reluctantly, "like so many alcholics, he has a certain charm. If he'd only make his messes off by himself somewhere—except right in people's laps. Just when somebody's taken him up and is making a big fuss over him, he pours the soup down his hostess' back, kisses the serving maid and passes out in the dog kennel with the debutante daughter. But he's done it too often. He's run through about everybody, until there's no one left."

"There's me," said Julia.

There was Julia, who was a little too good for anybody and sometimes regretted that she had been quite so well endowed. Anything added to beauty has to be paid for—that is to say, the qualities that pass as substitutes can be liabilities when added to beauty itself. Julia's brilliant hazel glance was enough without the questioning light of intelligence that flickered in it; her irrepressible sense of the ridiculous detracted from the gentle relief of her mouth, and the loveliness of her figure might have been more obvious if she had slouched and postured rather than sat and stood very straight, after the discipline of a strict father.

Equally perfect young men had several times appeared bearing gifts, but generally with the air of being already complete, of having no space for development. On the other hand, she found that men of larger scale had sharp corners and edges in youth, and she was a little too young herself to like that. There was, for instance, this scornful young egotist, Phil Hoffman, opposite her, who was obviously going to be a brilliant lawyer and who had practically followed her to

Paris. She liked him as well as anyone she knew, but he had at present all the overbearance of the son of a chief of police.

"Tonight I'm going to London, and Wednesday I sail," he said. "And you'll be in Europe all summer, with somebody new chewing on your ear every few weeks."

"When you've been called for a lot of remarks like that you'll begin to edge into the picture," Julia remarked. "Just to square yourself, I want you to introduce that man Ragland."

"My last few hours!" he complained.

"But I've given you three whole days on the chance you'd work out a better approach. Be a little civilized and ask him to have some coffee."

As Mr. Dick Ragland joined them, Julia drew a little breath of pleasure. He was a fine figure of a man, in coloring both tan and blond, with a peculiar luminosity to his face. His voice was quietly intense; it seemed always to tremble a little with a sort of gay despair; the way he looked at Julia made her feel attractive. For half an hour, as their sentences floated pleasantly among the scent of violets and snowdrops, forget-me-nots and pansies, her interest in him grew. She was even glad when Phil said:

"I've just thought about my English visa. I'll have to leave you two incipient love birds together against my better judgment. Will you meet me at the Gare Saint-Lazare at five and see me off?"

He looked at Julia hoping she'd say, "I'll go along with you now." She knew very well she had no business being alone with this man, but he made her laugh, and she hadn't laughed much lately, so she said: "I'll stay a few minutes—it's so nice and springy here."

When Phil was gone, Dick Ragland suggested a second *fine* champagne.

"I hear you have a terrible reputation?" she said impulsively.

"Awful. I'm not even invited out anymore. Do you want me to slip on my false mustache?"

"It's so odd," she pursued. "Don't you cut yourself off from all nourishment? Do you know that Phil felt he had to warn me about you before he introduced you? And I might very well have told him not to."

"Why didn't you?"

"I thought you seemed so attractive and it was such a pity."

His face grew bland—Julia saw that the remark had been made so often that it no longer reached him.

"It's none of my business," she said quickly. She did not realize that his being a sort of outcast added to his attraction for her—not the dissipation itself, for never having seen it, it was merely an abstraction, but its result in making him so alone. Something atavistic in her went out to the stranger to the tribe, a being from a world with different habits from hers, who promised the unexpected—promised adventure.

"I'll tell you something else," he said suddenly. "I'm going permanently on the wagon on June fifth, my twenty-eighth birthday. I don't have fun drinking anymore. Evidently I'm not one of the few people who can use liquor."

"You sure you can go on the wagon?"

"I always do what I say I'll do. Also I'm going back to New York and go to work."

"I'm really—I'm really surprised how glad I am." This was rash, but she let it stand.

"Have another *fine?*" Dick suggested. "Then you'll be gladder still."

"Will you go on this way right up to your birthday?"

"Probably. On my birthday I'll be on the *Olympic* in mid-ocean."

"I'll be on that boat too!" she exclaimed.

"You can watch the quick change—I'll do it for the ship's concert."

The tables were being cleared off. Julia knew she should go now, but she couldn't bear to leave him sitting with that unhappy look under his smile. She felt, maternally, that she ought to say something to help him keep his resolution.

"Tell me why you drink so much. Probably some obscure reason you don't know yourself."

"Oh, I know pretty well how it began."

He told her as another hour waned. He had gone to the war at seventeen and, when he came back, life as a Princeton freshman with a little black cap was somewhat tame. So he went up to Boston Tech and then abroad to the Beaux-Arts—it was there that something happened to him.

"About the time I came into some money I found that with a few drinks I got Irish and expansive and somehow had the ability to please people, and the idea turned my head. Then I began to take a whole lot of drinks to keep going and have everybody think I was wonderful. Well, I got plastered a lot and quarreled with most of my friends, and then I met a wild bunch and for a while I was expansive with them. But I was inclined to get superior and suddenly think 'What am I doing with this bunch?' They didn't like that much. And when a taxi that I was in killed a man, I was sued. It was just a graft, but it got in the papers, and after I was released the impression remained that *I'd* killed him. So all I've got to show for the last five years is a reputation that makes mothers rush their daughters away if I'm at the same hotel."

An impatient waiter was hovering near and she looked at her watch.

"Gosh, we're to see Phil off at five. We've been here all the afternoon."

As they hurried to the Gare Saint-Lazare, he asked: "Will you let me see you again—or do you think you'd better not?"

She returned his long look. There was no sign of dissipation in his face, in his warm cheeks, in his erect carriage.

"I'm always fine at lunch," he added, like an invalid.

"I'm not worried," she laughed. "Take me to lunch day after tomorrow."

They hurried up the steps of the Gare Saint-Lazare, only to see the last carriage of the Golden Arrow disappearing toward the Channel. Julia was remorseful, because Phil had come so far.

As a sort of atonement, she went to the apartment where she lived with her aunt and tried to write a letter to him, but Dick Ragland intruded himself into her thoughts. By morning the effect of his good looks had faded a little; she was inclined to write him a note that she couldn't see him. Still, he had made her a simple appeal and she had brought it all on herself. She waited for him at half-past twelve on the appointed day.

Julia had said nothing to her aunt, who had company for luncheon and might mention his name—strange to go out with a man whose name you couldn't mention. He was late and she waited in the hall, listening to the echolalia of chatter from the luncheon party in the dining room. At one she answered the bell.

There in the outer hall stood a man whom she thought she had never seen before. His face was dead white and erratically shaven, his soft hat was crushed bun-like on his head, his shirt collar was dirty, and all except the band of his tie was out of sight. But at the moment when she recognized the figure as Dick Ragland she perceived a change which dwarfed the others into nothing; it was in his expression. His whole face was one prolonged sneer—the lids held with difficulty from covering the fixed eyes, the drooping mouth drawn up over the upper teeth, the chin wobbling like a made-over chin in which the paraffin had run—it was a face that both expressed and inspired disgust.

"H'lo," he muttered.

For a minute she drew back from him—then, at a sudden silence from the dining room that gave on the hall, inspired by the silence in the hall itself, she half pushed him over the threshold, stepped out herself and closed the door behind them.

"Oh-h-h!" she said in a single, shocked breath.

"Haven't been home since yest'day. Got involve' on a party at—"

With repugnance, she turned him around by his arm and stumbled with him down the apartment stairs, passing the concierge's wife, who peered out at them curiously from her glass room. Then they came out into the bright sunshine of the Rue Guynemer.

Against the spring freshness of the Luxembourg Gardens opposite, he was even more grotesque. He frightened her. She looked desperately up and down the street for a taxi, but one turning the corner of the Rue de Vaugirard disregarded her signal.

"Where'll we go lunch?" he asked.

"You're in no shape to go to lunch. Don't you realize? You've got to go home and sleep."

"I'm all right. I get a drink I'll be fine."

Thankfully a passing cab slowed up at her gesture.

"You go home and go to sleep. You're not fit to go anywhere."

As he focused his eyes on her, realizing her suddenly as something fresh, something new and lovely, something alien to the smoky and turbulent world where he had spent his recent hours, a faint current of reason flowed through him. She saw his mouth twist with vague awe, saw him make a vague attempt to stand up straight. The taxi yawned.

"Maybe you're right. Very sorry."

"What's your address?"

He gave it and then tumbled into a corner, his face still struggling toward reality. Julia closed the door.

When the cab had driven off, she hurried across the street and into the Luxembourg Gardens as if someone were after her.

II

Quite by accident, she answered when he telephoned at seven that night. His voice was strained and shaking.

"I suppose there's not much use apologizing for this morning. I didn't know what I was doing, but that's no excuse. But if you could let me see you for awhile somewhere tomorrow—just for a minute—I'd like the chance of telling you in person how terribly sorry—"

"I'm busy tomorrow."

"Well, Friday then, or any day."

"I'm sorry, I'm very busy this week."

"You mean you don't ever want to see me again?"

"Mr. Ragland, I hardly see the use of going any further with this. Really, that thing this morning was a little too much. I'm very sorry. I hope you feel better. Good-bye."

She put him entirely out of her mind. She had not even associated his reputation with such a spectacle—a heavy drinker was someone who sat up late and drank champagne and maybe in the small hours rode home singing. This spectacle at high noon was something else again. Julia was through.

Meanwhile there were other men with whom she lunched at Ciro's and danced in the Bois. There was a reproachful letter from Phil Hoffman in America. She liked Phil better for having been so right about this. A fortnight passed and she would have forgotten Dick Ragland, had she not heard his name mentioned with scorn in several conversations. Evidently he had done such things before.

Then, a week before she was due to sail, she ran into him in the booking department of the White Star Line. He was so handsome—she could hardly believe her eyes. He leaned with an elbow on the desk, his fine figure erect, his yellow gloves as stainless as his clear shining eyes. His strong, gay personality had affected the clerk who served him with fascinated deference; the stenographers behind looked up for a minute and exchanged a glance. Then he saw Julia—she nodded, and with a quick, wincing change of expression he raised his hat.

They were together by the desk a long time and the silence was oppressive.

"Isn't this a nuisance?" she said.

"Yes," he said jerkily, and then: "You going by the *Olympic*?"

"Oh, yes."

"I thought you might have changed."

"Of course not," she said coldly.

"I thought of changing; in fact, I was here to ask about it."

"That's absurd."

"You don't hate the sight of me? So it'll make you seasick when we pass each other on the deck?"

She smiled. He seized his advantage:

"I've improved somewhat since we last met."

"Don't talk about that."

"Well then, you've improved. You've got the loveliest costume on I ever saw."

This was presumptuous, but she felt herself shimmering a little at the compliment.

"You wouldn't consider a cup of coffee with me at the café next door, just to recover from this ordeal?"

How weak of her to talk to him like this, to let him make advances. It was like being under the fascination of a snake.

"I'm afraid I can't—" Something terribly timid and vulnerable came into his face, twisting a little sinew in her heart. "Well, all right," she shocked herself by saying.

Sitting at the sidewalk table in the sunlight, there was nothing to remind her of that awful day two weeks ago. Jekyll and Hyde. He was courteous, he was charming, he was amusing. He made her feel oh so attractive! He presumed on nothing.

"Have you stopped drinking?" she asked.

"Not till the fifth."

"Oh!"

"Not until I said I'd stop. Then I'll stop."

When Julia rose to go, she shook her head at his suggestion of a further meeting.

"I'll see you on the boat. After your twenty-eighth birthday."

"All right. One more thing. It fits in with the high price of crime that I did something inexcusable to the one girl I've ever been in love with in my life."

She saw him the first day on board, and then her heart sank into her shoes as she realized at last how much she wanted him. No matter what his past was, no matter what he had done. Which was not to say that she would ever let him know, but only that he moved her chemically more than anyone she had ever met, that all other men seemed pale beside him.

He was popular on the boat; she heard that he was giving a party on the night of his twenty-eighth birthday. Julia was not invited—when they met they spoke pleasantly, nothing more.

It was the day after the fifth that she found him stretched in his deck chair looking wan and white. There were wrinkles on his fine brow and around his eyes, and his hand, as he reached out for a cup of bouillon, was trembling. He was still there in the late afternoon, visibly suffering, visibly miserable. After three times around, Julia was irresistibly impelled to speak to him:

"Has the new era begun?"

He made a feeble effort to rise, but she motioned him not to and sat on the next chair.

"You look tired."

"I'm just a little nervous. This is the first day in five years that I haven't had a drink."

"It'll be better soon."

"I know," he said grimly.

"Don't weaken."

"I won't."

"Can't I help you in any way? Would you like a bromide?"

"I can't stand bromides," he said almost crossly. "No thanks, I mean."

Julia stood up: "I know you feel better alone. Things will be brighter tomorrow."

"Don't go, for God's sake. If you can stand me."

Julia sat down again.

"Sing me a song—can you sing?"

"What kind of a song?"

"Something sad—some sort of blues."

She sang him Libby Holman's "This is how the story ends," in a low, soft voice.

"That's good. Now sing another. Or sing that again."

"All right. If you like, I'll sing to you all afternoon."

III

The second day in New York he called her on the phone. "I've missed you so," he said. "Have you missed me?"

"I'm afraid I have," she said reluctantly.

"Much?"

"I've missed you a lot. Are you better?"

"I'm all right now. I'm still just a little nervous, but I'm starting work tomorrow. When can I see you?"

"When you want."

"This evening then. And look—say that again."

"What?"

"That you're afraid you have missed me."

"I'm afraid that I have," Julia said obediently.

"Missed me," he added.

"I'm afraid I have missed you."

"All right. It sounds like a song when you say it."

"Good-bye, Dick."

"Good-bye, Julia dear."

She stayed in New York two months instead of the fortnight she had intended—because he would not let her go. Work took the place of drink in the daytime, but afterward he must see Julia.

Sometimes she was jealous of his work when he telephoned that he was too tired to go out after the theatre. Lacking drink, night life was less than nothing to him—something quite spoiled and well lost. For Julia, who never drank, it was a stimulus in itself—the music and the parade of dresses and the handsome couple they made dancing together. At first they saw Phil Hoffman once in awhile; Julia considered that he took the matter rather badly; then they didn't see him anymore.

A few unpleasant incidents occurred. An old schoolmate, Esther Cary, came to her to ask if she knew of Dick Ragland's reputation. Instead of growing angry, Julia invited her to meet Dick and was delighted with the ease with which Esther's convictions were changed. There were other small annoying episodes, but Dick's misdemeanors had fortunately been confined to Paris and assumed here a faraway unreality. They loved each other deeply now—the memory of that morning slowly being effaced from Julia's imagination—but she wanted to be sure.

"After six months, if everything goes along like this, we'll announce our engagement. After another six months we'll be married."

"Such a long time," he mourned.

"But there were five years before that," Julia answered. "I trust you with my heart and with my mind, but something else says wait. Remember, I'm also deciding for my children."

Those five years—oh, so lost and gone.

In August, Julia went to California for two months to see her family. She wanted to know how Dick would get along alone. They wrote every day; his letters were by turns cheerful, depressed, weary and hopeful. His work was going better. As things came back to him, his uncle had begun really to believe in him, but all the time he missed his Julia so. It was when an occasional note of despair began to appear that she cut her visit short by a week and came East to New York.

"Oh, thank God you're here!" he cried as they linked arms and walked out of the Grand Central Station. "It's been so hard. Half a dozen times lately I've wanted to go on a bust and I had to think of you, and you were so far away."

"Darling—darling, you're so tired and pale. You're working too hard."

"No, only that life is so bleak alone. When I go to bed my mind churns on and on. Can't we get married sooner?"

"I don't know—we'll see. You've got your Julia near you now, and nothing else matters."

After a week, Dick's depression lifted. When he was sad, Julia made him her baby, holding his handsome head against her breast, but she liked it best when he was confident and could set her up, making her laugh and feel taken care of and secure. She had rented an apartment with another girl and she took courses in biology and domestic science at Columbia. When deep fall came, they went to football games and the new shows together, and walked through the first snow in Central Park, and several times a week spent long evenings together in front of her fire. But time was going by and they were both impatient. Just before Christmas, an unfamiliar visitor—Phil Hoffman—presented himself at her door. It was the first time in many months. New York, with its quality of many independent ladders set side by side, is unkind to even the meetings of close friends—so, in the case of strained relations, meetings are easy to avoid.

And they were strange to each other. Since his expressed skepticism of Dick, he was automatically her enemy; on another count, she saw that he had improved, some of the hard angles were worn off; he was now an assistant district attorney, moving around with increasing confidence through his profession.

"So you're going to marry Dick?" he said. "When?"

"Soon now. When mother comes East."

He shook his head emphatically. "Julia, don't marry Dick. This isn't jealousy—I know when I am licked—but it seems awful for a lovely girl like you to take a blind dive into a lake full of rocks. What makes you think that people change their courses? Sometimes they dry up or even flow into a parallel channel, but I've never known anybody to change."

"Dick's changed."

"Maybe so. But isn't that an enormous 'maybe'? If he was unattractive and you liked him, I'd say go ahead. Maybe I'm all wrong, but it's so darn obvious that what fascinates you is that handsome pan of his and those attractive manners."

"You don't know him," Julia answered loyally. "He's different with me. You don't know how gentle he is, and responsive. Aren't you being rather small and mean?"

"Hm." Phil thought for a moment. "I want to see you again in a few days. Or perhaps I'll speak to Dick."

"You let Dick alone," she cried. "He has enough to worry him without your nagging him. If you were his friend you'd try to help him instead of coming to me behind his back."

"I'm your friend first."

"Dick and I are one person now."

But three days later Dick came to see her at an hour when he would usually have been at the office.

"I'm here under compulsion," he said lightly, "under threat of exposure by Phil Hoffman."

"Oh God!" she thought, her heart dropping like a plummet. "Has he given up? Is he drinking again?"

"It's about a girl. You introduced me to her last summer and told me to be very nice to her—Esther Cary."

Now her heart was beating slowly in her very womb.

"After you went to California I was lonesome and I ran into her. She'd liked me that day, and for awhile we saw quite a bit of each other. Then you came back and I broke it off. It was a little difficult—I hadn't realized that she was so interested."

"I see." Her voice was starved and aghast.

"Try and understand. Those terribly lonely evenings. I think if it hadn't been for Esther, I'd have fallen off the wagon. I never loved her—I never loved anybody but you—but I had to see somebody who liked me."

He put his arm around her, but she felt cold all over and he drew away.

"Then any woman would have done," Julia said slowly. "It didn't matter who."

"No!" he cried.

"I stayed away so long to let you stand on your own feet and get back your self-respect by yourself."

"I only love you, Julia."

"But any woman can help you. So you don't really need me, do you?"

His face wore that vulnerable look that Julia had seen several times before; she sat on the arm of his chair and ran her hand over his cheek.

"Then what do you bring me?" she demanded. "I thought that there'd be the accumulated strength of having beaten your weakness. What do you bring me now?"

"Everything I have."

She shook her head. "Nothing. Just your good looks—and the head waiter at dinner last night had that."

They talked for two days, and decided nothing. Sometimes she would pull him close and reach up to his lips that she loved so well, but her arms seemed to close around straw.

"I'll go away and give you a chance to think it over," he said despairingly. "I can't see any way of living without you, but I suppose you can't marry a man you don't trust or believe in. My uncle wanted me to go to London on some business—"

The night he left, it was sad on the dim pier. All that kept her from breaking was that it was not an image of strength that was leaving her—she would be just as strong without him. Yet as the murky lights fell on the fine structure of his brow and chin, as she saw the faces turn toward him, the eyes that followed him, an awful emptiness seized her and she wanted to say: "Never mind, dear, we'll try it together."

But try what? It was human to risk the toss between failure and success, but to risk the desperate gamble between adequacy and disaster—

"Oh, Dick, be good and be strong and come back to me. Change, change, Dick—change!"

"Good-bye, Julia—good-bye."

She last saw him on the deck, his profile cut sharp as a cameo against a match as he lit a cigarette.

IV

It was Phil Hoffman who was to be with her at the beginning and the end. It was he who broke the news as gently as it could be broken. He reached her apartment at half-past eight and carefully threw away the morning paper outside. Dick Ragland had disappeared at sea.

After her first wild burst of grief, he became purposely a little cruel.

"He knew himself. His will had given out; he didn't want life anymore. And, Julia, just to show you how little you can possibly blame yourself, I'll tell you this: He'd hardly gone to his office for four months—since you went to California. He wasn't fired because of his uncle; the business he went to London on was of no importance at all. After his first enthusiasm was gone he'd given up."

She looked at him sharply. "He didn't drink, did he? He wasn't drinking?"

For a fraction of a second Phil hesitated. "No, he didn't drink; he kept his promise—he held on to that."

"That was it," she said. "He kept his promise and he killed himself doing it."

Phil waited uncomfortably.

"He did what he said he would and broke his heart doing it," she went on chokingly. "Oh, isn't life cruel sometimes—so cruel, never to let anybody off. He was so brave—he died doing what he said he'd do."

Phil was glad he had thrown away the newspaper that hinted of Dick's gay evening in the bar—one of many gay evenings that Phil had known of in the past few months. He was relieved that was over, because Dick's weakness had threatened the happiness of the girl he loved; but he was terribly sorry for him—even understanding how it was necessary for him to turn his maladjustment to life toward one mischief or another—but he was wise enough to leave Julia with the dream that she had saved out of wreckage.

There was a bad moment a year later, just before their marriage, when she said:

"You'll understand the feeling I have and always will have about Dick, won't you, Phil? It wasn't just his good looks. I believed in him—and I was right in a way. He broke rather than bend; he was a ruined man, but not a bad man. In my heart I knew when I first looked at him."

Phil winced, but he said nothing. Perhaps there was more behind it than they knew. Better let it all alone in the depths of her heart and the depths of the sea.

RECORD OF VARIANTS

Emendations adopted from the various textual witnesses are recorded in the tables below, as are independent editorial emendations. The surviving evidence for each story is described in the headnote for that story. The following symbols and sigla are used:

~	the same word
^	absence of punctuation or paragraphing
¶	new paragraph
ed	an editorial emendation
ser	a reading in the serial text
TS/TSS	typescript/s
stet	refusal to emend, followed by an explanation
FSF	Fitzgerald
TAR	*Taps at Reveille*, the Scribners 1935 first edition
TITN	*Tender Is the Night*, the Scribners 1934 first edition
As Ever	*As Ever, Scott Fitz—* (Philadelphia: Lippincott, 1972)

"Crazy Sunday"

Two early triple-spaced TSS (35 pp. and 42 pp.) survive in the Fitzgerald Papers at Princeton. Both bear revisions in his hand, but neither is sufficiently close to the TAR text to be a source for emendation. Collation of the serial text from the *American Mercury* against the TAR text reveals a scattering of revisions, likely authorial, which must necessarily have been entered on the TAR setting copy or introduced in proof. A 26-page TS of the story, revised in FSF's hand, was offered by the Scribner Book Store in a 1946 sales catalogue at $55.00. The location of this TS is unknown. It was likely the setting copy for TAR, sent by FSF to Perkins and preserved in the Scribners files. Remarks in these headnotes concerning the sale of Fitzgerald's working drafts on the collector market are taken from Matthew J. Bruccoli, with Judith S. Baughman, *F. Scott Fitzgerald in the Marketplace: The Auction and Dealer Catalogues, 1935–2006* (Columbia: University of South Carolina Press, 2009). The text of "Crazy Sunday" in *The Best Short Stories of 1933*, ed. Edward J. O'Brien (Boston: Houghton Mifflin, 1933) shows no evidence of further authorial revision.

6.7	Davies] ser; Davies'
6.27	Joel] ser; Joe
6.32	that] ed; the
7.19	looked] ser; look
8.31	Joel] ser; Joe
13.5	good-looking—‸] ser; ~ - ~—"
13.30	outside] ed; ~ of
13.34	giggled] ser; giggle
15.4	pan] ed; pam
15.13	game.] ed; ~,
15.17	walked to] ser; walked
16.15	mouth.] ed; ~,

"Two Wrongs"

The text of "Two Wrongs" is discussed in section 6 of the Introduction above. A 55-page TS of the story, bearing heavy authorial revisions, is extant at Princeton and is the source for restorations to the Cambridge text. Fitzgerald almost completely rewrote the story for TAR; the revisions are so heavy that a fresh TS (no longer extant) must have served as setting copy for the collected text. Many of the revisions on the surviving TS remove material that had been used in TITN. Unless otherwise indicated, all emendations below are taken from the TS at Princeton.

24.12	anyhow . . . kyke.] anyhow.
24.28	two;] ed; ~,
26.29–31	in. ¶"Two . . . two."] in.
28.4	coffee . . . drink?] coffee?
30.1	she] she had
30.2	hadn't,] ~;
30.5	moodiness,] ed; ~‸
33.12	trap . . . kyke.] trap.
35.23	Like . . . it] It
36.11	her;] ed; ~,
37.15	man,"] ~";
38.20	"Oh . . . it's] It's
39.12	Tchaikovsky . . . Stravinski] ed; Tschaikowsky . . . Stravinksi
40.22	she took . . . she] she dressed. She
41.6	say?" . . . her mind] say?" Her mind
42.3	She . . . arm] She put an arm
42.8	cut . . . drinking] start cutting down smoking
42.19–20	winter, and . . . she] winter, she

"The Night of Chancellorsville"

Three TSS of this story survive at Princeton: an early 6-page ribbon copy typed on a pica typewriter; a 5-page ribbon copy typed on an elite typewriter (this TS served as the *Esquire* setting copy and is now among the Bertie Barr Additional Papers); and a 5-page carbon of the *Esquire* setting copy. The first and second of these TSS bear light revisions by Fitzgerald; the setting copy exhibits a few markings by the compositor (e.g., galley takes). Collations of the setting copy, and of the *Esquire* text, against the TAR text uncover heavy authorial revision between the *Esquire* text and the TAR text, carried out by FSF in proof. (See *F. Scott Fitzgerald in the Marketplace*, 75.)

45.4 Philly$_{\wedge}$] ed; ~,
47.30 Sedgwick's] ed; Sedgewick's

"The Last of the Belles"

A 31-page TS, revised heavily by FSF, is among his papers at Princeton. Collation of this TS with the *Post* text indicates that the TS was the last version revised by Fitzgerald before publication of the magazine text. Further collation with the TAR text reveals more authorial revision—and some editing of Southern idioms, likely carried out at Scribners. The original Southern speech forms, together with some punctuation and other pointing, are restored to the Cambridge text from the TS at Princeton. All emendations recorded below are taken from this TS.

51.22 How you] How are you
51.31 Come in, y'all] Come in
52.1 ordered] order
54.36 *An*-dy] An-dy
56.23 Ailie,] ed; ~;
56.25 about let's] about
57.7–8 that," continued Kitty.] ~."
57.9 Her] Miss Preston's
57.33 lay] lie
58.21 house,] ed; ~;
59.31 right,] ~;
60.30 Yes,] ~;
61.28 life—] ~:
62.17 dude-ish] dudish
62.30 card,] ~;
65.7 *course*] course

"Majesty"

No MS or TS survives for this story. Collation of the *Post* version against the TAR text uncovers a round of light revision, judged here to be authorial, including name changes for some of the characters and the deletion of the final three words from "thick blonde hair like a chow's" on p. 67 of the Cambridge text—a descriptive phrase that FSF had used for Nicole's hair in TITN. The repetition of the typo "base" in "base viol" on p. 7 of the *Post* text and p. 280 of the TAR text suggests that FSF sent marked tearsheets to Perkins to serve as printer's copy. The error is mended at 71.6 of the Cambridge text. The paragraph of dialogue by Harold Castleton at 73.21–22 of the Cambridge text appeared as a single paragraph in the *Post* but was erroneously set, by the Scribners compositors, as four separate lines (p. 283 of TAR). The arrangement from the *Post* has been restored. The emendations recorded below are editorial.

70.11 tips] ed; tip
70.35 simile] ed; metaphor
71.6 bass] ed; base
76.3 Greenwich] ed; Greenwhich
79.6 moving] ed; moved
80.3 past,] ed; ~$_{\wedge}$
80.18 said. Then] ed; ~; then

"Family in the Wind"

A full TS of this story, bearing numerous revisions and inserted passages in FSF's hand, is among his papers at Princeton. This 42-page document, sent by FSF to Ober, served as copy for the ribbon TS prepared at Ober's and submitted to the *Post*. Collations of this surviving TS with both the *Post* and the TAR texts reveal further revising by Fitzgerald between serial and collected appearances, including a reworking of the ending. (The collations indicate that FSF began his revising with *Post* tearsheets.) Before the story appeared in the *Post*, mild blasphemies ("By God" and "Christ!") were deleted; these have been restored to the Cambridge text. Unless otherwise indicated, the emendations below are taken from the TS at Princeton.

87.5	*totally*] totally
88.19	Listen,] ~;
89.1	Forrest,] ~;
91.10	twenty-five] 25
91.11	him—] ~;
92.36	By God, I'll] I'll
93.7	*you*] you
93.16	ain't] ant
94.14	itself,] ~;
94.33	*man!*] man!
96.16	"God, I] "I
99.20	*is*] is
99.35	*That's*] That's
101.23	'em] ed; ^em
102.37	"Christ!" . . . back."] "It's come back!" the doctor yelled.
103.12	"Oh, God, we] "We
104.6	back,] ed; ~;
104.16	would] ed; will
104.17	ceased] ed; cease
104.19	would] ed; will

"A Short Trip Home"

No MS or TS survives for this story. Collation of the serial version from the *Post* against the TAR text uncovers light revision and some cutting to speed up the narrative pace toward the end. In revising, Fitzgerald removed wording in the second paragraph of the story that he had used to describe Rosemary Hoyt in TITN—the words "magic suddenly in her pink palms" and the sentence "She was nearly complete, yet the dew was still on her." See the Cambridge edition of TITN, pp. 9 and 10.

FSF added the following note in proof; it appears at the bottom of p. 323 of the Scribners first edition: "In a moment of hasty misjudgement a whole paragraph of description was lifted out of this tale where it originated and properly belongs, and applied to quite a different character in a novel of mine. I have ventured none the less to leave it here, even at the risk of seeming to serve warmed-over fare." FSF is referring to the paragraph beginning "Vaguely I placed him . . . " which appears halfway through Part 1 of the story, at 109.34 of the Cambridge edition. Fitzgerald had used a version of this paragraph in TITN (p. 106 of the Cambridge edition of the novel). The apology, as part of the historical record of the text, is reproduced here but is not included in the critical text.

107.23 and,] ed; ~^
107.28 Key] ed; Keys
108.23 well—^] ser; ~—.
113.16–17 that on] ed; that
126.13–14 perspective of . . . bench also] ed; perspective also—something too faint for a man, too heavy for a shadow. Of *During galley corrections the printers shifted a linotype slug reading "of the night. There was something extended on the bench" to an incorrect position, below the line it was meant to precede. This emendation mends the error, which appears at 346.7–8 of the first edition.*

"One Interne"

A 33-page TS, heavily revised and augmented by FSF, is at Princeton. Collations with the *Post* and TAR texts demonstrate that this TS, though one stage removed from the serial text, can be used to resolve two confusing readings in the TAR version. See the emendations at 134.4 and 137.6 below. Three of the emendations below were introduced, by Fitzgerald's order, into the second state of the first impression.

129.29–31 need not . . . longer.] FSF; need not base himself on the adding machine-calculating-machine-probability machine-St. Francis of Assis machine any longer. *The corrected reading was introduced on the 349–50 cancellans.*
129.31 Assisi] ed; Assis
130.31 Michael] ed; Michael's
130.32 Ward] ed; Ward's
131.2 was] FSF; and was *The corrected reading was introduced on the 351–52 cancellans.*
131.15–16 "Oh . . . together."] FSF; "Oh, catch it—oh, catch it and take it—oh, catch it," she sighed. *The corrected reading was introduced on the 351–52 cancellans.*
132.32 Hel*lo!*] TS; Hello!
134.4 the man's] TS; his
137.3 tying] ed; trying
137.6 atmosphere] ed; ~ so

"The Fiend"

An 8-page TS of this story, bearing a few corrections by FSF, is preserved in the C. Waller Barrett collections of American literature at the Albert and Shirley Small Special Collections Library, University of Virginia. This TS served as setting copy for the *Esquire* compositors; it bears a few marks by a copy-editor and has galley takes marked on leaves 4 and 6. Collation of this TS with both the *Esquire* and TAR texts reveals no further authorial revision for the serial text and only a scattering of variants between the serial and collected versions. This last round of revision is judged to be authorial and has been incorporated into the Cambridge text. The emendations below derive from the TS unless otherwise indicated.

150.11 he] ed; it
150.19 prematurely] ed; permaturely
151.4 garroted] ed; garotted
151.18 of the] of
153.11 maneuvers] manœuvres
154.6 Fiend,] ~;
154.27 Yes‸] ~,

"Babylon Revisited"

For a discussion of the text of this story, see Christa E. Daugherty and James L. W. West III, "Josephine Baker, Petronius, and the Text of 'Babylon Revisited,'" *F. Scott Fitzgerald Review*, 1 (2002): 3–15. Several of the emendations suggested in this article have been superceded by examination of a carbon typescript of "Babylon Revisited" that Fitzgerald sent to Zelda's sister Rosalind. This TS appeared in the Bruccoli Collection at South Carolina after publication of the article. Unless otherwise indicated by a siglum or note, all emendations in this story are taken from TS1 (sent by FSF to Ober) and TS2 (sent by FSF to Rosalind); that is, the adopted emendations appear in both TSS.

157.7 Anyway‸ his friend‸] ~, ~ ~,
157.7 Schaeffer‸] ~,
157.23 habit, and then‸] ~; ~ ~,
157.23 rail‸] ~,
157.24 room—] ~,
157.29 Alix was] Alix
158.1 strong] strong a
158.27 girl?"] FSF; girl?" ¶Outside, the fire-red, gas-blue, ghost-green signs shone smokily through the tranquil rain. It was late afternoon and the streets were in movement; the *bistros* gleamed. At the corner of the Boulevard des Capucines he took a taxi. The Place de la Concorde moved by in pink majesty; they crossed the logical Seine, and Charlie felt the sudden provincial quality of the left bank. *FSF's instructions to cut this paragraph in proof were not carried out by the Scribners editorial staff. See the discussion in the Introduction above.*
158.31 "La Plus que Lente,"] ed; *Le Plus qu Lent*,
158.33 bookstore] ed; Book-store
159.1 onto] ed; on to
159.15 salon‸] ~,
159.27 relax—] ~;
159.37 subject.] ~:
160.5 eyes‸] ~,
160.25 afternoon‸] ~,
160.31 smiled—] ~;
161.15 familiarity—] ~;
161.19 *maître d'hôtel*] ed; maître d'hôtel
161.23 closed;] ed; ~,
161.24 local‸] ~,
162.11 coffee‸] ~,
163.1 First‸] ~,
163.17 *daddy*] daddy
163.33 *quite*] quite
164.2 *adorable*] ed; adorable *The murmurings would be in the French language.*
164.12 him.] ~!
164.14 Lorraine . . .] ~ . . . .

164.15 past—] ~:
164.16 lovely∧] ~,
165.6 Somehow∧] ~,
165.7 him∧] ~,
165.36 leaped—] ~;
166.11 Good-bye∧ . . . dads∧] Good-by, dads, dads, dads,
167.2 proportion—] ~.
167.6 Anyhow∧] ~,
167.8–9 me—] ~,
167.20 first.] ~:
167.33 grimly—] TS2; ~;
168.14 expected—] ~;
168.23 course∧] ~,
168.29 time—] ~,
169.3 himself—] ~;
170.20 apologetic.] ~:
171.9 white∧] ~,
171.15 dress∧] ~,
171.15 time∧] ~,
171.24 closely. Afterward] ~: afterward
171.27 bright∧] ~,
171.36 a cross Béarnaise] ed; cross Bernaise
172.17 *maîtres d'hôtel*] maîtres d'hôtel
173.20 saw∧] ~,
173.20 apartment∧] ~,
174.9 was∧ after all∧] ~, ~ ~,
174.14 *à tout*] ed; *de toute*
174.17 Lincoln] ed; Richard
174.22 astounded,] ed; ~;
174.35 shishi, cagy] stet *Both spellings were acceptable (though infrequently encountered) in 1935.*
175.18 *night!*] night!
177.14 snow∧] snow,
177.32 day—] ~;

"Outside the Cabinet-Maker's"

A 6-page TS bearing light revisions in FSF's hand is extant in his papers at Princeton. This is the TS that Fitzgerald sent to Ober for retyping and submission to magazine editors. (Fitzgerald was living in Wilmington, Delaware, when he wrote the story and sent it to Ober.) On p. 6 of the TS one finds this clause added in Ober's hand: "for she had been poor and had never had one as a child." The clause appears in the last paragraph of the published *Century* text. FSF likely sent this addition, an important one, to Ober by letter or other means; it was not Ober's practice to make substantive improvements in FSF's texts. Collation of the Princeton TS with the *Century* version brings to light further revisions. The phrase "in President Coolidge's collar-box" in the first section, before the first space break, is a revision over "under a mountain in Austria" in the TS. And the two sentences "Is that the Queen?" and "No, that's a girl called Miss Television." in the second section are substitutions for "There's the Queen." and "Yes, that's the Queen." These changes, which likewise appear first in the *Century* text, are judged here to be authorial, most likely introduced by Fitzgerald in proof or in a further communication to Ober or to the magazine editors. These changes are accepted for the Cambridge text. Two other emendations in the serial text are recorded below.

181.6 you got] TS; you
184.19 down the] ed; down

"The Rough Crossing"

Fitzgerald mailed a heavily revised 48-page TS of this story to Ober from Paris on 29 March 1929. For the story he had drawn upon fresh material—his and Zelda's voyage to Europe during the first week of March. Ober had a fresh TS of the story prepared and submitted it to the *Post*, where it was accepted and published in the 8 June 1929 issue, while the Fitzgeralds were still living in Paris. It is unlikely that Fitzgerald saw proofs. Variants between the revised TS, which survives at Princeton, and the *Post* text show a round of editing to remove several references to alcohol and drinking, and to excise some mildly offensive comments about the British. These readings have been restored for the Cambridge text. The *Post* restyled Fitzgerald's punctuation, replacing many dashes with semicolons and adding numerous commas. Fitzgerald's dashes have been restored; the extra commas have been removed. Emendations in the table below derive from the Princeton TS unless otherwise indicated.

186.1	long‸ covered piers‸] ~, ~ ~,
186.3	shouting‸] ~,
186.6–7	you—] ~;
186.7	ship—] ~;
186.9	gangplank‸] ~,
186.15–16	come—] ~,
186.16	loud‸] ~,
186.16	thing,] ~ —
186.17	mind,] ~ —
186.20	celebrity‸] ~,
186.21	name‸] ~,
186.22	blonde] blond
186.23	and‸] ~,
186.24	aerie‸] ~,
187.1	at 288 Park Avenue] at our door on Park Avenue
187.15	shops and things] shops
187.22	Eva‸] Eva,
188.21	ropes,] ~‸
188.24	low‸] ~,
189.5–6	such . . . existed] all activity
189.7	lunch] luncheon
190.3	that‸ and] that, and
190.8	that‸ too] that, too
190.30	self-consciousness,] ~ - ~;
191.3	him—] ~;
191.18	in‸] ~,
191.29	pitch—toss—roll] ~, ~, ~
192.35	bar for cocktails.] bar.
193.5	sleep, sleep . . .] ~, ~.
193.6	*Hey*] Hey
193.7	*crea-eak! wrench!* swoop!] Crea-eak! Wrench! Swoop!
193.8	later,] ~‸
193.22	graceful—] ~;
194.15	coming‸] ~,
194.25	sailing.] ed; ~:
194.33	lost‸] ~,
195.28	lay‸] ~,
195.28	him‸] ~,
196.11	There.] ~,
196.20	Unwilling,] ed; ~‸
196.25–28	child." ¶You're tight." ¶"No . . . party."] child."
196.37	please—] ~;
197.19	on. Please] ~, please
197.36	delicate‸] ~,
198.1	it—] ~;
198.7	lovely—] ~;
198.13	tossing‸ . . . wretched‸] ~, ~ ~ ~,
198.21	curb broker] broker
198.22	disappeared. For] ed; ~; for
198.26	spilt] spilled
198.33	the only haven, the bar.] the bar.

198.37	fact. Annoyance] ed; ~; annoyance
199.2	to,] ~ —
199.17–18	Adrian, her Adrian,] ~ — ~ ~ —
199.27	Adrian; for . . . child;] ed; Adrian; *The TS reads* "unwillingness to have"; *here* "unwillingness" *is editorially emended to* "reluctance" *because Eva has indeed given birth to a second child.*
200.31	no—] ~.
200.35–201.2	her." ¶"How?" Adrian gasped. ¶"Some . . . Empire."] her."
201.15	it—] ~;
201.17	lunch] luncheon
202.5	night—when] ~∧~
202.9	years—] ~;
202.12	Furthermore∧] ~,
202.19	lunch] luncheon
202.22	holding] ed; holding on
202.31	stiff∧] ~,
202.33	owned and lived] lived
203.1–2	Adrian—] ~;
203.6	her. To] ~; to
203.12	days. It] ~; it
203.18	want and then] ~, ~ ~,
203.26	me. I'm in love with him—"] me."
204.1	sullen∧] ~,
205.7	burden. Then] ~; then
205.33	Me∧] Me,

"At Your Age"

A 30-page TS of this story, with extensive revisions in pencil by FSF, was auctioned at Sotheby Parke Bernet, Sale 4355, on 9 April 1980. The same TS was auctioned at Christie's, New York, Sale 9178, on 9 June 1999; and the TS was subsequently offered by the dealer Kenneth W. Rendell in Catalogue 298, ca. 2003. The Rendell entry reveals that the working title for the story was "The Old Beau." The current location of the TS is not known.

207.23	said,] ed; ~∧
218.18	apartment,] ed; ~∧
220.30	later,] ed; ~∧
222.6	nineties,] ed; 90's,

"The Swimmers"

A 46-page TS, missing its first page, survives in the Bruccoli collection at the University of South Carolina. This TS bears heavy revisions by Fitzgerald, especially toward the end. It is two stages removed from the *Post* text; another TS must have intervened between this TS and the copy prepared at Ober's and submitted to the *Post*. (See Ober to FSF, 22 August 1929, *As Ever*, 142.) The TS has proved useful in recovering FSF's pointing and spelling.

Two passages critical of the behavior and appearance of Americans in Europe were altered before the story was published in the *Post*. These passages survive only in the South Carolina TS. Responsibility for the changes is difficult to assign. FSF was aware that these passages might cause problems for the *Post*. In a 28 August 1929 cable to Ober (sent after the *Post* had accepted the story) he offered, unbidden, to modify the passages if necessary (*As Ever*, p. 144). In a letter to Fitzgerald dated 3 September, Ober wrote that the *Post* did not have time to send a proof to him in Paris but that George Horace Lorimer, the editor, did not feel that the passages in question were "objectionable" (*As Ever*, p. 145). These passages were nevertheless altered before serial publication. They might have been changed at the *Post*; it is also possible that FSF decided on his own to delete the first passage and revise the second. He would have cabled instructions to do so to the *Post* offices in Philadelphia, or sent a communication to the *Post* through Ober. Given this possibility, and given the distance of the surviving TS from the published text, the passages have not been restored.

The first passage, not present in the *Post* text, is a full paragraph that appears in the TS just before the paragraph in the Cambridge text that begins, "Henry Clay Marston was a Virginian" (p. 227 of this edition). The deleted paragraph reads as follows:

Henry as usual was depressed by the sight of his race en masse. In ten years of prosperity he had watched many waves arrive—each wave rawer, less educated than the last, yet sitting ever more complacently in the cars that bore their faint faint smell of fried potatoes around the western world. He was thankful not to be in Paris now for this was the season of the buyers, when a liquid vulgarity seemed injected into the city's body that made it reel and stagger. All that was best in the history of man must succumb at last to these invasions, as the old American culture had finally exhausted its power to absorb the bilge of Europe.

The second passage involves the sentence which, in TS, follows the paragraph ending "the governing class" in the Cambridge text (p. 227). In TS the sentence reads: "The two young men coming out of the water as she went in bore with them the large shoulders, the empty face, the loud vacant laugh, the canned wisecrack, of the rich west—but not the girl." In the *Post* text (and the Cambridge text), the sentence reads: "The two young men, coming out of the water as she went in, had large shoulders and empty faces."

The emendations in the table below are taken from the South Carolina TS unless otherwise indicated.

223.2	slowly in] ed; ~ by
223.11	100,000] ed; 1000
223.13	100,000] ed; 1000
224.12	tall∧] ~,
225.25	*heard*] heard
226.3	doctor,] ~;
226.6	one hundred thousand] ed; one thousand
226.27	St∧-Jean-de-Luz] ed; ~. ~ ~ ~

227.23 told—] ~;
227.27 girl,] ~—
227.28 eighteen,] ~—
228.3 deserved,] ~—
229.36 St-Jean] ed; ~. ~
230.13 to even] even to
230.37 other‸] ~,
230.37 will‸] ~,
231.1 country‸] ed; ~,
231.23 *Amoricaine*] American *Fitzgerald means that Henry and Choupette know French cuisine in a sophisticated way. Lobster "Amoricaine" was a Gallicized term for Lobster "Américaine," a dish invented by a chef named Noel Peters in 1867. See* The Short Stories of F. Scott Fitzgerald: A New Collection, *ed. Matthew J. Bruccoli (New York: Scribners, 1989): 502n.*
232.18 she's—] ~‸
236.8 over with] ed; over
241.33 leapt] leaped
242.23 October‸] ~,

"The Bridal Party"

A 51-page TS, heavily revised by FSF, is among his papers at Princeton. This is the TS mailed to Ober in late April 1929; it would have served as copy for the TS prepared for and sold to the *Post*. Collation of the Ober TS with the serial text uncovers a restyling of punctuation, the bowdlerization of two mild oaths, and the removal of a reference to drinking. The oaths and the reference to alcohol have been restored, as has Fitzgerald's pointing. Emendations are taken from the TS.

244.3–4 marriage—which moreover] ~; ~, ~,
244.6 Cathedral Church] ed; Protestant Episcopal Church *The* "Protestant Episcopal Church of the Holy Trinity," *in the* Post *text, and in the TS, is located in Brooklyn Heights. Fitzgerald has confused the name of this church with the Cathedral Church of the Holy Trinity on Avenue George V—also known as the American Cathedral in Paris, a church frequented by American expatriates and the logical place for this marriage ceremony to take place.*
244.10 fine‸] ~,
244.20 York‸] ~,
244.21 because‸] ~,
244.22 world‸] ~,
244.25 great‸] ~,
245.14 *Michael!*] Michael!
245.26 *Michael*] Michael
245.26 *have*] have
246.5 West's—] ~;
246.36–247.2 impossible . . . sentiment . . . .] impossible.
247.14 month—] ~;
247.20 morning,] ~ —
247.25 Well, by God,] Well,
248.22 done—] ~;
248.27 dark‸] ~,

249.2	goods.] good.
249.3	and∧] ~,
249.3	side∧] ~,
250.16	up∧] ~,
250.16	saw∧] ~,
250.17	violently∧] ~,
250.19	"God, yes."] "Yes."
250.36	*pour*] pour
251.35	difficult—] ~;
254.25	but—] ~∧
254.25	there∧ too,] ~, ~;
255.20	in—] ~;
256.25	*swell!*] swell!
258.19	clean∧] ~,
258.22	lacy∧] ~,
259.19	flora—] ~;
259.21	drink—] ~;
260.37	appeared∧] ~,
261.1	ballroom∧] ~,
262.2	free—] ~;

"One Trip Abroad"

A 63-page TS bearing heavy revisions by Fitzgerald is at Princeton. This TS, close substantively to the *Post* text, would have served as copy for the typists at the Ober agency; their fresh TS would have gone to the *Post* for copy-editing and typesetting. Collation reveals a round of editing: mild blasphemies ("For God's sake") have been removed; punctuation has been restyled. Several typing errors from the surviving TS have been carried forward into print and are here emended. Blasphemies have been reinstated, and punctuation has been restored. Unless otherwise indicated the emendations recorded below derive from the Princeton TS.

263.7	bus] ed; car
263.15	stock exchange] Stock Exchange
263.21	Among] Amongst
263.24	couple∧] ~;
264.3–4	background—] ~,
265.6	emphatically,] ~;
265.11	girl her] girl of her
265.16	god] God
265.18	were, . . . so,] ed; ~∧ . . . ~∧
265.26	silence—] ~;
267.5	café] Café
267.12	show—] ~;
267.18	mammies—] ~;
267.21	comedian—] ~;
267.26	exacting,] ~ —
267.27	simple, languid,] simply languid
268.2–3	country. We . . . prudishness] country; a little prudishness shouldn't
268.21	giving it] giving
268.22	that] the fact that
268.34	world—] ~;
269.6	tranquility] tranquillity
269.14	tranquility.] tranquillity;
269.27	General Sir Evelyn Frazelle] Gen. Sir Evelyne Fragelle *And subsequent occurrences.*
269.27–28	Lady Frazelle] ed; she
270.4	uncertainly—] ~;
270.23	sound,] ~;
270.26	matter—] ~;
270.30	*he*] he
270.31	*he*] he
271.7	said. "We'll] ~; "we'll
271.18	which naturally] ~, ~,
271.19	chartered] ed; charted
271.20	cruises—] ~;
271.27	coast—] ~;
271.31	French,] ~;
271.32	do,] do;
271.32	husband,] ~;

271.34 ten-thirty] 10:30
272.8 ones,] ~;
272.22–23 even stranger] other
272.24 Well‸] ~,
272.36 Casino—] ~;
273.6 afterward‸] ~,
273.7 lunch] luncheon
273.13 her‸] ~,
273.15 lunch: the] luncheon: The
273.17 counted,] ~;
273.17 Frenchwoman] ~-~
273.20–21 Nelson—] ~;
274.19 stopped‸] ~,
274.31 cigarette, Noel‸] ~; ~,
274.32 turned‸] ~,
274.36 thing—] ~;
275.1 Say‸] ~,
275.9 water.] ~!
275.9 then‸ to Oscar‸] ~, ~ ~,
275.10 damn fool] fool
275.21 saw,] ~;
275.27 later‸] ~,
275.27 away‸] ~,
275.29 face.] ~;
276.1 *crazy*] crazy
276.3 square‸] ~,
276.4 did‸] ~,
276.12 "For God's sake, hasn't] "Hasn't
276.15 Oscar] ed; He
276.24 thing‸] ~,
276.27 reinforced] reëforced
276.30 hour‸] ~,
277.20 can,] ~‸
277.23 café—] ~;
277.26 forward—] ~;
277.27 now‸] ~,
277.32 home‸] ~,
278.10 sake,] ~ —
278.11 unrestrained,] ~ —
278.15 snobbishness‸] ~,
278.15 self-preservation—] ~,
278.25 genius‸] ~,
278.29 Duchamp] ed; Deschamps *See the explanatory note for this reading.*
278.30 mentioned‸] ~,
279.1 intelligent,] ~;
279.1 go‸] ~,
279.10 sodden—] ~,
279.13 decided,] ed; ~‸
279.23 Americans—] ~;
279.27 interested by] ~ in
279.29 lunch] luncheon
279.33 apartment] *appartement*
280.1 So‸] ~,
280.2 Hospital,] ~‸
280.5 status,] ~‸
280.19 aboard. As] aboard—as
280.20 French,] ~ —
280.21 that,] ~ —
280.32 Why—] ~,
280.34 weeks—] ~;
281.7 knew‸] ~,
281.7 tone‸] ~,
281.7–8 right—but‸ perversely‸] ~, ~, ~,
281.8–9 said‸ instead‸] ~, ~,
281.16 Somewhere‸] ~,
281.27 bottles‸] ~,
281.37 were coming] coming
282.13 box—] ~‸
282.14 nurse,] ~‸
282.24 then‸] ~,
282.24 cross-examination‸] ~,
282.25 out‸] ~,
282.33 gone—] ~,
283.1–2 *our* party—*our*] our party—our
283.26 While] Though
284.1 night—] ~;
284.16 alone, really alone,] ~ — ~ ~ —
285.3 disappeared;] ~ completely;
285.9 arrivals,] ~ —
285.9 that] the
285.13 saw the other couple] saw other couples
285.17 Later‸] ~,
285.23 thought‸] ~,
285.24 eyes,] ~;
285.26 expensively‸] ~,
285.29 whole‸] ~,

286.9 rose bushes] rosebushes
286.9–10 damp-sweet$_\wedge$] ~,
286.14 below,] ~ —
286.20 brightened—] ~;
286.34 last dark] last
286.36 turned—] ~,
287.1 thunder—] ~,
287.5 "God, Yes!"] "Yes!"

"The Hotel Child"

Among Fitzgerald's papers at Princeton is a 43-page TS, revised in his hand. This TS would have served as copy, at the Ober agency, for the fresh TS submitted to the *Post.* Collation of the extant TS with the *Post* text reveals numerous revisions and cuts. These alterations were made in order to remove references to drinking and to the taking of hasheesh; to change the slur "Sheeny" to "Jewess"; to remove mild profanity; and to mask the names of countries, cities, towns, and business establishments. (Fitzgerald's habit was to mix fictitious names with real names; the *Post* took no chances, cutting or altering them all.) The readings from the TS have been restored for the Cambridge text. Also restored is the paragraphing and much of the pointing from the TS. Emendations recorded below are taken from the TS at Princeton unless otherwise indicated.

288.18 fine$_\wedge$] ~,
289.14–15 Swiss city] city
289.37 handsome$_\wedge$] ~,
290.3 Kentuckians] people
290.10 "career"] $_\wedge$~$_\wedge$
290.15–16 Balkan-like] Balkanlike
290.21–25 bar. ¶"Most . . . Capps-Karr strolled] bar, and strolled
290.32 Fifi—] ~,
291.3 hotel—] ~;
291.16 night. And] ~$_\wedge$ and
291.19 a corner] a dark corner
291.29–30 the thrones of France and Brazil] European thrones
291.34 Mama] Mamma *And subsequent occurrences.*
292.2 tall$_\wedge$] ~,
292.3 Capps-Karr$_\wedge$] ~,
292.4 him.] ~:
292.5 *say!*] say!
292.7 "Good God, Capps . . . you."] "Fancy running into you, Capps."
292.12–14 sofa, took . . . two,] sofa$_\wedge$
292.15 was going over the Simplon pass] was leaving
292.25–26 demanded, surreptitiously . . . Pekingese.] demanded.
292.26 Sheeny.] Jewess?
292.30 stripe—] ~;
293.7 her—] ~;
293.22 to$_\wedge$ maybe$_\wedge$] ~, ~,
293.22 Then maybe] ~, ~,
293.22 married,] ~;
293.30–31 over the Simplon pass] to Milan
294.7–11 duel." ¶Annoyed . . . war.] duel."
294.20 him?] ~.
294.26–27 the Café Central] a café *And subsequent occurrences.*
294.31 fur$_\wedge$] ~,
295.14–15 sitting quite drunk] sitting
295.29 taxi-stand . . . François] taxi stand
295.35 as club and] as cloud and

295.36–296.1 wrong. Did . . . cars?] wrong.
296.7 saw‸] ~,
296.7 late‸] ~,
296.12 was‸ perhaps‸] ~, ~,
296.17 answer,] ~;
296.31 But—] ~‸
296.32 in Dayton] back home
298.17 schools,] ~ —
298.17 schools,] ~ —
299.19 obsequious‸ but hostile‸] ~, ~ ~,
299.22 life,] ~;
299.25 down,] ~;
300.6 Now‸ listen. What] ~, ~; what
300.12 Fifi‸] ~,
300.26–27 hesitate." ¶Fifi . . . shut.] hesitate.
300.29 assured] answered
300.30–31 her. In . . . law.] her.
300.31 But if] If
301.8 over the Simplon pass] to Milan
301.20 "Goodby-ee"] "Good-by-e-e"
301.23 in her] ed; of her
302.2 said. "And] ~, "and
302.14 I‸ naturally‸] ~, ~,
302.23–25 here. He . . . tonight."] here."
302.29 happy‸ too—] ~, ~;
302.33 back to Dayton] back
302.34 stay in Dayton] stay
302.35 wanted‸] ~,
302.35 could‸ maybe‸] ~, ~,
303.5 Borowki at the Perroquet] Borowki
303.15–16 uptown . . . Nussneger's.] uptown.
304.9 periodic] ed; periodical
304.26 watch,] ~ —
305.9 dozed—] ~‸
305.21 and, as] ~‸ ~
305.23 Indian-like] Indianlike
305.24 later—] ~;
305.25 cantons.] country.
305.29 dogs—] ~;
306.1–2 manager . . . Mondes] manager
306.19 bed—] ~;
306.22 answered—] ~;
307.10 Café Central] café
307.11 *say*] say
307.21 Luckily‸] ~,
307.30 Lausanne] the city
308.3 to Switzerland] here
308.3 consulate,] ~‸
308.5–6 Office, and . . . mine."] Office."
308.9 should] could
308.10 but a Swiss—or an] but an
308.25 the Meurice Hotel] a hotel
309.1 glass. The] ~; the
309.4 Bye-bye. I've] ~-~; ~
309.9 hopes, her . . . clothes—] hopes,
309.12 whether they] ed; if they
309.12 her‸] ~,

"Indecision"

An earlier version of this story, entitled "Other Winter Sports," survives in TS among FSF's papers at Princeton. This version was rejected by the *Post* in February 1931; FSF revised the story extensively, and the magazine took it one month later. A heavily revised 47-page TS of this later version, with the title now "Indecision," is also extant at Princeton. It includes mild profanity ("Get the hell out of here!") and slang ("broads" for "girls") that is missing from the *Post* appearance. These readings have been restored. Fitzgerald's preference for the dash over the semicolon and his habit of omitting the comma between two adjectives of equal weight have been followed. Emendations below originate in the "Indecision" TS unless otherwise indicated.

310.5	dark‸ convict-like] ~, convictlike
310.7	‸ickle durls‸] "~ ~" *And subsequent occurrences.*
310.12	much,] ~;
310.15	it—] ~;
310.17	her,] ~‸
311.1	seven-thirty] 7:30
311.18	that,] ~‸
311.19	days,] ~‸
311.22	free—] ~;
311.23	night‸] ~,
311.26	Emily‸] ~,
311.28	added them] added
311.34	eighteen.] ~‸
311.37	"Nawlins 'riginly,"] "N' Awlins rigin'ly,"
312.4	She was sitting] ed; Sitting
312.4	man. He] ed; man, he
312.8	his.] him.
312.8	something—] ~;
313.6	God, you're] You're
313.8	lovely‸] ~,
313.9	carnations‸] ~,
314.1	rarebit] rabbit
314.7	Andalusia;] ~ —
314.8	Harvard] Cambridge
314.8	Whitby;] ~,
314.12	nineties] 90's
314.14	the smoke] and smoke
314.27	off—] ~;
314.34	noise—] ~;
315.3	years—] ~;
315.23	annoyed.] ~:
315.30	him!] ~.
315.30	ride—] ~;
316.5	Moros—] ~;
316.8	snow‸] ~,
316.10	small‸] ~,
316.17	Boches] boches
316.18	gathered‸ and,] ~, ~‸
316.20	complicated. The] ~: the
316.28	Get the hell] Get
316.30	sleigh. Shut] sleigh. . . . Shut
316.35	broads] girls
317.23	horrible—] ~;
317.27	sincerity—] ~,
318.12	me—] ~;
318.25	Honestly‸] ~,
318.28	marches‸] ~,
318.31	turn—] ~,
319.1	Oh‸] ~,
319.11	her—] ~;
319.25	Whitby—] ~,
320.10	once—] ~,
320.22	hours—] ~;
320.29	Why‸ no,] ~, ~;
321.12	moment, perhaps *the*] ~; ~ the
321.19	meeting. He] ~, he
321.25	*true*—] ~‸
321.33	apart—] ~;
322.1	evening—] ~;
322.2	thought . . .] ~.
322.18	saw‸] ~,
322.18	glance‸] ~,
322.22	started—] ~;
322.24	Cola—] ~;
322.28	women—] ~;
322.28	I takem.] I take 'em
323.5	*smelled*] smelled
323.11	durl;] ~‸
323.13	around‸] ~,
323.16	searching—] ~;
323.17	as finally] ~, ~,
323.36	way—] ~;
324.13	"*O bei Gott*, I] "I *Idiomatic German would be "Ach mein Gott," but FSF probably wanted the English-language cognate here.*
324.24	apologized—] ~;
324.24	feeling—] ~;
324.33	finished—] ~;
324.36	overshoes. The] ~; the

325.12	sleigh?] ~.
325.27	hopeless—] ~;
326.15	breath . . .] ~;
326.17	valley . . .] ~,
326.21	back—] ~;
327.2	one?] ~.
327.10	guitar—] ~.
327.14	move—] ~;
327.19	now$_{\wedge}$] ~,
327.22	sharp$_{\wedge}$] ~,
327.24	cried, quickly,] cried$_{\wedge}$

"A New Leaf"

A 27-page TS of this story, bearing revisions in FSF's hand, is extant at Princeton. This TS was sent to Ober by Fitzgerald; a fresh TS was made at the agency for submission to the *Post*. Collation of the extant TS with the magazine text reveals the same pattern of editing that is apparent in other Fitzgerald stories published in the *Post* during this period. Mild blasphemies have been removed; the words "in her very womb" in Part III of the story have disappeared; a suggestion that the Irish are prone to drink has been expunged. These readings are restored here, together with FSF's preference for the dash over the semicolon and his use of italics in dialogue to indicate emphasis. Unless otherwise indicated the emendations below have been taken from the surviving TS at Princeton.

328.22	onto] on to
329.2	Nonsense. He] ed; ~; he
329.9	Good Lord—drink, women] Drink, women
329.17–18	kennel with the debutante daughter.] kennel.
329.25	enough$_{\wedge}$] ~,
330.27	minutes—] ~;
330.29	a second *fine*] a *fine*
331.3	bland—] ~;
331.8	abstraction,] ~ —
331.19	really—I'm really surprised] really surprised
331.26	change—] ~;
332.1	Arts—] ~;
332.4	I got Irish and expansive] I got expansive
332.13	*I'd*] I'd
332.21	again—] ~;
333.14	wobbling] wabbling
333.18	him—] ~;
333.29	her. She] ed; ~; she
333.36	Thankfully a passing] A passing
334.16	shaking.] ~:
335.9	He was so] He was as
335.12	clear$_{\wedge}$] ~,
335.14	Julia—] ~;
335.31	you've] you have
336.3	can't—] can't,
336.8–9	feel oh] ~, ~,
336.17	right. One more thing.] ~: one ~ ~:
336.27–28	invited—] ~;
337.13	Don't go, for God's sake. If] Don't go, if
338.6	intended—] ~,
338.20	other small] ~, ~,
338.21	had fortunately] ~, ~,
339.5	Station] station
339.12	know—] ~;
339.13	nothing else] nothing
339.16	set] cheer
339.19	at] ed; in
339.26	friends—] ~;
340.6	ahead.] ahead with it.
340.23	"Oh God!" she thought, her] Her

340.24	up? Is] up?" she thought. "Is	341.20	days,] ~‸
340.27	slowly in her very womb.] slowly.	341.29	her—] ~;
340.31	difficult—] ~;	341.32	dear,] ~;
		343.9	bend;] bent;

Hyphenated Compounds

The compound words in the table below are hyphenated at the ends of lines in the Cambridge text. The hyphens should be preserved when quoting these words. All other compound words hyphenated at the ends of lines in this edition should be quoted as a single word.

8.6	good-humored	122.26	low-animal
9.9	Indian-like	153.25	respectable-looking
12.28	good-humored	176.23	Good-night
15.27	life-tired	181.1	dingy-looking
17.12	pale-blue	182.21	cabinet-maker's
20.16	twenty-four	189.23	flat-nosed
21.35	half-asleep	195.13	now-covered
29.15	fine-looking	213.25	short-sightedness
90.4	well-kept	224.26	one-dimensional
94.22	half-conscious	286.9	damp-sweet
98.22	dirt-filled	286.14	full-bodied
102.30	fish-white	290.15	Balkan-like
113.19	run-down		

EXPLANATORY NOTES

The annotations below identify important persons and places, literary and dramatic works, movie and stage stars, sports heroes and celebrities, popular songs, restaurants, and hotels that are mentioned in the stories.

"Crazy Sunday"

5.10 Puppenfeen

In the one-act ballet *Die Puppenfee* (*The Fairy Doll*) by Austrian violinist and composer Josef Bayer (1852–1913), the toys in a toy shop come to life after the store has closed for the night. "Die Puppenfee," which had its premiere in 1888, was the most popular of Bayer's many ballets and was performed frequently by the Vienna Court Opera Orchestra. "Puppenfeen" is the plural form of the word.

5.14 writing continuity

In Hollywood film production, continuity involves keeping track of props, makeup, costumes, and sound effects as camera angles shift and scenes change. Inconsistencies must not appear when shots, taken at different times, are merged to create the final movie. The continuity writer works closely with the director to preserve the visual flow of the film.

5.28 a Eugene O'Neill play

Fitzgerald probably has in mind O'Neill's *Strange Interlude*, which had its Broadway premiere in 1928, with Lynn Fontanne and Glenn Anders in the featured roles. The play was made into a movie by Metro-Goldwyn-Mayer in 1932, the year in which "Crazy Sunday" was published. The film starred Norma Shearer and Clark Gable.

6.6–8 Marion Davies . . . Dietrich and Garbo and the Marquise

Marion Davies (1897–1961), a movie actress who appeared mostly in light comedies, is today remembered for her liaison with the publishing tycoon William Randolph Hearst (1863–1951). They lived together at his estate La Cuesta Encantada (the Enchanted Hill) in San Simeon. Marlene Dietrich (1901–92) was among the most highly paid actresses in Hollywood during the 1930s. Her movies *The Blue Angel* and *Morocco*, both of which premiered in 1930, are still shown today. Like Dietrich, Greta Garbo (1905–90), a native of Sweden, worked in European films before coming to America. Her most famous movies are *Anna Christie* (1930), *Grand Hotel* (1932), *Queen Christina* (1933), and *Anna Karenina* (1935). The Marquise is likely a reference to the English playwright and performer Noel Coward (1899–1973), whose play *The Marquise* (an eighteenth-century costume drama) was first produced in 1927. Coward served several stints in Hollywood.

8.2 Napoleon's mother

Letitia Bonaparte (b. 1750), mother of Napoleon, was known for her common sense and for living conservatively and quietly. Widowed young, she raised eight of thirteen children to adulthood; most of them rose to ranks of power or royalty within the French government. Letitia did not attend her son's coronation; nevertheless, Napoleon had the artist Jacques-Louis David give her a prominent position in an enormous painting commemorating the event.

9.20 the Great Lover

After the death of Rudolph Valentino (1895–1926), his film role as the Great Lover was filled by John Gilbert (1897–1936), whose suave good looks first brought him attention in *Monte Cristo* (1922). Gilbert failed to make the transition from silent films to talkies in the late 1920s because of his high voice.

9.24 a Menjou type

Adolphe Menjou (1890–1963) was frequently cast in movies as a debonair and heartless ladies' man. His appearance was distinctive: a longish nose, wide dark eyes, a high forehead, and an uptilted black moustache. Menjou played opposite such stars as Mary Pickford, Norma Shearer, Louise Brooks, Marlene Dietrich, Irene Dunne, and Barbara Stanwyck. Charlie Chaplin called him "the perfect French tripe."

9.24–25 a sort of Michael Arlen

Michael Arlen (1895–1956), born Dikran Kouyoumdjian to Armenian parents, was best known for his short-story collection *These Charming People* (1923) and his novel *The Green Hat* (1924), both of which featured outspoken, sexually adventurous heroines. Urbane and sophisticated, Arlen was married to a Greek countess and was conspicuous in London society during the 1920s and 1930s.

11.4 Grauman's

Sid Grauman (1879–1950) owned and operated several motion-picture palaces in downtown Los Angeles during the 1930s. His best-known film venues were the Egyptian Theatre and Grauman's Chinese Theatre, both of which still stand on Hollywood Boulevard. Fitzgerald has the latter of these two in mind in this passage. The Chinese Theatre resembles a large red pagoda. Many Hollywood stars have put their handprints, footprints, and signatures in wet concrete in the forecourt of this theatre.

15.12–13 the Notre Dame-California game

Notre Dame and the University of Southern California, two American football powerhouses, began their long rivalry in 1926. Miles Calman is flying to South Bend, Indiana, to see the game on the Notre Dame campus.

17.27 Jack Johnson

The pugilist Jack Johnson (1878–1946) was the first African American world heavyweight champion. He was also among the first celebrity athletes; he endorsed numerous products and invested in businesses, restaurants, and nightclubs.

21.15 Lois? Joan? Carmel?

Joel is suggesting the names of movie stars who might be called upon for help. Lois Moran (1909–90) appeared in both silent movies and talkies. Fitzgerald met her at a Hollywood party shortly after her film debut and was smitten by her youthful exuberance and freshness. She served as the model for Jenny Prince in his story "Jacob's Ladder" (1927) and stood for Rosemary Hoyt in *Tender Is the Night* (1934). Joan Crawford (1904–77) danced her way from Texas to Broadway, where she was noticed by MGM while performing in a chorus line. She was among the most famous stars of her era: she played opposite Lon Chaney and Douglas Fairbanks in the 1920s and appeared in several movies with Clark Gable during the 1930s. Carmel Myers (1899–1980) was a leading actress on the silent screen, known for her vamp roles opposite Rudolph Valentino and Ramon Novarro. She played the seductress Iras in *Ben-Hur* (1925), a film in which she wore a magnificent costume by Erté. During the making of that movie in Rome, she struck up a friendship with the Fitzgeralds, who were temporarily residing in the city.

"Two Wrongs"

24.27 Theatre Guild

The Theatre Guild was established in 1918 to produce high-quality plays for New York audiences. Plays were chosen by a board rather than a single director. Performances during the guild's first two decades included O'Neill's *Strange Interlude* (1928) and *Mourning Becomes Electra* (1931), and the Heyward–Gershwin collaboration *Porgy and Bess* (1935).

25.1 Take Ames, take Hopkins, take Harris

Bill is naively (or boastfully) comparing himself with the leading producers of the time. Winthrop Ames (1870–1937), a Broadway producer and director, was also a playwright and screenwriter. He personally funded the building of the Little Theatre in New York City as a performance venue for experimental plays. He also organized a group that paid for actors to travel to Europe and perform for American troops stationed there, and created a renewed interest in Gilbert and Sullivan by staging extravagant performances of their comic operas. Arthur Hopkins (1878–1950) directed and produced plays in the American Expressionist theater, including Maxwell Anderson's war play *What Price Glory?* (1924) and Sophie Treadwell's surrealistic *Machinal* (1928). During the 1920s the Yale-educated Jed Harris (1900–79) produced a run of hit shows—*Broadway* (1926), *Coquette* (1927), *The Royal Family* (1927), and *The Front Page* (1928). These garnered him fame before he turned 29 years of age. His productions starred many of the leading players of the time, including Laurence Olivier, Basil Rathbone, and Lillian Gish.

25.31 Reinhardt

When "Two Wrongs" appeared in the *Post*, the energetic Max Reinhardt (1873–1943) was managing one theater in Berlin and another in Vienna. In 1920 he helped to found the long-standing Salzburg Festival, a venue for music and drama. Reinhardt was associated with Expressionism, an avant-garde style developed in Germany during the early twentieth century.

26.28 the Bedford

The Bedford Hotel, favored by movie and stage people, was a European-style establishment located near Fifth Avenue and Grand Central Station.

26.35 Jack Dempsey

The professional boxer Jack Dempsey (1895–1983), nicknamed the "Manassa Mauler," won the heavyweight title in 1919 and held it until 1926. Later he became a restaurateur in New York City. Dempsey is also mentioned in "One Trip Abroad."

26.36 the Harvard Club

A club for faculty and alumni of the university, located at 27 West 44th Street. The neo-Georgian building was designed by the architect Charles F. McKim (1847–1909).

27.5 Gold Coast boys

The establishment of a rail service between Penn Station and Long Island in the early 1900s encouraged wealthy New Yorkers to build large estates on the Island's North Shore. The area became known as the "Gold Coast."

27.17 Pavlova's a hoofer

Bill is attempting irony. Anna Pavlova (1881–1931) was the most famous classical ballerina of her time, principal dancer in both the Imperial Russian Ballet and in Diaghilev's Ballets Russes. The slang term "hoofer" was used for a female tap dancer who improvised her routines.

29.5–6 in a Grand Street apple cart

Bill is referring to Brancusi's Jewish background. Grand Street, on the Lower East Side of New York, passed through a Jewish immigrant neighborhood, with open-air markets and peddlers who sold fruit, vegetables, and other goods.

31.23–24 New York agencies were making big buys

That is to say, ticket agencies in New York City that bought up blocks of tickets to promising Broadway shows, sporting events, and cultural attractions. These agencies operated from hotels, tobacco shops, and other locations in the city. Initial success would be guaranteed by "big buys" from these agencies, which sent representatives to dress rehearsals in Atlantic City.

32.16 the Savoy Grill

One of the favorite restaurants for Americans in London was the grill room of the Savoy Hotel on the Strand—known as the "American Bar" after 1926. George Gershwin and Ernest Hemingway, among many others, patronized the Savoy Grill.

34.9 a hit at the New Strand, a hit at the Prince of Wales
The New Strand, which opened in 1905, was connected to the Waldorf Hotel on Aldwych. The Prince of Wales was built in 1884 on Coventry Street in the West End. Both theaters featured popular shows, especially light dramas and musical comedies.

34.12–13 his Hyde Park house
Hyde Park is one of four city parks of central London. Originally used by Henry VIII as a hunting ground for deer, it consists of some 350 landscaped acres divided by a man-made lake known as the Serpentine, which provides a sanctuary for waterlife. The park has been a venue for national celebrations and performances since the 1800s. To live in a Hyde Park house during Fitzgerald's era would have indicated a high income and a tolerance for the common public.

36.17 her Mayfair house
Named after the annual May Fair held in this region from 1686 until 1764, this tony section of London is near Hyde Park. At one time it was largely owned by the Duke of Westminster and became part of the Grosvenor family estate. Regent's Park is in Mayfair, as are the London Zoo and the Royal Academy of Arts.

39.13 *Chopiniana . . . The Ring*
The romantic ballet *Chopiniana*, by the Russian choreographer Michel Fokine (1880–1942), featuring the music of Chopin, was presented in 1909 by the impresario Serge Diaghilev (1872–1929) under the title *Les Sylphides*, with Anna Pavlova and Vaslav Nijinsky in featured roles. The composition of *Der Ring des Nibelungen* took Richard Wagner (1813–83) more than twenty-five years. The work includes four individual operas; the characters (gods, mortals, giants, dwarves, and Valkyries) are drawn from Norse mythology.

40.26 the Metropolitan
This would be an excellent opportunity for Emmy. The Metropolitan Opera House, then at Broadway and 39th Street, was one of the most prestigious performance venues for American music and dance.

41.18 to the Adirondacks or to Denver

Hospitals and sanitariums for consumptives were located in the Adirondack Mountains (in upper New York State) and in the city of Denver, Colorado. Both locations offered cold, clear mountain air and warm mineral springs.

44.17 reading *Variety* and *Zit's*

Two leading entertainment and scandal magazines of the period. *Variety*, a weekly, covered vaudeville and the stage; its distribution was international. *Zit's Theatrical Newspaper* was an American gossip rag edited by the flamboyant Carl Florian Zittel, who apprenticed with the *New York Morning Telegraph* and the *New York Journal*.

"The Night of Chancellorsville"

45.— CHANCELLORSVILLE

The Battle of Chancellorsville in the American Civil War took place from 30 April to 6 May 1863 in Spotsylvania County, Virginia. Confederate troops commanded by Robert E. Lee (1807–70) engaged the Army of the Potomac under Joseph Hooker (1814–79). Lee, who was outnumbered, divided his forces twice and outflanked Hooker, putting him on the defensive. Losses were heavy on both sides.

45.28 Hooker's army

Prostitutes who followed Hooker's troops and consorted with them came to be known as "hookers"—hence the modern slang term.

46.30–32 The Seven Days . . . Gaines' Mill

This series of battles lasted from 25 June to 1 July 1862. The Army of Northern Virginia under Robert E. Lee took the offensive against the Army of the Potomac, commanded by George B. McClellan (1826–85), and prevented the Union troops from attacking Richmond. In the Battle of Gaines' Mill on 27 June, Lee dislodged the Union Fifth Corps from its defensive posture and drove its men north across the Chickahominy River.

47.30 Sedgwick's Corps

The Union general John Sedgwick (1813–64) commanded the Sixth Corps at Chancellorsville; his men stormed and took Marye's Heights above Fredericksburg, Virginia, but could not prevent an overall defeat for the North.

"The Last of the Belles"

51.21 Camp Harry Lee

The name of this fictitious camp is meant to bring to the reader's mind "Light-Horse Harry" Lee (1756–1818), an American cavalry officer in the Revolutionary War. Lee attended Princeton before the war; later he became governor of Virginia. In a December 1799 eulogy he described George Washington as "First in war, first in peace, and first in the hearts of his countrymen." Henry Lee was the father of the Confederate general Robert E. Lee.

51.33–34 heard Ruth Draper or read "Marse Chan"

American storyteller Ruth Draper (1884–1956) was a *diseuse*—an actress who specializes in monologues and, with minimal props, creates theatrical performances involving multiple characters. Draper made her debut on Broadway in 1916 and performed for nearly forty years; she acquired several languages and could imitate the Southern accent convincingly—hence the reference here. "Marse Chan" (1884), a sentimental short story by the Virginia native Thomas Nelson Page (1853–1922), tells of an ill-fated love affair in the postbellum South. The story is narrated by the hero's worshipful manservant, in African American dialect.

52.26–27 a Leyendecker forelock

The American illustrator J. C. Leyendecker (1874–1951) was best known for his renderings of the Arrow Collar Man. His typical male figure was tall, handsome, polished, and aloof. A drooping forelock was in evidence on some of the Leyendecker men.

52.34 ten consecutive steps

Men from the stag line would have cut in frequently on Ailie, a popular girl with a good line of conversational patter.

53.28 "After You've Gone"

In 1918, shortly before the end of the First World War, the female crooner Marion Harris (1896–1944) made this song—with words by Henry Creamer and music by Turner Layton—enormously popular. Amory Blaine hums the tune in *This Side of Paradise*, after his romance with Rosalind has come to an end (p. 193 of the Cambridge edition).

55.22 Tech

Georgia Tech, in Atlanta, was known for rowdy fraternity parties and a winning football team. Zelda Sayre, along with other girls from her home town of Montgomery, Alabama, attended some of the dances there.

58.11 an ensign from Pensacola

A junior officer, training at the U.S. naval air station at Pensacola, Florida, to fly seaplanes, dirigibles, and free kite balloons. Anson Hunter in "The Rich Boy" (1926) trains at Pensacola.

60.4–5 "My Indiana Home"

Fitzgerald probably has in mind "Indiana" (also known as "Back Home Again in Indiana"), a popular song with lyrics by Ballard MacDonald (1882–1935), a Princeton graduate. In 1917 the Columbia Gramophone Company released "Indiana" on the flip side of "Darktown Strutters' Ball." Both tunes were performed by the Original Dixieland Jazz Band.

60.35 Camp Mills

This installation was a major embarkation point for American troops headed to Europe during the First World War. It was located on Long Island, near the town of Mineola. Fitzgerald was stationed there at the end of the war, waiting to be deployed to France.

62.34 at the Montmartre in New York

The Montmartre was a popular *faux* Parisian nightspot at Broadway and 50th Street, near the Winter Garden. The proprietors, Paul Salvin and Jim Thompson, operated two similar clubs, the Palais Royal and the Moulin Rouge, at other locations in New York.

"Majesty"

67.12 Briarly School

A veiled reference to the Brearley School, an expensive private girls' school founded in 1884 in New York City by Samuel A. Brearley, Jr., a Harvard graduate and former tutor. The *Post* text reads "Miss Thatcher's School."

67.13 Tuxedo Park

This 5,000-acre community for the wealthy, located some forty miles north of New York City, was built by the tobacco millionaire Pierre Lorillard IV.

Tuxedo Park had its own police station, clubhouse, and shopping district. The New York debutante season usually began with a formal ball at the clubhouse; it was here that Pierre's son, Griswold, first appeared in a satin dress coat that eventually became known as the tuxedo.

68.20–21 St. Bartholomew's

St. Bartholomew's Episcopal Church, in its third incarnation in New York City, was (and still is) located at 325 Park Avenue. The cornerstone for the enormous Byzantine-style church, with seating for 1,500, was laid in 1917; its first service was held in the autumn of 1918.

71.37 'At Dawning'

This popular romantic song of the early 1900s, in which "I love you" is repeated after nearly every line, was the work of the composer Charles Wakefield Cadman (1881–1946). Cadman was prominent in the Indianist movement, which promoted Native American themes and melodies. "At Dawning" was first recorded in 1912 by the tenor John McCormack for the Victor label.

72.4 wilting collar after collar

The first detachable collars appeared in the 1820s; they were worn by American men several decades into the twentieth century. The basic styles were poke, wing, spread, lap front, fold, and turn-down. Detachable collars were held in place by studs and buttons. In hot weather one could have a fresh collar without changing one's shirt. Dick Diver wears detachable collars in *Tender Is the Night*.

75.34 Park Row

Park Row, in the financial district of Manhattan, was known during this period as Newspaper Row. Offices for most of the prominent papers in the city, including the *New York World*, the *New York Tribune*, and the *New York Times*, were located there, within walking distance of City Hall and the municipal police department.

76.3 Greenwich

This town in southwestern Connecticut is a relatively short train ride from Grand Central Station. Brevoort is in a hurry: according to state laws then in force, couples wishing to wed in New York were required to wait at least twenty-four hours from the time a license was issued until they could marry. Connecticut, with no waiting period or residency requirement, was a popular place for impulsive nuptials.

77.8 Southampton, Lake Forest or Back Bay

These communities for the wealthy and fashionable—the first on the southern tip of Long Island, the second a suburb north of Chicago, and the third a neighborhood in Boston—are suitable places of origin for the Paris newcomers mentioned here. Ginevra King (1898–1980), Fitzgerald's first serious love, was from Lake Forest.

78.21 Westbury Hills

Olive's new house is being erected in one of the most exclusive and expensive suburbs of New York City, located on Long Island, some twenty miles east of Manhattan. Many of the mansions in Westbury Hills featured formal gardens, indoor swimming pools, and similar amenities.

81.18 Going to Jerusalem

Another name for the children's game known as Musical Chairs. Going to Jerusalem is fully described in *The Bobbsey Twins at School* (1910), the fourth book in the popular children's series published by the Stratemeyer Syndicate.

81.30 Ellis Island

This small island in the upper bay of New York City was a processing site for immigrants arriving in the United States during the great flood of European immigration of the late nineteenth and early twentieth centuries. After the First World War quotas were imposed by the federal government to slow the influx of immigrants.

"Family in the Wind"

93.26 Chilton County

This county in central Alabama is named after William Parish Chilton, Sr. (1810–71), leader of the first Confederate Congress. Other place names in the story are inventions by Fitzgerald.

95.8 it was a tornado

"Family in the Wind," published in the *Post* on 4 June 1932, was based on an outbreak of tornadoes in the Deep South on 21–22 March of that year.

Fitzgerald was living in Montgomery, Alabama, when tornadoes hit the middle portion of the state, causing some 268 deaths and great destruction of property, crops, and livestock.

"A Short Trip Home"

107.27–28 New Haven . . . Scroll and Key

Joe Jelke attends Yale University in New Haven, Connecticut, and belongs to Scroll and Key, one of the six senior societies at the university. The most prestigious of these societies was Skull and Bones; the others were Berzelius, Book and Snake, Wolf's Head, and Elihu.

110.5 one of Tad's more savage cartoons

Fitzgerald reused this paragraph in Book One, Chapter 21, of *Tender Is the Night* (p. 106 of the Cambridge edition). "Tad" was Thomas Aloysius Dorgan (1877–1929), a journalist, boxing authority, and cartoonist for the *New York Journal*. He used slang terms of the period in his cartoons, including "twenty-three skidoo," "the cat's meow," and "for crying out loud."

111.11 witch-hazel and court-plaster

Witch-hazel is an astringent used to treat bruises, cuts, and swelling. By "court-plaster" Fitzgerald means an adhesive bandage, or a "band-aid" or "sticking plaster." The term originates with the small round adhesive patches (mimicking beauty spots) worn by members of the British court during the late eighteenth century.

112.33 like Stuart's plume

James Ewell Brown (Jeb) Stuart (1833–64) was a daring and flamboyant cavalry commander who served under Robert E. Lee in the civil war. In photographs of the period he is shown with an ostrich plume in his hat.

113.5 Seven Corners

The Seven Corners region of St. Paul was located between the hilly residential section and the business district along the shoreline of the Mississippi River. Fitzgerald would have passed through Seven Corners as he walked from Summit Avenue toward the riverfront.

113.11–12 Hoot Gibson and Wonder Dogs and Wonder Horses

Born Edmund Richard Gibson (1892–1962) in the horse country of Nebraska, as a teenager Gibson picked up the nickname "Hoot Owl," later shortened to "Hoot." Gibson competed on the summer rodeo circuit and appeared as a stuntman in early western movies. Eventually he became a leading man in both silent films and talkies. Cowboy stars of his era often had canine and equine sidekicks with special talents.

113.13 "Old King Brady" . . . "The Liberty Boys of '76"

Characters in popular fiction of the period. Old King Brady was the protagonist of numerous pulp-style detective adventures published between 1885 and 1912. Dime novels about the Liberty Boys of '76 often featured Captain Dick Slater, leader of a group of young freedom fighters during the American Revolutionary War.

116.10 the University Club

When he was visiting St. Paul, Fitzgerald often socialized at the University Club, which still stands on Summit Avenue. To break the winter monotony, he and Zelda organized a "Bad Luck Ball" at the club on 13 January 1922, a Friday.

117.12 Pump and Slipper dance . . . Princeton Prom

This spring formal dance for Yale undergraduates was usually held at the Hotel Taft in New Haven. Fitzgerald mentions the dance also in "May Day" (1920) and "Bernice Bobs Her Hair" (1920). The Princeton Prom was a comparable spring dance at Fitzgerald's university.

120.4–10 Lake Shore Drive . . . the Blackstone

This thoroughfare, known as "The Drive," runs through Chicago alongside Lake Michigan. The Blackstone Hotel, a small and elegant establishment, was a favorite caravansary for wealthy visitors to the city. Amory Blaine stays there in *This Side of Paradise* (p. 154 of the Cambridge edition).

"One Interne"

129.1 the Coccidian Club

Medical humor at Johns Hopkins in Baltimore, where the story is set—though neither the university nor the city is named in the text. Coccidia are single-celled, spore-forming parasites that infect the intestinal tracts of beasts and humans, causing diarrhea and other such difficulties.

130.15 If you forget Alfonso

Fitzgerald is referring here to Alfonso, Prince of Asturias (1907–38), heir to the throne of Spain from 1907 until 1931. Alfonso and his brother Gonzalo were afflicted with hemophilia; both wore tailored and padded clothing to protect them from injury. Alfonso died in Florida from injuries sustained in a car accident.

132.23 a gigantic Christ

A reference to the large statue of Christus Consolator which stands in the rotunda of the administration building of Johns Hopkins Hospital. The statue, unveiled in October 1896, was executed by the Danish sculptor Bertel Thorwaldsen. Fitzgerald would have passed it frequently during the months in which Zelda was being treated for mental disorders at Johns Hopkins.

133.19 a P. E. and a history

Shorthand for a personal examination and a history of previous illnesses and treatments.

134.10 Hoover's speech

Herbert Hoover (1874–1964) was U.S. president when "One Interne" was published in the *Post* (5 November 1932). The reference in the story is probably to one of Hoover's campaign speeches for the fall 1932 presidential election, which he lost to Franklin D. Roosevelt (1882–1945). Hoover's speeches were broadcast over the radio, as were Roosevelt's, giving both men much wider audiences than previous candidates had enjoyed.

137.36 Peabody Institute

The Peabody Institute, on Mount Vernon Place in Baltimore, was founded in 1857 as a conservatory for the training of composers, conductors, and musicians.

139.19 actinomycosis

The term denotes a long-term chronic bacterial infection affecting the face and neck.

141.1–2 a Duncan Phyfe table, a brass by Brancusi
The table, if originally manufactured in the shop of the Scottish American cabinet-maker Duncan Phyfe (1770–1854), would have been quite valuable. The Romanian-born sculptor Constantin Brancusi (1876–1957) was a pioneer of modernism; his early works include *The Kiss* (1908) and *Bird in Space* (1922–23).

145.17–146.6 mesenteric thrombosis . . . hypodermoclysis . . . pancreatitis
The first is a clot blocking blood flow in a mesenteric vein, one of two veins through which blood leaves the intestine. The second is infusion of fluids under the skin to treat dehydration. Pancreatitis, several paragraphs along, is inflammation of the pancreas.

"The Fiend"

152.21 a German doctor's thousand case histories
Probably a reference to the Austro-German psychiatrist Richard von Krafft-Ebing (1840–1902), whose *Psychopathia Sexualis* was first published in 1886. The volume presents case studies of sexual behavior, much of it deviant in character. The book was deliberately written in a dry, factual style.

152.23 New England Divine
Fitzgerald has in mind the American theologian Jonathan Edwards (1703–58), whose most famous sermon was "Sinners in the Hands of an Angry God," first delivered in 1741. Edwards was a prominent figure in the First Great Awakening of the 1730s and 1740s.

152.28 the Newgate Calendar
This compilation of tales about thieves and murderers, and the punishments administered to them, had its origins in the monthly bulletin of executions issued by the keeper of Newgate Prison, in London. The narratives, colorful and bloody, typically ended with admonitions against vice and lawlessness. *The Newgate Calendar* was said to be one of the three books most often found in the average home during the late eighteenth and early nineteenth centuries, the other two being the Bible and Bunyan's *Pilgrim's Progress*.

"Babylon Revisited"

157.14 the Ritz bar

The best known of the gathering places for expatriates in Paris, especially in the afternoons and early evenings, located in the Ritz Hotel on the Place Vendôme. Abe North spends an entire day at the Ritz bar in Book One of *Tender Is the Night.*

158.31 "La Plus que Lente"

A slow waltz for solo piano by the French composer Claude Debussy (1862–1918), first performed in 1910.

158.33–34 Brentano's . . . Duval's

This branch of the New York-based bookstore chain, located on the Avenue de l'Opéra, was a popular gathering place for American expatriates. Fitzgerald was a regular visitor during the 1920s. Duval's, a restaurant chain with locations throughout Paris, offered small portions of excellent food at low prices.

161.8–9 *strapontin* . . . Josephine Baker

A *strapontin* is a small folding chair. Charlie is watching a performance by the African American dancer and *chanteuse* Josephine Baker (1906–75), known during the 1920s in Paris for her *Danse banane*, which she performed at the Folies Bergères wearing only a banana skirt.

161.15 Bricktop's

The African American performer and cabaret-owner Ada Smith (1894–1984), known as "Bricktop" for her bright red hair and freckles, operated a popular nightclub in Paris during the 1920s. Among the stars who performed there were Ethel Waters, Noel Coward, and Cole Porter. The Fitzgeralds caroused at Bricktop's during their periods of residence in Paris. For Ada Smith's recollections of Fitzgerald, see her memoir *Bricktop*, written with James Haskins and published by Atheneum in 1983.

161.23 Zelli's

Joe Zelli's establishment on the rue Fontaine, known as the Royal Box, featured an underground dance hall surrounded by elevated box seats. Zelli's attracted a rough clientele and was raided from time to time by the police. Fitzgerald mentions it also in "The Bridal Party," a later story in this volume.

161.26 the Café of Heaven and the Café of Hell

Le Café de l'Enfer was a popular night spot on the Boulevard de Clichy in the Pigalle. The decorations were bizarre. One entered through a gaping demon's mouth; the ceiling inside featured plaster representations of souls in torment. Next door was a café called Le Ceil (which Fitzgerald calls the Café of Heaven here) with heaven-themed ornamentation. The Poet's Cave, mentioned also in this sentence, has not been located.

162.16 Le Grand-Vatel

This first-class restaurant, on the Right Bank at 275 rue Saint-Honoré, not far from the Place Vendôme, specialized in oyster dishes.

163.3 the Empire

The Théâtre de l'Empire on the avenue de Wagram, near the Étoile, was a popular venue for variety shows and cinema.

172.3 Griffons

Fitzgerald is thinking of Griffon, a small restaurant at 31 avenue de l'Opéra, near the Boulevard des Capucines.

172.21 a *pneumatique*

A message enclosed in a capsule and delivered through a pressurized air tube. The pneumatique system in Paris, comprising some 467 kilometres of tubing, was in use from 1866 until 1984.

174.14 *bonne à tout faire*

A servant who took care of general duties in a household.

177.5 "Selling short."

"Selling short," a term used by investors on the stock and commodities markets, is a risky technique. One deals in "futures" and gambles against other investors. Selling short was unregulated during the 1920s and was one of the major causes of the Wall Street Crash of 1929. If the market rises, an investor who attempts to sell short will lose heavily. This happens to Charlie: he sells his daughter short when, in a weak moment, he gives up guardianship to the Peters. Perhaps he thinks that he can "buy back in" whenever he cares to, and that the price will be approximately the same. Now, however, he finds that the price has gone up. Honoria's value to Charlie has risen much more than he anticipated; he cannot buy her back with money. He has treated her, and perhaps others, in an emotionally thoughtless way. The strategy of "selling short" would be familiar to Charlie, who is himself an investor. Many of Fitzgerald's readers in 1931, when this story appeared in the *Post*, would have known the meaning of the term.

"Outside the Cabinet-Maker's"

182.27 President Coolidge's collar-box

The taciturn Calvin Coolidge (1872–1933) served as U.S. president from 1923 to 1929. During this period, men who wore detachable collars kept them in collar-boxes, usually made of wood or gutta percha, to protect them from crumpling.

183.2–3 transformed, like Mombi in 'The Land of Oz'

Mombi, the Wicked Witch of the North in *The Marvelous Land of Oz* (1904), the second of L. Frank Baum's Oz books, is defeated by Glinda the Good Witch of the South. Glinda forces Mombi to drink a potion that strips her of her magic powers.

"The Rough Crossing"

186.10 smaller than Andorra

This tiny principality in the eastern Pyrenees between Spain and France was a popular destination for tourists. The official language of Andorra is Catalan.

187.12 the *Majestic* or the *Aquitania*

Construction on the German liner *Bismarck* was halted by the First World War. The ship was completed by German builders after the armistice and, as one of the provisions of the peace settlement, was handed over to the British as compensation for the *Britannic*, which had been sunk by a German mine in 1916. The liner was rechristened the *Majestic* and began to work the North Atlantic trade in the White Star line. It is referred to again by Fitzgerald in "The Swimmers," p. 242 of this volume. The *Aquitania*, launched in 1914 by the Cunard Line, was the sister ship of the *Lusitania*. During the war the *Aquitania* was used as both a hospital ship and a troopship.

198.12 the *Vestris* disaster

On 11 November 1928 the Cunard liner *Vestris*, en route to the River Plate from New York City, encountered a severe storm off the coast of Virginia and developed a severe list to starboard. The list worsened as coal and cargo began to shift below decks. On 12 November the ship sank off Norfolk with a loss of over one hundred lives.

198.20–21 a Groton-Harvard lawyer . . . curb broker . . . Gyp the Blood

A mixed group. The lawyer prepped at the exclusive Groton School in Groton, Massachusetts, and finished his education at Harvard. A curb broker was a dealer, often of shady repute, who sold stocks and bonds not listed on the stock exchange. The broker probably resembles Harry Horowitz (1889–1914), known as Gyp the Blood, a Jewish American gangster who was executed on 13 April 1914 for his part in the murder of the gambler Herman Rosenthal outside the Metropole Hotel on 16 July 1912. Meyer Wolfshiem offers his recollections of the incident in *The Great Gatsby*.

198.30–31 tortured hundreds below

Those in third-class accommodation in the lower decks, where conditions would have been wretched during a storm.

202.15–16 the *Mauretania*

This Cunard liner, known as the "Maury," was the fastest ship of her class when launched in 1906. She was used as a troop carrier during the Gallipoli campaign of 1915–16 and later as a hospital ship. The *Mauretania* resumed service in the transatlantic passenger trade in September 1919.

"At Your Age"

207.11–12 hands that folded powders into papers

Prescription drugs were sometimes dispensed in powdered form rather than as pills or liquids. The powders were measured out and folded into small squares of waxed paper.

215.19 the Junior League show

The Junior League was an organization of young married women who carried out volunteer work and organized social gatherings and theatrical events. Annie, if she were to follow the path of convention, would eventually become a member.

"The Swimmers"

223.11 100,000 Chemises

This chain of three shops in Paris (all carrying the name "100,000 Chemises") offered an enormous selection of men's shirts. The stores were located on the rue La Fayette, the rue de Rivoli, and the rue de Rennes.

223.14–15 Constance Talmadge in *Déjeuner de Soleil*

Constance Talmadge (1898–1973) and Don Alvarado (1900–67) starred in this silent French farce, shot at Universal Studios in 1927. The title in English is *Breakfast at Sunrise.*

226.15 male cabbage

Fitzgerald is playing with the French language. The masculine noun *le chou*, meaning "cabbage," is often used as a term of endearment. Choupette would say "*mon chou*" here; normally the word is applied to a child: "*mon petit chou.*" Choupette's own name can be read as an ironic variant of the word, given her behavior in the story.

227.7–8 from Manassas to Appomattox

That is to say, from the first battle of the American Civil War in July 1861 to the end of the conflict in April 1865. Like other Virginians who opposed slavery, Henry's grandfather freed his slaves before the outbreak of war but remained loyal to his state. Henry is named for the prominent Virginia statesman Henry Clay (1777–1852).

231.22–23 lobster American . . . lobster *Amoricaine*

"Lobster *Américaine*," a dish invented in 1867 by the chef Noel Peters, was known as "lobster *Amoricaine*" to French restaurateurs and their patrons.

240.17 Gerbault

Between June 1923 and May 1929 the French aviator and tennis champion Alain J. Gerbault (1893–1941) made a single-handed circumnavigation of the globe in the English racing cruiser *Firecrest*. At various points in the journey he was beset by equipment failure and was forced to drift with the currents.

243.15–16 Shiloh . . . Argonne

Fitzgerald is referring to the Battle of Shiloh in the American Civil War, which took place in southwestern Tennessee on 6–7 April 1862, and to the Battle of the Argonne Forest, the last extended engagement of the First World War, fought along the entire Western Front between 26 September and 11 November 1918. Jay Gatsby fought at the Argonne.

"The Bridal Party"

244.6 Cathedral Church of the Holy Trinity

This church, more familiarly known as the American Cathedral in Paris, is located in the 8th arrondissement, between the Seine and the Champs-Élysées. It was a favorite place of worship for American Episcopalians in Paris during the 1920s and 1930s and would have been the proper place for this fashionable wedding to take place.

244.12 Smith's

The bookshop of the British bookseller W. H. Smith, established in Paris in 1903, was a gathering place for English-speaking readers in the city.

245.1 "Among My Souvenirs"

This weepy ballad by Horatio Nicholls (1888–1964) and Edgar Leslie (1885–1976) was first recorded in 1927 and became popular in both Britain and America, reaching the top of the U.S. charts in February 1928. "A few more tokens rest within my treasure chest, / And though they do their best to give me consolation, / I count them all apart, and as the teardrops start, / I find a broken heart among my souvenirs."

245.7 Graf Zeppelin

This Germain airship, built by the manufacturer Luftschiffbau Zeppelin, made its maiden flight in September 1928. It circled the globe in August 1929, taking twelve days to make the journey and stopping only five times. During the First World War, the Germans used dirigibles in the Luftwaffe; Paris was bombed from an LZ-38 Zeppelin in the summer of 1915.

245.29 bought a seat

That is to say, purchased a seat on the New York Stock Exchange.

246.2 Hôtel George V

The George V, which opened in 1928, was among the newest and most luxurious hotels in Paris at the time. It was built by the hotelier Joel Hillman at a cost of $31 million on avenue George V, just off the Champs-Élysées.

246.4 Chez Victor

Fitzgerald probably has in mind Victor's, a restaurant on the rue de Compiègne. A *Baedeker* of the period notes that Victor's is "quite as good" as restaurants of the highest class, but that it is "less pretentious."

249.31 the "Painted Doll"

"The Wedding of the Painted Doll" was a hit song by Nacio Herb Brown and Arthur Freed from the 1929 MGM movie *Broadway Melody*—a film which won an Academy Award for Best Picture that year.

259.9 Eton suits

These outfits, originally worn by the junior boys at Eton College, in England, were popular apparel for American boys from upper-class families during the late nineteenth and early twentieth centuries. The suit consisted of a short jacket, a stiff white collar with bow tie, short pants, knee socks, and leather oxfords.

261.2 The Old Mill

The Old Mill was a water ride found at state fairs and amusement parks during Fitzgerald's youth. Small boats for passengers were propelled or drawn through a dark tunnel that featured lurid lighting and scary sound effects. The Old Mill gave young couples a chance to kiss and touch.

"One Trip Abroad"

264.17–20 the little oasis town of Bou Saada . . . Hôtel Transatlantique

This market town in northeastern Algeria was a center for the production of jewelry and metalwork. Bou Saada was surrounded by extensive date groves. Fitzgerald and Zelda visited there in February 1930. In the next sentence Fitzgerald is using the name of a real hotel in Bou Saada, the Transatlantique, a forty-room establishment designed in the Moorish style, with a spacious terrace shaded by fruit and palm trees.

264.30–31 Also he painted a picture of a smokestack.

Fitzgerald is likely referring here to Gerald Murphy's painting *Boatdeck*, a large canvas depicting the funnels of an ocean liner. Murphy executed the painting in 1923 and exhibited it in February 1924 at the Salon des Indépendants in the Grand Palais, Paris.

265.21 the wail of Magian prayer

The Magians, members of a religious sect that traced its origins to ancient Persia, were fire-worshippers and followers of the prophet Zoroaster. The Magians studied astrology and alchemy and were said to practice magic.

266.36 The Ouled Naïls

Young women from the Ouled Naïls, a Berber tribe, traveled to coastal cities and worked as dancers and prostitutes in order to acquire money with which to purchase property at home. Fitzgerald and Zelda attended a performance of Ouled Naïl dancers in February 1930; Fitzgerald mentions the experience in his 1933 essay "One Hundred False Starts."

269.36–37 "Waiting for the Robert E. Lee"

Al Jolson first performed this rollicking Dixie steamboat song at the Winter Garden in 1913. The lyrics tell of waiting "on the levee in old Alabamy" for "the good ship Robert E. Lee" that will "carry the cotton away." The music was written by Lewis F. Muir, with lyrics by L. Wolfe Gilbert.

270.13 the relief of Ladysmith

In the Second Boer War of 1899–1902 some eight thousand British troops were entrapped in a fort at Ladysmith, a city in the Uthukela district of South Africa. The Boers laid siege to the fort; British troops under General Sir Redvers Buller eventually arrived and broke the siege in February 1900.

273.29 Sepoys at the gate

Indian soldiers in the British Army were called Sepoys. Initially these were Hindu or Muslim soldiers without uniforms and without much training; eventually the Sepoy regiments became effective fighting units for the British, helping them to achieve many of their victories in India.

273.32 wear the green hat

A reference to Michael Arlen's 1924 novel *The Green Hat*, glossed in the annotations for "Crazy Sunday."

278.28–29 Brancusi and Léger and Duchamp

The Romanian sculptor Constantin Brancusi (1876–1957), glossed above in the notes for "One Interne," was an important sculptor in the development of modernism. Fernand Léger (1881–1955) began as a proponent of cubism but soon adopted a more figurative style and became famous as a sculptor, painter, and filmmaker. The dadaist and surrealist artist Marcel Duchamp (1887–1968) is remembered for his painting *Nude Descending a Staircase* (1912) and for exhibiting a porcelain urinal as a work of art (1917).

282.2 the Café de Paris

This café was a popular meeting-place for artists, writers, and dancers. The Russian ballet impresario Sergei Diaghilev dined there frequently during his time in Monte Carlo.

283.35 Bonivard's dungeon and Calvin's city

Fitzgerald is referring to the dungeon, at the Château de Chillon near Montreux, in which the monk François Bonivard was imprisoned from 1532 to 1536. Lord Byron's *The Prisoner of Chillon* (1816) was based on a visit to the château. The theologian John Calvin (1509–64) lived in Geneva from 1536 to 1538. He attempted to establish a theocracy there but failed and was forced to flee to Strasbourg.

284.26 *Kursaal*

A public building at a health resort. In German the word translates to "cure room."

284.27–28 Tauchnitz editions . . . Edgar Wallaces

The German publishing firm of Tauchnitz issued paper-bound editions of popular English-language works in their Collection of British and American Authors. These inexpensive volumes were purchased by travelers on the Continent. The British novelist and playwright Edgar Wallace (1875–1932) produced detective stories and thrillers for the popular market; copies of his novels, often in yellow wrappers, were available in European bookstores that catered to the English and American trade.

286.18 Dents du Midi

The Dents du Midi are seven mountains in the Chablais Alps, located in the canton of Valais. These mountains are visible from most locations in the Rhone Valley.

"The Hotel Child"

288.8 Hôtel des Trois Mondes

A fictitious hotel. Its name suggests the Hôtel des Deux Mondes on the avenue de l'Opéra in Paris. The Fitzgeralds stayed at this hotel for several nights in May 1924 before leaving Paris for the Riviera. A Hôtel des Trois Mondes also appears in *Tender Is the Night* (p. 274 of the Cambridge edition).

288.27 Chanel . . . Molyneux . . . Patou

Fashionable designers of the period. Coco Chanel (1883–1971) operated boutiques in Paris, Deauville, and Biarritz; Edward Molyneux (1891–1974), a London designer, opened his own house in Paris in 1919 and expanded eventually to Monte Carlo and Cannes; Jean Patou (1880–1936) dressed Lady Diana Cooper and Barbara Hutton; he established his headquarters in Paris on the rue Saint-Florentin.

289.14–15 this little Swiss city

The story is set in Lausanne, in the French-speaking region of Switzerland. Fitzgerald lived there in the fall of 1930 at the Hôtel de la Paix.

291.30–31 mediatized German principalities

By mutual agreement, mediatized principalities or dominions were annexed to larger states. In this way the dynastic rights of their sovereigns were not disturbed.

292.15 over the Simplon Pass

This high mountain pass between the Pennine and Lepontine Alps in Switzerland connects the Swiss town of Brig with Domodossola, a city in the Piedmont region of northern Italy.

295.27 "*Ich bin von Kopf bis Fuss*"

This song by the German composer Friedrich Hollaender (1896–1976) was performed in *Der blaue Engel*, the 1930 movie that launched Marlene Dietrich's career as a screen star. An English version, with lyrics by Sammy Lerner (1903–89), became her signature song.

298.4 *Almanach de Gotha*

This directory of European royalty and aristocracy, first published in 1763, was an authoritative source for information about monarchies, dynasties, and royal families present and past.

298.6 the Crown of St. Stephen

Beginning in the thirteenth century, this crown, also known as the Holy Crown of Hungary, was used in coronation ceremonies for monarchs of Hungary.

303.2 the Villa d'Este at Como

This Renaissance villa, which stands on the shores of Lake Como, was originally built between 1565 and 1570 as the summer residence of the Cardinal of Como. It became a luxury hotel in 1873. The villa complex includes a large park and a formal garden.

308.25 the Meurice Hotel

Le Meurice, a luxury hotel on the rue de Rivoli, is located opposite the Tuileries Garden. At the time of the story it was known as the Hotel of Kings; guests included prominent statesmen, film stars, and artists.

"Indecision"

310.8–9 "I'm Getting Myself Ready for You"

A song by Cole Porter (1891–1964), performed first on Broadway in the musical *The New Yorkers* (1930) and recorded in March 1931 by Blanche Calloway and Her Joy Boys. The first verse goes: "I cut out necking, cut out petting, / And with the boys I'm all through, / 'Cause I'm gettin' myself ready for you!" Additional lyrics from the song appear later in the story.

316.17 Boches

French soldiers during the First World War referred to the Germans as "les Boches"—from the French slang word for rascal. British and American troops adopted and used the term.

326.3–4 the Wildstrubel

This mountain, part of the Bernese Alps, is still a popular destination for hikers and novice climbers.

"A New Leaf"

328.1–2 Bois de Boulogne

This wooded area of some 2,000 acres, located to the west of Paris, was created in the 1850s by Napoleon III as a place of amusement for the upper classes. By the first decade of the twentieth century it had been transformed into a public park for the bourgeoisie—for riding, rowing, dancing, and picnicking.

328.10 —*the purple noon's transparent might*

Lines 4–6 of "Stanzas Written in Dejection, near Naples" by Percy Bysshe Shelley (1792–1822). Fitzgerald has misquoted slightly. Shelley's text reads: "The purple noon's transparent light: / The breath of the moist earth is light / Around its unexpanded buds . . . "

328.22 the *Bremen*

With its twin high-speed turbine engines, this German ocean liner was among the fastest passenger ships of its day, crossing the Atlantic during normal weather in only five days.

331.24 the *Olympic*

This British liner, launched in October 1910, was dazzle-painted and fitted with armaments during the First World War for service as a troopship. After the war it was refitted as a passenger vessel and put back into transatlantic service. In 1934 the *Olympic* became part of the newly formed Cunard–White Star Company.

331.36–37 a Princeton freshman with a little black cap

First-year students at Princeton during Fitzgerald's time were required to wear small black caps. The cap, called a "dinky," made it easy for upperclassmen to identify freshmen and to administer hazing and mild harassment.

331.37–332.1 Boston Tech . . . the Beaux-Arts

Dick has attended Boston Tech, a prominent college of engineering and technical studies located near Copley Square in the city. In 1916 the college moved to nearby Cambridge and changed its name to the Massachusetts Institute of Technology, though it continued to be known informally as Boston Tech for the next decade or so. Dick has continued his architectural studies at the École des Beaux-Arts in Paris.

332.28 the Golden Arrow

This luxury boat train, which offered only first-class accommodations, was operated by British Railways. The train linked London via Dover with the Calais ferry.

335.9 White Star Line

One of the two best-known British transatlantic passenger lines of the period, the other being Cunard. White Star liners were known for their distinctive black-topped funnels. The most famous of their passenger ships were the *Olympic* (mentioned several lines below on this page), the *Brittanic*, and the ill-fated *Titanic*.

337.18 Libby Holman

The American torch singer and Broadway actress Libby Holman (1904–71) was notorious for her bisexuality and for irregularities in her personal life. In 1932 she was accused of murdering her husband, Zachary S. Reynolds, one of the heirs to the Reynolds tobacco fortune in North Carolina, but the charges were dismissed.

ILLUSTRATIONS

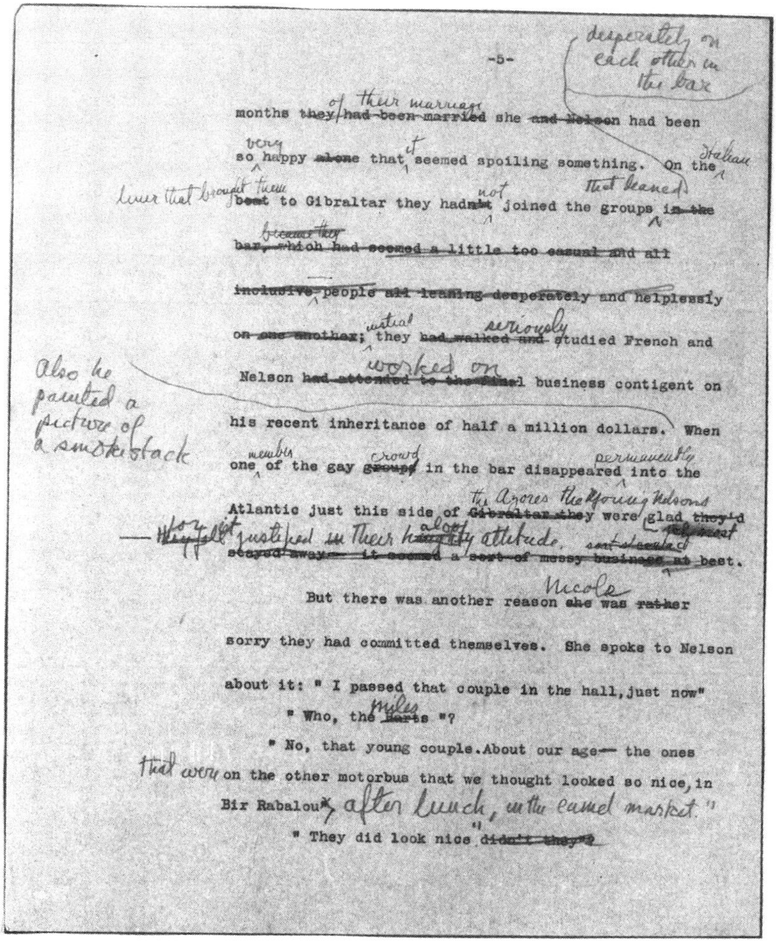

-5-

months they had been married she and Nelson had been so happy alone that seemed spoiling something. On the boat to Gibraltar they hadn't joined the groups in the bar, which had seemed a little too casual and all inclusive, people all leaning desperately and helplessly on one another; they had walked and studied French and Nelson had attended to the final business contigent on his recent inheritance of half a million dollars. When one of the gay groups in the bar disappeared into the Atlantic just this side of Gibraltar they were glad they'd stayed away— it seemed a sort of messy business at best.

Also he painted a picture of a smokestack

But there was another reason she was rather sorry they had committed themselves. She spoke to Nelson about it: " I passed that couple in the hall, just now"

" Who, the Harts "?

" No, that young couple. About our age— the ones on the other motorbus that we thought looked so nice, in Bir Rabalou, after lunch, in the camel market."

" They did look nice didn't they"?

Plate 1 Page 5 of the working typescript of "One Trip Abroad." The "picture of a smokestack" (inserted in the left margin by Fitzgerald) is a reference to a lost painting by the American expatriate Gerald Murphy, a friend of Fitzgerald's and one of the models for Dick Diver in *Tender Is the Night*. F. Scott Fitzgerald Papers, Princeton University Libraries.

-7-

" Bopes! Bopes! "

Their exclamations and laughter filled the room and the bartender whispered to an inquisitive American that ~~it~~ the new arrival was ~~Lord Arthur Gallum.~~ The Marquis Kinkallow.

Bopes stretched himself out in several chairs and a sofa, took a hasheesh tablet from a silver box which he proferred to the other two and called for the barman. He announced that he had driven from Paris without a stop and was going over the Simplon Pass next morning to meet the only woman he had ever loved in Milan. He did not look in a condition to meet anyone.

" Oh Bopes, I've been so blind," said Lady ~~Helen,~~ Rapps-Karr pathetically. " ~~I've been dringking and dringking and dringking.~~ Day after day after day. I flew here from Cannes meaning to stay one day and I ran into Rafe here and some other Americans I knew and its been two weeks, and now all my tickets to Malta are void. Stay here and save me -- oh Bopes! Bopes! Bopes!"

~~Lord Arthur~~ The Marquis Kinkallow glanced with tired eyes about the bar.

"Ah, who is that?" he demanded, surreptitiously feeding a hasheesh tablet to the pekinese, " the lovely Sheeny. And who is that item with her?"

" She's an American," said the daughter of a hundred Earls, ~~in a confiding whisper.~~ " The man is a scoundrel of some sort but ~~he seems to be~~ apparently he's a cat of the stripe -- he's a great pal of Schenzi in Vienna. I sat up ~~with him~~ till five the other night playing ~~double~~ two-handed chemin-de-fer with him here in the bar and he owes me a mille Swiss."

~~(Exactly the sum Lady Helen she had borrowed from him, thought Ralph Barry. He wondered if he would ever see it again.)~~

Plate 2 Page 7 of the working typescript of "The Hotel Child." Bopes, a decadent British expatriate, feeds a hasheesh tablet to his dog. This detail was cut by the *Post* editors. The word "Sheeny" in the same sentence became "Jewess" in the *Post* version. F. Scott Fitzgerald Papers, Princeton University Libraries.

- 17 -

→ you and Hamilton's like each other."

~~He wondered if~~ The engagement was making her stupid — he had never heard her make such a series of obvious remarks before.

"~~Of course,~~ I could ~~tell~~ kill him without a qualm," he said pleasantly, "but he looks like a good man. He's ~~all right.~~ fine. What I ~~want to~~ know is what happens to people like me who aren't able to forget."

~~Despite his efforts~~ As he said this he could not prevent his mouth from drooping suddenly, ~~and~~ glancing ~~looking~~ up ~~she~~ Caroline saw and her heart ~~did a little pirouette~~ quivered violently as it had the other morning.

"Do you mind so much, Michael?" ~~she asked gently.~~

~~"Oh, Caroline."~~ "God, yes."

For a second as he said ~~her name~~ this in a voice that seemed to have come ~~from every part of his body~~ up from his shoes they were not dancing, they were simply clinging together. Then ~~the moment was over~~ she leaned away from him, and twisted ~~as her mouth~~

Plate 3 Page 17 of the working typescript of "The Bridal Party." The *Post* cut the mildly blasphemous "God, yes." F. Scott Fitzgerald Papers, Princeton University Libraries.

-12-

to see Paris by night with ~~cooler~~ clearer and more judicious ~~different eyes than those of two~~

eyes ~~years~~ ~~ago~~. ~~It was late but~~ He bought a strapontin for the

Casino and watched Josephine ~~Butler~~ Baker go through her chocolate

arabesques but he felt that her stuff was poor. ~~it seemed that she had lost ground.~~ She was

followed the same contorted patterns ~~of five years ago~~ but

~~now~~ they lacked something. She needed America, she needed

refreshment — The bloom was going because the roots were

dry.

After an hour he ~~had enough~~ left and he strolled ~~along~~ toward

~~up~~ Montmartre, up the Rue Pigalle ~~toward~~ into the Place Blanche.

The rain had stopped and there were ~~people in the streets~~,

a few people in evening clothes disembarking from taxis in

front of cabarets, and cocottes prowling singly or in pairs, and

many negroes. He passed a lighted door from ~~behind~~ which issued

music and stopped with the sense of familiarity — it ~~having seen it before.~~

~~Then he remembered it~~ was "Bricktop's" where he had parted with

so many hours and so much money. A few doors further on

he found another ancient rendezvous and incautiously put

Plate 4 Page 12 of the working typescript of "Babylon Revisited." The comments about the African American entertainer Josephine Baker are more extensive here than in the published text. F. Scott Fitzgerald Papers, Princeton University Libraries.

APPENDIX 1

THANK YOU FOR THE LIGHT

Fitzgerald composed this vignette in the late spring of 1936 while he was living in Baltimore. He sent it to Harold Ober on 19 June with this note: "Do you think this is any good? I thought it might amuse the *New Yorker* and pick up a few dollars. It's an old idea I had hanging around in my head for a long time and didn't do justice to it when I came to write it, but it seems to me too good to go back in the file. Do what you can with it."[1] Ober took Fitzgerald's suggestion and submitted the story to the *New Yorker*, but without success. He tried at least four other magazines—*College Humor, Harper's Bazaar, Vanity Fair*, and *Vogue*—but was unable to sell the story. "Thank You for the Light" is atypical of Fitzgerald's magazine work; possibly magazine editors saw it as faintly irreligious or blasphemous. The final typescript of the story was preserved by Fitzgerald's heirs until 2012, when they decided to offer some of the materials in their possession to collectors. "Thank You for the Light," rediscovered among these materials, was offered again to the *New Yorker* on 13 June 2012 and accepted several days later. It was published for the first time in the 6 August 2012 issue of the magazine. The story is included here as one of the brief, Chekhovian vignettes that Fitzgerald produced in the 1930s. He taught himself to write in this form, partly for commercial reasons and partly to introduce a new tightness and understatement into his style. "Thank You for the Light" belongs with such other late stories as "Three

[1] Quoted in "The Lost Months: New Fitzgerald Letters from the Crack-Up Period," *Princeton University Library Chronicle*, 65 (2004): 479–501. This article publishes for the first time ten letters from Fitzgerald to Ober that were removed from the Ober files at some point after the author's death in 1940. Photocopies of these letters (some of which were subsequently auctioned at Sotheby Parke Bernet and Christie's New York) were donated anonymously to Princeton University Library in 2004.

Acts of Music" (1936), "The Long Way Out" (1937), "The Lost Decade" (1939), and "Dearly Beloved" (written in 1940 but not published until 1969).

THANK YOU FOR THE LIGHT

Mrs. Hanson was a pretty, somewhat faded woman of forty who sold corsets and girdles, traveling out of Chicago. For many years her territory had swung around through Toledo, Lima, Springfield, Columbus, Indianapolis and Fort Wayne; and her transfer to the Iowa, Kansas, Missouri district was a promotion, for her firm was more strongly entrenched west of the Ohio.

Eastward, however, she had known her clientele chattily and was often offered a drink or a cigarette in the buyer's office after business was concluded. But she soon found that in her new district things were different. Not only was she never asked if she would smoke but several times her own inquiry as to whether anyone would mind was answered half apologetically with:

"It's not that *I* mind, but it has a bad influence on the employees."

"Oh, of course, I understand."

Smoking meant a lot to her sometimes. She worked very hard and it had some ability to rest and relax her psychologically. She was a widow and she had no close relatives to write to in the evenings, while more than one moving picture a week hurt her eyes, so that smoking had come to be an important punctuation mark in the long sentence of a day on the road.

The last week of her first trip on the new circuit found her in Kansas City. It was mid-August and she felt somewhat lonely among all the new contacts of the past fortnight, and she was delighted to find at the outer desk of one firm a woman she had known in Chicago. She sat down before having herself announced and, in the course of conversation, found out a little about the man she was going to interview.

"Will he mind if I smoke?"

"What? My God, yes!" said her friend. "He's given money to support the law against it."

"Oh. Well, I'm grateful for the advice—more than grateful."

"You better watch it everywhere around here," her friend said. "Especially with the men over fifty. The ones that weren't in the war. A man once told me that nobody who was in the war would ever object to anyone smoking."

But at her very next stop Mrs. Hanson ran into the exception. He seemed such a pleasant young man, but his eyes fixed with so much fascination on the cigarette that she tapped on her thumbnail that she put it away. She was rewarded when he asked her to lunch, and during the hour she obtained a considerable order.

Afterwards he insisted on driving her to her next appointment, though she had intended to spot a hotel in the vicinity and take a few puffs in the wash room.

It was one of those days full of waiting, everyone was busy, was late, and it seemed that when they did appear they were the sort of hatchet-faced men who did not like other people's self-indulgence, or they were women willingly or unwillingly committed to the ideas of these men.

She hadn't smoked since breakfast, and she suddenly realized that was why she felt a vague dissatisfaction at the end of each call, no matter how successful it had been in a business way. Aloud she would say: "We think we cover a different field. It's all rubber and canvas of course, but we do manage to put them together in a different way. A thirty per cent increase in national advertising in one year tells its own story."

And to herself she was thinking: "If I could just get three puffs I could sell old-fashioned whalebone."

She had one more store to visit now, but her engagement was not for half an hour. That was just time to go to her hotel, but as there was no taxi in sight she walked along the street thinking: "Perhaps I ought to give up cigarettes. I'm getting to be a drug fiend."

Before her she saw the Catholic Cathedral. It seemed very tall—suddenly she had an inspiration: if so much incense had gone up in the spires to God, a little smoke in the vestibule would make little difference. How could the Good Lord care if a tired woman took a few puffs in the vestibule?

Nevertheless, though she was not a Catholic, the thought offended her. It didn't seem so important whether she had her cigarette, because it might offend a lot of other people too.

Still—He wouldn't mind, she thought persistently. In His days they hadn't even discovered tobacco...

She went into the church; the vestibule was dark and she felt for a match in the bag she carried but there wasn't any.

"I'll go and get a light from one of their candles," she thought.

The darkness of the nave was broken only by a splash of light in a corner. She walked up the aisle toward the white blur, and found that it was not made by candles and in any case it was going out soon—an old man was on the point of eliminating a last oil lamp.

"These are votive offerings," he said. "We put them out at night. They float in the oil and we think it means more to the people that give them to save them for next day, than it would to keep them burning all night."

"I see."

He struck out the last one. There was no light left in the cathedral now, save an electric chandelier high overhead and the ever-burning lamp in front of the sacrament.

"Good-night," the sexton said.

"Good-night."

"I guess you came here to pray.

"Yes, I did."

He went out into the sacristy. Mrs. Hanson knelt down and prayed.

It had been a long time since she had prayed. She scarcely knew what to pray for, so she prayed for her employer, and for the clients in Des Moines and Kansas City. When she had finished praying she knelt up. She was not used to prayer. The image of the Madonna gazed down upon her from a niche, six feet above her head.

Vaguely she regarded it. Then she got up from her knees and sank back wearily in the corner of the pew. In her imagination the Virgin came down, like in the play "The Miracle," and took her place and sold corsets and girdles for her and was tired just as she was.[*] Then for a few minutes Mrs. Hanson must have slept . . .

. . . She awoke at the realization that something had changed; and only gradually she perceived that there was a familiar scent that was not incense in the air and that her fingers smarted. Then she realized that the cigarette she held in her hand was alight—was burning.

Still too drowsy to think, she took a puff to keep the flame alive. Then she looked up again at the Madonna's vague niche in the half darkness.

"Thank you for the light," she said.

That didn't seem quite enough, so she got down on her knees, the smoke twisting up from the cigarette between her fingers.

"Thank you very much for the light," she said again.

Emendations in the final typescript

398.5 pretty,] ~∧
398.6 traveling] travelling
398.8 Wayne;] ~∧
398.29 and,] ~∧
398.30 conversation,] ~∧
399.7 man,] ~∧
399.8 thumbnail] thumb-nail
399.9 lunch,] ~∧
399.16 hatchet-faced] ~∧~
399.16 self-indulgence] ~∧~
399.19 breakfast,] ~∧
399.27 whalebone] whale-bone
399.28 now,] ~∧
399.29 hotel,] ~∧
399.34 God,] ~∧
400.20 overhead] over head
400.25 Yes,] ~∧
400.35 Miracle,"] ~",
401.6 cigarette∧] ~,

* Fitzgerald is alluding to *Das Miracle* by the German-American playwright Karl Gustav Vollmoeller (1878–1948). Vollmoeller wrote this play in collaboration with the director Max Reinhardt (1873–1943). The script is based on a twelfth-century Spanish legend; it tells of a medieval nun who flees from her convent with a knight, has adventures of a mystical nature, and is accused of witchcraft. While the nun is absent, a statue of the Virgin Mary in her convent chapel comes to life and replaces her, performing her devotions and fulfilling her duties. When the nun returns, the statue resumes its lifeless form. *Das Miracle* had its premiere in Germany in 1911; in 1924 it was staged in English, as *The Miracle*, in both London and New York. Fitzgerald was probably familiar with Vollmoeller's cinema work: the German playwright was best known for writing *The Blue Angel*, the film that made Marlene Dietrich a star in 1930.

APPENDIX 2

AUTHOR'S FOREWORD

Fitzgerald wrote a foreword for *Taps at Reveille*, which Perkins had set in type. In a 26 December 1934 letter to the editor, however, Fitzgerald directed that the foreword be withdrawn from the collection. He feared that it had a "snappy-snooty sound" and that it might strike the wrong note with book reviewers. The foreword survives in a proof copy revised by Fitzgerald; this proof was offered to collectors at Sale 23, Waverly Auctions at Quill & Brush, 15 May 1983. The proof was facsimiled in the catalogue for this sale. The present location of the document is unknown. The facsimile is reproduced in *F. Scott Fitzgerald in the Marketplace*: 76. The revised text of the foreword appears below.

AUTHOR'S FOREWORD

Before the last of these stories were written the world that they represented passed. In consequence the reviewer may be tempted to apply the title harshly to the fate of the collection. Yet almost all these stories, the winnowing of fifty odd, meant a great deal to the author at the time of writing: all of them tried for an arduous precision in trying to catch one character or one emotion or one adventure—which is all that one can do in the length of a short story.

APPENDIX 3

COMPOSITION, PUBLICATION, AND EARNINGS

Amounts earned and dates of publication have been taken from Fitzgerald's professional ledger and from his correspondence with his literary agent, Harold Ober. Price and publication are for the first serial appearances; the fees are those paid before Ober deducted a 10 percent commission.

Fitzgerald's habit was to deal directly with magazine editors whom he knew personally. Ober was not used as an intermediary on these sales. Fitzgerald sold "Crazy Sunday" to H. L. Mencken at the *American Mercury*, and he sold "The Night of Chancellorsville" and "The Fiend" to Arnold Gingrich at *Esquire*. He paid no commissions on these sales.

Much of the information in this appendix appeared first in Bryant Mangum, *A Fortune Yet: Money in the Art of F. Scott Fitzgerald's Short Stories* (New York: Garland, 1991). In the listings below, *AmMerc* stands for the *American Mercury*, and *Post* stands for the *Saturday Evening Post*.

TAPS AT REVEILLE (1935)

Title	*Composed*	*Published*	*Price*
"Crazy Sunday"	Jan. 1932	*AmMerc* 27 (Oct. 1932)	$200
"Two Wrongs"	Oct.–Nov. 1929	*Post* 202 (18 Jan. 1930)	$4,000
"Chancellorsville"	Nov. 1934	*Esquire* 3 (Feb. 1935)	$250
"The Last of the Belles"	Nov. 1928	*Post* 201 (2 Mar. 1929)	$3,500
"Majesty"	May 1929	*Post* 202 (13 July 1929)	$3,500
"Family in the Wind"	April 1932	*Post* 204 (4 June 1932)	$3,500

"A Short Trip Home"	Oct. 1927	*Post* 200 (17 Dec. 1927)	$3,500
"One Interne"	Aug. 1932	*Post* 205 (5 Nov. 1932)	$3,500
"The Fiend"	Sept. 1934	*Esquire* 3 (Jan. 1935)	$250
"Babylon Revisited"	Dec. 1930	*Post* 203 (21 Feb. 1931)	$4,000

ADDITIONAL STORIES

Title	***Composed***	***Published***	***Price***
"Cabinet-Maker's"	Dec. 1927	*Century* 117 (Dec. 1928)	$150
"Rough Crossing"	Mar. 1929	*Post* 201 (8 June 1929)	$3,500
"At Your Age"	June 1929	*Post* 202 (17 Aug. 1929)	$4,000
"The Swimmers"	July–Aug. 1929	*Post* 202 (19 Oct. 1929)	$4,000
"The Bridal Party"	May 1930	*Post* 203 (9 Aug. 1930)	$4,000
"One Trip Abroad"	Aug. 1930	*Post* 203 (11 Oct. 1930)	$4,000
"The Hotel Child"	Nov. 1930	*Post* 203 (31 Jan. 1931)	$4,000
"Indecision"	Jan.–Feb. 1931	*Post* 203 (16 May 1931)	$4,000
"A New Leaf"	Apr. 1931	*Post* 204 (4 July 1931)	$4,000